T0400390

THE
KING'S ONLY
CHAMPION

THE
KING'S ONLY
CHAMPION

JAMES GRAHAM,
FIRST MARQUESS OF MONTROSE

DOMINIC PEARCE

AMBERLEY

First published 2023

Amberley Publishing
The Hill, Stroud
Gloucestershire, GL5 4EP

www.amberley-books.com

British Library Cataloguing in Publication Data.
A catalogue record for this book is available from the British Library.

ISBN 978 1 4456 9519 8 (hardback)
ISBN 978 1 4456 9520 4 (ebook)

1 2 3 4 5 6 7 8 9 10

Typesetting by SJmagic DESIGN SERVICES, India.
Printed in the UK.

Contents

Author's Note

Dates
My narrative follows the convention that the new year starts in January (also but not invariably followed in the early modern period). Because the action is almost wholly in Scotland and England, the ten-day difference between the Gregorian and Julian calendars does not intrude. The former was used in Catholic countries at this time. Consistent with English and Scottish usage, I use the Julian calendar, except when noted.

Quotations
Much of the contemporary material is written in Scots or in English influenced by Scots. On the whole I have updated quotations linguistically, so they can be clearly understood by the reader of modern English. Quotations from the Bible are from the King James Version, a product of the early seventeenth century.

Legal terms
The technically correct vocabulary governing aspects of land ownership is not an easy read. For instance, the term 'landowner' when applied to the various nobles and lairds is anachronistic because the only landowner in Scotland in Montrose's day was the king (also, before the Reformation, the Catholic Church).

A noble such as Montrose held his land in 'feu' (more or less equivalent to 'perpetual lease') from the king as a 'vassal in chief'. There was a developed system under which land was held by lesser men and by the towns (burghs) all involving legalese. Similar issues arise with the system of 'teinds' (tithes) which were meant to finance the Kirk (Church of Scotland).

I have used modern words, even if they are inexact, for the sake of clarity. For example, I describe the nobility as landowners, the term we would use today. Where it matters, I have tried to spell things out.

The risk is that the power relationships could be glossed over, as if the people of the seventeenth century lived in a world governed by today's rules. However, it was a reasonably stable system – land held from the king was normally held in perpetuity – so hopefully modern shorthand is not too distorting.

Alasdair/Alexander MacDonald/MacColla

Montrose's most important officer has been called by different names. I chose Alasdair MacDonald. I am genuinely unsure of the most correct version, but it seemed important to understand that this man was at the same time a royalist officer and an island chief and one of the putative heirs to the medieval MacDonald Lords of the Isles.

Marquess/marquis

I have used the spelling 'marquess' for the second most senior noble rank, which Montrose and others attained. There is a tradition that the Scottish nobility used 'marquis' (French spelling) but I decided to standardise.

List of Illustrations

Map of Scotland, John Speed (1610).

1. John Knox preaches to the Lords of the Congregation in 1559. (Rijksmuseum)
2. Dunfermline Palace, where Charles I was born on 19 November 1600. (Author's collection).
3. The Ruthven brothers, Montrose's uncles, meet their fates on 5 August 1600. (Rijksmuseum)
4. James VI and I is described here as King of Great Britain, France and Ireland, although he never united England and Scotland into Great Britain. The claim on France was a historic dream. (Yale Center for British Art)
5. The Winter King and Queen, living in Dutch exile, riding with members of the Orange-Nassau family. (Rijksmuseum)
6. Within a coin's outline, on the back of an illustration in his copy of Raleigh's *History*, Montrose wrote most of the Lord's Prayer – a spiritual doodle. Probably during his student days. (Author's collection, with permission of the Governors of Innerpeffray Library)
7. Holyroodhouse, showing the ruined abbey church, where Charles I was crowned King of Scots in June 1633. (Author's collection)
8. Montrose's personal Bible measuring about three by five inches. (Author's collection, with permission of the Governors of Innerpeffray Library)
9. Title page of Montrose's Bible: a Protestant French language text, published in 1633. (Author's collection, with permission of the Governors of Innerpeffray Library)
10. The castle at Angers. Montrose attended the military academy in the town in 1633. (Wikipedia)

11. The statue of the philosopher-emperor Marcus Aurelius was among the classical antiquities that Montrose would see in Rome, probably in 1635. (Rijksmuseum)
12. A decorative arch of the kind erected for court entertainments, and for triumphal entries, such as that of Charles I into Edinburgh in 1633. (Yale Center for British Art)
13. Montrose in full armour. Probably painted while he was in Oxford in 1643-1644. (Flickr)
14. The saltire, or Cross of St Andrew. Scotland's national flag, thought to be the oldest national flag in Europe. (Author's collection)
15. Mary Ruthven, Montrose's niece, wife of Sir Anthony van Dyck. The inscription says she was born in Scotland but that is unlikely. (Rijksmuseum)
16. 'Cutty Stool' by Merilyn Smith (1992). This one is bronze. The original was wooden, thrown, according to tradition, by Jenny Geddes at the Dean of Edinburgh, when he started to read from the new prayer-book in St Giles' on 23 July 1637. It was still heavy. (Author's collection)
17. Montrose's signature on the title page of a 1637 edition of Camden's *Britain, a chorographical description*, usually called *Britannia...* (Author's collection, with the permission of the Governors of Innerpeffray Library)
18. A seventeenth-century musket. (Rijksmuseum)
19. Blair Castle was Montrose's base during his glorious year 1644-1645. At the time the building was much smaller, a fortress rather than stately home. (Author's collection)
20. A drummer boy, like the child killed before the Battle of Aberdeen. (Rijksmuseum)
21. King Charles I. The inscription describes him as King of England, Scotland, France and Ireland (Yale Center for British Art)
22. Statue of Montrose in Montrose High Street. (Author's collection)
23. Inverlochy Castle, the scene of Montrose's defeat of the Marquess of Argyll on 2 February 1645. (Yale Center for British Art)
24. Dunnottar Castle, where the Earl Marischal, surrounded by ministers of the Kirk, sheltered in March 1645 while Montrose burned his land. (Author's collection)
25. Site of the Auldearn battlefield, looking from Castle Hill onto Garlic Hill. (Author's collection)
26. Montrose as Lieutenant Governor of Scotland. (Rijksmuseum)
27. Seals of Montrose from 1639 and 1650, the latter with cypher of the lion poised to leap across an abyss. (Author's collection, with the permission of the Governors of Innerpeffray Library)

28. The Heart of Midlothian, a pavement mosaic marking the old Tolbooth of Edinburgh, very close to St Giles' Cathedral. (Author's collection)
29. Today's junction of East Preston Street and Dalkeith Road, Edinburgh, where Montrose's mutilated trunk was buried in May 1650. (Author's collection)
30. On 23 May 1660 (Julian calendar) Charles II set off from Scheveningen for England to reclaim his throne. Huge crowds watched. (Rijksmuseum)
31. The elegant memorial to Montrose in St Giles' was built in 1887-1888 after Queen Victoria indignantly asked why there was nothing in the church worthy of him. (Author's collection)

Introduction

There have been several modern accounts of the first Marquess of Montrose, although nothing comprehensive in the past forty years. There is plenty more to say now because more is known.

The first thing to say is that he created a legend. Since the fascination of history is trying to work out what *really* happened, the legend must be examined. Was Montrose the archetype of chivalry? And what is that? Was this period all antagonism and contrast, good king followed by bad king, rebels against oppression, saints against sinners?

Since the 1980s, so much meticulous work has been done by scholars delving into the civil war years. Our understanding of the period is transformed. This is new. I think it leads to a better understanding of Montrose, why he made the choices he did and where they led.

I want to fill in the essential and very striking faith and the nationalist background. Previous biographers assumed earlier history is well known to the reader. Given the unique Scottish development, that is a lot to assume. I think his travels in the Catholic world of France and Italy in the period 1633-1636 help explain his behaviour on return.

Earlier biographers insist on a boy's-only story. But even in the seventeenth century, things were not quite so simple. Captain Francis Dalyell was a woman (dressed as a man) who joined Montrose in command of her own troop of men, flying a provocative banner. One of his most faithful adherents was his niece, Elizabeth Napier. Queen Henrietta Maria was extremely influential, as was her sister-in-law, Elizabeth of Bohemia. If anyone made history, it was working women in the prayer-book riots of 1637.

King Charles I was, to use the words of a reviewer of my previous book,[1] 'a decent man'. But as his son's governor said, it is possible to be a good man but a bad king. His government of Scotland, while he had the power to govern, was clumsy. It directly and decisively shaped events in England (Scotland was the first to rebel) with massive consequences. I have done my best to weave the royal story of three kings – James VI and I, Charles I and his son Charles II – around that of Montrose. These are reflections on power.

And there is the fascination of the land. In the early seventeenth century Scotland was a very old kingdom long accustomed to independence: the national flag, the Saltire (Cross of St Andrew) is thought to be the oldest national flag in Europe. Scotland is defined by the highland-lowland divide. Perhaps this accounts for a romantic, myth-creating strand in Scottish history. There was a double consciousness. Thanks to the rainy, western high country, Scotland is also a land of rivers, not just in the highland area with its well-known lochs, but throughout the lowlands. These created barriers more than they connected, but any visitor can see how much they are part of the fabric. Lords even took their titles from rivers. The rivers North Esk and South Esk gave their names to two earls (who were brothers), and Lord Almond (later Earl of Callendar) took his title from a river. There is a story of geography as well as history.

Montrose was a spoiled, generous, charismatic man who tended to run before he could walk but matured after his experience of the late 1630s. He was both exceptional leader and poetic dreamer. That combination made him a celebrity, a figure almost of myth in his own time, one of the historic heroes. In some ways he saw all too clearly. Yet his vision was sometimes clouded by his own courage and by an intense, increasingly deeply felt loyalty to the Stuarts. In the end – and it was an end which seizes the imagination – his victimhood was self-willed.

By comparison with today's public figures the leaders of the seventeenth century were young. Montrose married at seventeen; made his mark politically first in 1637 when he turned twenty-five; in 1644-1645 fighting his major battles in his early thirties. He was dead at thirty-seven. How did that happen?

Main Characters

Immediate family of James Graham, fifth Earl and first Marquess of Montrose (1612–1650)

Magdalen (Carnegie). Montrose's wife, married in 1629, died in 1645. A mysterious figure in his life. Despite the survival of plenty of archive material about Montrose himself, including the huge collection of Mark Napier (1798-1879), no correspondence between the Montroses survives.

John, Lord Graham. their eldest son and heir, died in 1645 at the age of fourteen.

James, Lord Graham after his brother's death. He became the second Marquess of Montrose. He recovered his father's estates but also had to deal with his debts. Known as 'the good marquess', probably because he refused to vote for the execution of his father's enemy, Argyll.

Robert. The third son is known to us because of official correspondence about his care after the forfeiture of his father. He also appears in the 1660 state funeral procession.

Jean. When in 1650 Montrose was a prisoner on his way to execution, he visited two of his children at Kinnaird Castle. James was in the care of Lord Dalhousie at the time (not at Kinnaird). Robert was in his mother's care, presumably now at Kinnaird. From other hints, this fourth child, a girl, has been assumed. The main sources do not mention her.

Harry Graham. Montrose's illegitimate half-brother. One of the most stalwart of Montrose's followers. He survived the failure of the 1650 campaign and retired to Flanders. Harry came back to Scotland where he was in the 1660 state funeral procession for Montrose.

Extended family

Patrick Graham the younger of Inchbrakie. Montrose's kinsman and constant supporter in the 1644-1645 campaign, commander of the troops raised in Atholl; known as Black Pate because of a gunpowder accident.

Archibald, first Lord Napier. The older brother-in-law of Montrose, married to his sister Margaret. A successful politician who worked at the English court of James VI and I, then in Scottish government. A moderate presbyterian, a political thinker, widely respected.

Archibald, second Lord Napier. Son of first Lord Napier, nephew of Montrose. An ardent royalist who escaped house arrest in 1645 to fight on Montrose's side, and by 1648 was on the continent with him. He became his uncle's intimate. In his own words they were 'like the Pope and the Church, who would be inseparable'.

Elizabeth, Lady Napier. Wife of the younger Archibald Napier. Daughter of the Earl of Mar, her father-in-law's political enemy, she was a devoted wife, who at first stayed in Scotland after Montrose went into exile in 1646 so that she could manage the family finances. After Montrose's death, she did something remarkable...

James, Lord Ogilvy. Montrose's cousin (Ogilvy's Ruthven grandmother was Montrose's great-aunt) and close friend from university days at St Andrews, said to have been a rival for Magdalen's hand. With his father, the **Earl of Airlie**, Ogilvy was a constant royalist. He was not involved in Montrose's 1650 campaign but had been part of Thomas Mackenzie of Pluscarden's royalist attempt earlier that year.

Ruthvens. Through his mother, Montrose had Ruthven relations. None was closely involved in his career. His uncle **Patrick Ruthven** survived the 1600 Gowrie Conspiracy. His daughter, a Catholic lady at court, married the painter Anthony van Dyck, the protégé of Henrietta Maria.

Earl of Southesk (and Lord Carnegie). Father of Magdalen, therefore Montrose's father-in-law. There are several recorded quarrels between the two men. Southesk was a privy councillor, a moderate who wanted a peaceful Scotland. One daughter married Montrose and another the Earl of Traquair, who became Treasurer and was painfully caught in the middle of the escalating antagonism.

Stirling of Kier, Sir George. Husband of Margaret Napier, Montrose's niece. A loyal supporter of Montrose, imprisoned with him in 1641.

Politicians

Covenanters. The noblemen who did most to create the movement were the **Earl of Rothes, Lord (later Earl of) Loudoun,** and **Lord Balmerino, Lord Lindsay (later Earl of Crawford-Lindsay).** With the emergence of the **Earl (later Marquess) of Argyll** as covenanter leader, the movement changed for two reasons: first, Argyll drew in both the burghs (i.e. town businessmen) and more activist ministers in support; and second, his own clan interests compromised the ideology. Another important covenanter was the lawyer **Archibald Johnston of Wariston** (usually called Lord Wariston).

Moderates. In the early stage the **Earl of Traquair** counts as a moderate, trying in vain to act as royal servant without provoking the king's critics. The even more controversial **Marquess (later Duke) of Hamilton,** and his brother **William, Earl of Lanark (later second Duke of Hamilton),** tried and failed to find a balance, leading to the 1648 Engagement which sealed the fate of Charles I. Although he frequently acted in the covenanter interest and damaged the king by opposing his ecclesiastical policy, **Sir Thomas Hope,** the Lord Advocate, supported the king's civil prerogative. In that sense he had moderate beliefs.

Fighting men

Covenanters. A number of magnates took the field against Montrose, or opposed him in other ways: **Lord Elcho, Lord Balfour of Burleigh, the Earl of Sutherland** and, although at a distance – including when he was present in battle – **Argyll.** Professional generals on the covenanter side were the **Earl of Leven (Alexander Leslie),** who was active in the two Bishops' Wars but during 1644-1645 commanded the Scottish army in England, **William Baillie** and **David Leslie.**

Royalists. The most effective of Montrose's officers, fighting in every victory in 1644-1645 except Alford, was the Catholic Hebridean Scot **Alasdair MacDonald.** The **Gordons** were important to Montrose, the sons of the **Marquess of Huntly.** Of these, only **Viscount Aboyne** was always royalist (his two brothers joined Montrose in 1645). Lesser Gordon chiefs, such as **Gordon of Haddo,** were always royalist. A number of other Gordons fought on the royalist side, amongst whom **Nathaniel Gordon** is prominent. The **Ogilvy (Airlie) family** was royalist throughout.

Changed sides. In 1645 the first to come over to Montrose from the covenanters, very important, was Aboyne's eldest brother **Lord Gordon,** bringing their difficult younger brother **Lord Lewis Gordon.** The two young men probably sided with the National Covenant to begin with because Argyll was their uncle. In 1646 **Sir John Hurry** joined Montrose, having fought him at Auldearn. Another prominent turner, too late to help Montrose (and always unpredictable), was the **Earl of Seaforth** who first opposed the royalists but in 1645 signed Montrose's Kilcumin Band, and in 1649 left Scotland to join the royalists on the continent.

Churchmen

Scotland. In the original Scottish Reformation (1559-1560), **John Knox** was the key churchman. During the Scottish reign of James VI and I,

Andrew Melville (1545-1622) was an important figure. The first shaped sixteenth century Scottish reform more than anyone, the second led the separatist party in the Kirk in frequent confrontations with King James.

John Spottiswoode, Archbishop of St Andrews, was the most important royalist churchman of the 1620s and 1630s. He also controversially became Chancellor. During the 1630s and 1640s the leading minister for the covenanters was **Alexander Henderson**. Important for Montrose was his chaplain and biographer **George Wishart** (not to be confused with the sixteenth century Protestant martyr of the same name).

England. The most important English churchman was **William Laud**, Archbishop of Canterbury, one of the key officials of Charles I. Although he had no involvement in Scottish affairs, **William Juxon**, Bishop of London, was important as a political bishop who became English Treasurer.

PART ONE

BEGINNINGS

'His eyes sparkling and full of life...'
Patrick Gordon of Ruthven

1

A Pot of Gold

Slightly before seven o'clock in the morning of 5 August 1600, Alexander Ruthven, brother of John Ruthven, Earl of Gowrie, arrived at Falkland Palace in Fife. The young man approached King James VI, who was about to mount his horse for the morning's hunt. There was a conversation between Alexander and James observed but not overheard by others. It lasted about fifteen minutes. The king then rode out with his courtiers and hunted for three or four hours.

On return he asked his cousin the Duke of Lennox to accompany him on a ride to Gowrie House in Perth. It was seventeen miles, a little more than two hours each way taken at a trot. The king explained Alexander had met a man with a pitcher full of golden coins. The treasure was now safe at Gowrie House. James wanted to look at it, or more likely he wanted to claim it.[1]

The royal party set off at about eleven o'clock, consisting of no more than the king, Alexander Ruthven and Lennox. Alexander apparently requested this. However, they were joined by fifteen or twenty more on the way, including the Earl of Mar and Dr Herries, the king's physician. Everyone was armed.

On arrival in Perth the king and his entourage were met by the Earl of Gowrie. Alexander had ridden ahead to warn his brother of their sovereign's approach. Nonetheless at Gowrie House no preparations had been made. It was something like an hour before James VI had anything to eat or drink. The king at last was served in a chamber on the ground floor next to the great hall. Of course he was served first. Gowrie invited the courtiers to eat in the hall itself. While they ate they watched the king, with Alexander at his side, walk from this adjoining chamber into the hall, and disappear up the house's main staircase, a spiral stair or turnpike at the side of the house.

Lennox and others jumped to their feet to attend their lord, but Gowrie said his Majesty was going about private business. Alexander called back from the foot of the stairs saying the king did not want anyone else to come. Since King James was in earshot there was no reason for doubt.

When they had finished eating the courtiers dispersed, some walking in the garden, others staying inside on the ground floor. The question arose, where exactly was the king? It was a more unusual question than may appear. The head of state, the fount of law, the owner of all the land in Scotland (under feudal tenure) was never lost. His courtiers always knew, day and night, exactly where he was and who was with him.

Surprisingly, a member of the earl's household said James VI had left the house through a yard at the back and was now riding away. Gowrie confirmed it even though his own porter, who had the keys to all the gates, denied it. Gowrie called for horses, so they could follow the king. Actually his own horse – had he forgotten? – was some miles away at Scone. Confusion. Several courtiers ran into the street.

A yell from the house brought them back. King James's scarlet face appeared at a first-floor turret window. 'I am murdered! Treason! My lord of Mar, help, help!' he shouted. A hand could be seen gripping the king's cheek and mouth, according to one witness. Another said his Majesty was pulled suddenly backwards.

Some ran up the main staircase to the gallery. They could not reach the gallery chamber, this being the room with the turret window – and the king. There was a door between the gallery and the gallery chamber. It was locked. They started to break it down. Back in the street Sir Thomas Erskine and his brother James took hold of Lord Gowrie, accusing him of treason. He cried innocent. His servants came forward to protect him.

The king's page of honour, John Ramsay, had the wit to see there was another staircase from the ground to the first floor, the so-called black turnpike, which took him directly into the gallery chamber. He rushed up the black turnpike, a hooded hawk still on his wrist, from the hunting party.

Ramsay found King James VI and Alexander Ruthven locked together, the king holding Alexander's head under his arm, Alexander clutching at the king's face. Further confusion came from the presence of a third man. It was an equal struggle. While Alexander was the younger, about twenty, at thirty-four the king was in his prime.

The king shouted at Ramsay to strike Alexander 'low' because he was wearing a protective coat beneath his clothes. Ramsay released the hawk and knifed Alexander in the face and neck. At this point the unknown third man ran away. The king pushed the wounded Alexander away, down the staircase (the black turnpike). Sir Thomas Erskine and

22

Dr Herries met Alexander as they ran up the stairs. One or both struck at him, this time fatally.

Recovered from his tussle with the Erskines, Gowrie charged back to the house, a sword in each hand. He was followed by members of his household. He found his brother's body at the foot of the Black Turnpike. He tore upstairs. There was a fight. Dr Herries lost two fingers. Sir Thomas Erskine was wounded in the right hand. Ramsay challenged Gowrie, ran him through and killed him. The Gowrie household retreated. The door between the gallery and the gallery chamber was at last broken down. The king, who had been locked for safety in the turret, was relesaed. James VI and his courtiers thanked God for his delivery.

Nothing more was said of the pot of gold.

That day King James VI cannot have arrived back at Falkland Palace much before ten o'clock at night. As the news of the fighting in Gowrie House spread through Perth, the townspeople gathered. That took time to calm. The royal party did not leave until eight o'clock in the evening. We can assume the king was exhausted on return but instead of going to bed he at once wrote a letter to the privy council in Edinburgh giving his version. The violent death of two young and prominent noblemen in peacetime was not something to be brushed under the carpet.

The disgrace of the Ruthven family followed. On 15 November the Scottish parliament found Gowrie and Alexander posthumously guilty of treason. Their estates were forfeit to the crown and distributed to crown supporters. Their descendants were disinherited. Their corpses were dismembered. Body parts were displayed publicly in Edinburgh (the heads) and Perth (the limbs). The 5th of August was declared a day of commemoration to be celebrated throughout Scotland from then on. Even the name Ruthven was abolished.[2]

The stranger in the gallery chamber was named as Andrew Henderson, a Gowrie servant. He was locked up but released after testimony that he had tried to help the king. The king obviously was a witness.

When he inherited the crown of England in 1603, the commemoration of his deliverance from the Ruthven brothers travelled south with King James. A set of prayers was commissioned for use by the Church of England. These prayers did not mince words. They lamented 'the wicked designments of those bloody wretches the Earl Gowry and his brother, and their desperate confederates...' They appealed to the king of heaven: 'Oh Lord... smite his (the king's) enemies upon the cheekbone, break their teeth, frustrate their counsels.'[3]

In his pursuit of the remaining Ruthven brothers, William and Patrick, both very young, the king was vindictive from the word go. In 1600 they fled to England and poverty. When James become King of England,

William fled to France, while Patrick, who remained, was thrown into the Tower of London.

—◦◦◦—

The Gowrie Conspiracy, as these events became known, was a moment of destiny. John Gowrie was a powerful young man, a skilful swordsman armed to the teeth. You would expect him to win his fights. But he froze and dropped his guard when, in the gallery chamber, John Ramsay, high on adrenalin, said something untrue. 'You have killed the king our master, and will you also take our lives?' he shouted. [4]

A second of hesitation. Gowrie's shock, when he was told the king was dead, gave Ramsay his chance. Such is the power of fake news. The violence speaks for itself. But who was deceived? According to the official version, the king was lured into an ambush. Was this what happened? Or was it an elaborate royal conspiracy against the Ruthvens? According to others, for instance the presbyterian ministers of Edinburgh, the earl and his brother were victims.

After all, the Ruthvens were a family inclined for many years to challenge King James. They stood with the presbyterian faction within the Kirk (Church of Scotland) which fought the king's attempts to interfere in church government. As recent family history showed, the Ruthvens repeatedly stepped out of line. The grandfather of John and Alexander, Lord Ruthven, led the men who attacked and killed David Rizzio (or Riccio), secretary of Mary, Queen of Scots, in Holyroodhouse on 9 March 1566. In the next generation, the Ruthven family struck again. With other nobles, the first Earl of Gowrie, son of Lord Ruthven, in 1582 kidnapped the sixteen-year-old James VI in order to separate him from his advisers, mainly the Catholic Esmé Stuart, Duke of Lennox (father of the duke who went to Gowrie House in 1600).[5] No physical harm was intended, but the plan was to make it plain that James VI could not give favour where he chose: the first Earl of Gowrie and his supporters intended to control him. This was called the Raid of Ruthven.

The kidnap was an immediate success. Esmé Stuart left Scotland and died in Paris the following year after a collapse in his health. But in the end James VI asserted himself and escaped. In his late teens he took up the mantle of government personally. He did not forget. It is safe to assume that among the violent and frightening experiences of James VI's life the Raid of Ruthven ranked very highly. The first Earl of Gowrie was executed on treason charges in 1584.

On his way back to Scotland in 1600, after several years spent on the continent of Europe, his son, the third earl, John Gowrie (succeeding his short-lived brother), travelled through London where he was received more than once, and with favour, by the unpredictable Elizabeth I. For King James any unscheduled meeting between the Queen of England and one of his nobles was a worry.

Reaching Scotland in May, Gowrie made a triumphal entry into Edinburgh, surrounded by friends and relations. He went on to oppose James VI's pet project of raising an army (to be financed by tax), which would protect the king's position as claimant to the throne of England. This was in June, just two months before the events in Gowrie House. On top of this, the king was literally in Gowrie's debt. He owed a substantial sum, £48,000 Scots, the amount loaned to the crown by the first earl while he was Treasurer.[6] The death of Gowrie and obliteration of Ruthven power was a win for the king on several fronts.

Other explanations of the events of 5 August 1600 include an attempted seduction by James VI of the attractive Alexander. Further romantic slants have been found in the favour supposedly shown to the Ruthven family by Anne of Denmark, wife of King James, whether to Gowrie or Alexander.[7] The Ruthvens were a good-looking family.

Today, historians tend to agree that the king told the truth. That there was, a second time, a Ruthven plot to kidnap him – not to kill him, hence Gowrie's astonishment – and hold him until he agreed changes in policy towards England, and in religious affairs.

Standing back, one sees how the Gowrie Conspiracy throws a flickering light on the high politics of the time, in particular on the relationship between the King of Scots and his nobility:

1. The king commanded the obedience of his nobles but...
2. ... they felt they had the right to defy him, even turn on him personally.
3. The king was always short of money
4. England was always a factor
5. Religion always mattered.
6. The king's (and his family's) sex life came into it[8]

These factors persisted. Over time they festered, thanks to the King of Scots becoming the King of England in 1603; thanks to the marriage in 1625 of James VI's son Charles – King Charles I – to the Catholic, formidable and French Henrietta Maria; and thanks to the character of Charles I. The Gowrie Conspiracy is a vignette, a synecdoche of everything, a curtain-raiser to the Scottish seventeenth century.

The career of James Graham, first Marquess of Montrose, developed in the 1630s and 1640s but the questions would be the same. The duties of subjects, royal responsibility and the royal prerogative – the rights of the king – royal finance, bedroom influence, the relation between Scotland and England, the path to Salvation, all would feature.

During the time Montrose came to adulthood another confrontation developed between the nobility of Scotland and the King of Scots. It would be vastly consequential. As events piled on events, that quarrel turned into something new, something more complicated than a purely aristocratic complaint but it was, at the start, a fight between the king and his nobles. Montrose played his part precisely because he was a Scottish noble. The results of that confrontation are felt to this day.

Whose triumph would it be this time? Whose head would be lifted for the crowd to see? A more intimate connection is not to be missed. When the limbs and heads of Lord Gowrie and his brother were put on public display, the Ruthven family continued to exist. Two brothers survived as we have seen. Their sister Margaret was unlikely to forget the events of 5 August 1600. She was soon married to the fourth Earl of Montrose. This book is about her son.

2

The Royal Family

Among the pictures in the Great Gallery of Holyroodhouse, the royal palace in Edinburgh, is one of a contemporary of Alexander the Great. The man wears a simple metal helmet that leaves his handsome face unprotected. His thick, curly, black hair flows free. He is armoured, wearing a breastplate and greaves. His right hand loosely grips the handle of a broadsword, the tip rests on the ground behind his right foot. Over his shoulders he has flung a crimson cloak, lined with ermine. A simple gold crown is placed over the helmet, snug against his temples. It is the portrait of a king.

According to a long historical tradition, Fergus I was the first King of Scotland. He ruled for a short time around 330 BCE but was unfortunately drowned crossing the sea between Scotland and Northern Ireland, where Carrickfergus is named after him.

King Fergus descended from that famous Egyptian princess, Pharaoh's daughter, who found the baby Moses in a basket in the Nile. Historians explained that she – Scota was her name! – moved to Ireland with her husband Gathelus, son of a King of Athens. Generations passed. Their descendant Fergus, son of Ferchard, moved on to Scotland where he established a new ruling dynasty from whom all later Scottish sovereigns descended. Before the Romans arrived in Britain, before the life of Christ, Scotland was born. This is the myth: national and royal.

This account was accepted by Scots high and low at the time when King James VI of Scotland became King James I of England in 1603, and when his son Charles I succeeded to the thrones of both kingdoms in 1625. A line of historians had made the case for unique antiquity: John of Fordun (fl. mid-fourteenth century), Walter Bower (1385-1449), Boethius (Hector

Boece) (c 1465-1536), George Buchanan (1505-1582). Essentially, they did so in order to show that Scotland was older than England.[1]

The portrait of Fergus I, a king who did not exist, and similar depictions of his legendary successors on the throne – so similar that the seventeenth-century artist who painted them probably used the same model for every one[2] – were commissioned and hung in the second half of the seventeenth century. These Scottish icons, including kings called Domadilla, Ederus, Athirco, Crathilinthus, remain in the royal picture gallery in the twenty-first century. That is staying power.

Modern historians have taken a slightly different tack. They believe the Kings of Scotland, or Kings of Scots, descended – whether by blood, adoption, marriage, or other agreement – from a dynasty established in the sixth century AD.

The sources for such truly distant events are fragile, consisting largely of king lists, that would be recited at enthronements, and folk tales that might, for instance, emerge in the chronicles that monks wrote. Nonetheless, it is agreed that some things can be known with reasonable certainty; and that the true beginnings of Scottish royalty were with with a man called Fergus son of (Mac) Erc who arrived in about 500 AD on the west coast of Caledonia, to use the Romans' name for northern Britain. He led a band of 'Scots' (the word then meant 'Irish') from Ireland to found a colony which survived as, originally, the small kingdom of Dalriada. This Fergus was in reality the first 'King' of Scots.

In his time the majority population of Caledonia consisted of Celtic Picts occupying the whole eastern side of the country. Through obscure passages of history, which probably included intermarriage with the ruling Picts, the Scottish kings came to dominate and indeed rename the whole country. By the Middle Ages Scotland was ruled by kings who claimed descent, depending on the king list, from Fergus son of Erc and/or the Picts.

The last few of this royal line are called the Dunkeld dynasty.[3] When King Alexander III of Scots died in 1286, thrown from his horse – possibly over a cliff edge – that dynasty came to an end in the male line. The death of Alexander III started a chain of events leading to the first great conflict of historical Scotland.

As his only direct descendant he left his granddaughter, Margaret, the Maid of Norway. This child was daughter of the King and Queen of Norway, the latter being the daughter of Alexander III. Thanks to her grandmother, who had been Queen of Scotland, the Maid of Norway also had English blood because she, the grandmother, was daughter of King Henry III of England. It was a slightly confusing case of three Margarets. Grandmother, mother and child had the same name. By 1286 the two older Margarets were dead. The Maid of Norway was three when her grandfather died. She was now the rightful heir to Scotland, but also, as a relative, she gave her great-uncle King Edward I of England a wonderful opportunity to intervene in Scottish politics.

Over the heads of local magnates, who had installed a regency council called the Guardians of Scotland, he and King Erik agreed first that the Maid of Norway was indeed heir to Scotland, and second that she should marry his son Edward of Carnarvon (the future Edward II), who was even younger than the Maid.

However in September 1290 the little girl fell ill and died at the age of seven. She was in Orkney on her way to England, where she could be safely housed in one of the royal castles ready for marriage in due course. The Plantagenet plan to secure a personal union between Scotland and England was blocked by a child's death. There was no shortage of claimants to Scotland after this. No less than fourteen stepped forward to succeed the Maid of Norway.[4] Two stood out. One was Robert de Brus, the other was the much younger John Balliol.[5]

Invited by the Scots to oversee the selection of their next king, Edward I, now pursuing plan B, demanded Scottish fealty. Events followed thick and fast. Balliol became king briefly but was ineffective in difficult circumstances, which included a campaign of ferocious harassment by Edward I, who tried to bully him into accepting English overlordship. The magnates intervened with another regency council and a treaty with France, the first move in what became know as the *auld alliance* between Scotland and France. That led to an English invasion of Scotland in 1296 and the defeat of the Scots at the Battle of Dunbar that year.

After mopping up, Edward I returned south, taking back to Westminster with him the Stone of Scone on which for centuries Scottish kings sat when they were crowned.[6] A ten-year period followed during which Edward I ruled as the Scots' feudal overlord and king. This was the first stage of the Wars of Scottish Independence.

Thanks to persistent if varying Scottish resistance, English imperialism failed. The fight-back was led in its early stages by William Wallace (d 1305) then by Robert de Brus – Robert the Bruce – grandson of the original Bruce claimant.

In 1306 de Brus became King Robert I of Scotland (1274-1329) by virtue of his descent from King David I. In this period major events included the Battle of Bannockburn (1314) won by Robert I against Edward II of England, and the Declaration of Arbroath. Dated 6 April 1320 the medieval Declaration is a key document of Scottish history. It was drafted to make the case for both the independence of Scotland and the kingship of Robert I. Addressed to Pope John XXII, the Latin Declaration made the following claims:

1. Scotland had always been independent, indeed had lived under 'one hundred and thirteen kings of their own race, the line unbroken by any foreigner'.

2. Edward I of England – *princeps magnificus* – had attacked Scotland without provocation committing 'unjust deeds, massacre, violence, theft, arson, imprisoning prelates, burning monasteries, robbing and killing monks and nuns... sparing nobody by virtue of age or sex.'

3. Robert, 'our king and lord,' had delivered Scotland from this attack, 'like another Macabaeus or Joshua meeting toil and fatigue, hunger and danger.'

4. However, his position as king depended on the job he did. The declaration said that the Scots – as represented by the nobles who sent it – were bound to King Robert by law and also 'by his personal merit'. Nonetheless, if he were to change tack and attempt to make Scotland subservient to England, they would drive him out and choose another king in his place. In those circumstances he would become 'an enemy and subverter of his own rights and ours'.

5. The relationship with England was hammered home: *quia quamdiu centum ex nobis vivi remanserint, nuncquam Anglorum dominio aliquatenus volumus subiugari* – 'for as long as a hundred of us remain alive we will never consent to be subjugated to English rule.'[7]

The text was sent above the seals of eight earls and forty-five barons, including three members of the Graham family, one of them David Graham of Kincardine, ancestor of the Montrose Grahams.

Once said, some things cannot be unsaid. The Declaration of Arbroath stated a principle so deeply felt it could not be forgotten. This was the idea that being king of Scots did not depend on heredity alone, that there was a Scottish national interest. The independence of Scotland was the king's charge. Kingship was identified with nationhood not with the blood royal or not the blood royal alone. Scotland was not the only medieval country in which the barons asserted their opinions, but the Declaration of Arbroath is strikingly national.

The pope accepted the arguments to the extent that he lifted the excommunication of Robert I imposed by an earlier pope. That eased the pressures. Thanks to this tactic and despite further English invasion (under Edward III) on behalf of a new Balliol claimant, the Plantagenets were barred. Other complications arose during the reign of David II. Nonetheless, Scotland continued to be independent of England. In 1371, a new family took the throne.

—∿∿—

It was from their hereditary office as Stewards of Scotland that the family name came – first written as Stewart, then in the sixteenth century as Stuart.[8] The first Stewart king was Robert II who became King of Scots at the age of fifty-four, old for the time. His father was Walter Stewart, one of the most powerful medieval Scots, but it was Walter's wife Marjorie Bruce, daughter of King Robert I, who provided their son with the necessary royal blood.[9]

Robert II and his son Robert III died in their beds (respectively in 1390 and 1406, both in their late sixties or early seventies). As the years went by, the ride was rockier. The third Stewart king, James I of Scotland, was assassinated in a noble conspiracy (in 1437, aged forty-three). When a cannon exploded at the siege of Roxburgh Castle, his son James II was standing nearby, and may have ordered it to be fired. The King died soon after of his wounds, aged twenty-nine (1460).

There were family quarrels. English intrusions continued. In 1488 James II's son, James III (aged thirty-six) was killed at the Battle of Sauchieburn (1488), fought against rebellious nobles who had set up his son as their not unwilling leader. This son now became the Renaissance prince King James IV who died (aged forty) in 1513 at the Battle of Flodden, fought against the English.

His son James V died in 1542 (aged thirty) shortly after the defeat of his troops by an English army at the Battle of Solway Moss. James V's daughter Mary, Queen of Scots, was forced to abdicate her throne in 1567 (aged twenty-four). She was beheaded twenty years later as the prisoner of her English cousin Elizabeth I. They were cousins because they both descended from Henry VII, the first Tudor king.

Like his mother, Mary's son James VI was a cradle king. He succeeded as a one-year-old when she abdicated and did a good job of governing Scotland as an adult. Still relatively young in 1603, the year of his thirty-seventh birthday, he became king of the much bigger and richer southern kingdom on the death of Elizabeth I of England in March 1603.

The sky lightened. James VI had longed to be King of England, had planned and prayed for it for years. As James I of England he travelled south in state to claim his new realm. Finding luxury at his disposal in the massive royal palaces mainly located around in the south-east around the River Thames – Whitehall, Richmond, Greenwich, Hampton Court, Nonsuch, Oatlands, Theobalds – there he stayed.

England and Scotland did not merge in 1603. Each was and remained a long-established and independent political unit with its own institutions. The change was that the same man was king of both. James VI and I's skill and his policies made him a different sort of king, one dedicated to diplomacy and the maintenance of peace. To his contemporaries he was *rex pacificus*.

3

The Scottish Reformation

Among the challenges facing King James was Scottish religion. In the world of the Stuart kings, certain things were taken as fact, not to be queried. The realm of Scotland was one, that of God another. The two went together. A contemporary of Charles I wrote the Kings of Scotland were Christians 'ever since Donald I in whose reign the Emperor Severus in the year 211… extended the Bounds of the Empire.'[1] The consequences of the sixteenth-century Reformation would be the essential background, and all too often the foreground, of James VI and I's reign and that of his son Charles I. James was a peacemaker but the Reformation was not.

The Reformation was grounded in centuries of religious thought. Martin Luther (1483-1546) was not the first to reappraise Catholic traditions, to be critical of the beetling edifice that the Church had become, but his own energies, the time in which he lived and the rejection of his ideas by Pope Leo X made him the pivotal figure.

The Reformation was an intellectual movement of great rigour, but the consequences could not be purely intellectual or spiritual because the practice and teachings which reformers challenged were bound in with material power, both that of the Catholic Church and that of Catholic kings. So non-theologians dictated the way the new thinking affected European society: hereditary sovereigns.[2]

The second wedding of King James V of Scotland provides an introduction to the staggering complexity that resulted. James V was the son of James IV and Margaret Tudor, the older sister of Henry VIII. Unless Henry VIII produced an heir, James V was in line to inherit not just Scotland but England, too.

On 1 January 1537 James V married Madeleine de Valois, daughter of King François I of France. He had gone to France to find his bride, was offered and refused a lesser princess, and seems to have prevailed with Madeleine by charm and good looks. The wedding took place on a raised platform outside the cathedral of Notre Dame in Paris, followed by Mass inside. The couple sailed back to Scotland with delays because of Madeleine's poor health. Aged seventeen, she died on 7 July the same year in Holyroodhouse.

The fix was finding another bride. The king still wanted a French connection. François I was still agreeable because the ultimate French policy was surrounding England. The King of France proposed the widowed twenty-two-year-old Duchesse de Longueville. She is normally known as Marie de Guise (Mary of Guise) using the name she was born with. Marie was not the king's daughter, but she was from a sovereign family. The Guises were a cadet branch of the independent Dukes of Lorraine. Her mother, Antoinette de Bourbon, was from an outlying branch of the French royal family (as her short-lived husband had been). Through her father Marie de Guise claimed descent from Charlemagne.

She married the King of Scots first in a proxy wedding at Châteaudun on 9 May 1638 and then on 18 June in St Andrews Cathedral. Both services were Catholic of course. Forty days of celebrations followed, hunting, hawking, tournaments. Marie had arrived with a French entourage who made a good impression during the festivities and received one, too. In August 1638 they returned home spreading the word about Scottish generosity.

After an anxious wait the new queen had two sons, both of whom died in infancy. On 8 December 1542 she gave birth to the third child of her second marriage, a daughter named Mary, who was very soon Queen of Scots by right of birth, because her father, James V, died six days later.

By now Scottish politics were again turbulent. Religious complexity was building thanks to Henry VIII's break with Rome in 1532-1534.[3] In response to James V's francophile foreign policy the King of England put pressure on his nephew, spurred by worry about his ultimate heir. Until 1537, when Queen Jane Seymour bore a son (the future Edward VI), Henry only had two daughters to succeed him and their status was confused by his marriages – an illegitimate child would not normally inherit the throne. On 1 July 1543 the Treaties of Greenwich provided for peace between England and Scotland, and for the marriage of the children Prince Edward and Mary, Queen of Scots.

Fast shifting Scottish politics led to a denial of the Treaties of Greenwich by the Scottish parliament the following September, which in May 1544 provoked the first of a series of aggressive English raids on Scotland, called the Rough Wooing. This the Scots withstood with much pain. Ten years later Marie de Guise became Regent of Scotland. By this time England was governed by Queen Mary I who returned her country to Roman Catholicism. Nothing was constant.

In this period important events occurred within the Holy Roman Empire. The essence is that a group of German Lutheran princes fought the Emperor Charles V in order to win their freedom to worship as they wished. The Reformation was originally German, starting with Luther's teaching in Saxony, which risked unbalancing the empire when some princes remained Catholic and others took up the new thinking. Charles V wanted the empire to remain solidly Catholic but in the Peace of Augsburg (1555), which ended this first outburst of religious war, he accepted a compromise. This is summarised by the Latin tag *cuius regio eius religio*, which can be paraphrased as 'whoever rules a territory can impose his/her religious choice on it.'

That meant the empire was the first political unit in which religious tolerance was sanctioned by law after the Reformation. For instance, Saxony could be Lutheran while Bavaria could be Catholic. After the Augsburg treaty there was work to do to keep the peace, and the slow-burn complication was that the more recent form of Protestantism – Reformed Protestantism, or Calvinism, named after the leading Reformed thinker, John Calvin (1509-1564) – was not taken into account; but the settlement worked well enough for sixty years.

As for events outside the empire, the deal was a confirmation. It helpfully expressed a wider acceptance that the ruling prince decided religious practice. In England it was Henry VIII and his children Edward VI and Elizabeth I who, in their different ways, determined the Protestant religious settlement. Regardless of the message of the New Testament, religion was dynastic.

Since 1548, when she was six, Mary, Queen of Scots, had been living in France under the agreement that she would marry the Dauphin. Their wedding took place on 24 April 1558 seven months before Mary I of England died (17 November 1558), to be succeeded by her half-sister Elizabeth, who was an uncertain prospect.

While she was the one remaining child of Henry VIII, Elizabeth's legitimacy could be questioned because she was the daughter of his second wife, born while his first wife was still alive. If Elizabeth were illegitimate, then she could not be queen, especially when there was another possible heir. Mary, Queen of Scots, was definitely legitimate, the daughter and granddaughter of orthodox Catholic and royal marriages, the descendant of Henry VII of England and his wife Elizabeth of York.[4] Pinning it down, one can say Elizabeth I was legitimate only in the Protestant world. If she accepted Catholicism, she would lose her throne.

Before the eyes of some, an alluring vista hazily unfolded. If the Dauphin and Mary had children, or rather if they had a boy – the French succession only went to men – then that child could claim three historic kingdoms: France, England, Scotland (also Ireland, classed as a kingdom since the days of Henry VIII). The Valois government did nothing to dispel the vision. When they appeared in state – in other words most of the time – the Dauphin and his wife displayed the arms of England with their own.

Protestants everywhere prayed for Elizabeth I. In Scotland there was an increase in Protestant agitation, tightened by an aristocratic group called the Lords of the Congregation. They agitated for the Calvinist version of Protestantism, but they also stood, in the best Scottish tradition, for national independence. Which of the two was more important to them, the political aim or the religious one?

As regent, Marie de Guise was running a pro-French policy in Scotland. She appointed Frenchmen to senior offices including the Treasury. The French ambassador sometimes attended meetings of the Scottish privy council. She seems to have been surprised by the opposition all this aroused. She seems truly to have seen Scotland as an independent nation, allied to France but not part of a French empire. Yet the regent's tactics terrified Scottish grandees, who could see a future in which French garrisons and a French administration would deprive them of income and influence, to say nothing of the horde of Catholic priests everywhere. Scotland for the Scots.

—◦◦◦—

Born in Haddington in the southern Scottish lowlands in about 1514, John Knox was ordained in the late 1530s and became involved in the Scottish reform movement in the 1540s. He lived in Geneva briefly in 1554, then again from September 1556 to January 1559 with some interruptions. By this time he had been expelled from Scotland as a Reformed Protestant agitator; spent nineteen months as a galley slave in France; and several years in England when he was one of the royal chaplains of Edward VI and nearly became Bishop of Rochester. His pastoral work indicated some of the moderation which his writings lacked, but Knox increasingly lived in a black and white world, mostly black.

Knox had a way with words. He neatly expressed the Reformed trust in the Bible, the utter rejection of any other authority:

> In religion there is no middle. Either it is the religion of God, and that in everything that is done it must have the assurance of His own Word, and is his Majesty truly honoured, or else it is the religion of the Devil.[5]

'His own Word' here means Holy Scripture.

Being a galley slave nearly killed him, but Knox came through nurtured by pain. He later described how he refused to show devotion to an image of the Virgin Mary as his jailors demanded. Instead, he threw it overboard (probably unobserved), spat on it and told it to float. Knox exulted in delivering sermons that lasted two hours or more. He knew Calvin at the time when Calvin's theology was reaching maturity. He embraced confrontation. His rejection of all that he disagreed with at first included a furious denial of his own vocation as a preacher. As time passed, he saw that he was called to broadcast truth to power, that is to say the truth as seen by John Knox.

It was in Geneva that he nailed his colours to the manly mast with the publication of *The First Blast of the Trumpet Against the Monstrous Regiment of Women* (1558). This now notorious text begins: 'To promote a Woman to bear rule, superiority, dominion, or empire above any Realm, Nation, or City, is repugnant to Nature.'[6] It took blistering aim at women rulers – 'regiment' meaning 'rule' – on the grounds that God meant women to be subordinate to men. Knox had several close women friends and a wife whom he loved. His scorn for women raised to be rulers was not the same as contempt for women, but his world order could not accept female political authority.

The First Blast of the Trumpet sounded mainly against the Catholic Mary I of England in her dying days. Knox was preoccupied by England at this time, but Scotland also reeled from the decibels. After all, Marie de Guise, whom Knox detested, was another ruling Catholic woman, as her daughter quite soon would be. By Knox's logic the young queen's French husband would be his preferred King of Scots, a prospect so awful that it changed history.

John Knox returned to Scotland in May 1559 to inspire and support the rebellion of the Lords of the Congregation. Even if had wanted to be in England he could not, because Elizabeth I refused him permission to enter her realm. In a way *The First Blast of the Trumpet* sealed his future as a Scot.

His furious sermons in Perth and St Andrews in early summer provoked iconoclastic riots. He encouraged attacks on priories with the words 'pull down the nests that the crows might not build again.'[7] In July, Henri II of France died after a jousting accident. Dauphin François succeeded his father as King of France. Mary, Queen of Scots, became Queen of France. It was the nightmare scenario.

In early 1560 the Lords invited an English army to support their wavering cause. Elizabeth I could not risk French dominance of Scotland, so she sent a fleet and troops. Marie de Guise fought back with both

French and Scottish troops. The English put the port of Leith under siege, an operation which exhausted both sides. Utterly worn down, Marie became seriously ill and died on 11 June 1660. On 5 July 1560 the Treaty of Edinburgh was signed, bringing peace. The signatories were Scotland as represented by the Lords, France and England. It was agreed that both English and French troops would leave Scotland. The Protestants won.

Two comments can be made. First, England guaranteed the Scottish Reformation. In the light of the events that are the main subject of this book, that is one of the ironies of history. Second, had Mary Tudor lived longer – she died aged forty-two – the events of 1560 could not have happened. She would never have supported Scottish Protestantism. So much hung by a thread.

The Scottish Reformation was at once launched by the parliament that in August 1560 followed the peace. This is the essential point. Parliament reformed religion. In Scotland *cuius regio eius religio* did not apply. It was not the regent, nor her daughter the rightful Queen of Scots who decided what faith the Scots would follow. The French were widely resented, so the Lords of the Congregation found support among ordinary people. And the sermons of Knox set loose a popular fury. The voice of the people made its contribution on the winning side. The Scottish Reformation was not royal. It was both aristocratic and popular. In other countries faith was dictated from the throne. In Scotland it was the people's choice.

That gave religion in Scotland a distinctive flavour. The new Scottish church, the Kirk, became an emblem of Scottish, not of dynastic, identity, in fact *the* emblem. From the beginning the Kirk stood for something separate from the crown.

The Reformation Parliament passed revolutionary legislation, the main but not the only measure being the Papal Jurisdiction Act. The text includes the words:

> ...the three estates then being present understanding that the jurisdiction and authority of the Bishop of Rome called the Pope used within this realm in times past has been very hurtful and prejudicial to our sovereign's authority and commonwealth of this realm. Therefore it is ordained that the Bishop of Rome have no authority in this realm in times coming.

The title used, the Bishop of Rome (genuinely the Pope's title), reduced papal authority to the middle of Italy. But it did more. It pointed out that the Pope was yet another bishop, something which Calvinist preachers would more and more inveigh against. The cause of the bishops, they said, was not godly, it was worldly.

Naturally Mary, Queen of Scots, did not think that the Pope's authority was hurtful and prejudicial to hers. She never endorsed the Papal Jurisdiction Act. She and her husband (as King of Scots) had allowed the parliament but had vainly forbidden debate of religion. What did the parliament make of her?

There was an ingenious attempt to sideline their sovereign. The parliament tried to pursue the marriage of James Hamilton, Earl of Arran, with Elizabeth I of England – which might have created an alternative royal family, since the Hamiltons came after the Stuarts in the line of succession. To this proposal Elizabeth 'gave no answer at all'.[8] But parliament did not deny the Scottish queen. Until her husband died (aged sixteen) in December 1560, Mary was still most undesirably the Queen of France, but nobody at this time argued she should not be Queen of Scots. Yet in a purely constitutional sense the Reformation parliament broke new ground. In August 1560 Mary was still in France and under-age. The regent was dead. Who governed Scotland?

It was a good question. The legality of the many acts of the Lords of the Congregation was doubtful because they had rebelled against the sovereign power. They were not shy. They rallied support and the Reformation parliament declared everything they had done legal. Here was parliamentary assertion – and back-dating – well in advance of England.

The Reformation Parliament ratified a Reformed Protestant confession of faith, drafted by a group of ministers including John Knox: the Scots Confession. This text eloquently expresses the essential humility of Protestantism. Evidently it is a document of its time. Interspersed with its commitment to a selfless and rather communal spirituality are notes of denial, defiance, despair, anger and at one point an aggressive emphasis on the subordinate role of women (with an interesting comment on Catholic practice).

The gist can be understood from the following.

The remembrance of the which day [the Day of Judgement] is not only a bridle to us whereby our carnal lusts are refrained but also such inestimable comfort, that neither may the threatening of worldly princes, neither yet the fear of temporal death... move us to renounce... that blessed society [with Christ].

... of nature we are so dead, so blind and so perverse, that neither can we feel when we are pricked, see the light when it shines, nor assent to the will of God when it is revealed.

...The Law of God we confess and acknowledge most just, most equal, most holy, and most perfect... But our nature is so corrupt, so weak, and imperfect, that we are never able to fulfil the works of the Law in perfection.

...we flee the society with the Papistical Kirk in participation of their Sacraments; first, because their ministers are no ministers of Christ Jesus; yea (which is more horrible) they suffer women, whom the Holy Ghost will not suffer to teach in the congregation, to baptise.

Since the context was and had to be political, it is notable that the Scots Confession starts with a warning against 'the threatening of worldly princes'. On the other hand, the final sections commit to support of the civil order.

We confess and acknowledge empires, kingdoms, dominions, and cities to be distincted and ordained by God: the powers and authorities in the same (be it of Emperors in their empires, of Kings in their realms, Dukes and Princes in their dominions, or of other Magistrates in free cities), to be God's holy ordinance...we further confess and acknowledge, that such persons as are placed in authority are to be loved

...to Kings, Princes, Rulers, and Magistrates, we affirm that chiefly and most principally the conservation and purgation of the Religion appertains; so that not only they are appointed for civil policy, but also for maintenance of the true Religion, and for suppressing of idolatry and superstition. [9]

It was not until King James VI took personal control of government from 1583 that the Kirk had to face an assertive and politically skilled Protestant king. Meanwhile the key date was 1578 when the Second Book of Discipline was adopted, which set out a presbyterian (congregational) church structure, one that was bottom up – the opposite of a church run by bishops. The Kirk would be formed of local presbyteries, regional synods and the national General Assembly. Everything started with the presbyteries, parish organisations run by ministers and lay elders. Where did 'Kings, Princes, Rulers, and Magistrates' fit into this scheme? In a presbyterian church, who decided what was 'true Religion' and what was false?

4

Lord Graham

For eight years in the second century AD, the northern border of Roman Britain was the Antonine Wall, built between the Firth of Forth and the Firth of Clyde. It was not defensible. The Romans soon drew back to Hadrian's Wall to the south. Apparently, the war leader who broke though the Antonine Wall from the north was Graym or Gramus. Supposedly he was father-in-law of King Fergus II and ancestor of the patrician Graham family.[1] Remnants were later called Graham's Dyke.

Early Grahams may have been Scandinavian, although historians tend to think the family was Anglo-Norman in origin, settling in Scotland during the reign of William I (1143-1214) – William the Lion. They became high-ranking nobles. By the fifteenth century the ancestors of the Montrose line had assembled large estates. Their base was in the central part of the country, lowland estates bordering the highlands. We do not know the exact numbers but by the seventeenth century the ground covered can be guessed at upwards of a hundred thousand acres. According to the standards of their rank the Montrose Grahams were not especially rich but according to everyone else's standards they were. Always they were part of the great game of politics.

Their main residence was Kincardine Castle, near Auchterarder in what was then Strathearn, now Perth and Kinross. Kincardine lies about fourteen miles to the south-west of the city of Perth. It was a moated fortress built on a plateau in a wide valley. On one side the land slopes steeply down to Ruthven Water, a tributary of the River Earn. To the south-east the Ochil hills can be seen, the Grampian Mountains lie to the north. Today the building is a romantic ruin in gentle countryside.[2] The Montrose Grahams had other big houses, the most important being Old Montrose, a little to the south of modern Montrose in Angus, and Mugdock Castle, Stirlingshire.

The family motto is *ne oublie* ('do not forget') which is apt. There is plenty to remember. There were family casualties in the Wars of Scottish Independence: Sir Patrick Graeme was killed at the Battle of Dunbar in 1296; his brother Sir John was close to William Wallace and died at the Battle of Falkirk in 1298. Sir David Graham, signatory of the Declaration of Arbroath in 1320, has already been noted.

Not everything was straightforward. The men who killed King James I in February 1437 were led by Sir Robert Graham of Kinpont. Clearly, Sir Robert was opposed to the king if not to the system (the context was a quarrel within the royal family). The Grahams were close to the royal Stuarts. In the early fifteenth century Sir William Graham married Mary Stewart, daughter of King Robert III. His brother married Euphemia Stewart, granddaughter of King Robert II.

Notwithstanding their regicide, the family thrived through service to the crown. In 1445 Patrick Graham was recognized as a Lord of Parliament with the title Lord Graham. In 1503 Patrick's grandson William was made Earl of Montrose. The first earl died in 1513 at the battle of Flodden. The second Earl of Montrose was a member of the privy council during the minority of Mary, Queen of Scots, and after her 1561 return to Scotland. Although he supported her as a Queen's man, and was probably Catholic, he was not prepared to fight in her favour, so in the end he trimmed. The third Earl of Montrose was the second earl's grandson.[3] He became Treasurer and Chancellor of Scotland, the two most senior government posts. His son John Graham, fourth Earl of Montrose, was admitted to the privy council at the age of thirty-one (1604) and became its president in 1626. He died soon after. As regards Reformation politics, the Montrose Grahams became conventionally Protestant (presbyterian) with the third earl.

Supplementing the medieval marriages, the seventeenth-century Montrose Grahams had a few drops of royal blood running in their veins ever since the second Lord Graham married Lady Helen Douglas. Her father was Earl of Angus, a descendant of King Robert III through his daughter Mary. Similar distinction marked other noble families, especially the Hamiltons, who descended from another Mary Stewart (1453-1488), daughter of King James II. Within their already elevated rank, families like these could claim to be part of an inner élite.

We do not have the date of Lady Margaret Ruthven's marriage with the fourth Earl of Montrose. Judging from the dates of their children's weddings their own was probably in the first years of the new century shortly after the Gowrie Conspiracy – 1602 or 1603.[4]

The more things change, the more they stay the same. Margaret was from a family so disgraced that it lost everything, including its name, whereas her husband's family basked in the king's favour. One would think the two young people had quite different status but that is a misapprehension. Even disgrace on the Ruthven scale left surviving Ruthvens, especially the unthreatening women, as aristocrats fully worthy of the normal life progression.

John and Margaret had several children, of whom one was a boy. James was born in 1612, probably in October. The exact date is not known.[5] We read that Margaret consulted witches (fortune-tellers) at his birth.[6] The Ruthvens as a family were repeatedly associated with illegal[7] folk practices like this – soothsaying, witches. At least once, Margaret's son would return to that tradition.

James had the courtesy title Lord Graham as eldest son and heir to everything. Almost nothing is known of his childhood, but we do know that he was raised in the presbyterian faith and as a cavalier: by the age of eight he had two horses of his own.[8] It is safe to assume the little boy was left in the charge of servants at Kincardine while his parents would move between their houses and the royal court; and that it was an outdoor life to a great extent. The traditions of the masculine nobility, and especially the old nobles like the Grahams, were weighted toward physical activity. The main service owed to the king, in return for tenure of land, was military.

Margaret died in 1618. John did not remarry. He had at least one illegitimate son, Harry Graham, who may have been born around this time. Perhaps James's sisters – Lilias, Margaret, Dorothea, Katherine, Beatrix – compensated as female company after they lost their mother. Though as a boy James would have been raised very differently from them. And there was often a distance between noble children and parents, which reflected the deadly seriousness of family. Children were the fruit of love no doubt, but much more important they had a job in the world, a job which required professionalism. They had to secure the future.

The power of Scottish magnates within their lands was palatine, like that of a sovereign: 'The real basis of the great landholder's local power lay in his grant of regality, which gave him judicial authority over those who lived within it.'[9] The child Lord Graham was raised to exercise massive authority. As an adult he must be capable of exercising it in such a way that the Grahams would continue their historic role without damaging the family position, and ideally enhancing it.

In pursuit of that essential end, the fourth earl provided for his son's schooling. From the Martinmas, or Christmas, term of 1624, James lodged in Glasgow with a personal tutor. Aged twelve he was in his own bespoke boarding-school.

5

Exit King James

The end of an era approached. The king was ailing. In September 1624 his arthritis became more severe. For the Scots a testing time lay ahead. His son Charles would be the first King of Scots ever not to live as an adult in Scotland. Nor had he been raised to know the country. For what came later, King James carries a fair portion of responsibility. He lived up to his reputation as a peace-loving king but sowed the seeds of conflict.

The loose ends from his time in Scotland included a religious agenda which developed when he had experience of working with the Church of England, of which he was Supreme Governor. From England James pursued the Kirk, first by restoring more fully what had not quite been abandoned, a working Scottish episcopacy.

The king made the Scottish bishops royal officials more than showy spiritual princes, the figures so particularly offensive to the presbyterian Scots. By the time of the General Assembly of 1610 diocesan episcopacy had been restored.[1] Nonetheless, that meant that the bishops were if anything more closely associated with royal authority. King James's experience of the Church of England persuaded him more than ever of the importance of episcopacy. It was in England, quite soon after his succession, that he uttered the heartfelt words 'No bishop, no king'.[2]

Although raised in the Reformed theology, which all his life he upheld, James VI and I while in Scotland had to handle tenacious and clever Kirk opponents, led by Andrew Melville (1545-1622). The king was not head of the Kirk, he was not governor, he had no place formally except as a worshipping Christian like anyone else, which Melville loved to point out. Nonetheless, James won a great point by maintaining – and enshrining in

43

law (in 1584), and therefore passing to his son – his right, as king, to call a General Assembly of the Kirk, and to decide where it would meet, which nobody else could do.

These tensions included a showdown in 1596 when the king for a short time abandoned Edinburgh (threatening its economy) after riots that he described as 'treasonable and seditious uproar.'[3] The king's divine right convictions resulted: the idea that the king was chosen by God and therefore had an unequalled authority over his kingdom in everything; and the belief that Scottish presbyterians (and English puritans) undermined that authority, even that they were naturally treacherous.

> How learned, how wise, and judicious was that great king, Jacobus Pacificus… who had been brought up a Puritan since his infancy… yet when he had passed his adolescence, and was come to have reigned thirty-six years, then did his far and deep reaching judgement pierce the most hidden secrets of the Puritans; and, therefore, did ever hold this general maxim, that it was impossible for any man to be both a Puritan and a faithful subject to his prince.[4]

While King James operated on this basis in combination with real political skill, it remained to be seen how his son Charles would work. The son took on divine right wholesale.

Nor could James VI and I leave the Kirk to its own devices. He wanted the Kirk to be like the Church of England, which was playing with fire. The congregational nature of the Kirk was the main difference between the two, but the form of service also differed. England worshipped according to a defined liturgy, prayers and services spelled out in the Book of Common Prayer; for the same purpose Scotland used another text, the Book of Common Order written by John Knox.

Knox's liturgy was written in Geneva. It was pure Reformed Protestant, including its provision for the 'Lord's Supper' (the Eucharist, or Communion) where there were conflicting theologies; and it allowed *extempore* preaching and prayer. The English Book of Common Prayer was more permissive theologically, but more restrictive in the forms of prayer. It sought to control what the minister/priest said and did – within the defined services he might have a spiritual freedom, a freedom within himself, but he could not define the services.[5]

James VI and I knew the Scots well enough to understand that imposing on them an English prayer-book would not be accepted. Instead, he tried keyhole surgery. He wanted to nudge them in the right direction.

His compromise was to ask the Scots to accept five practices commonly found in England:

1. Private baptism;
2. Communion to be taken privately by the sick;
3. Confirmation of young people by a bishop;
4. Holy days of Christ's life to be celebrated (for instance Christmas);
5. Kneeling to receive communion.

The 'Five Articles' were debated and accepted first by the General Assembly (at Perth, in 1618) and later by parliament (1621). Because of the location of the General Assembly, they became known as the Five Articles of Perth.

To prepare the ground the king visited Scotland in 1617, the only time he ever returned from England. During his visit the royal chapel in Holyroodhouse was repaired, 'wherein was a glorious altar set up, with two closed Bibles, two unlighted candles, and two basins without water set thereon, brave organs and choristers require to sing, and the English service ordained to be said daily.'[6]

It was thanks to tough management of both General Assembly and parliament by his officials that the king pushed the Five Articles through, but it was a Pyrrhic victory. At the General Assembly a number of nobles, due to attend as laymen, failed to do so, pleading sickness. Archbishop Spottiswoode of St Andrews knew what that meant and commented 'I think their minds were more sick than their bodies and are so still.'[7] There was huge opposition.

The last article, kneeling to receive communion, was the hardest for both ministers and parishioners. Kneeling implied worship. Reformed theology insisted that the communion bread and wine were symbols of the Last Supper, they never transformed into a holy substance, from first to last they remained bread and wine. The Scots were not going to worship a loaf and a drink. Because of the fifth article above all, the Five Articles were hated.

Because they were hated, they were not enforced. Whose antennae twitched? Historians have ascribed government back-pedalling to the wisdom of James VI and I. Recent research suggests something different: that it was the Scottish privy council, not the king, which saw that the articles could not be enforced – in Edinburgh in particular.

The councillors could see what was happening. Opposition to the fifth article took the form of parishioners, in their thousands, walking outside the city to churches where minsters could not be scrutinised.[8] Just as dangerously, the growth of private prayer meetings – conventicles – was another reaction. Conventicles could not be controlled. In a private house anything could be said.

The Privy Council's reluctance to drive home the king's instructions opened another crack in the wall. If the king imposed an unpopular policy but his top advisers judged it too risky, where was the cohesion of government? The king who boasted that he governed Scotland by the pen was perhaps not governing Scotland at all. By the time he realised that his instructions were not in force, James VI and I's own time was up. He died on 27th March 1625, at Theobalds in Hertfordshire.

In May 1625 the Archbishop of St Andrews travelled south to represent the Kirk in the procession for King James's funeral. He turned up in the sober dress of the Scottish clergy but was asked to add lawn (fine linen) sleeves like the English bishops wore. He refused and withdrew.[9] That spoke volumes about the Scottish attitude to English religious practice.

The truth was that both nations had prejudices about the other, not just in religion. We have a flavour of the worst English scorn in remarks by a courtier who went with the king to Scotland in 1617:

> ...for the country I must confess it is too good for those who possess it, and too bad for those that will be at charge to conquer it; the air might be wholesome but for the stinking people that inhabit it, the ground might be fruitful had they wit to measure it, their beasts are generally small.[10]

Ruminating on the nature both of Scottish people and the natural environment, the author continues: 'As for fruit, for their Grandmother Eve's sake they never planted any, and for other trees, had Christ been betrayed in this land, as doubtless he should have been, had he come as a stranger among them, Judas had sooner found the grace of repentance than a tree to hang himself on.'

For Edinburgh the writer has nothing but contempt, calling it a parish, 'for City I cannot call it.' And the Scottish women are to him repellent: 'The ladies are of the opinion that Susanna could not be chaste because she bathed often... their breath commonly stinketh of pottage, their linen of piss, their hands of Pigs' turds.'

Scots understood this kind of attitude very well. They thought their own informal society more honest, more free, and with a better pedigree than England. In particular, the distancing formality of great Englishmen, their de haut en bas attitude, was a joke, and they did not like to see any of their own copy it.

> For once that English devil, keeping of state, got a hold amongst our [Scottish] nobility, they began to keep a distance as if there were some divinity in them, and gentlemen must put off their shoes, the ground is so holy where they tread... It is true that in England the keeping of state is in some sort tolerable for that nation (being so often conquered) is become slavish, and takes not evil to be slaves to their superior...[11]

On both sides was an overwhelming perception of otherness. The remark about 'being so often conquered' referred to 1066 and the Norman Conquest – pretty much a one-off. This is the starting point for the ensuing politics: exaggeration on both sides and the hostility of warring neighbours. These factors made the legacy of James VI and I in 1625 much shakier than it seemed at the time.

The relative size of the two countries naturally counted. It meant the king was bound to give the priority to England. At the beginning of the seventeenth century the English population was four million. The population of Scotland was less than a quarter of that. Crown revenues from England were more than correspondingly bigger because of the more advanced economy, including far more international trade.

Royal finances and financial decisions (for instance on monopolies) were a huge feature of James VI and I's reign, as they would be for his son. Crown revenues from Scotland were modest – less than the revenues of Ireland.[12] James and his son both tried to increase the Scottish revenue (ie increase tax). One of the underlying causes of discontent in Scotland, a discontent that only became visible very slowly, was a new tax on the interest on loans in 1621, which particularly hit the businessmen of the burghs, Scotland's budding bankers.[13]

On 5 May the king's funeral was celebrated without the presence of the Scottish primate. He was buried in the Henry VIII chapel of Westminster Abbey. Both England and Scotland were at peace when he died.

His other great duty, to provide the succession, was also fulfilled. His son Charles had no children but had just married, in a proxy ceremony in Paris, the French princess Henrietta Maria (the two had not yet met). His daughter Elizabeth, Electress Palatine and, controversially, Queen of Bohemia,[14] was pregnant with her sixth child. On his deathbed at Theobalds, the old king had asked his son to protect the church, his sister and his beloved Duke of Buckingham.

The accession of the new king invited no controversy.

6

Kinnaird Castle

The Glasgow schoolboy cannot have paid too much attention to pious discussion. Perhaps the king's funeral had a mournful appeal, but Henrietta Maria's colourful arrival at Whitehall by river on a very wet June day must have been the best story.[1]

Normally the queen would have a triumphal entry through the streets but there was a bad outbreak of plague in London. On the royal barge, dressed in green, the king and his wife were splendidly isolated. Londoners liked the watery epiphany. Insofar as she could be glimpsed through the pouring rain Henrietta Maria was cheered and applauded – a nice-looking if very small girl.

James lodged with Sir George and Lady Elphinstone, a couple with court connections. He had his own tutor, William Forrett, and two pages. As Provost of Glasgow, Sir George was very much involved in city politics. An archdiocese since 1492, Glasgow's other power centre was the archbishop's palace. Archbishop James Law was a supporter of the king's religious policy, kneeling at communion and all.

Thanks to two surviving inventories we glimpse Lord Graham's lifestyle. His possessions included a sword 'got from Merchiston' (the home of his sister Margaret, married to Archibald Napier), a brass arquebus (muzzle-loaded gun) and a crossbow inlaid with mother-of-pearl. These weapons were beautiful objects finished to a high degree. Also listed is a scarf, a gift from his father. The second inventory includes silver and silver gilt cups and spoons, a silver salt cellar, linen napkins, red 'figurato' (embroidered) curtains, yellow curtains worked with red thread, tablecloths and a brown velvet cushion to be used at church.[2]

James was living a life both energetic and comfortable, probably quite public too. He was heir to a great house. He lodged with the Provost.

His father was Lord President of the privy council. He would know Archbishop Law. He would be recognized in the street and would not go out unattended.

The young Lord Graham was educated as a classical humanist, a system which emphasised the Latin language first of all; then history of the ancient world; then its thought. In humanist imagination the modern world came last. He had editions of the Latin silver age dramatist and philosopher Seneca, famous for his service as the Emperor Nero's tutor and for the suicide that resulted. James also had a Latin translation of the 'History of Xenophon', the work now called the *Hellenica* (originally in Greek), a history of war in Greece of the fifth and fourth centuries BCE.[3]

Other books were more recent: the *History* of Marcus Sabellicus (fifteenth century), the works of Joachim Camerarius (sixteenth century) – although these were probably his Latin translations of Greek authors; a treatise on the orders of knighthood; William Strangvage's recent life of Mary, Queen of Scots (1624); and *Geoffrey de Boulogne*, a translation of Torquato Tasso's sixteenth-century epic about the First Crusade – the hero being Godfrey of Bouillon. [4]

The work for which James clearly had an attachment was Walter Raleigh's *History of the World*. He personally transported it to St Andrews University when he went in 1627. On the back of one of the illustrations in the copy that survives from his library is a doodle: within the traced circumference of a coin is written, in Montrose's handwriting, a version of the Lord's Prayer, tiny, precise letters suggesting a meticulous and disciplined mind. We also have his signature written on another of his books, again elegant, italic, polished.

Raleigh's *History* consisted of several volumes. Hugely popular at the time, Raleigh's *History* is a bit of a showy moral tract filled with improving stories – appealing to the teenage mind. Raleigh had written his *History* when he was quite comfortably imprisoned in the Tower of London from 1603 to 1616 on treason charges. The first edition came out in 1614. The *History* was never finished. It covered the ancient world, with only some anecdotes and comments on the modern.[5] The message, a commonplace of philosophers, was do not worship power.

There is a story in which Pope Sixtus V (1521-1590) is asked by a friend how had he become Pope. If his friend had only seen 'by what folly this world is governed, thou would wonder at nothing' replies Sixtus. Other comments on princes include criticisms of 'the crimes of monarchs,' a depiction of Henry VIII as the type of the 'merciless prince,' examples of the overthrow of tyrannies, a suggestion of the constitutional limitations on monarchs.[6] From the ancient world two soldiers emerged as praiseworthy: Epaminondas of Thebes and Hannibal of Carthage. Both had dramatic deaths: the first in battle, the second in exile, thought to be suicide.

James read Julius Caesar, writing about his own military success in ancient Gaul in famously limpid prose; and the Roman poet Lucan, whose great work was the *Pharsalia*, a verse epic about the historic war in the first century BCE between Caesar and Pompey, a civil war. It begins with a tragic declaration which would quite soon apply to the affairs of Scotland:

> We sing of wars over the Emathian plains worse than civil,
> Of right given to crime, a powerful people turning a sword
> Into its own guts with the hand of victory, armies all related,
> And the realm's broken treaties...[7]

The fourth Earl of Montrose died on 14 November 1626 (aged fifty-three). James returned to Kincardine in time to see his father still alive. On 3 January 1627 the burial took place. The house was filled with relations. In their grief they consumed venison, beef, mutton, lamb, veal, goose, capons, moorfowl, woodcock. They drank claret, white wine, ale.[8] From this time James was earl and can be called Montrose. Because he was under-age, guardians, or curators, were appointed, including his brother-in-law Archibald Napier, 'a most indulgent parent'[9] to the new earl. Napier would later be his political ally.

By 1626 Montrose's two elder sisters, Lilias and Margaret, had been married for several years. Dorothea married not long after her father's death. Lilias was the wife of Sir John Colquhoun of Luss (wedding in 1620), Margaret, a little younger but married earlier (1619), was Lady Napier. Dorothea would marry Sir James Rollo (or Rollock) of Duncrub in 1628. Beatrix, the (very much) youngest, would marry David Drummond, third Lord Maderty in 1641. That only leaves Katherine, to whose story we will return.

We have information about the Montrose finances at this time. At the end of March 1627, the young earl sold the estate of Airthrey near Stirling to an uncle. Other outlying estates were sold in the period 1630-1632. He also raised mortgages, as his father had, on the (substantial) property which he kept. Evidently, debts had been inherited and had to be recycled. The transactions did not clip his wings, but they show that he was not cash rich when he inherited and had to sell capital.[10]

Aged fifteen Montrose moved from his Glasgow schoolroom to St Andrews University, the university traditionally patronised by the Scottish aristocracy. His name is found on the register of students dated 26 January 1627.[11] Here he remained not quite three years. It looks like an acceleration of his preparation, now that he was head of the family. Everything happened to him young.

At St Andrews Montrose had a new tutor, John Lambye. New books were bought including a Greek grammar. A copy of the works of the humanist George Buchanan was in his St Andrews collection. Buchanan had a European reputation as a master of Latin prose and was one of the tutors to King James VI. His *De Jure Regni apud Scotos* (1579) argued that the king had supreme power subject to acceptance by the people, that resistance to tyrants was lawful. Buchanan did not accept divine right theory; he thought king and people lived under a contract which put obligations on both (like the men who signed the Declaration of Arbroath). Montrose also owned William Struthers' *Meditations* and the *Sacred Meditations* of the Lutheran John Gerhard, both contemporary devotional works.

Probably at this time Montrose started to write his own poetry. And at university, for the first time he was the subject of poetic admiration: an anonymous Hungarian poet was paid fifty-eight shillings for verses dedicated to the student earl. [12]

One has the impression that at St Andrews study faded. The young man was constantly travelling across Scotland to see friends and relations. His business accounts mention trips to Edinburgh, Leith, Bruntilling, Braco, Morphie, Clanberkie, Kinnaird, Dundee, Orchill, Rossdhu, Scone, Garscube, Stirling, Inchbrakie, Cumbernauld, Dumbarton. Various nobles and men of business are mentioned, some from his age group, some older, including Lord Lindsay, Lord Sinclair, Lord Sutherland, Lord Colville, Sir Thomas Hope (Lord Advocate of Scotland). It was a round of entertainment and networking.

We have the financial accounts from this period. Not surprisingly, a good deal of money was spent on horses: 'hire of two horses', three horses to the ferry', 'for my Lord's horse corn and straw'; he bought 'a pair of gilt spurs'. Sport was important. Lindsay is mentioned as a hunting companion, Colville as recommending a falconer, Sutherland as a fellow archer. Montrose competed successfully for the silver arrow that the university awarded to its best archer, winning it in both 1628 and 1629.[13] He played golf. He had both his arquebus and sword professionally refurbished. Both must have been in use in sport. The most constant accounts items are cloth and clothes including ribbons, lace, gloves, shoes. A lot of money went on these. Show was essential. Montrose had a public. He paid a drummer to celebrate the silver arrow competition. He hired minstrels, drummers, pipers. Food features in quantities that can only be explained by rounds of entertaining: 'six pairs of chickens... a gigot of mutton... fruits and milk... wild goose ...a pound of raisins'.

With conspicuous consumption went charity. Again and again, the accounts report money given by Montrose to those in need, of whom in a subsistence society there were many. There were payments to the 'poor at the port of Dundee', 'the poor that week at the kirk door', 'another poor woman', 'the poor at the kirk of Goven' and many more, also money given to 'a Frenchman (a fellow student) to help bear his charges'.[14] Not only was Montrose generous, but he was also a reliable churchgoer. He regularly gave money to poor people at the church door.

Although the subject was raised later in an attempt to discredit him as immoral, we know nothing of Montrose's relations with women. In the course of his rounds he certainly met girls other than his sisters. He was young, athletic, handsome, rich, well-dressed, sociable, single, an earl. Presumably he went down well. What we do know is that aged seventeen he married Magdalen Carnegie in late 1629.

Evidently the marriage reflected the determination of Montrose's guardians that the next generation of Grahams should arrive as soon as possible. It is not out of the question that Magdalen was pregnant at the time she married. Their eldest son John would die in March 1645 aged fourteen (so he could have been born any time between April 1630 and February 1631).[15] The wedding day of Montrose and Magdalen was 10 November 1629.

Magdalen was the youngest daughter of Lord Carnegie and his wife Margaret Lindsay. Her father was one of the royal commissioners at the General Assembly of 1617 when the Five Articles of Perth were forced through (and he attended the subsequent parliament, again agitating for royal policy). Carnegie was a member of the Scottish privy council. His title was awarded in 1616, possibly to buy his support for the Five Articles. He was the first Lord Carnegie, though the Carnegies were an established élite family having lived in Kinnaird Castle over two hundred years.[16]

Because they were both so young it was agreed the Montroses would live at Kinnaird with Lord Carnegie for the first three years of marriage (Magdalen's mother had died). It was a success. Magdalen quickly gave birth to two sons in a row, John and James, achieving everything the guardians and the young parents themselves could have hoped.

Kinnaird gave no cause for complaint. It was 'a great house having excellent gardens, parks with fallow deer, orchards, hay meadows wherein are extraordinary quantities of hay, very much planting, an excellent breed of horse, cattle and sheep, and extraordinary good land; without competition the finest place in the shire.'[17]

7

Charles I, King of Scots

A few miles off the A9, in the stretch running north-east from Sterling to Perth, lies the village of Braco. From March to October the castle gardens are open to the public. The house stands five hundred feet above sea level. While the elevation is enough to increase the winter chill it has not stopped the owners from creating a beautiful garden. Twenty acres are planted with trees and shrubs. There is a laburnum grove, a lake, walks through wooded areas, a wall covered with clematis stretching thirty feet. Today's Braco Castle includes parts of the original sixteenth-century tower house but has been extended considerably.

Not long after the Scottish Reformation, the Bishop of Dunblane granted – 'feued' – the Braco estate to his cousin the third Earl of Montrose, whose Kincardine estate was very near. We have the information because the grant led to a petition to parliament in 1578 by tenants who feared they would be dispossessed.[1]

What the bishop did was a normal transaction. The transfer of church lands to new landlords for a one-off down payment ('grassum'), and a fixed annual rent, was a long-established way – since the thirteenth century – for bishops and other ecclesiastical proprietors to raise money.[2] The Reformation expanded an existing practice, because after the Reformation the king took on the rights to Kirk lands.

So the tenants' petition maddened the earl. He was being treated 'against all order in such cases... the like whereof was never used against any nobleman within this realm who had got feu of the Kirklands.'[3] He argued there was nothing unusual in his deal. In the end, at an additional cost, he kept the land, which in due course he gave to one of his sons. While the exact extent of the Braco estate at the time is hard to know, the number of tenants was large. About a thousand were involved in the petition.

By the time of Charles I, the Braco estate was held by a Graham cousin. As such it was an important family property, the main property (ie. livelihood) of the Braco Grahams. You would not want to lose something so valuable. It was a shock when the loss of Braco was exactly what King Charles announced in October 1625 just seven months after he ascended the throne.

He issued a Scottish Act of Revocation. In this he reclaimed as crown property all grants of land in Scotland made since 1540 including all Kirk lands. We do not know how much the Montrose patrimony had been enlarged by other purchases like this, but there is every likelihood that by 1625 there were other blocks from the Kirk held by the extended family. Without warning, not having consulted his Scottish privy council, the king threatened massive repossession on an unprecedented scale. There were lords whose entire wealth consisted of land which had originally belonged to the church. They were 'lords of erection', so-called because their estates had been 'erected' from Kirk lands into secular lordships (Graham of Braco was one). Hundreds of lords and lairds were involved. Nearly half the income-generating land in Scotland was affected. What was going on?

Historians tend to let the king off the hook. First it is argued that Charles I was acting properly up to a point. It was accepted custom that a new king of Scots could revoke land grants made during his minority. That was because of the risk of regents or favourites enriching themselves and their supporters at the king's expense while he/she was too young to stop them. The revocation must be made before his twenty-fifth birthday which, for Charles, was 19 November 1625. To make his Act of Revocation he had to move fast.

Nor did Charles I act without advice. He took his Scottish privy council by surprise, but there were Scots at Whitehall. The Earl of Nithsdale was his main adviser on Scotland at this time. Nithsdale was openly Catholic and part of Buckingham's patronage circle, having married a cousin of Buckingham's. Neither of these salient facts was going to win this particular earl friends back home, but of course the king had not acted all alone, and there were other Scots at court involved.[4] Thirdly, Charles I issued the Act of Revocation to do a good deed. He wanted to help Kirk ministers. He wanted to raise money so that ministers could be properly paid and properly educated, and to finance colleges, schools and hospitals.[5] There was a need. He intended to reassess and reorganize teinds (tithes – the proportion of rent intended for the Kirk) to increase Kirk revenue. His plan was to give compensation to anyone who lost land, in fact his intention, having taken possession, was to re-grant the land to many. He did not mean to impoverish the lords of Scotland, he meant to secure the Kirk.

Insofar as it goes that shows good intentions, but the sheer clumsiness of the 1625 Act tells us everything about Charles I's political skills at this time. Yes, a revocation was normal. But the king's wish to travel back eighty-five years was unheard of. Charles's actual minority *as king* was eight months.[6]

Nor was it forgivable to ignore entirely the privy council. It existed for a reason. In January 1626 – this incidentally was the first time the privy council was allowed to see the text of the Revocation[7] – a delegation came to London to explain the difficulties. One of the members was the Earl of Mar. He wrote a record of the meeting. From this we know that Charles I received his privy councillors in the withdrawing chamber of Whitehall. When someone addressed the king, he had to kneel. The king was not taking their advice, he was graciously – or not very graciously – granting an audience. In one blow Charles I stunned his Scottish nobles with the Revocation; then when they met him, he required them to behave like Spaniards.

Another quickfire reform at the same time was the king's ruling that members of the Court of Session, the highest civil court in Scotland, could not also be privy councillors and *vice versa*. The separation would stop the same people defining the law and advising on it (perhaps to their private benefit). There was wisdom in the change, but it could not be popular. The king also issued a decree by which he would take back into his hands all the heritable (and remunerated) offices in Scotland.[8]

On his knees at the age of sixty-eight, Mar suggested to his master that he take his time in the matter of dismissals from the Court of Sessions and privy council. Charles replied 'My lord it is better the subject suffer a little than all lie out of order.'[9]

The solution to the teinds problem took years to thrash out. Charles I stepped back, which helped. In February 1626 he issued a proclamation that explained some of the thinking behind the Revocation. In July another said that those who lost assets would be compensated. In February 1627 a Commission of Surrenders and Teinds was set up consisting of nobles, lairds and clergy. From then on, the *modus operandi* was to proceed by negotiation and voluntary surrender. Braco remained in Graham hands. The commission met until 1637. It achieved a reform of the teind system which lasted, with some later refinements, until the 1920s![10]

In a way the king's project was after all a great success; but what a price he paid. He looked aggressive, taking, heedless. The worst damage was beneath the water line. Subliminally – always the important part – his Act of Revocation announced that the Reformation did not matter when it came to property rights, that the huge land transfers since 1560 counted for nothing. But property rights were the most important subject there was. Experience throughout northern Europe showed huge problems in dealing with land originally owned by the Catholic Church. Land was wealth.

Did King Charles think the Reformation did not matter? And/or the wellbeing of his nobles meant nothing to him? Was it their Protestantism which offended? After all, he had just married a Catholic.

One further comment. Scotland and England were governed separately. We have seen how the English tended to regard the Scots as inferior and distant and thoroughly foreign. But news trickled between the countries. The Revocation must have sounded alarm bells to those English families enriched by the Dissolution of the Monasteries under Henry VIII. The English did not know Scottish custom and law, but the bare bones of the Revocation looked like pure autocracy.

———◦◦◦———

On 2 February 1626 Charles I was crowned King of England in Westminster Abbey. The date was a compliment to his wife, Queen Mary. It was Candlemas, the feast of the Purification of the Virgin Mary. Yet Henrietta Maria refused to be crowned with her husband. In line with French policy, she could not accept coronation at the hands of a Protestant bishop. What the teenage queen did or did not do carried no weight north of the border. The more she was marginalised the better. What the Scots observed was how England came first by a long way.

Until 1633 Charles I simply did not find the time to visit the country where he was born, which he had left aged three. Because of the delay in his Scottish coronation there was also a delay in calling the Scottish parliament. By custom the first parliament of the reign would be a coronation parliament, so the Scots had to wait for that, too.

What was permitted earlier was a Convention of Estates. This was very similar to parliament. The different estates were represented, the clergy, the nobility, the lairds or barons, the burgesses (representatives of the towns). Both convention and parliament were called by the sovereign. In both, grievances could be aired and taxes agreed, but only a parliament could pass legislation. The 1630 Convention of Estates met in Holyroodhouse from 28 July to 7 August. By custom, a convention did not require the king's presence and of course he remained in England. New taxes were agreed, although the convention refused to extend the period of taxation. There was a serious but civilised debate on the Revocation, which was an improvement.

Two petitions on religion were put to the convention. The first was against ceremony, the target being the Five Articles of Perth. The second urged full implementation of a 1612 Act of Parliament which gave lay patrons (presbytery elders) rights in the introduction of new ministers. Here was a 'petition against bishops'. Bishops should have no rights in the introduction of new ministers. Both petitions were sponsored by a number of lords including the Earl of Rothes, Lords Loudoun and Balmerino. Other noble signatories were the Earls of Seaforth and Cassillis; and Lords Yester, Ross and Melville. These petitions were not recorded officially. The official record was restricted to items that required action. Because Chancellor Viscount Dupplin dismissed both petitions, they fell away to nothing. They failed. No action, no record.

There were unofficial records. One is found in presbyterian sources, which show the detail. This is how we know what happened. Another was a 'diary', an informal account, possibly written by Sir Thomas Hope, lord advocate and privy counsellor, and probably intended as an aide-mémoire for the Earl of Menteith (who did not attend every session). Menteith was president of the privy council. He explained Scotland to the king, and the king to Scotland. He certainly debriefed the king on the proceedings. We do not know whether Charles I himself read any of the diary.

Oddly, the diary describes the petitions without naming their noble sponsors. Lord Balmerino alone was named, because he introduced the second petition – he had to be named. The diary did not say that other nobles sponsored both petitions. Was that deliberate? Did the author want to downplay things? With the benefit of hindsight, we can see this amounted to putting the king's head in the sand. By keeping names out of the record the author of the diary surely was protecting friends. Charles I did not favour the presbyterian spirit. So nobody told him how many presbyterians there were among the nobility and that they were ready to step forward. But he needed to know.

In 1630 Montrose would celebrate his eighteenth birthday. He was emerging into adulthood. Naturally, he was dreaming. On his copy of Caesar's *Commentaries* is a scribbled couplet:

> Though Caesar's paragon I cannot be
> Yet shall I soar in thought as high as he.[11]

Would he really be happy to soar only in thought?

He had role models, first his father and especially his Graham grandfather, also Lord Carnegie, men working for the royal government. That was the royalist path. His Ruthven relations were conventional in a different way, trying to turn the clock back to the days when noble factions controlled the crown. They did this in the interests of the ultra-presbyterians. It was open to Montrose to side with men like Lord Balmerino. How often did Montrose think of his dead Ruthven uncles? And his living one, Patrick (then living in Somerset)?[12] Did he reflect on Raleigh's remarks about unjust kings?

His brother-in-law, the father-like Archibald Napier, from an intellectually distinguished family,[13] was probably the influence that counted. He had been a senior court politician. Thirty years before, Napier had gone into England with James VI and I in 1603 had pursued a court career, but he failed to join the Buckingham faction when it grew from 1617. He returned to Scotland, married Lady Margaret Graham in 1619, and became Scottish Treasurer Depute (the second ranking financial offical) in 1622.

In 1627, Charles I made him Lord Napier of Merchiston, which was the zenith. He fell from grace because he quarrelled with his chief, the Lord Treasurer the Earl of Mar. Another of his enemies was the Earl of Menteith. In 1631 he resigned his charge and relinquished various benefits, retiring to a well-heeled private life. Napier had been fighting accusations of corruption, which evaporated once he was out of the picture.

Napier was a constitutional and practical thinker who wrote about 'the affairs of court, which are never long stable',[14] and believed that 'a King and people make up one politic body, whereof the King is the head... neither can the one subsist without the other, but both must go to ruin with the other.' He knew the English court and both King James and his son Charles personally. We can assume he talked with his young brother-in-law about everything. Possibly, chats with Napier put Montrose off the royal court, although it is likely that the athletic, outdoors young noble always thought of a military career.

His king did not exactly help him. In a characteristic zigzag, Charles I started his reign as a warrior but turned peacemaker. In 1625 he authorised an attack on Spain that was carried out with ineptitude. He then started a campaign against France, the other superpower. Both were failures, expensive in money, lives and reputation. By the end of the 1620s the king managed to sign peace treaties with both France and Spain. The peace made it possible for him to govern England for the next eleven years without calling parliament. It looked as though Charles I wanted to live his father's dream of pacifism.

8

Hopeful Youth

At seventeen, the Earl of Montrose did not attend the 1630 Convention of Estates. Three years later he was old enough for the coronation of Charles I as King of Scots and a parliament at last.

Charles I set off for Scotland in early May 1633. He took advantage of the trip to make a public progress through England, enjoying the hunting on the way, making his triumphal entry into Edinburgh on 15 June. With him came a huge English establishment including the Lord Chamberlain (Earl of Pembroke), the Lord Treasurer (Earl of Portland), the Earl Marshall (Earl of Arundel). To entertain the king, the Scots moved mountains. Beggars were removed from the Edinburgh streets, Holyroodhouse was repaired and swept clean of human and animal sewage, piled up by the walls.

As Charles I entered Edinburgh, an elaborate pageant greeted him. There were seven arches with tableaux including the genius of the city of Edinburgh, the American colony of Nova Scotia (New Scotland), the Scottish countryside, the 107 (*sic*) Kings of Scots preceding Charles I, various Olympian gods and goddesses, the heavens including Endymion 'apparell'd like a shepheard' – he was associated with astrology – and finally his father King James VI with personifications of Fame and Honour. King Fergus I and others made speeches to Charles I. There was poetry and pure fantasy in the vision of Scottishness; for instance, claims on 'Nova Scotia' were delusional since the territory was first colonised and at this time occupied by France.

The pageant was not all grovelling. There was an opportunity to make some points. Hopefully and in vain Jove told the king not to raise taxes. Saturn confidently told his Majesty he (the king) would 'no paranymph raise to high place' which could not be mistaken. It was about favourites.

In fact, Charles I did not have real favourites after the death of the Duke of Buckingham, assassinated in 1628. But he had a wife. Henrietta Maria was in fact at this time a pregnant nymph. She had her husband's love and trust and attention. The words meant the Catholic queen. The finger-wagging did not stop there. A number of Scottish worthies were depicted including George Buchanan, whose well-known views on kingship were anathema to Charles I.[1]

He lodged first in Holyroodhouse then moved on 17 June to Edinburgh Castle. On 18 June in a six-hour ceremony he was crowned King of Scots in the abbey church of Holyroodhouse.

On 20 June the king opened the Scottish parliament, 'the most strictly controlled meeting of the Estates that there had ever been.'[2] Throughout the proceedings Charles I was present to deflect opposition. Parliament obediently voted for 186 pieces of legislation, increased taxation further and concluded on 28 June. Most of the members had no opportunity to scrutinize the detail of the legislation before they were asked to vote it into law.[3]

Charles I then went on a tour of his Scottish palaces – to Linlithgow, Falkland, Sterling, his birthplace Dunfermline. After that he went back to the Thames valley where his wife would shortly give birth to the future King James II. They already had two healthy children, Charles and Mary. With a third he would have done his duty in terms of the succession.

Was the visit a success? Throughout, Charles I showed himself much more comfortable with his English courtiers than with the Scots he met. Possibly the scripts of Jove and Saturn, Buchanan's ghost, unsettled him. He signally failed to connect with the Scots that he did not already know. That was sheer bad manners, which is not a trivial accusation.

If the micro-aggressions of the triumphal entry annoyed him, there was worse to come. Returning to Edinburgh in July, Charles I had to cross the Firth of Forth, the wide estuary with Edinburgh on its south side. The king used two ships to sail from Bruntisland to Leith. He sailed in the first. The baggage, including his silver plate, followed in the second with members of his household. In sight of the king, this second ship foundered and sank with loss of life and all the treasure.

It was a summer's day. Our sources are unclear about what happened. The king's ship, the first of the two, crossed safely. There might have been a squall, the second ship might have been too heavily loaded, there are explanations, but anyway Charles was shaken. One of the reasons he so quickly set off for England afterwards was to forestall rumours of his death.[4] 'That night the King was very melancolious; and returning homeward, out of Edinburgh, he made mention, that at his entry he had met with fire; for some houses in Dalkeith were burnt; and now about the time of his removal the water in his own sight had drowned some of his servants.'[5]

As for his Scottish subjects, the coronation and parliament made one thing evident: their king was English. The coronation itself took place with un-Scottish ceremony. At the door of the abbey church the king, protected by an English bodyguard, was met by the Archbishop of St Andrews and five other bishops dressed in white rochets with white sleeves (such as Spottiswoode had refused for King James's funeral), decorated with loops of gold, and wearing blue silk stockings. The Communion table was arranged like an altar, which the presbyterians detested, covered with a tapestry. On it were two books, two candles and a gold basin. Behind this altar a rich tapestry was hung showing the Crucifixion. The form of the service was English, which included the bishops kneeling.

The following Sunday the king went to Edinburgh's main church, St Giles', to worship. Again, the English form of service was used. The Bishop of Moray presided, again dressed in linen, again looking, to the Scottish gaze, papist.[6] After the service was a great feast at which 'so great was the noise in it of men, musical instruments, trumpets playing, singing, also the shooting of canons, that no sermon was had in the afternoon, either in the greater or the lesser Kirk of St Giles.'[7]

In October the king, back home in England, would order the English liturgy to be used always in the Scottish Chapels Royal, the private chapels of bishops and at St Salvator's, the chapel of St Andrew's University. The following year he would order it to be used for all university chapels and cathedrals in Scotland.

The parliament also began with magnificence, when Charles rode in a procession wearing the 'robe royal' of his great-great-grandfather James IV (husband of Margaret Tudor) which was 'of purple velvet, richly furred and laced with gold, hanging over his horse's tail a great deal, which was carried up from the earth by five grooms of honour.'[8]

Parliament followed the king's agenda with no discussion of grievances, the essential safety valve. Tax was increased, which alone might have been acceptable – there must be compromises – but in return the king gave nothing. It was a program in which the king won every point and the interests of the subject were ignored: 'Of 31 Acts and States concluded... not three of them but were most hurtful to the liberty of the subject.'[9]

We read that there was an argument about how the votes were cast. The Earl of Rothes accused the Clerk Register, Sir John Hay, of wrongly giving a majority to the royal agenda. If so, in front of the king, a good many votes were visibly cast against him. The story is that Charles I himself intervened, telling Rothes that he would pay with his life if he could not prove his accusation. Wisely Rothes sat down.[10]

The people of Edinburgh must have enjoyed the theatricals, but they too made sacrifices. As part of the privy council's tidying up there was a particularly onerous requirement: from 31 March, two and a half months before Charles I actually arrived, nobody was permitted to 'slay, sell, buy or eat deer or fowl'[11] in order that there should be plenty of meat available for the royal party. Since the King of Scots came with a large retinue, at least two hundred (English) people, it was practical thinking, but it prioritised foreigners. It would be hard to make a worse impression.

―――⁓⁓⁓―――

Montrose did not turn up at the coronation. In the Lord Lyon's list of nobles attending, Montrose is marked as absent.[12] The head of a prominent family, an earl (member of parliament), had a strict obligation to attend his sovereign at the coronation. It is agreed that Montrose did not. Admittedly, he was not yet twenty-one, but he was married, a father, and should have been there to show his support for Charles I. Instead on 6 September 1632 he received a licence to travel abroad.[13] When the coronation was held he was not in Scotland.

We know Montrose was expected to attend because of some verses written by William Lithgow. This man was well known as a traveller in foreign countries, as an adventurer. By 1633 Lithgow had visited Paris, Rome, Cairo, Constantinople, the Hague, Vienna, Stockholm, Tunis, Algiers, Fez. He had in 1620 gone to southern Spain where he was imprisoned, according to himself, and tortured as a spy and heretic on the orders of the governor of Malaga. On return to England Lithgow exhibited his wounds to King James at Theobalds, having been transported there on a feather bed. He received royal support as a result.[14] In short, Lithgow was a celebrity.

In 1633 he produced a more or less rhyming welcome to King Charles on the eve of his coronation. Lithgow had received support from Montrose's father and grandfather, so his effusions included lines which singled out Montrose:

As for that hopeful youth, the young Lord Graham,
James, Earl of Montrose, whose warlike name
Sprung from redoubted worth, made manhood try
Their matchless deeds in unmatched chivalry,
I do bequeath him to your gracious love...[15]

Since Montrose was not there, these oily compliments did not help, but they show that Lithgow assumed he would be. Whether Charles I read the patchy lines there is no way of knowing, but it seems certain that he would have noticed that one of his more prominent earls was not supporting him. The tribute of Lithgow would make Montrose's absence clear as day. Lithgow's status attracted a readership. Around a king, gossip is never in short supply.

What went wrong? The explanation lies in family scandal.

After the death of the fourth earl in 1626 his three unmarried daughters had to be respectably housed. While there were several large Montrose houses available, their brother was far too young to supervise the girls. He was not a safe pair of hands. Other arrangements must be made. Dorothea went to live with the Napiers at Merchiston, while Lilias (Lady Colquhoun of Luss) invited Katherine and Beatrix to live with her husband and her at Rossdhu on the banks of Loch Lomond. Because Montrose and his wife were at Kinnaird, because they themselves needed adult supervision, these arrangements continued after his own wedding. Over the next four years, Lilias's husband fell for Katherine.

In September 1631 Sir John Colquhoun, Lady Katherine Graham and Sir John's servant Thomas Carlippis (described as German) disappeared from Rossdhu. More than a year later, in October 1632, Sir Thomas Hope initiated a prosecution against Sir John and his servant, but not against Lady Katherine. The grounds for prosecution came from a 1567 Act against cohabiting within forbidden degrees. Katherine was the sister-in-law, equivalent to a sister. Her seduction was incest. The crime was not hers but Sir John's.

The prosecution also drew on the 1563 Witchcraft Act. Sir John tried to seduce Katherine, but she would not submit. He therefore 'addressed himself to certain witches and sorcerers, consulted and dealt with them for charms and incantations'. Carlippis was a necromancer who provided his employer with 'a jewel of gold, set with diverse precious diamonds or rubies, which was poisoned and intoxicate by the said necromancer; and had the secret and devilish force, of alluring and forcing the person receiver thereof to expose her body, fame and credit to the unlawful will and pleasure of the giver.' There were potions.[16] Bewitched by the jewel, the potions – by Sir John? – Katherine gave in. They eloped; or Sir John Colquhoun abducted her.

At the end of 1632, these accusations were proclaimed at the market-cross of Edinburgh and in Leith. The whole awful scandal was public. Was Katherine a victim or a woman in love? Was the victim really the abandoned Lilias? Possibly Colquhoun and his mistress went to live abroad. Possibly they disappeared in London. Katherine from then on is lost to the pages of history (while Colquhoun much later reappeared in Scotland).

Timing is everything. First, Sir John and Katherine and Carlippis left Rossdhu. A year later the prosecution was announced. So Montrose was on the rack for at least fifteen months. *Three* of his sisters had been together in Sir John's house. Katherine was abducted. Lilias was abandoned. Beatrix was an unmarried girl. Above all, her reputation had to be protected. Was Katherine even alive? For the brother, the man responsible for their well-being, it could not be more serious, or more distressing. Nor was it kept behind closed doors. Everybody knew about the disgrace of the Grahams. Did Montrose think of personal revenge?

He left redress to Sir Thomas Hope and set off from Scotland at the end of 1632 or a little later, escaping the worst of the publicity. Possibly he thought Sir John had taken Katherine to the continent; or he just needed to be in another place. His own family life, his wife, his children, were evidently not enough. He went to France. He would be away three years.

Montrose could have returned for the coronation in the summer. The king's plans were known. There was a mail service. He did not. Apart from the horror of confronting his fellow lords, there was the fine tuning with the king, how the king would receive him. Charles I liked a high moral tone at court.[17]

Would he hold Montrose responsible? What to say to such a monarch? Better say nothing. Better be somewhere else.

9

Opening the Mind

On their way to Madrid, wearing bad disguise (fake beards), the Prince of Wales and Buckingham passed through Paris in March 1623 and visited the Louvre, whose buildings 'stretched out along the Seine like a mismatched necklace'.[1] They stood in the crowd watching the royal ladies dance.

Ten years later the twenty-year-old Earl of Montrose could hardly resist that. Bits of the jigsaw are missing but some things can be assumed. When he arrived in France, he went to Paris to see the theatre of the court. There, too, was the Scottish Guard of Louis XIII. For two hundred years the King of France's personal bodyguard had included a Scottish unit. It originated in the Hundred Years War. From 1560, Scottish Protestantism weakened the tradition, but in the early 1630s the *Garde Écossaise* was revived by Lord Gordon (also called the Earl of Enzie), son of the first Marquess of Huntly.[2] Gordon/Enzie was now living with such magnificence in France that he nearly bankrupted himself. Montrose possibly hoped for a position as an officer of the guard.

He cannot have missed the latest on the Bourbons. At this time the French royal family offered a masterclass in how to fracture a nation.

Shortly before he was beheaded (November 1632 – just before Montrose arrived in France) the Duc de Montmorency revealed a secret to Louis XIII and Cardinal Richelieu. He said the king's brother, Gaston, had at the beginning of the year married Marguerite of Lorraine, an ideal bride except for two things. First, her brother the sovereign Duke of Lorraine was the enemy of France; and second, Louis XIII had obviously not given his permission. Nor was permission granted now.[3]

Montmorency was the highest ranking lay noble. He was Constable of France, commander-in-chief of French forces, Governor of Languedoc. His sister was married to the Prince de Condé, the most senior of the Princes of the Blood (men in line to the throne, the king's cousins). His crime was to be caught up in Gaston's rebellion against his brother the king. There was no doubt about Montmorency's guilt. Displaying exceptional courage, the Constable of France personally led a cavalry charge against royal troops at the Battle of Castelnaudry on 1 September 1632. He was wounded in the neck, captured and lost the battle. Although a rebel, Montmorency was not certain to die. There were attempts to rescue him before his trial. After the sentence King Louis found himself surrounded by gentlemen on their knees 'weeping and begging him to show mercy'.[4]

Provided you came from the highest nobility, or from the royal family, there was a French tradition of forgiveness. You were literally bought with money and land and office.[5] Lesser traitors would be executed but ranks closed around the top people. As his brother's heir, Gaston survived everything and Montmorency was also grand enough to spare, but traditional toleration was now gone. Louis XIII showed a new ruthlessness when he insisted on Montmorency's death.[6] The story was huge.

The run-up to this tragedy was a fast-moving soap opera: in 1630 the King of France had outwitted his highly political mother, Marie de Médicis, in defence of Richelieu, of whom she was furiously jealous, on whom he relied, and drove her into exile. The net result was an attempt by the mother to unseat her elder son the king, in support of her second son Gaston. The further complication was that neither Louis XIII nor Gaston had sons at this time – although long married, the king had no children at all.[7] Because of the ruling family, France seemed always on the brink.

As for faith, the Bourbons were split. France was Catholic but there was a Reformed Protestant minority, the Huguenots. They included great nobles. The Condé family were Reformed Protestant. As the senior Prince of the Blood, the Prince de Condé would inherit the throne if the king and Gaston died without producing sons, which was entirely possible. Yet the core royal family was devotedly Catholic. Louis XIII's campaigns against Huguenot strongholds were the hallmark of his early years. His (and Henrietta Maria's) mother, the half Italian and half Habsburg Marie de Médicis,[8] now living in exile, led the party of the *dévots*, the Catholics most closely tied to Rome.

For a visiting presbyterian Scot, it was a case of 'put not your trust in princes.'

Gordon/Enzie did not offer a commission. Instead, Montrose went to the military school at Angers 185 miles south-west of Paris. The city stands just north of the Loire, on the banks of its tributary, the Maine.

Castle, cathedral and precincts were built on a hill dominating the Anjou landscape. Housed since 1629 in the Hôtel de Cazenove, the military school was one of the new European academies[9] that formalised the preparation of young officers.

French equestrian skills were considered the most advanced in Europe. Angers was a riding-school, but we know that more was studied there. As well as horsemanship, the students learned mathematics, the use of arms and apparently dancing, the latter being something the athletic Montrose probably passed on. A contemporary wrote: 'I never heard he had much delight in dancing.'[10]

The Angers students learned how generals had developed new technology-driven tactics. Hand-held guns had been in use for a hundred years but they were difficult things. A musket was heavy. The barrel had to be supported by a forked rest driven into the ground. Early muskets were defensive weapons used to protect fortifications. To take aim and fire, a soldier would rest his musket on the top of a wall – or branch, or rocky outcrop. Yet the power of the musket was desperately needed in battle when soldiers moved around.

The musket was also slow to fire. The burning match had to fall on priming powder thus igniting the charge. Using a prop made the musket mobile but having fired, the musketeer of course must reload. Any pause gave the enemy a chance to attack, which meant that range was also critical: soldiers might fire early with no effect and expose themselves to attack while desperately reloading.

The necessary insight was that of Count Wilhelm Louis of Nassau-Dillenburg who wrote to his cousin Prince Maurice of Orange in 1594 to explain. He had been reading the second-century *Tactics* of Aelian (in Greek). From the description of spear-carrying soldiers in a Roman legion William Louis saw that musketeers could also be deployed in rotating ranks and thus maintain a wall of fire.[11] This was called 'extraduction' whereas a blast from all the musketeers at once was a 'salvee'. It produced an effective battlefield formation, although muskets were also vulnerable to the elements, mainly rain. In the 1620s the cartridge was developed, which combined the shot with the gunpowder in a single package. That would accelerate loading when (later) it came into widespread use, although the cartridge still had to be torn and the powder poured in, so loading was never rapid, especially by inexperienced soldiers.

Handguns (pistols) also had the trigger mechanism. They were used in battle in the *caracole*, a tactic intended to damage and intimidate or provoke the opposing army without risking a full cavalry charge. One by one cavalry would ride up to the enemy ranks and fire into them, then canter away leaving their place to the next man. Handguns were also used in close fighting.

The old-fashioned pike was a heavy, thrusting spear which needed highly trained and incredibly physically strong soldiers. A lone pikeman could accomplish nothing. Grouped, as in the *tercios* (regiments) of the Spanish armies of the previous century, pikemen were formidable. A *tercio* was like a Roman legion, a bristling, marching square. Musketeers placed around the edges increased the reach of the *tercio*. Opposing troops were shot, run down, skewered.

The momentum of the *tercio* limited manoeuvre. Leading the Dutch revolt against Spain, the various heads of the Orange-Nassau family, and especially Prince Maurice, developed new ideas to defeat the Spaniards. Maurice thinned the line, which made it broader. Musketeers were placed between pikemen, protecting them and firing from more points in the field.

King Gustavus Adolphus of Sweden built on Dutch innovations. At the Battle of Breitenfeld (17 September 1631) the king's army faced an imperial army under Count Tilly. Tilly grouped his men in squares thirty deep while Gustavus Adolphus grouped his in an extended line of just six ranks. The deployment made it easy to outflank the imperials. Gustavus Adolphus also worked on field artillery. Foundries were now able to produce relatively small cannon that could be transported easily. At Breitenfeld, a crushing Swedish victory, he outgunned Tilly.[12]

Drill was becoming part of the soldier's life. Article 286 of the French Code Michau (1629) instructed that drill was to be done at least once a week by soldiers in garrisons.[13] Prince Maurice had introduced his men to regular exercises before that. Full uniform was not yet provided, but you had to know your friends in battle. Generals expected their men would wear a sash, plume or ribbon of the same colour (orange in the case of the Dutch). At Breitenfeld, the Saxon and Swedish allies plucked branches from the forest and put them in their hats.

The study of war rested on one key principle: the battle of resolve. The aim of the general was to break the spirit of the enemy. His greatest skill was judging when to engage and when to avoid. We do not know how much siege craft was studied at Angers. According to the Earl of Orrery there were 'twenty sieges for one battle'.[14] But mathematics was applied to engineering, to architecture, to ballistics and so forth, so it seems reasonable to assume this important branch of early modern warfare was covered. All this Montrose learned.

In France he also acquired a (very) portable Bible. Measuring about three by five inches, it is a French language edition, beautifully printed in Sedan, a Huguenot centre. As a translation into the vernacular, it is an elegant and practical product of Reformed Protestant culture. The Bible has comments by Montrose written on it, was clearly much perused, and has survived to the present day. It bears witness to his religious faith and to his culture: he read Holy Scripture in French.

———◉◉◉———

After Angers, the empire was the obvious draw for Montrose. Many Scots went to fight there in a war without end.

For example, in summer 1627 Lord Nithsdale tried to raise 3,000 soldiers to support King Christian IV of Denmark.[15] He raised fewer but still went. The Marquess of Hamilton enlisted under Gustavus Adolphus from 1631 to 1632 bringing with him 6,000 soldiers. In an advance up the Oder valley he was supplemented, on the king's orders, by the experienced Alexander Leslie, also Scottish. The 'black baron' Robert Monro led a regiment of Mackays at Breitenfeld on the Protestant side.[16]

Having prepared himself for war, Montrose changed his mind, decided on tourism, arriving in Italy probably in spring 1634. Seeing the sights – the sites – of the classical past was usual for aristocrats then. Here was a dedicated presbyterian, from a country bristling at the name of Rome, immersed in the culture of the enemy.

Perhaps the weirdest encounter was when Montrose met the Earl of Angus at dinner in the English College (a Catholic seminary) in Rome. In the Pope's city two loyal Scots caroused in a training house for enemies of their king, their faith, their country. To be exact, the English College trained Englishmen for the Catholic priesthood with the aim of returning them to England to catechize. There was also a Scots College in Rome that did the same for Scotland.

From a slightly later description, we have a sense of the young man, now feeling the southern wind in his hair. We read that Montrose had 'a body not tall but comely and well composed... complexion nearly white with flaxen hair... a staid, grave and solid look and yet his eyes sparkling and full of life, of speech slow but witty and full of sense.'[17]

He would have visited the Renaissance city of Florence, where Henrietta Maria's grandfather Grand Duke Francesco I of Tuscany (1541-1587) had practised alchemy in his *studiolo*, both laboratory and picture gallery, in an inner room in the Uffizi Palace. The current Grand Duke of Tuscany was the queen's cousin. Other princely courts, Mantua, Ferrara, Modena, dazzled with displays of modern art.[18] In Scotland, nothing came close to the visual culture of the Italian states; nor to the political culture.

At the time Italy was shaped by more than sixty years of war in the previous century. A French Valois claim to the throne of Naples set the ball rolling in 1494. The Habsburgs with local allies responded successfully in the end. Foreign armies marched through the peninsula for decades. In 1527, Rome was sacked by imperial troops. The negotiated 1559 peace held, but there was a further Habsburg-France confrontation in the north in 1628 over the Mantuan succession, concluding in 1631 to the advantage of France.

Montrose cannot have failed to pass through Milan, governed by a Spanish viceroy with all the Spanish paraphernalia. Taxation was rising throughout the Spanish world to fund their attempt to defeat the Dutch rebels. In 1626, Sardinia paid six times as much tax as it had paid only thirteen years before. The Kingdom of Naples in 1645 would pay fourteen times as much as it had in 1616.[19]

In France he had made friends with Lord Feilding, a man three years older, who, in these years, was the English Ambassador Extraordinary to the Venetian Republic. We read that Montrose and Feilding together consulted 'all the astrologers they could hear of' to learn the future, and that Feilding took the exercise totally seriously.[20] Did Montrose do the same?

Feilding provided a personal introduction to Europe's most beguiling state. Venice astonished the eye, glimmering palaces rising from the lagoon. At the time there was no land connection. It really was an island city. Politically, it was a republic. The city state had never been ruled by a single family. Venice was an oligarchy of rich business families that elected the Doge as leader, supported but also tracked him, and could dismiss him. Venice looked east. As well as its very large Italian mainland territory, the *terraferma*, it had possessions on the Dalmatian and Istrian coast (now parts of Slovenia and Croatia); and in the east Mediterranean, once including Cyprus, Crete, and parts of the Levant (at this time all lost to Ottoman expansion).

Pulling the other way was the court of England. Basil Feilding's father was the first Earl of Denbigh, who owed his title and status to his marriage with Susan Villiers, sister of the Duke of Buckingham. Susan was a lady of Henrietta Maria's bedchamber and close friend of the queen. Basil had married the daughter of the Lord Treasurer, the Earl of Portland; exceptional connections.[21] By nature, Basil was no diplomat but would show himself independent-minded in all things. He was a man of culture, adept at sourcing paintings for the king.

In Rome the Forum and the Colosseum could be visited. Compared with today's carefully preserved tourist sites they were a mess, being used as quarries and markets, but they were there. Nero's vast palace, the Golden House (built in the first century AD), was also partially excavated. This was a complex so vast, so extravagant that it embarrassed subsequent emperors, which is saying something of a Roman emperor. In the century after it was built large parts of the Golden House were filled in with earth (and built over) and therefore preserved. Here were dreams made visible. Montrose had read classical works, now he could see what was left in stone.

There was the Christian past too, examined in the *Roma sotteranea* of Antonio Bosio published in 1632 just before Montrose arrived. The book described the history and identity of the Christian catacombs. They were recently rediscovered. Bosio, a Maltese, had the patronage of the ultra-Catholic Knights of Malta but paradoxically his work on the early church played to Protestantism, which wanted to go back to the beginning. And there was Renaissance Rome, the new city. Naturally there was a connecting theme between the staggering buildings. For example, the Palazzo Farnese, built during the sixteenth century, owed its magnificence – so much greater than that of Holyroodhouse – to Pope Paul (Farnese) III. Similarly, the Palazzo Borghese was superbly expanded in the early seventeenth century thanks to the patronage of Pope Paul (Borghese) V.

In fact, papal patronage was everywhere. If it was not the Pope, it was some cardinal not infrequently belonging to the Pope's family. There was nothing in Edinburgh or Glasgow like these palaces, nothing to compare with the Church of the Gesu, designed in the new baroque style, consecrated back in 1584 as headquarters of the Jesuits, funded again by the Farnese family. Where did all the money come from?

By this time the Catholic landmark, St Peter's cathedral, was completed structurally but embellishment went on. When Montrose was in Rome finishing touches were being applied to the *baldacchino* (canopy) over the high altar, a new and still today extraordinary statement of religious confidence. The whole structure stands about ninety-five feet high and perhaps thirty feet square. Forget about the unimaginably vast cathedral in which it stood, a smaller Scottish parish church would have fitted the space held by the *baldacchino* alone. Four twisting columns support a massive – but apparently weightless – roof, pointing up to heaven. The whole structure is bronze. On the corners stand four angels and the whole is surmounted with a cross.

Rome had another privileged electorate, the cardinals, who voted in the Pope but could not vote him out. Once in, the Pope was an autocrat for life. The practice was to enrich the family of the incumbent while there was time. The papacy was not hereditary but could be dynastic. Pope Urban (Barberini) VIII, elected in 1623, was known for nepotism. The cardinals were mostly extravagant power players. In Rome, money, power and faith marched together and you could see it all.

Nor was Pope Urban a listener.[22] Foreign ambassadors found it hard to transact business with him because he talked over them. That was assertion. He ruled as a prince, ready for war. In 1625 he had fortified the Castel Sant'Angelo with new breastworks. He used the vaults under the Vatican library as an arsenal. In 1631 he occupied and took possession of the Duchy of Urbino, north of the Papal States.

There was thought control. Having supported the earlier work of Galileo Galilei, Urban turned against the astronomer when in 1632 he presented arguments for a heliocentric astronomy.[23] Galileo was tried by the Inquisition in 1633 because Catholic doctrine taught that the sun went around the earth. He was not found guilty of heresy, which merited a death penalty. But he was judged 'suspect of heresy', the book was banned and the astronomer lived out his remaining years under house arrest.

We cannot know how Montrose reacted to what he saw and heard in Italy. But it is not too much of a stretch to assume its brilliant culture both astonished and appalled him. In his own family (the Napiers) was a tradition of scientific research which surely predisposed him towards Galileo's side of the intellectual debate, for instance. As for the buildings, the sculpture, the paintings, there is not the slightest sign at any time in his life that he was much attracted. Montrose liked books, he wrote poems, he liked ideas perhaps, but he does not seem to have been especially visual. Probably he thought about the cost and the militancy.

The Catholic tide was rising, the exuberance of Counter Reformation.

PART TWO

REBELLION

'Build your nest upon no tree here for ye see that God hath
sold the forest to death'

Samuel Rutherford

10

Noble Lords

Why do things happen? Historians look for explanations of war especially. In the case of Charles I's reign, the consensus tends to character analysis of the king: he lacked empathy, so he could not see the other side of the argument; he was insensitive, so he made things worse; he was both stubborn and an improviser; he thought, as king, he was always right. Archbishop Laud said that Charles I was 'more willing not to hear than to hear.'[1] An opposing school blames his uncompromising opponents. And how could anyone govern in peace when the most important thing in the world, the path to salvation, was so bitterly contested?

The court made its contribution, a field of competition. The career and especially the end of the career of William Graham, seventh Earl of Menteith, fits that line of thought: the reign of Charles I was thrown off course by court intrigue. The Earl of Menteith came to the king's attention because of the Revocation. Before this he was mainly distinguished by a reputation for breeding terriers.[2] In 1626 he persuaded Charles I to receive one of the delegations that wanted to plead the cause of the Scottish landowners. To date, Menteith, a man nine years older than the king, had shown no interest in royal service. In fact, he voted against the Five Articles of Perth in 1621. Nonetheless there was chemistry between Menteith and the king, who, unusually, listened to his advice. The earl had rare diplomatic skills.

He appears to have been the man who persuaded Charles I to proceed by establishing a committee to tackle the Revocation – and that was the path to tranquillity. He also helped the king in the difficult matter of the Treasurer Depute Lord Napier who could not work with the Earl of Mar.

In January 1628 Menteith was made president of the privy council. He presided over the 1630 convention of estates. He undertook other business always obedient to the king, always mediating between Charles I and the nobility, which included regular trips between Whitehall and Edinburgh. Menteith was not a classic politician. He did not look for power. He was conservative. He did not build a following. He shared the interests of his Scottish peers. While Menteith headed the council there was a functioning system for Scotland that satisfied both king and nobles.

In 1633 he fell from favour for the most astonishing reason, this being that he wanted – and was granted – a further earldom, that of Strathearn, a royal title in origin. Menteith made no territorial claim, although he did buy additional land (which he could barely afford) to support his new dignity. It was a matter of honour. Menteith argued that the earldom of Strathearn could rightfully descend through the female line. If so, it should be his by virtue of his descent from the granddaughter of King Robert II.[3] Why would anyone bother with this sort of thing? Why would the seventh Earl of Menteith also want to be Earl of Strathearn? It was a grander title and that seems, from his point of view, to have been that.

At first Charles I supported his friend. Of course, it was the king who granted him the earldom of Strathearn (July 1631). But the claim gave an opportunity to Menteith's opponents. After all, it was impossible to have influence without enemies. Charles I came to credit what they said and lost confidence in the man who made the government of Scotland work. The intrigue is one of the best pieces of evidence we have for the psychological insecurity of Charles I.

Charles I descended from King Robert II through his eldest son by his first wife, who became King Robert III. The boy was born before his parents were married in church but was later legitimized. Clearly, any doubts about his rights had been cleared before Robert III succeeded in 1390. His descendants inherited the throne for the next two hundred and fifty years.

The campaign against Menteith included landowners afraid the new double earl would make a claim against them. They said he said he had 'the reddest blood in Scotland'. They warned he wanted to be Earl of Strathearn as a precursor to claiming the throne.

Menteith descended from Robert II's eldest son of his *second* marriage, Earl David of Strathearn. If the children of the first marriage were set aside as bastards, then the descendants of the second marriage would be kings. He was the senior of these.

The notion that Menteith wanted to be king was preposterous. He had no political following. He did not agitate for power. How was he meant to overthrow the Stuarts? What firepower did he have? None. Menteith was not Macbeth.

His claims to the Strathearn earldom were first made in 1629. By early 1633 Charles I turned. The earldom was taken back (March 1633).[4] A commission investigated. Menteith was ordered to retire to one of his houses. He was not permitted to see the king during the coronation visit. In October 1633, his offices and pension were taken away. Was it coronation nerves unsettling the king? Although later restored to the privy council, Menteith's career was finished. The magic touch was gone. The king's mistrust was corrosive.

It was not the only change. Since 1622 the entrepreneurial George Hay had been Chancellor of Scotland. He became Viscount Dupplin (1627) and Earl of Kinnoull (1633). When he died in December 1634 Kinnoull was replaced as Chancellor by John Spottiswoode, Archbishop of St Andrews (aged sixty-nine). Having sacked an essential go-between who was trusted by the Scots, Charles I wanted to work with bishops.

Not much later the royal government made an example of John Elphinstone, second Lord Balmerino. The interventions of Charles I in this episode show the king as a micromanager blind to justice.

First there is Balmerino himself. In the 1621 parliament he voted against the Five Articles. In 1627 he annoyed Charles I when he visited Whitehall with others and tried to water down the Revocation. Balmerino was himself a Lord of Erection and therefore first in the line of fire. His title and his main estate came from a Cistercian abbey in Fife (whose ruins can still be visited, opposite Dundee on the southern bank of the River Tay). He could not afford to lose this land. Then came his 1630 religious petition.

At the 1633 parliament he did it again. Among the parliamentary bills which government managers forced through was a measure which empowered the king to rule on clerical dress. Balmerino spoke against it in the presence of Charles I. We have seen how Archbishop Spottiswoode had to withdraw from the funeral of James VI and I in 1625 because he refused to dress like an English bishop. The elaborate, by Scottish standards, outfits of the bishops attending the king at his Scottish coronation caused dismay. Presbyterians did not want their ministers dressing like Catholic priests. When Balmerino vainly opposed this measure in parliament he was speaking for many and putting his own head above the parapet. About forty years old in 1633, he knew exactly what he was doing. It was provocation. That was not all. There was the previous generation.

Although Catholic, his father James Elphinstone, first Lord Balmerino, was a loyal servant of King James VI and I. He worked both for the queen, Anne of Denmark, and for James VI himself, being appointed Scottish

Secretary of State in 1598. In 1604 he was rewarded with his title and estate. So far it was a success story.

In 1606, as King of England, James introduced an oath of allegiance in order to flush out the disloyal and box in the waverers. If you took the oath, you were solemnly committed to its words. It would be a sin if you went against it. Swearing the oath was signing a contract.

The oath declared King James was 'lawful and rightful king' and committed the person who swore it to obedience. It denied the deposing power of the Pope (used in 1570 by Pope Pius V when he published the bull *Regnans in Excelsis* declaring Elizabeth I a usurper). It was a response to the Catholic Gunpowder Plot of 1605 even though that famous conspiracy was not supported by the Pope. In trying to dispel one cloud, the king brewed up a new storm.

A propaganda war between England and Rome broke out, because the Pope could not let his nuclear option, the power of deposition, be wrenched from his grasp without a fight. The various statements that followed included a pamphlet written by James VI and I himself, called *Triplici nodo, triplex cuneus*.[5] In response Cardinal Bellarmine pointed out that King James had not always been anti-Catholic. In fact, in 1599, as King of Scotland, he had written to Pope Clement VIII declaring his admiration for the Catholic Church. That was dangerous. It was true.

What happened in 1599 was as follows: James VI had indeed sent a letter to the Pope asking for a cardinal's hat for his subject William Chisholm, Bishop of Dunblane and Vaison (in France). He wanted a favour for a Catholic Scot. So he showered compliments on the Pope. By 1606, having just survived a Catholic attempt on his life, that was a bad history. Denial was the only option. Denial was a lie, but in matters of state...

The loyal first Lord Balmerino stepped in. When the letter was written, he was Secretary of State. Balmerino said that he concealed the letter in a pile of innocuous documents for the king's signature, and the king unwittingly, carelessly, unreading, deceived by Balmerino, had signed. Chisholm was a family connection of Balmerino. Himself a Catholic, he wanted his cousin to be a cardinal. The idea was hopeless. The hard-working King James VI read everything. But Balmerino got him off the hook and got himself firmly and painfully, indeed almost fatally, on the hook in his master's place.

To make the mess good in the eyes of Europe, Balmerino must suffer. He was put on trial for treason (1609). He was found guilty and sentenced to death. He survived but suffered forfeiture and disgrace. He lost his title and estate; this after lifelong loyalty to the king. That would be enough to worry any son. Nor was it all.

A year after his father's death the second Lord Balmerino married Anne Kerr, sister of Robert Kerr (anglicized to Carr), the first great male favourite of James VI and I during his English reign. By 1613, Robert was Earl of Somerset. The brother-in-law of the king's favourite should have won huge material awards, but a novelistic chain of events shattered his hopes. In the Overbury case, Somerset was convicted, with his wife Frances Howard, of murder. A royal pardon saved the lives of both Robert and Frances. Probably Robert was innocent and probably Frances was not. Hot on the heels of his father's disgrace was a second example of the perilous seductions of the court for the second Lord Balmerino.

In short, from youth Balmerino the son was set up to doubt royal bona fides. Title and property were restored to him after his father died. He did not pay materially. But here were two members of his family raised to the heights then dashed to the depths. Add his sincere Reformed religious belief and he was set up to distrust the Stuart court. The king knew it.

After Charles I returned to England in 1633 a group of Scots arranged for a petition to be written, that would go to the king to explain the grievances which should have gone before the coronation parliament but had not. The lawyer who drafted it was William Haig of Bemersyde.

Balmerino received a copy of the petition. Haig's draft seemed to him too much of a confrontation. He wrote corrections to tone it down. He showed his new version to a lawyer called John Dunmure who took another copy without telling him. Dunmure showed this copy to a friend. This man showed it to the Archbishop of St Andrews who took it to Charles I in Whitehall. The diplomacy of Menteith was now needed. But Menteith was disgraced.

In June 1634 Balmerino was summoned to appear before the Royal Council in Edinburgh after which he was held in prison. Before his appearance he warned Haig, who fled to the Netherlands. On 3 December 1634 Balmerino was put on trial for 'scandalous libel' against the king. Three of the Lords of Session were chosen as assessors for the trial, Chancellor Spottiswoode, Sir John Hay and Sir James Learmonth, 'men sworn to the bishops'.

In January 1635 a blazing comet was seen in the night sky.[6] The winter lasted much longer than usual in the north. In March 1635 the Dee was still frozen and there were heavy snowfalls – all at the time the trial came to its climax.[7]

The defence argued that Balmerino had not distributed the petition, he had only shown it to a lawyer to ask his opinion, having watered it down. He wanted it to be respectful. However, the prosecution established that at least one other copy had been made from Balmerino's copy by his servant Robert Dalgleish, and he had shown it to at least one other person.[8] The prosecution also said that Balmerino had not disclosed the existence of the draft to the privy council. That was true.

When it came to a jury vote (20 March 1635) there was a tie, seven votes on each side. The casting vote from the Treasurer, the Earl of Traquair, came down on the prosecution side. Balmerino was guilty. These people knew each other very well. Traquair, in his previous incarnation as Sir John Stewart, had accompanied Balmerino in 1627 to Whitehall to protest together the Act of Revocation.

The king's government did not treat their prisoner well, a lord, a member of the Scottish parliament. During his imprisonment Balmerino was denied preacher, physician and exercise in the yard. Nor was it fair play. The king intervened directly. Before the trial Charles I wrote to Sir John Hay 'to recommend the continuance of your accustomed diligence… which we will take as acceptable service.'[9] Just as he had attended the parliament to force his Bills through, so the king now put pressure on the supposedly independent assessor.

The sentence was death. Balmerino accepted it 'with a smile… and a low curtsey'.[10] Sir John insisted that the sentence be given without further reference to Charles I, then pushed for the execution of Balmerino the same day.

Balmerino survived. Traquair ignored the savage urgings. He advised Charles I not to insist on the sentence. The trial was no secret. Presbyterian street organizers were at work. 'The common people avowedly with loud and high lifted up voices were praying for my Lord Balmerino… and from doing this the magistrates could not possibly get them stayed.'[11]

Incidentally, popular protest had some economic foundation. There was discontent because of higher taxation. There were sporadic rises in the corn price, so high at times that some people probably starved: this happened twice in the 1630s.[12] It was an unusually bad decade for the poor.

In July 1635, Balmerino was released from Edinburgh Castle and permitted to return to Fife subject to restrictions. In November his full liberty was restored. Probably the privy council had always meant this to be the outcome, much was show. An example would be made of a persistent offender, but no real harm was meant, it was a message. Now it looked like a storm in a teacup but… some storm, some teacup. A Scottish lord was sentenced to death for being in possession of a document that he had not written, that he wanted to moderate. And the paper trail pointed to the bishops, because it depended on the Archbishop of St Andrews. How did it look? It looked as though government by bishops was a conspiracy against the established aristocracy.

> Both the Nobility and the People were grievously offended at the Respect the King had for the Clergy. The Confidence he had in the Bishops… provoked them to the highest degree.[13]

11

Meeting the King

Charles I was devout. He believed in the divine realm, an all-encompassing reality. He gazed humbly at a vision of God. As an earthly king he was in a unique position. In his coronation oaths he swore to 'grant and keep... the true profession 'of the gospel' and 'to maintain the true religion of Christ'.[1] He had responsibilities. They deserved respect. He was owed obedience. Out of religious self-abasement came royal entitlement and this was the paradox of sovereignty.

He could not doubt his instincts. They were reinforced by the clergy he favoured such as Spottiswoode in Scotland and William Laud in England (Bishop of London from 1628 to 1633, then Archbishop of Canterbury). The outcome was a virtuous circle in which his senior bishops confirmed his approach, which they also favoured: an orderly, seemly, contemplative practice in church through liturgy, prayers and services spelled out by the authorities to be used everywhere by everyone. This was the beauty of holiness and the holiness of beauty. Both in England and Scotland the king introduced measures accordingly, which have been much discussed by historians. Today it looks like groupthink.

With matching sincerity, the English puritans and Scottish presbyterians wanted their ministers to read the Bible then preach to congregations *extempore*. The pulpit was the most important structure in a presbyterian church, but it was also good to preach in other buildings, just as prayer meetings (conventicles) could be held in private houses – or to preach and pray outside. These people wanted simplicity and enthusiasm. They minimised sacrament: transcendent events, holy places, transforming ceremony.

One of the telling differences was two ideas of discipline. The king needed religion in its literal sense: *religio* in Latin originally meant a bond. He needed cohesion, social glue, something that could be observed, that could almost be measured. He was governing to bring his people together. That was his discipline. He wanted a church with defined and required practice both in England and Scotland.

Whether Charles I was an Arminian in theology was not quite the same question. That school of thought could be called diluted or permissive Calvinism, something closer to Catholic theology. For instance, by contrast with the Reformed embrace of predestination, Arminians accepted that free will and the decision of God about personal salvation were compatible – that individual behaviour is relevant to God's judgement.[2].

Hard-core presbyterians rejected royal interference. But they loved *moral* discipline. Reformed discipline was living your daily life obedient to the Bible as supervised by the local presbytery. Senior clergy like the bishops could not tell the presbyterians anything about being good. Presbyterians were saints on earth. They had no time for saints in heaven. On neither side did spiritual conviction deny violence.

In a showdown after the Synod of Dort (1618-19) the Dutch Republic offered a foretaste of where the disagreements pointed. In May 1619, the distinguished Dutch patriot Jan van Oldebarnevelt, who supported the Arminians, was executed for treason at the age of seventy-one. The man behind the trial and sentence was the Stadholder and Captain General of the Dutch army, Prince Maurice of Orange, who supported the Gomarists, another version of exacting Calvinism, predestination included. It was a brutal proceeding against an old man who had lived a life of exemplary public service.

—❦—

In the early 1630s Charles I ordered new statement buildings for the middle of the Scottish capital, Edinburgh, on a sloping site next to St Giles' church. Designed by James Murray in a classical style, these would house a meeting chamber for the parliament with rooms for the privy council and the Court of Sessions. In this way a precinct advertising royal government was to embellish Edinburgh. The outside space was called Parliament Close, later changed to Parliament Square. It has been there for four hundred years. Parliament Hall, the actual parliament building, also survives. More than anything the scheme was a celebration of popular representation. St Giles' too would be updated – the symbolic church.

The old town of Edinburgh looks up at one end to the royal castle, a fortress on a rock and at the other down to the royal palace, Holyroodhouse. The connecting Royal Mile, the High Street and continuation, is on a slope that runs roughly south-west to north-east towards the Firth of Forth. Because of the site, houses were built many storeys high – there was not much room on the ground. The layout was a perfect visual expression of the Stuart ideal: at one end a castle, at the other a palace, the people (parliament, the houses), the church (St Giles') held in a royal embrace.

At this time Holyroodhouse was mainly sixteenth century, boasting a 'Great Tower' which contained the royal apartments, French in style with steeply angled roofs and circular corner turrets. Surrounded by gardens and orchards and protected from the worst of the weather by location, the palace was a royal paradise. The adjoining abbey church had been much damaged by English raids and then by Reformation changes and now consisted only of the nave framed by gothic-arched windows, but it proclaimed continuity.

Shortly after his coronation the king conferred an honour on Edinburgh, raising it to the status of diocese, so that it needed a bishop. The first Bishop of Edinburgh was William Forbes, who preached before the king during his 1633 visit. Not everyone saw the elevation as the king did. Edinburgh was full of radical presbyterians who did not want any bishops at all. Apart from anything else, everyone knew that one more bishop was one more vote for the king in parliament.

Charles I went further. If there was a bishop there must be a cathedral. It must be St Giles'. But if St Giles' was to function as a cathedral, changes were necessary. After the Reformation, the interior of St Giles' had been partitioned to produce three separate places of worship adapted for the preaching ministry (and space for a school and administrative offices). The king now commanded it to be 'ordered as is decent and fit for a church of that eminence and according to the first intentions of the erectors and founders thereof'.[3] Work began at the end of 1633. The partition walls came down. Galleries built in the choir to accommodate listening worshippers were removed. Less controversially, except to those who made a living from them, shops adjoining the church were demolished.

Other cathedral churches were restored: St Andrews, Dornoch, Dunkeld, Kirkwall, Whithorn. These buildings were bishop centres, or bishop platforms, that is what a cathedral is. As such, they had been neglected. Presbyterianism made parish churches the focus, and indeed new ones were built. Charles I wanted to change things. He wanted bishops in place, visible, elevated, presiding over the kind of worship he favoured in a cathedral.

The new works in Edinburgh put the city's budget under strain. As well as the king's demanding commission, two new churches were needed to make up for the space lost when the St Giles' partitions came down. The church had housed three congregations and would now house one. Similar considerations applied in the other Scottish refurbishments. Money had to be found which meant a levy on the people.

Architecture was not enough. Charles I wanted to reorder the Kirk's manner of worship. He wanted the Church of Scotland to operate in every way similarly to the Church of England that Archbishop Laud was so energetically shaping. He wanted a Scottish liturgy that conformed to his idea of religion, not to the Scots'. He wanted to replace Knox's Book of Common Order.

A new Book of Canons was issued in January 1636. This was the rulebook for the Kirk. It changed everything:

> The first Canon defined and determined such an illimited power and prerogative to be in the King, according to the pattern (in express terms) of the kings of Israel, and such a full supremacy in all causes ecclesiastical, as hath never been pretended to by their former kings or submitted to by the clergy and laity of the nation.[4]

It forbade *extempore* preaching, nor would ministers be allowed to preach outside their own parish without a licence. It required the communion table (altar) to be placed decorously at the east end of the church (not communally in the middle as presbyterians liked). It re-enacted the Five Articles of Perth. There was no mention of presbyteries. Despite all this, there was no protest against the Canons, which reassured the king.

A new prayer-book had been in the air since the days of King James, if not pursued by him, but it was Charles who ordered work to begin. Use of a new liturgy was included in the new Canons. None of this could be a surprise to a nation which had witnessed the 1633 coronation and received the king's commands about the English liturgy in Chapels Royal and elsewhere.

By early 1636 the drafting was advanced. Originally, the king wanted a Scottish version of the English prayer-book to be used, but he accepted the advice of some of the bishops that Scotland required its own text. Two of them did the bulk of the work with the king almost literally reading over their shoulders, writing comments on the text, always emphasising sacrament, for instance replacing 'minister' with 'priest'.[5]

The draft was tightly controlled but the project was not secret. Stories spread about the horrors. Older bishops rightly worried about its reception. Spottiswoode wrote to Archbishop Laud of Canterbury, suggesting he intervene with the king to delay the introduction. Some of the younger bishops, ambitious to serve the king, made sure Laud was reassured that Scotland was ready. They were wrong. Scotland was not ready.

By the end of 1636 people heard what they feared, the worst of all things, that the prayer-book even included 'a very ambiguous prayer... looking much to transubstantiation'.[6] Papist.

—⚬⚬⚬—

At this juncture Montrose returned to Scotland. He was back in 1636 and probably travelled in the summer (the sailing season). He had not intended to come back. We read of plans to travel further east to see the Ottoman world – Greece, Constantinople ('the Sublime Porte'), Cairo. His curiosity was not satisfied. Nor does he appear to have had any great desire to see his wife and children. We can assume he was not celibate during his travels – earthly pleasure was part of these extended trips. Did he like the bachelor life?

Friends wrote. They wanted him in Scotland. We do not have the letters but there can be little doubt that they urged his return because of the state of the country. Whatever the detail – and the 'friends' must have been Lord Napier and others of his close family – he took it seriously.

We know Montrose had an audience with Charles I before returning to Scotland. So he came back through England and probably crossed from Calais to Dover, the shortest crossing. If he saw the king in Whitehall, he must have been impressed by the largest palace in Europe. Located on the riverside, Whitehall had 1,500 rooms and rambling gardens. It looked like a town, not a single building. There were endless ranges, roofs, walls, courtyards, gardens. There was a large sports complex (cockfighting, royal tennis, jousting). If Montrose did not go to Whitehall he found the king in another of the royal residences, all spectacular. Hampton Court, Richmond, Nonsuch, Greenwich or Theobalds are the obvious locations. In the summer especially, the king travelled. And it was a plague year. As the death toll rose in London, the court would flee Whitehall.

We read that the king, at this first meeting, having permitted his hand to be kissed, looked away. We read that Montrose was 'much discontented' when he returned to Scotland. Why the cool reception? The old explanation was court intrigue. According to one source the Marquess of Hamilton warned the king against Montrose as a powerful and popular noble 'of such esteem among the Scots by reason of an old descent from the royal family' who might endanger the king's cause in Scotland. He must be 'nipped in the bud'.[7] Hamilton had done it before. He was one of the enemies of the Earl of Menteith deploying exactly the same argument. He was highly political. But it seems likely that the king was already biased against Montrose because of his failure to attend the Scottish coronation.

As for the unhappiness of Montrose, there is more to be said. At court he saw the advance of bishops. Following the death of Richard Weston, Earl of Portland in March 1635, William Juxon, Bishop of London was made Lord Treasurer. William Laud, Archbishop of Canterbury, had wanted this post for himself. Any visitor would hear how close Laud was to the king. Montrose had seen episcopal power in action in France and Italy. He never liked bishops much in the first place. He agreed with Archibald Napier's words:

> That churchmen have competency, is agreeable to the law of God and man. But to invest them into great estates, and principal offices of the state, is neither convenient for the Church, for the King, nor for the State... Our reformed churches having reduced religion to the ancient primitive truth and simplicity ought to beware that corruption enter not in their church.[8]

The ancient, primitive truth. Historians today agree that Scotland was converted to Christianity by Irish missionaries, men within the same cultural orbit. Mediterranean domination of liturgy and creed came later. Many early modern Scots thought the Reformation rightly discarded centuries of Roman interference: presbyterian beliefs were not new, they were old.

Sure enough another warning sign at court was Catholic presence. Montrose was back in a Protestant realm, but it did not look like it. In December 1634 a legate from Rome had arrived – after a request from Henrietta Maria.[9] This was Gregorio Panzani. In July 1636 George Conn was attached to the queen's court as official representative of the Holy See. Conn was a Catholic from Aberdeenshire and author of a history of Scottish Christianity. Charles I enjoyed his company.

This was the time when Pope Urban VIII deluged the king and queen with presents such as oil paintings, costly rosaries and a cross, Henrietta Maria's favourite, which she wore all the time, decorated with diamonds in the shape of bees (the emblem of Urban's family, the Barberini). Whether the glittering bounty was visible before or after Montrose attended court, he would learn of it. Centred on the shadowy figure of Eleazar Borthwick, an intelligence system had developed in London that briefed presbyterian leaders in Scotland.

And there was a family connection. Montrose's cousin Mary Ruthven was one of the children of Patrick Ruthven,[10] the youngest of the Ruthven brothers. She was probably in her late teens in 1636, Patrick having married before he was released from the Tower. Mary was Catholic, a lady in Henrietta Maria's household. Montrose surely must have seen her at court. She would soon marry a famous Catholic husband, the image creator of the Caroline court, Sir Anthony van Dyck.[11] A meeting between Montrose and Mary is pure conjecture, but it is extremely likely. What would he have made of her?

His discontent as he travelled north probably was the result of a bungled audience with the king, but it is tempting to suppose that the royal court had not suited Montrose anyway. Charles I was influenced by Spanish etiquette. His wife was a sophisticated Bourbon with an exotic style. There were bishops everywhere. Even Montrose's cousin was Catholic. Montrose found the King of England when he wanted a King of Scots.

12

'An holy nation'

In the unusually dry summer of 1637, a new age dawned. It was what Charles I, King of Scots, had worked for. He had every reason to look forward. He had been crowned king. His government had raised tax both in 1630 and 1633. Scottish cathedrals were being restored. There were more bishops than ever. Dissent (Balmerino) was suppressed. The Kirk accepted new Canons with no mention of presbyteries. With the prayer-book coming into use, a prayer-book which was a compliment to the Scots – written specially for them, when there was already a perfectly good English prayer-book – everything fell into place.

But everything fell to bits.

We can look at the king's actions in the coming months with some sympathy for his predicament. It was cruel to find that, after all, it was not to be *his* new age. It belonged to his enemies. What exactly was this enmity? How far would Charles I's critics go? It can at once be said they would go the distance.

On 23 July 1637 the Scottish prayer-book was used in Sunday service for the first time. The fuse had been lit and the bomb exploded. The scenes sound comical but must have been very frightening for those on the receiving end. When the Dean of Edinburgh, James Hannay, started to read at the service in St Giles' 'a multitude of wives and serving-women... rose in a tumultuous way.'[1] There were catcalls, there was wailing: 'they are bringing in popery among us.' A 'creepie stool' – a portable stool, quite heavy – was hurled at the dean by Jenny Geddes, according to later tradition. Was she Johnny Geddes in disguise? The power of the women amazed. More stools were hurled. People later asked if there were young men in the congregation dressed like their mothers. Perhaps that underestimates the strength of a working woman.

Including a sermon, the service finished somehow. Afterwards Bishop David Lindsay was attacked in the street. He presided over a second service in the afternoon from which the women were excluded. After that he was chased by a crowd but survived thanks to the protection of the Earl of Roxburgh, in whose coach he made it back to his Holyroodhouse lodgings.

'Survived' is not putting it too strongly. The crowd threw stones at Lindsay shouting 'Kill the traitor!'[2] The earl's footmen kept the people back with drawn swords. Other ministers in other churches faced the same trial by mob. Nobody died. Everyone was scared. The Bishop of Brechin got through his readings by the simple expedient of arriving in church with two loaded pistols which he kept in sight of his congregation, but that was a high-risk strategy he did not dare repeat. He, too, struggled to return home because of the mass of people.

It was defiance of the king – rebellion. The bishops, instructed by Spottiswoode of St Andrews, told their ministers to use the prayer-book. Spottiswoode was Primate of Scotland and president of the privy council. He was the king's servant. Everyone knew the prayer-book was written and introduced at Charles I's command. The minister Robert Baillie wrote 'All the people think popery at the doors... no man may speak anything in public for the king's part, except that he should have himself marked down for sacrifice to be killed one day.'[3]

It was perfectly organized. These outrages had been long planned.[4] The ability to sort things would be the hallmark of the Scottish revolution, real competence. Day one was a success. Now the rebels needed to communicate as widely as possible what they stood for.

When he heard the news, King Charles was cool. He told the privy council that he meant to be obeyed. Nonetheless, his councillors had taken a different tack. They suspended the prayer-book on 29 July while awaiting instructions. But the protest had only just begun. In August a petition to the king was organised by the minister of Leuchars in Fife, Alexander Henderson. The petition complained that the prayer-book had not been agreed by the General Assembly and that it introduced a crypto-Catholic liturgy. The first was a reasonable and true point. The prayer-book had not gone through the Kirk's usual decision-making process. The second could be debated, but it fired the spirit.

Distance made it hard for the royal government. The privy council was in Edinburgh while the king was four hundred miles away in the south of England. A man could, at the absolute quickest, if he had a great deal of luck, make it from Whitehall to Edinburgh in two days perhaps, changing horses, but that was exceptionally optimistic. It was better to allow three and that would still be incredibly quick. The roads were much worse in winter, the rider must rest, he would not want to travel in the dark, there was the risk of accident.[5] So the bare minimum turnaround time was a week for news to be delivered to the king and his instructions to be reported back. In fact, the normal winter turnaround for the post was two weeks.

As summer turned to autumn the weather duly made things harder. In October there were floods in the north, in Aberdeen four ships were wrecked (with loss of life), and in December the mouth of Aberdeen harbour was briefly blocked by sand, which threatened the life of the town, but the same bad weather happily unblocked it.[6]

From Whitehall the situation in distant Scotland was therefore hard to assess. It seemed random, chaotic. And Charles I had his hands full in England where John Hampden was being tried for his refusal to pay Ship Money – a critical test case for the king's English finances (and military defences), so much more important than Edinburgh riots.

Scotland was hard to understand, it was distant, it was on the margins. So the king reduced these events to the easiest thing to understand. He saw an illegal, impious challenge to the authority God gave him. Charles I and the London Scots did not have the least idea about the preparation behind the prayer-book riots. They were badly informed. Alexander Henderson, while he did not act alone, was at the heart of things: 'Upon Mr Henderson all the ministry of that judgement depended, and no wonder, for in gravity, learning, wisdom and state-policy he far exceeded any of them.'[7]

Women's activism was Henderson's idea in collaboration with another leading minister, David Dickson. In April 1637 the two of them contacted Lord Balmerino and Sir Thomas Hope. Having 'gotten their approbation thereto', Henderson and Dickson met, most unusually, with several women of Edinburgh: Euphame Henderson, Bethia and Elspeth Craig, 'and several other matrons'. From this meeting came the events of 23 July. Yet another first from Scotland.

The movement increasingly took on the character of a noble revolt. Other names coming forward were the earls of Rothes, Lindsay, Cassillis, Eglinton, Home, Sutherland and lords Loudoun, Yester, Cranstone. These men were sincere defenders of presbyterianisn, but there was a further irritant to the magnates in plans drawn up by Sir James Balfour for the Principality of Scotland to be increased.[8] These were the lands set aside to provide an income for the king's eldest son. If the principality were increased, then existing landowners must lose something – it was a badly timed reminder of the 1625 Revocation.

And a women's revolt? Since the position of women in law was marginal, their leadership of the St Giles' uproar was hard to oppose. And what a shock. Women were not meant to complain about royal policies, or complain at all, they were not meant to throw furniture at churchmen and threaten bishops with dismemberment.

In October 1637 in Edinburgh 'women fell to work again and assembled on the street to the number of 200... and their first attempt was on Bishop Sydserf.'[9] Sydserf was at risk of being 'torn in pieces' but was rescued by the armed attendants of a friendly noble. The women went on to besiege the city council, which was then sitting, and threatened to 'burn the house about their ears'. The provost and bailiffs escaped having agreed to appoint two commissioners to join the supplicants (show support).

From Henderson's petition came a signed 'Supplication' (18 October) – how submissive it sounds. That was for the privy council to see, and the king. Then very radically an alternative government for Scotland was formed (6 December) called the Tables. This was fast work.

The Tables were committees. There were four Tables reflecting the parliamentary division of the nation into nobles, barons (lairds), clergy and burgesses (the towns), and a fifth executive committee (like the Lords of the Articles). Deftly the rebels created a nucleus which looked like parliament. That was clever. Parliament could not meet unless the king summoned it, but the rebels just side-stepped him with their alternative representative body.

The Earl of Montrose was invisible during the summer agitation but quite soon decided to stand up for the Kirk. He signed the Supplication. In November 1637 Montrose came to an Edinburgh meeting with other nobles who, as he did, initially reserved judgement. His appearance 'was most taken note of, yea, when the bishops heard that he was come there to join, they were somewhat affrighted, having that esteem of his parts, they thought it time to prepare for a storm when he engaged.'[10]

From this time Montrose was closely involved in the rebellion against Charles I.

Charisma earned him a place in the Tables. In the Table of Nobles were four members only. The older members were the Earl of Rothes (thirty-seven), Lord Lindsay (forty-one) and Lord Loudoun (thirty-nine). At twenty-five, Montrose joined them. It was a distinction that marked him as a trusted, valued member of an extraordinary movement. At last he had his cause, if not yet his war. His nephew by marriage Sir George Stirling of Keir (husband of Margaret Napier) was a member of the Table of Barons. That was a considerable family interest.

What Montrose did not know was that some colleagues had already reached out across the border to like-minded men in England. One of our sources, usually reliable, says that before the prayer-book rebellion, or about the same time, certain Scottish nobles had an agreement with Englishmen who also opposed the Arminian spirit of Charles I. The signatories, if there really was a document, wanted one reformed religion in both England and Scotland; the abolition of bishops in both countries; a reduction in the king's powers.[11]

———osso———

In February 1638 the Treasurer, the Earl of Traquair,[12] returned to Scotland. He had instructions to insist on the prayer-book by proclamation; in short, no compromise. Charles I put himself in the front line. The proclamation said the king had 'seen and approved' the prayer-book.[13]

Before this it was possible for the Scots to hold to the traditional view about bad advice, which exonerated their king: advisers were responsible for the king doing something wrong, you could not blame Charles Stuart. From now on there was no concealing the king's personal responsibility. That certainly was what he wanted, believing his personal *imprimatur* would win the argument. It is another clue to the way his mind worked. Charles I did not lack courage, he lacked judgement.

The presbyterian rebels reached for their copies of the Bible where they found agreements between God and man which trumped the instructions of a mere mortal king. For instance, the 'Old Covenant' was with the prophet Moses: 'Now therefore, if ye will obey my voice indeed, and keep my covenant, then ye shall be a peculiar treasure unto me above all people: for all the earth is mine: And ye shall be unto me a kingdom of priests, and an holy nation.'[14]

And there was the New Covenant announced but not delivered in the Book of Jeremiah: 'Behold the days come, saith the Lord, that I will make a new covenant with the house of Israel, and with the house of Judah… for I will forgive their iniquity and I will remember their sin no more.'[15]

If the Israelites could do it, so could the Scots. They, too, were in search of the promised land. The response of the Tables to their king's threats was to commit themselves to the Lord and He would protect them.

The National Covenant of Scotland of 1638 was drafted by Alexander Henderson and a younger man, the feverish Archibald Johnston of Wariston, 'the only advocate who in this cause is trusted.' It was launched on 28 February 1638 in Greyfriars Kirk in Edinburgh.

Here the text was read out to a large crowd, whose members were asked to subscribe. As far as we know they did so to a man. The nobles signed first, starting at four in the afternoon. The lairds came next and so forth. The work went on while it was light and finished about eight – four hours of people signing.[16]

Few can have read the words for themselves. That showed the feeling, but the National Covenant was far from pure emotion, it had a calculated logic. It was a carefully structured statement that had to bear the scrutiny of enemies. The opening words were as follows:

> The confession of faith of the Kirk of Scotland, subscribed at first by the King's Majesty and his household in the year of God 1580; thereafter by persons of all ranks in the year 1581, by ordinance of the lords of the secret council, and acts of the general assembly, with a general band for the maintenance of the true religion and the King's person, and now subscribed in the year 1638...

So the protest went back to the King's Confession of 1581 signed by James VI. That was a commitment by the young king to maintain the Scottish Reformation. He issued it because he faced opposition to the favour he gave his cousin Esmé Stuart, Duke of Lennox (born Catholic in France). In 1581, James VI wanted to clear himself of the charge of Catholic leanings. That royal commitment was now repeated in 1638. That is all, said these opening words – nothing revolutionary. The opposite in fact.

While it may have looked as though they were defying their present king, the people subscribing to this new (but old) band pledged support for the 'maintenance of the King's person'. Repeatedly the text declared loyalty to Charles I:

> We protest and promise with our hearts under the same oath, hand-writ, and pains, that we shall defend his person and authority with our goods, bodies, and lives...
>
> Like as all lieges are bound to maintain the King's Majesty's royal person and authority... in the same cause of maintaining the true religion and His Majesty's authority.

The text listed the many Acts of Parliament since the Reformation which supported 'maintenance of the true religion'. This National Covenant was consistent with these: it was constitutional. The Tables, the non-conforming ministers, the nobles and other people in Greyfriars Kirkyard were just saying again things already agreed by parliament. The rebellion was not a rebellion. Not least, 'persons of all ranks' had signed in 1581, just as they were going to now. The movement was national.

It was clever to insist that the King's Confession of 1581 had passed the General Assembly. In 1638 there had been no General Assembly for twenty years. Charles I called a convention of estates in 1630 and a parliament in 1633. But he had not called the General Assembly – the parliament of the Kirk.[17] And he had issued the Book of Canons and then the prayer-book. But if the rules governing the Kirk were not to be debated by the General Assembly, what was it meant to debate?

To come to the heart of the matter, the National Covenant was a manifesto against Catholicism: 'But in special we detest and refuse the usurped authority of that Roman Antichrist upon the Scriptures of God.' The Pope and everything he stood for were rejected, such as 'his erroneous doctrine against the sufficiency of the written Word' and 'his holy water, baptizing of bells, conjuring of spirits, crossing, sayning, anointing, conjuring' and of course 'his worldly monarchy and wicked hierarchy'. The last word meant bishops.

Above all, the Tables wanted to shred the Book of Canons and consign the detested prayer-book to the dustbin of history. So there was a pledge against 'innovations already introduced in the matters of worship of God' and a commitment against changes in government 'until they be tried and allowed in the free Assemblies and in Parliament'.

The movement now formally launched combined reason and unreason. Reformed theology was very carefully, rationally argued. The tactics of the prayer-book rebellion were planned and managed. But there was revulsion and fear too. People at the time believed in the strength of evil, of satanic forces. When the Pope was called Antichrist it was not a figure of speech.

Politically, this was deliberate and obvious opposition to the king, nonetheless what stands out is thoroughly researched support for a Reformed Protestant king. The brilliance of the National Covenant lay in this insistence, because a Reformed Protestant king was exactly what Charles I was, just like his father – whether he liked it or not; even in England. The Church of England was not Lutheran, it was Calvinist. The Kirk could be labelled *more* Calvinist perhaps, but both countries followed Reformed Protestant theology. The king need only reflect. The king need only agree that the Kirk was right, he need only support its presbyterian structure by doing what his father had failed to do and get rid of the bishops.

Montrose was in Greyfriars kirkyard on 28 February 1638. His flamboyant signature appears shortly below the end of the text. He was one of the first to sign.

13

Thrusting Through

In the house of Archibald Johnston of Wariston a young woman came to visit. Her name was Margaret Mitchelson. He welcomed her because of something they had in common and that was enthusiasm, or perhaps it was mania. This was October 1638, eight months after the first signing of the National Covenant.[1]

Margaret was a prophetess. She was living, speaking proof. There she sat 'transported in heavenly raptures' enthusing about the rightness of the Covenant and the falsity of everything else. Her 'soul was full to the brim and to the overflowing of the most sensible conceptions and expressions of the greatness, goodness and glorious excellency of King Jesus...'[2] 'She spoke of Christ and called him Covenanting Jesus'.[3]

She was to be admired; she was an inspiration. 'Great numbers of all ranks of people were her daily hearers; and many of the devouter sex, the women, prayed, and wept with joy and wonder, to hear her speak.'[4] Margaret was a flash in the firmament, a holy woman who came and went. We know nothing of her life before and after. It was fifteen minutes of fame.

The teeming thoughts of Wariston himself survive in his diary, which is one of the memorials of early covenantism. They include fears about sex and marriage. His first wife Jean Stewart was fourteen when they married (1632) and died within a year of the wedding. His second marriage (1634) with Helen Hay produced several children. He decided to remarry because he needed a woman in his life, which can be understood, but it tells us something about the experience of his very young first wife. Both girls were the daughters of lawyers. They came from educated, affluent homes.

Wariston was equally devout and needy. He prayed for hours on end, on one occasion being lost in prayer from six in the morning to eight at night. His nephew wrote he 'could seldom sleep above three hours in the twenty-four... he would often pray in his family two hours at a time.'[5] He was terrified that he might not be one of the elect. He detested Catholicism as 'Romisch superstition.' He was dedicated to 'the overthrow of episcopacy, that great grandmother of all our corruptions'. His relationship with God was passionate. On one occasion he 'roared, groaned, sobbed unutterably... shouted' to God.[6]

Without this man what would the Scottish revolution have been? The leaders otherwise were variously pious and high-principled, self-serving and political, but the intelligent, diligent Wariston brought a particular focus. A seething mass of personal uncertainty and godly certainty, he played a critical role in holding the rebel leadership together in 1638. He drafted the National Covenant with Henderson, gave moral support in spades, if moral is the word, and was a workaholic in the cause.

From March the Tables gathered signatures. They wanted the country lined up. In March, April, May, copies of the National Covenant were sent all over Scotland. People were asked to sign usually by an insistent lord or laird. When there was reluctance the soldiers of God did not hesitate. In some places there were 'threatenings, tearing of cloths, drawing of blood'.[7]

In the south-east and southern lowlands, the tactics worked. Tens of thousands of signatures were gathered.

Not every part of Scotland co-operated, however. In the 'north parts... many opposed'.[8] The area around Aberdeen (the north-east) was dominated by the head of the Gordon clan, the second Marquess of Huntly. This was the man who as Lord Gordon/Earl of Enzie had lived magnificently in France. Huntly did not support the rebellion. He was royalist and crypto-Catholic although he never confirmed Catholic belief publicly.[9] His two main residences Strathbogie (now Huntly Castle) and Bog o' Gight (Gordon Castle) stood fifteen miles from each other, north-west of Aberdeen. They formed an axis of control over the surrounding country. The Gordon clan was one of the largest in Scotland. Huntly was new to its leadership because he only returned to Scotland after his father died in June 1636. By coincidence he and Montrose came back about the same time.

The city of Aberdeen was firmly Protestant, independent-minded, educated (the university was founded in 1495), generally episcopalian. The civic influence of Aberdeen reached into surrounding areas.

North of Aberdeenshire was more fertile ground for the Covenant, helped by lies: 'They went through all the north... through Murray, Ross, Sutherland and Caithness, making the people believe that the king was to bring in popery and the mass, and that the king was to take the kirklands or abbacy land from them that had them in heritage.'[10] Here one sees the damage of the 1625 Revocation. In the more westerly Highlands and Islands we do not have good information. Inaccessibility probably meant that much of this part of Scotland was untouched. There was a strong Catholic tradition in these parts.[11]

Argyll was always a region apart. It was the huge swathe of territory in the southernmost part of the Highlands reaching out to and including some of the western isles, altogether more than two thousand square miles. The great part was the territory of the Catholic Earl of Argyll. Not that he lived in Scotland. He lived in London. His son Archibald, Lord Lorne, did live in Scotland, and was a privy councillor, bound to obey the king. He held the Campbell patrimony, he had authority to manage it all thanks to a deal with his father, so Argyll power was really his power. Nonetheless, while his father lived Lorne was constrained by the risk of that authority being reclaimed – by the earl himself or on the instructions of Charles I.

By contrast with his father, Lorne was an orthodox Scottish presbyterian. The king thought him reliable. He had discussed the Scottish situation with him, a full hour and a half of talks, in early 1638. Afterwards Lorne continued on the privy council.

When he heard the news of the National Covenant, Charles I saw that a group of fishwives was not the problem. On the other hand, he had senior noble support from Lorne, from Huntly, from his cousin the Duke of Lennox, from his friend the Marquess of Hamilton. He might fairly assume much more. In summer 1638 the king agreed to call a General Assembly of the Kirk. He could see that sticking to his guns would not win his point. He would have to play for time.

Montrose was in the thick of it. In March 1638 the Tables started to collect money to finance their campaign. We have a record of the noblemen who contributed at once. Montrose heads the list with a contribution of twenty-five dollars, the highest level of individual gift (the same as Rothes, Balmerino, Loudoun, Lindsay). His brother-in-law Lord Carnegie contributed fifteen dollars (Carnegie's father was still alive as Earl of Southesk, a coronation honour).

The same month Montrose was one of the six lords tasked with being in Edinburgh to await the king's response to the latest communication. A few days later, a letter was sent to the privy council signed by seventeen lords – Montrose was the second to sign after Rothes.[12] As the year went on, he kept this very senior position.

In June or July 1638, he went to Aberdeen with Henderson, Dickson and others to treat with the city. It was time to sort the north-east. At the same time the experienced soldier Robert Monro met the Marquess of Huntly to ask for his support. The co-ordinated missions both failed. Huntly told Monro he was a dedicated royalist who owed everything to the crown, and Montrose's mission fell flat. He returned to Edinburgh with a handful of signatures.

With exasperating disorder, the General Assembly of the Kirk opened in Glasgow Cathedral on 21 November 1638. The building would be well known to Montrose from the days he lodged with the Elphinstones. It was a grand medieval church, well preserved. The rood screen survives today, this being the carved stone screen separating the priest from the congregation. Catholic structures housed the presbyterians. The meeting was arranged thanks to Hamilton. His trips to Edinburgh and back, to consult with his king, trying for a way forward, inspired not only politics but also verse:

> My Lord, your unexpected post
> To court, made me to miss
> The happiness which I love most,
> Your lordship's hands to kiss.[13]

Glasgow was full to bursting. Delegates and others flocked to give support. Room rates were sky-high.[14] Before the opening, a fast was observed with preaching and prayer. People then went to find their places in the cathedral, which was a battle. There was 'much delay of time and thrusting through'.

One of the parish representatives wondered whether the struggle was due to the 'rudeness of our nation' or to the excitement of 'this latest reformation'. He remarked 'It is here alone, I think, we may learn from Canterbury, yea from the Pope, yea from the Turks or pagans, modesty and manners.'[15]

Somehow, people sat down. Representing the king, Hamilton was raised high on a chair of state – essentially a throne sporting the royal arms. On either side and immediately in front of him were members of the privy council. On the floor of the nave a long table was placed to accommodate the lords including Montrose (always named in second place after Rothes), and the lairds. All of these had been selected as elders to represent parishes. Montrose represented Auchterarder. Seating was built up around the long table to hold the university delegates and ministers. There were more than two hundred delegates, both elders and ministers.

Beyond was a smaller table for the Moderator (Alexander Henderson) and the clerk (Wariston). These two officials were meant to be neutral in the discussion. Opposite Hamilton at the end of the church was seating mainly for the 'young noblemen'. The galleries were packed with spectators including 'ladies and some gentlewomen'.[16]

The discussion was between the Royal Commissioner and the delegates. The others were there to watch and listen. The privy councillors were there for the king. Almost everyone else was there for the National Covenant. Hamilton understood perfectly.[17]

The marquess was a very senior noble in England and Scotland. He was a member of the English as well as the Scottish privy council. As Earl of Cambridge, he was a member of the English House of Lords. He was the king's Master of Horse and a Gentleman of the Bedchamber – both much envied court positions that guaranteed physical access to the king almost all the time. Having known the king since they were both children, Hamilton had come as close as any courtier to being a second Buckingham, the trusted favourite. Like Charles I, Hamilton was an art collector. The king and queen were even said to have secured the consummation of Hamilton's marriage. He had a unique personal understanding with Charles I.

In addition, Hamilton knew Scotland. For a start, his estates were managed by his mother Anna, presbyterian to her fingertips. There could be no closer Covenant link. Second, like other nobles, he sincerely disliked bishops. So he was sympathetic. Third, when he arrived in Scotland in June 1638 as Royal Commissioner, a hundred of his relatives and retainers failed to greet him at Dalkeith as he asked. Of course, Hamilton saw the situation for what it was. But he had his instructions. On 11 June Charles I wrote to him 'I give you leave to flatter them with what hopes you please...' and two days later, 'I shall follow your advice in staying the public preparations for force; but in a silent way I will not leave to prepare that I may be ready.' The king struck the highest pitch: 'I will rather die than yield to those impertinent and damnable demands.'[18]

In brief, by summer 1638 the king had decided to fight. War was inevitable. At whatever cost, *cuius regio, eius religio.*

Long procedural discussions started the assembly. The question arose whether the assembly was competent to rule on bishops. Hamilton had already questioned the competence of all those laymen to rule on theology. He was outmanoeuvred by the supposedly neutral Wariston producing documents that 'proved' the opposite.[19]

When it became clear that he could not prevent a vote on the bishops, Hamilton used the weapon of last resort. He spoke with emotion of his duty to God and the king: 'This was the Commissioner's last passage, he acted it with tears and drew, by his speech, water from many eyes.' After further exchanges he said, 'no act there should import his consent, and that naught done by the voices of the present members was lawful... he discharged them to proceed any further.'[20]

The Royal Commissioner closed the assembly down. This was 28 November 1638, a week after the opening.

In Glasgow Cathedral, Montrose did not distinguish himself. He made one fierce intervention. There was a dispute over the representation of the Brechin presbytery. The Tables had given instructions that the Laird of Dun was to be sent for Brechin; while the majority vote was for Lord Carnegie, Montrose's brother-in-law. Montrose supported Erskine of Dun against Carnegie by having a shouting match with his father-in-law Southesk: 'The contest between Montrose and Southesk grew so hot that it terrified the whole Assembly.'[21]

Had it happened before at Kinnaird Castle? These men were close family, the people he had lived with in the early years of marriage. What did this sort of thing do to help anyone? Since Carnegie was dedicated to the new national movement – he had given money – while his father was a privy councillor, Montrose might be expected to show at least a degree of courtesy. One thinks of the position of his wife.

By contrast, Hamilton's behaviour was exemplary. As presiding official, he earned plaudits for his grace and good manners through the give and take. Later, he reported to the king. He named the rebel leaders as Rothes, Balmerino, Lindsay, Lothian, Loudoun, Yester and Cranstone. He did not blame the ministers. Hamilton did not name Montrose as a leader. In fact he regarded the young man with contempt: 'There are many others forward in show – amongst them none more vainly foolish than Montrose.'[22]

Publicly, Hamilton was so much the diplomat that his sympathies became suspect. In July he had apparently reached out during a meeting with a group of covenanting leaders. Montrose reported that Hamilton had said to them, 'If you go on with courage and resolution you will carry what you please, but if you faint and give ground in the least you are undone.' This, from the king's close friend! Whose side was he on? We read that Montrose told the story with surprise, he did not know what to think. Yet the truth is we do not know what the king's commissioner said. It was the covenanters (Rothes, Loudon, Henderson) who spread the word. They had every reason to lie.[23]

Before Hamilton swept out, Lord Lorne, newly authoritative as eighth Earl of Argyll thanks to his father's recent death, made a short speech. He spoke quietly. Not everyone heard. His personal style, it can be seen, was very different from Montrose's (he was just five years older). There are different accounts.

In one version he said he regarded the assembly as lawful. In another he said having laymen as well as ministers made sense because 'these two made up one complete body.' While Hamilton summoned the privy council the same day, 28[h] November 1638, and issued a proclamation that those continuing to sit after the formal dissolution were traitors, Argyll did not sign.[24]

The assembly did not go away, it continued. Moderator Henderson said there was a war to be fought with the 'Kingdom of Satan and Antichrist'. The gloves were off. The delegates voted to continue in session and did so for several weeks unchecked. Although not a parish delegate, Argyll continued to attend, always cloaked in ambiguity. He said almost nothing and what he did say was cautious. Many delegates thought his presence meant royal approval for what they were doing. In reality, the king's greatest subject was beginning to show his hand against the king (he had his reasons).

The assembly formally abolished episcopacy and convicted the bishops personally of crimes including debauchery and corruption (no bishops were present). The delegates declared the previous six assemblies invalid. They declared the Five Articles of Perth invalid. They condemned the prayer-book, the Book of Canons, the Court of High Commission. They voted for a permanent Commission of the Church invested with the full powers of the assembly. If this new committee functioned, the king's power to call and close the General Assembly mattered little.

Hamilton retreated to Glasgow Castle, then to Holyroodhouse where he stayed several weeks. He ordered the king's tapestries, especially loved by Charles I,[25] and his silver plate to be packed up and sent into England. After Christmas he, too, left the country.

14

Salve regina

Between the Mull of Kintyre and the Ulster coast lie the straits of Moyle, at the narrowest point twelve miles of sea. The peninsula of Kintyre reaches back thirty miles to the north-east connecting with the Scottish mainland at Tarbet, a village bordered on the south by Kintyre itself, on the north by the uplands of Knapdale and to the east and west by the sea. The islands of Jura and Islay lie several miles north-west of Kintyre, and beyond them Colonsay. To the south-east, separated by the Kilbrannan Sound, is Arran, located in the body of water which becomes, as it enters the landmass in a passage that narrows to the breadth of a mile or two, Loch Fyne. This substantial inlet continues another forty miles leading to the headquarters of the Campbell Earls (today Dukes) of Argyll at Inverary Castle.

The Kintyre peninsula rises to heights of 1,000 feet and more at points on its central spine, and features cliffs, bays, beaches. At no point is it more than eleven miles wide. The low-lying parts are fertile and productive. By the seventeenth century Kintyre had been inhabited for millennia. It contains neolithic standing stones and burial cairns, an iron age hillfort, a medieval abbey and tombs.

While the Romans occupied the southern part of Great Britain, migrants from Ireland crossed to Kintyre and established a statelet of islands and shorelands that was taken over by the Vikings. In the twelfth century the warlord Somerled, probably of mixed Gaelic and Norse origins, created the kingdom of Argyll and the Isles. His descendants included the MacDonald family who in the fourteenth century created the Lordship of the Isles, an entity linked by sea lanes (traversed by galleys). That lasted about a hundred years before it was challenged by the Scottish kings in the fifteenth century, and the last hopes of an independent lordship disappeared with the death of Donald Dubh MacDonald in Ireland in 1545. However, branches of clan MacDonald survived in the region.

In the early years of the seventeenth century Kintyre was the object of a struggle between Campbells and MacDonalds, the former with crown support. In 1617, the seventh Earl of Argyll at last subjugated the MacDonalds.[1] The grant to him of the peninsula was ratified by the king and parliament.

Evidently the peninsula was a big and valuable property. Before 1620 the old earl settled it on his son by his second marriage, James Campbell, younger half-brother to Archibald. James was made Lord Kintyre in 1626. During their father's lifetime Archibald used the courtesy title Lord Lorne, as we have seen. So Lord Kintyre had the peninsula, while Lorne was to inherit – in fact, as it happened, would before his father's death by agreement take possession of – the other, more enormous family estates.

That led to another dispute in the course of which Lorne, partly through the tactic of buying church lands, partly by buying his half-brother's mortgages, became the *de facto* manager or controller of Kintyre. In 1636 the rights to the disputed lands were given by the king to Lorne's young son, an act which recognized they were part of the whole Argyll inheritance, not to be separated.

Nonetheless, James, Lord Kintyre, nearly sold the peninsula to the family of the Irish Earl of Antrim in 1635. Antrim was one of the largest Irish landholders, a Catholic possessing huge expanses in Ulster. The family name was MacDonnell (an Irish form of MacDonald[2]). This transaction was blocked by the Scottish government.

For these reasons Kintyre was a sensitive subject by the time of the Glasgow Assembly. There was therefore a fantastic clumsiness in the war plan adopted by Charles I.

We have seen the king wanted to crush the rebellion by force. His preparations started early. It was to be a three-pronged attack: Hamilton would lead a flotilla up the east coast to meet the loyal Marquess of Huntly and his Gordons and so assemble a northern army; the king would lead the main army through England to the Borders and attack from the south; and the (new) Earl of Antrim, 'a tall, clean-limbed, handsome man with red hair',[3] then twenty-nine years old, would lead a third army from Ulster by sea to Kintyre and attack from the west. Antrim's reward would be the possession of Kintyre and Jura and other parts of the disputed lands. The king's Scottish fortresses, including Edinburgh Castle, would support the attacks from outside.[4] How bad can planning get?

The king's offer of Kintyre to a family enemy forced Argyll to support the covenanters. It was the king himself who destroyed the loyalty which he appears to have taken for granted. As a privy councillor, and despite his own presbyterian convictions, Argyll went so far as to sign the King's Covenant – Hamilton's decoy which did not reject the new measures – but it was impossible for him to ignore the threat to Kintyre, which was in addition a Catholic threat.[5]

What kind of a man was Lord Lorne, the new Earl of Argyll? After his first wife's death (the mother of Lorne), Lorne's father had married a Catholic Englishwoman, started a second family, converted to Catholicism himself, this being announced in 1618 (Lorne was a young teenager), and went into the service of the King of Spain. His title was forfeited in 1619 with the threat of sequestration of all or part of the estate. That did not happen. There was a reconciliation, the title was restored, but Lorne was raised under the protection of his cousin the Earl of Morton, far away from his father, who returned from the continent to England but not to Scotland. All this explains why the old earl agreed to renounce responsibility for the Argyll patrimony in favour of Lorne. In 1626, Lorne married his near relation, Margaret Douglas. Two years later the king forced him to relinquish the hereditary office of Justice-General of Scotland.

In 1628 Lorne was appointed to the privy council in compensation. The following years were taken up with the consolidation of the estate. By the second half of the 1630s Lorne was highly experienced in life at the top and must have won some considerable degree of confidence. In 1637 he was about thirty years old. This gilded career did not come easy. It required work. Emotionally Lorne had to be tough. He was not physically glamorous although the sheen of wealth and power, the habit of command, made up for that.

The bruises of privilege made Argyll a formidable operator. According to a contemporary:

> For his external and outward disposition he was of homely carriage, gentle, mild, and affable, gracious and courteous to speak to. Internally he had a large and understanding heart, a jealous and far-reaching apprehension, and yet his presence did show him of such plain and homely aspect, as he seemed rather inclined to simplicity than any ways tempted with a lofty and unsatiable ambition, although he proved the deepest statesman, the most crafty, subtle and over-reaching politician, that this age could produce.[6]

Another wrote 'Though by the ill placing of his eyes, he did not appear with any great advantage at first sight, yet he reconciled even those who had aversion to him very strangely, by a little conversation.'[7]

In Whitehall Palace Henrietta Maria continued her efforts to raise the tone, as did Charles I. Almost since the time she arrived in 1625 she had mounted a series of theatrical entertainments for the court in which she appeared in leading roles – as Chloris, a nymph raised to heaven, as Bellessa (beauty) and so forth.

The masques featured music, poetry, singing, dancing, glamorous costumes, mind-challenging stage sets. They showcased lofty ideals: love in its most sublime expression, social harmony, Stuart kingship. Inigo Jones was usually the designer. The words came from poets of differing gifts. During this part of the reign, it was usually William Davenant who provided the libretto.

In January 1637, Charles and Henrietta Maria had presented *Britannia Triumphans* (Britain in triumph) at Whitehall, either in the Great Hall or the recently built Banqueting Hall.[8] The name of the masque was important: it was about Britain, not England or Scotland but the two combined.[9] This was six months before the prayer-book rebellion, but the masque shows how important the king's plans for Scotland already were. He fully intended to reign over a unified Great Britain. The name *Britannia Triumphans* would turn out to be unprophetic for Charles I, but in early 1637 it was a statement of intent.

The raised stage, opposite which Henrietta Maria sat in the Chair of State, was surrounded by ornamentation which emphasised the maritime power of King Charles and therefore referred to his controversial Ship Money campaign in England. At the front beneath the level of the stage were figures on pedestals, representing bound captives. Above on either side was a niche, one with a woman wearing pale blue and silver, holding a ship's rudder in one hand and a winged figure and a garland in the other. She stood for naval victory. The other niche held a man wearing an antique cloak of blue and crimson, holding a sceptre and a book, his feet treading the head of a serpent. He was right government. The frieze above the stage showed children riding seahorses and fishes, and young Tritons 'and other maritime fancies'.

The curtain rises to reveal an English scene, houses old and new with trees between them, and a view of London with the Thames flowing through, which 'might be taken for all Great Britain' (the Scots would not agree). The dialogue in the first scene is between 'Action', 'Imposture' and Merlin, the latter wearing a long robe of light purple and holding a silver wand. The wizard summons a vision of 'a horrid hell' because he wishes to 'straight collect from dismal corners there/the great seducers of this Isle...'

There is a musical entertainment in which various figures appear dancing, the anti-masquers. They include a ballad singer, a kitchen maid, a 'crier of mouse traps', a harlequin, 'four old-fashioned parasitical courtiers' and 'rebellious leaders in war'.

Bellerophon enters on Pegasus, 'riding up into the middle of the room', so not on stage. He wears a plumed helmet. Pegasus is covered in white. His mane and tail are silver. He has large wings. The saddle and reins are carnation trimmed with silver. Bellerophon challenges Imposture for being what he is. Merlin summons a play within a play, the Romance, set in a forest with a castle in the background.

In the Romance a lady, her dwarf, a chain-mailed giant, a knight and his squire exchange banter, the upshot of which is that the lady has unwittingly picked berries in the forest claimed by the giant, who therefore wants to make her his cook. The knight defends her. The giant takes nothing lying down and says he will fight back:

> Then I perceive I must lift up my pole,
> And deal your love-sick noddle such a dole
> That every blow shall make so huge a clatter,
> Men ten leagues off shall ask, Hah! What's the matter?

Merlin resolves the quarrel with further dancing. Action tells Imposture that he must go and hide in a dark place:

> The light is killing, cause it doth reveal
> Thy thin disguise...
> Thou art a shadow...
> So thou dost thrive in darkness, waste in light.

A sumptuous palace rises from below, all silver and gold. On a high tower is the figure of Fame (reputation), a lady with white wings and blonde hair, dressed in red and gold holding a trumpet and an olive garland. This is therefore the Palace of Fame. Imposture has been banished because he cannot stand up to the truth. With a song, Fame summons Britanocles, a name meaning Britain's glory, who stands not only for the unified state so much desired but also for the light of day and the light of wisdom: 'we all in darkness mourn till thou appear.'

Although it is not quite spelled out in the text, there can be no doubt that Britanocles was played by Charles I. He enters. The masquers dance triumphantly. The palace sinks leaving the stage to the king and his attendants. Fame floats aloft, still singing, and disappears into the clouds.

A group of dead but resurrected poets that has been on stage for some time now address Henrietta Maria in the audience. The queen, too, is a figure of light who literally opens their eyes:

Our eyes (long since dissolved to air)
To thee for day must now repair
Though raised to life by Merlin's might
Thy stock of beauty will supply
Enough of sun from either eye
To fill the organs of our sight!

The British triumph is not yet done. There is yet another scene change in which the sea appears at the back, with a citadel and harbour on one side and rocks on the other. A dolphin swims out carrying the sea-nymph Galatea on his back. She wears chains of pearls around her neck and arms. She is dressed in white and partly veiled and her fair hair is dishevelled in the sea breeze. Having arrived at centre stage Galatea sings the praises of Britanocles. When she has finished the dolphin carries her away. Individual boats and then a whole fleet appear, and take refuge in the harbour, as the masquers dance.

The valediction comes urging spectators to depart to bed and not to sleep for among the continued praises of the king he is called a 'royal lover': vigorous, fertile (four children so far, and the queen was pregnant again). Supporting Charles I various courtiers appeared in *Britannia Triumphans* including Scots: the Duke of Lennox and his brother Lord Ludovic Stuart, the Earl of Carlisle, the Earl of Elgin, Lord William Hamilton (brother of the marquess).

A year later, in the winter season of 1638 – the court was at Whitehall during the winter, the Christmas period passed in a round of entertainment – the PR barrage continued, although *Luminalia,* staged for the first time on 6 February of that year, was indirect politically. It is tempting to put this down to the queen's touch. Henrietta Maria initially wanted a peaceful settlement in Scotland. She had seen civil war in France as a child. Her own mother was a more recent political casualty (and would soon arrive in England).

Luminalia has Henrietta Maria written all over it. As the name suggests, it was a celebration of light, building on the imagery of *Britannia Triumphans*. Light was divine. The creation myth at the beginning of the Book of Genesis begins with a watery world sunk in darkness. 'And the Spirit of God moved upon the face of the waters; and God said "Let there be light;" and there was light. And God saw the light, that it was good. And God divided the light from the darkness.'[10]

It was a production of ravishing visual appeal, all glowing lanterns and candles, illumination symbolic and physical. The queen appeared as 'an earthly deity' dressed in a cloth decorated with stars and surrounded by glowing rays. The story, as slender as any of the other masque narratives, was about the nine muses, the goddesses of culture – of history, comedy, tragedy, dance and so forth – who flee Greece for Italy and then travel further, driven out from both by barbarians, and arrive at last in the secure and peaceful Great Britain (not England) where the king and queen welcome them.

The sub-text was Marian. The first performance of *Luminalia* was four days after Candlemas, the Catholic Feast of the Purification of the Virgin Mary, celebrated with hundreds of flickering candles in church. As usual, a celebratory Mass in the queen's chapel had been held in 1638, attended by Catholic ladies, several of them recent converts.[11] The religious festival and the court masque which followed broadcast one and the same message about light and dark, enlightenment and its opposite.

Henrietta Maria, Queen Mary, now stood back-to-back with the other Mary, the mother of Jesus, the woman who bore Him, protected Him as a child, raised Him, and was present at the crucifixion. The Virgin Mary – 'Our Lady' – was already and increasingly became the greatest Catholic mystical symbol of human intimacy with the divine. It was some statement from the queen.

15

Silver Bullet

In August 1638, a group met in the house of Mrs Cromewell in Shire Lane, off Fleet Street, London. They talked politics. The man with the news was the Scottish Captain Nappier (or Napier). The other guests were a local vicar Mr Swadlin, a physician Dr Edward May, and Mrs Grace Southcott, possibly connected with the landowning Southcotts from Devon, who fielded at least one member of the House of Commons. In short, they were from the professional ranks.[1]

Nappier reported on the Scottish situation. He explained there was a Scottish army 200,000 strong that would combine with an English army of 40,000 to summon parliament both in England and Scotland 'to reform all things'. He thought the problem was Archbishop Laud, which is telling, because Laud in fact had little input into the handling of the Scottish situation at this time. The king, said Nappier, 'is deluded, and seduced and made a Baby'.

In the end his friends denounced him to the authorities for treasonous talk. Nappier was wrong about the numbers and Laud and the king, and he was ahead of the game... but the gist was unnervingly accurate. We see that gossip was everywhere, in London as much as Edinburgh. Similarly, in July 1638 the Venetian ambassador to the court of King Charles, writing home, had reported fear of a Scottish invasion of England.

No Scottish smoke without English fire. In May-June 1638 Sir Jacob Astley was in the Dutch Republic advising King Charles on arms purchases. On 26 July 1638 – well before the Glasgow General Assembly, in the period when Hamilton was busy with shuttle diplomacy between Edinburgh and Whitehall – the English privy council voted funds to kickstart support for the king's war against the Scots.[2] They were encouraged by the government's success in winning the Ship Money judgement (12 June 1638).[3] By November, Astley was in England assessing border defences.

On their side, the Scots started war preparations late in 1638. The big step forward for them was the return of Alexander Leslie from the German wars (January 1639). Alexander was a distant relation, somehow, of the Earl of Rothes. It was probably Rothes who persuaded him to come. In fact Alexander was illegitimate by birth. Either he was illiterate or had very limited writing skills. Probably he had no formal education whatever, but he had made his way by guts and brainpower. He had many years' experience both as a fighting officer and as military governor (of Stralsund on the Baltic coast from 1628 to 1630). He won the confidence of King Gustavus Adolphus and reached the rank of Major-General in the Swedish army. He had worked with the Marquess of Hamilton in Germany, knew him well (and regarded him for several years as his patron) which was also an attraction. Starting from nothing, Leslie made a lot of money and in 1635 invested it in a Scottish estate at Balgonie, Fife, where his wife and children lived.

Sailing in a small boat to avoid the attention of the English fleet, which had instructions to intercept him, Alexander Leslie arrived in Scotland towards the end of 1638. The Swedish government gave him a pension, also two cannon and 2,000 muskets. This is the first evidence of international support for the presbyterian cause.

At first Leslie was an adviser to the Tables with no formal position but soon became key to the military preparations. The Tables also called on the Scottish merchants based overseas to raise funds, just as Leslie would attract Scottish officers back from the empire.

The year 1639 was when fighting began. Preparation took time.

Expecting the main attack to be from the army of Charles I on the Borders, the covenanters protected the rear, starting with the south-west. Kintyre was garrisoned. The Castle of Brodick on Arran (the Marquess of Hamilton's property) was occupied. Dumbarton Castle on the Clyde River was taken, safeguarding Glasgow. Antrim's Irish troops were blocked from the start and never even attempted the landing. Edinburgh Castle itself had been occupied by a force led by Leslie. Near Edinburgh, Dalkeith Castle with its arsenal was also taken (from the Earl of Traquair). The king's Scottish strongholds, on which his plans relied, were rapidly lost by Charles I. This was in March 1639. Very quickly the king's plans fell short: no invasion from Ireland and no help from the royal castles. The king still had options. He had his own southern army and Hamilton's amphibious expedition. The three-pronged attack was not to be; but a royal pincer remained.

Now in his first war, Montrose was a military commander active in north-east Scotland. In these early stages he won a victory of a sort. In February 1639, hearing of the Marquess of Huntly's plans to make a pre-emptive move against the Tables by occupying Turriff, a small town thirty-five miles north-west of Aberdeen, Montrose led a small force in a dash from Forfar. Remarkably, he arrived before Huntly and with local reinforcements took up a position in the walled churchyard. That was a quick decision, rapid action over a distance of eighty miles – and superb communication. Finding a strong defensive position against him, Huntly withdrew. There was no fighting.

In March Aberdeen returned to the fore. The Tables sent Montrose with an army to neutralize the city and surrounding area. When the men from the south were added to local forces, he had 6,000 men, a considerable army for Scotland. Montrose displayed a personal ensign marked 'For Religion, the Covenant, and the Country'.[4] The troops all wore something blue, a ribbon, a scarf, a sash. 'This was Montrose's whimsy.'[5] When the men marched south to the Borders later they stuck to his colour wearing bunches of blue ribbons in their hair, often throwing away their original caps.

With Montrose came Alexander Leslie as deputy, who appeared to young officers 'an old, little crooked soldier' but held effortless sway because of what he knew about war. Not only did Montrose, who had not yet fought a battle, have an exceptional lieutenant, he had a teacher both in the grind of campaigning and in diplomacy – also a supervisor. Leslie was known for his ability to manage the arrogant nobility and to keep them working together. Montrose had a lot to learn from him.

Having retreated from Turriff, Huntly (who was appointed the king's Lieutenant in the North) led his men south to Aberdeen where they dug in for a month. They built earthworks around the city. Montrose won the second stand-off too. When the large covenanting army arrived, Huntly abandoned Aberdeen and went back to Strathbogie, then to Bog o' Gight. The deciding factor may have been artillery. Montrose and Leslie came with fourteen pieces of cannon. Abandoned by their natural protector, the citizens of Aberdeen were terrified the city would be looted, but Montrose did not allow it. The anxieties of Huntly himself were perhaps a factor. The commissioners he sent to talk with Montrose were convinced they saw 'the sun shining in a perfect blood colour', which was not a good omen.[6]

Having occupied Aberdeen on 30 March 1639, without a blow struck, Montrose installed a garrison. In his suite were several noblemen including Lord Carnegie, who had swallowed the pride dented in Glasgow,[7] and the Earl of Kinghorn, now made governor of Aberdeen.

When the keys to the city were ceremoniously handed to Kinghorn by Lady Pitfodells[8] a shot rang out, there was a general panic, nobody was hurt but afterwards Lady Pitfoldells found her purse, containing rings and money, had disappeared.[9] If Lady Pitfoldells lost her purse, the covenanters at least had control of Aberdeen for the first time. On the other hand the Marquess of Huntly was at large in his fortresses, a man who could potentially summon thousands – who might be a war leader, who ought to be a war leader. The Tables did not want that threat in the north when they confronted the king in the south.

There could have been fighting, Montrose could have wasted Gordon lands, one or both of the big castles could have been besieged, but he chose negotiation. A parlay took place near Bog o' Gight. Huntly and Montrose met at Lewes of Fyvie, each with an escort.

One of the gentlemen from each group searched the opposite party for hidden firearms, then Huntly and Montrose conferred at length out of earshot. That concluded with Huntly peaceably riding with Montrose to the camp at Inverury under a safe conduct. Here he signed not the covenant but a document which committed him to 'maintain the King's authority, together with the liberties both of Church and State, Religion and Laws'. The deal included an exemption from signing for Catholics provided they undertook to respect the laws and liberties of Scotland. In short in early April 1639 Montrose made a gentleman's agreement to pacify the north.

More covenanting nobles arrived in Aberdeen. Among them was James Crichton of Frendraught, who had a furious family quarrel with Huntly and the Gordons. Montrose's deal was discussed. Now it was management by committee, majority vote. Clearly Montrose was satisfied so far, but his colleagues were not. He fought 'with all his might' but in the end felt obliged to accept their opinions. They turned his deal on its head.

Having guaranteed Huntly's safety, Montrose asked him to return for more talks in Aberdeen. This Huntly did to find he was no longer talking one on one but with the whole group. A friendly dinner followed the discussion. Huntly went to bed in his lodgings, which in the night were surrounded by an armed guard. The next day, talks resumed in a different style. Huntly was asked to contribute to the cost of the rebel campaign. He refused. He was asked to give his friendship to Crichton of Frendraught. He refused. Montrose then said Huntly should come with them back to Edinburgh. Huntly asked whether this meant he was a prisoner, or whether he could go voluntarily. 'Take your choice,' said Montrose.

The marquess opted for co-operation. On 13 April they set off for Edinburgh, leaving garrisons in Turriff and Aberdeen. The citizens of Aberdeen had unwillingly signed the National Covenant and also been heavily fined for supporting Huntly.

Some historians think that Huntly was happy to be shut up in Edinburgh Castle, which is what happened when they reached the capital. It made his position easier. Notwithstanding, there is every reason to think that Montrose's about-turn offended Huntly to the core.

The marquess was sincerely a royalist but also a proud and distant man: 'He seemed desirous to keep a distance with his inferiors... For friends and followers were equalled with domestics.'[10] At this time he was also still mourning his wife. Lady Huntly (Lorne's sister) had died on 14 June 1638, less than a year before.[11] In the opinion of a French envoy Huntly was guided by the stars:

> Being born in a country in which ignorance has always produced a large number of soothsayers [Huntly] has from his youth been an adept in that somewhat trivial branch of mathematics that teaches to judge of people's fortune by the study of the stars, and has persuaded himself that he had a complete knowledge of what was, so that he has always been very hopeful in his transactions.[12]

Huntly was cut-off, prickly.

Now his eldest son Lord Gordon (twenty-three) stayed with him. His second son, Viscount Aboyne (twenty) was permitted to return to Strathbogie in order to fetch clothes and money for his father. When he arrived there, Aboyne discussed the turn of events with relatives. They said it was out of the question for him to return to Aberdeen and captivity. So Aboyne broke his parole and rode south into England to find the king at Newcastle. These events in spring 1639 were the opening of a long Gordon drama.

—ৎৎৎ—

In the second week of May 1639 George Ogilvy of Banff with other royalists drove the covenanter garrison out of Turriff in a cavalry raid. The 'Trot of Turriff' was the first, if slight, engagement of the civil wars. The royalists continued to Aberdeen and on 15 May expelled Kinghorn and his men. The north-east was back to square one.

In reaction, two covenanter forces were deployed. The Earl Marischal was at Dunnottar Castle due south of Aberdeen. He had 800 men with him. From the south Montrose marched back to Aberdeen with 4,000 men. By the time he arrived (25 May) Aberdeen was back in covenanting hands. Banff had fallen ill. Marischal had negotiated for the city. The royalists left. The uncertain balance continued with a royalist victory in a minor stand-off at Elgin but the lack of leadership in Banff's absence told, and the royalists dispersed.

For a second time Montrose installed a garrison in Aberdeen. He exacted a second fine on the unfortunate citizens but did not allow plunder. The soldiers were unhappy with that. Some of them killed all the dogs they could find. Montrose left Aberdeen to confront the Gordons and other royalists. He invested Gight Castle (not Bog o' Gight) but withdrew when news came that Viscount Aboyne was back with reinforcements supplied by Charles I.

.This led to Aberdeen being re-occupied by the royalists, although events were deceptive at first. In fact, Aboyne arrived by sea with only two ships and a collier. There was a third ship carrying artillery, but that was blown off course. He had few troops, but news of his arrival spread and the Gordons assembled. Within a week he had 4,000 infantry and 600 cavalry. He also had two professional officers, Colonels Gunn and Johnstone. Aboyne was even younger than Montrose. Neither had experience of war. Over three months Aberdeen had changed hands repeatedly. Montrose had come and gone and come and gone. The only fighting was the quickfire exchange at Turiff.

Further south things were no further advanced. As agreed with Charles I, the Marquess of Hamilton led nineteen ships carrying 5,000 men, arriving in the Firth of Forth at the beginning of May. If Hamilton had come later he might have threatened the south of Scotland from the east at the same time as Charles I arrived with his army on the Borders. Within reach of Edinburgh, covenanter forces would have split. But in early May the king was still in York. A smallpox outbreak in Newcastle delayed his move further north.

Or Hamilton could have sailed further north to join the Gordons as first envisaged. Yet the situation in the north-east changed by the day. He could not land at Aberdeen if the enemy held it. His interim measure, and it was a half measure, was to send Aboyne – whom Charles I had sent on to him from Newcastle – with the three or four boats and a few troops as described.

So Hamilton could not work together with the king's army in May, because it was not there. Nor did he try to link with the Gordons. He anchored between the islands of Inchkeith and Inchcolm in the middle of the Firth of Forth – only possible during the summer and risky even then. His troops disembarked on the islands for safety and health and provisions. On 23 May he sent 3,000 of them back to the king[13] probably because of the difficulty of feeding them.

Among Hamilton's enemies onshore was his energetic presbyterian mother, Anna. She had not learned to write until she was adult but having married Hamilton's father, the second marquess (who died in 1625), she brought up their eight children and ran the estates including doing much of the accountancy herself, using both Arabic and Roman numerals (mixed). Anna visited everything in person, ran coalmines and saltpans, redecorated the family mansions, restocked the deer park at Hamilton Palace.

Anna did not hate her son, but she hated the king's reforms. When Hamilton arrived with his fleet she raised a regiment against him (spending his money), slept with pistols and a carbine at her side, and said she would shoot him with a silver bullet if he landed on the mainland.[14]

Back in the Aberdeen area, opposing forces in early June 1639 were more or less matched, although Montrose had the advantage in artillery.[15] The next encounter was at Stonehaven, the village just north of Marischal's Dunnottar (16 June 1639). On Colonel Gunn's orders, the royalists deployed on an exposed hillside. That deployment left the men open to artillery attack. It was a psychological blow since highlanders, as many Gordons were, had a particular fear of cannon. There were not many casualties, but Aboyne's infantry panicked and ran. There were desertions. Aboyne regrouped in Aberdeen with a reduced army. Another Montrose victory, modest admittedly.

The real struggle began for Aberdeen itself. While Aboyne partly made up his losses with citizen militia, the numerical advantage was with Montrose who also had his artillery and good luck. But the geography equalised things. In order to take the city Montrose had to advance along the road from Stonehaven which, when it reached Aberdeen's southern limit, crossed the River Dee. It would therefore be a battle for the bridge – the Brig o' Dee. The Dee was too wide and deep to ford. It was swollen by recent rainfall. The bridge must be crossed. It was a bottleneck.

On 18 June Aboyne marched out of Aberdeen and fortified the position before the arrival of Montrose's army. Earthworks were dug in front of the crossing on the south side. The gate across the road was fortified with turf. Infantry were stationed on the bridge itself. The beauty of the position was that few were needed to mount an effective defence. The royalist cavalry under the command of Colonel Gunn were stationed on the north side of the river. This left them free to charge across the bridge, if needed, but also to patrol the northern bank in case covenanting troops tried somehow to cross the river.

Montrose began his attack with an artillery barrage. Then he ordered two assaults on the bridge, both beaten back. For the royalists Colonel Johnstone was in command on the ground and his professionalism showed. The casualties were mainly on the covenanter side. Night fell.

Overnight Montrose ordered his artillery to be moved closer to the bridge. In the morning of 19 June his cavalry moved conspicuously upriver as if looking for a place to ford the Dee. Locals knew there was no such place for many miles. Colonel Gunn for the royalists was not a local. He thought the risk had to be faced. He sent his own cavalry off to shadow the departing troopers, just in case. This meant that neither side had full cavalry support at the bridge, which favoured Montrose since he had the bigger army.

The artillery attack resumed at close range and with more success. The turning point was a direct hit which dislodged a heavy chunk of masonry that fell on Colonel Johnstone's leg, shattering the bone. The man was in agony, his leg useless. He was carried from the bridge. The spirit of the defence suddenly was broken. The story circulated that the unpopular Gunn said Johnstone was dead and that caused a panic. Montrose's men took the bridge and poured across. Their greater numbers were irresistible. The Gordons retreated to their own country and Aberdeen was in covenant hands once more.

This victory was all Montrose's, since by now Alexander Leslie was leading the rebel army in the south of Scotland. He showed himself apt for war and for peace, too. Montrose had instructions this time to sack royalist Aberdeen. Marischal and other nobles said it should be allowed. They knew how much the soldiers gained by plunder. Most citizens would survive a sack. But survivors would be scarred, impoverished, abused. Some would die – men, women, girls, boys. Montrose was against. He said they should sleep on it.

The next day brought news came by sea. Down on the Borders the Pacification of Berwick, a treaty between Charles I and the Tables, had been signed on 19 June, the day of Montrose's breakthrough.[16] That meant an end to all hostilities. It saved Aberdeen – but so did the clemency of Montrose. Nonetheless the citizens received their third fine of the year. Montrose ordered the army to disband and returned to Edinburgh.

These were the main military events of the First Bishops' War. On the Borders there were also confrontations. They take us back to the theatre.[17]

16

Theatre of War

On 30 March 1639 the king arrived at York. Here he had summoned the nobility of England with the aim of raising an army 30,000 strong. Cavalry would be supplied by the nobles, or else cash payment. Infantry would come from a levy and from county militias. The York meeting was a rally. There was little discipline or drilling. The king enjoyed riding beyond the city walls to the fields called Clifton Ings, attended by his nobles.[1]

What Charles I refused to do was call parliament, the way to raise additional finance (by agreement with the House of Commons) and – war being crisis – to build national purpose. But at this time Charles I did not need additional finance, or rather, he did not need it acutely. After years of peace and thanks to non-parliamentary money-raising measures such as Ship Money, Charles I was solvent. As for national purpose, what was needed? The king was national purpose incarnate.

He thought it better to force loyalty. A new military oath of allegiance had been devised in which 'life and fortune' were pledged against those who rebelled in the name of religion. All the peers were expected to take it. Unhelpfully, at this time, in spring 1639, the king was not open. The letters summoning the nobility to York had spoken only of a defensive war against Scottish incursion. But if the king really led a large army against the rebels, how else would it be used than in an invasion of Scotland? How could he force his will in Scotland by staying in England?

Two peers, Lords Saye and Brooke, refused the new oath on 23 April 1639. They took the view that English lives and fortunes should not be lost in a foreign war, and especially this foreign war, and especially when the king was not even telling the truth. They considered that Scotland had not in fact invaded England, so there was no defensive war. They were arrested and questioned independently but stood their ground. Brooke said that the war should be debated by parliament. He was not the only one. Sir Thomas Wilsford from Kent made the same point direct to the king, telling his sovereign that he should trust the 'wise men' in parliament to handle the 'knaves'.[2]

Saye and Brooke refused to recant. They were brave enough to go public. Others swore the oath and supported the king nonetheless many did so despite the suspicion gnawing at their stomachs. In total, Charles I raised about 15,000 troops, half his target.

—⁂—

On 6 May 1639 the king at last arrived in Newcastle (where Aboyne met him). There he waited two weeks. An advance followed to Berwick, the northernmost English fortress, about sixty miles from Edinburgh. On 22 May, as the troops travelled north, there was an eclipse of the sun during the late afternoon, which made their journey 'dark and misty'.[3]

The quality of the royal troops was mixed. Militia men came from trained bands raised by the lords lieutenant (originally for the defence only of their own locality). However, the lords permitted substitution if, as often happened, the trained men argued that they had many children, or their occupation was essential locally. Men pressed for service could come from anywhere. So the regiments contained many untrained, undisciplined men.

The commander-in-chief, the Earl of Arundel, and the commander of horse, the Earl of Holland, had never campaigned before. Holland was a friend of Henrietta Maria. He owed his position to her. Arundel was the very rich scion of medieval nobility and yet another art collector. According to a contemporary witness he was chosen 'for his negative qualities: he did not love the Scots; he did not love the Puritans; which good qualifications were allayed by another negative, he did love nobody else.'[4]

Nothing stopped the king from enjoying himself: 'he rode from four in the morning till five in the evening... wearing out two horses.'[5] Two confrontations then occurred in rapid succession.

On 3 June 1639 June the king received intelligence that the main Scottish army under Alexander Leslie had arrived at Kelso, on the Scottish side of the border, about twenty-five miles south-west of Berwick. The next day Holland was sent at the head of a force that consisted of 1,000 cavalry and 3,000 infantry to drive them back. The 4th was a very hot day. There was a considerable trek before reaching Kelso. The infantry were slower than the cavalry and obviously suffered more from the heat as they were on foot: 'The day was so hot and the way so long that a number of them fainted by the way and could not possibly march any further.'[6] When Holland arrived before the town he effectively commanded the cavalry only as a vanguard. The infantry with their heavy muskets and pikes were miles behind.

In front of the English stood the walled town. To the left was the River Tweed. To the right was a marsh.

A line of Scottish infantry appeared, which confirmed the presence of Leslie's army. Holland unsheathed his sword and prepared to charge. More Scottish infantry appeared in battle array, with lancers. Then more. So many drew up that they started to outflank the English cavalry. Dust clouds could be seen above the massed infantry, which showed the depth of the ranks.

If the Scottish infantry could fire from both sides as well as the front, the chances of a cavalry charge were poor. Having outpaced his own infantry, Holland lacked protective musketeers. Even if Holland's men broke the line they would be up against the walls of Kelso and vulnerable to musketeers placed above. If they had been fighting fewer men, regrouping after the charge would be straightforward. Before their eyes an army of thousands was deploying.

Holland sheathed his sword and sent a herald, which started a dialogue of the deaf. Holland asked why the Scottish army was within ten miles of the border (which the king had forbidden); and Leslie asked why the English army was in Scotland (foreign invasion). Holland conferred with his officers, who advised their position was too weak. Having led his men to force the Scots back, he had evidently failed. He ordered a retreat, leading them back to the royal camp, another long, hot march. where he reported on enemy strength.

Later it was thought that Leslie had spread his line very thin and deliberately flown many colours, which gave the appearance of many regiments, a much larger force than he really had. And 'by the showing of great herds of cattle at a distance'[7] the dust was raised as if by the feet of soldiers. The military *ingénu* Holland was deceived.[8] Perhaps he was also worried by the quality of his army.

The next day the skills of Leslie were displayed a second time. At six o'clock in the morning of 5 June the Scottish army appeared on the heights of Duns Law within sight of the main English camp – within sight of the king's own pavilion. That was a *coup de théâtre*. It was considerable cheek and also a feat of generalship. Leslie had led his men overnight, almost on the heels of Holland's retreat, ready to take up position within striking distance of his sovereign.

The king was so cool in the face of the threat that some of his officers thought he had expected it but had kept it to himself. After a few hours in which both sides stood ready to advance, Charles I sent one of his personal attendants (probably Will Murray who had family connections with the covenanters) to suggest negotiation. Leslie agreed. So much for the fighting.

The theatricals intensified when the two sides met for talks on 13 June. The intervening time had been taken up in exchanges about selection of the Commissioners who would speak for each of the parties. When the Scots arrived at Berwick they expected to be talking with their English equivalents. To their consternation, and they must have jumped to their feet, snatching their hats from their heads, his Majesty entered the room with a well scripted line: 'My lords,' said Charles I, 'You cannot but wonder at my unexpected coming hither; which I myself would have spared, were it not to clear myself of that notorious slander laid upon me, that I shut my ears from the just complaints of my people of Scotland.'[9]

Over several days the king debated with the Scots with conspicuous success and won their admiration. This king (whom they had not seen for six years) was not at all a baby. One of the points he made was that the 1638 assembly was heavily populated with lay members, which did not make sense for a church assembly: the assembly was invalid for that reason alone, not to mention Hamilton's dissolution. Another of the puzzles of the man is his cleverness.

Yet he was a poor negotiator. When it came down to brass tacks the Scots forced the pace. On 18 June they said that unless agreement was reached that day they would fight it out. It was bluff added to bluff. Leslie had exactly the same problems with his army as the English. It was smaller than he had hoped. It was hard to feed. The quality of men was not especially good and there were desertions. Whereas the English army, bedraggled and slow when it arrived on the Borders, was increasing in size as new troops came, both cavalry and infantry. By the time of the Berwick negotiation Charles I had more soldiers than his opponents but did not know it. Had he tried battle, he would probably win. He decided to settle.

From the chivalry of York to royal nonchalance as he gazed at Duns Law to his *deus ex machina* appearance at Berwick, Charles I showed himself also to be a trickster – in his own royal sphere, he outplayed the ingenious Leslie. He was a performing king. Almost, at this time, he outperformed himself. He required his nobles to risk life and fortune in war against the Scots but stopped short when the chance came.

Terms were agreed. Both sides would disband their armies. The royal castles would be returned to the king. Prisoners (such as Huntly) would be freed. There would be a General Assembly (the king refused to accept the validity of the 1638 assembly). There would be a parliament to sort the detail and government as usual could return (no Tables).

With this rather open deal came an end to the 1639 military confrontation. Other than Montrose's Aberdeen campaign, nothing really happened in the First Bishops' War.

—◦◦◦—

According to verses circulating at the time,

... the factious Scot
His ancient spleen is ne'er forgot
He long hath been about this plot.[10]

In other words, the Scots hated England and were continuing an ancient conflict. That was how it seemed on the English side perhaps, yet it was not a quarrel between England and Scotland but between the Tables and the king. Actually, it was a brand-new conflict. The Berwick treaty did not deal with the root problem, that Charles I had a reform agenda which his subjects could not accept, with the result that the whole thing unspooled.

On 1 July 1639 the General Assembly was announced. Bishops, said the royal proclamation, would attend. According to Charles I the bishops must be there because their position would be debated, indeed attacked. They must attend to put their case. What he really thought was that bishops should attend because they were bishops. But according to the other side, bishops had no place in a General Assembly. They were not elected by parishes, they were not lay elders. Bishops were outside the Kirk.

The result of the proclamation was riots in Edinburgh on 2 and 3 July. Charles I commanded the rebel leaders to come back to Berwick to explain. Only five obeyed: Rothes, Loudoun, Lothian, Dunfermline and Montrose. Alexander Henderson came too, which was honest and brave. Notably, Argyll stayed away. That was a pointer. The soft-spoken earl was good at not doing things, dodging bullets. The covenanters played other tricks. They had handed over Edinburgh Castle and the other royal castles to the king's troops having first removed the cannon and ammunition. The Tables were still functioning. The privy council was still powerless.

At this second Berwick meeting, Rothes and the king exchanged opinions very much in the Scottish style. Charles I candidly explained that the wording of the 1638 General Assembly resolution, that bishops were unlawful, implied they were unlawful everywhere. If that resolution stood, then English and Irish (Protestant) bishops could also be considered unlawful. So he could not accept it. It was an interesting debating point although perhaps pushing the logic. In the king's favour, he was at least trying to explain himself.

Rothes argued back. He said the only concern was Scotland. Charles I lost his temper and told Rothes he was a liar. The insulted earl told the king that the Scots, if they were not permitted their deeply felt decision on Scottish bishops, would 'rip up' the wickedness of the English and Irish bishops. The king might have arrested the covenanting lords on the spot, but he did not. It was a telling moment. Charles I was slippery, he was deceptive, but he was not in the end a tyrant.[11]

The problem was momentum. The further the rebels pushed, the more difficult it was for them to back down. They feared repercussion.[12] It is at moments like this that one senses their hardness – no retreat. 'Toleration was impossible for men who saw life as a narrow path through a land shaken by the fires of hell.'[13]

At Berwick, Montrose for the second time saw King Charles face to face, but here the king was coming to life. He had not seen that before. Now he had a better feel for his sovereign. A historian of the next generation, closely connected to the events, said that Montrose 'was much wrought upon' at Berwick. 'He (Charles) also gained the Earl of Montrose, who was a young man well learned, who had travelled, but had taken upon him the part of a hero too much.'[14] From this time Montrose's position shifts – as does the king's attitude to him. In December 1639 he would receive an invitation to court (which he declined).

The General Assembly met in Edinburgh on 12 August 1639. It was the second meeting of the assembly since the prayer-book riots. Charles I sent the Earl of Traquair as his commissioner. The delegates passed again the resolutions of the previous year's assembly including declaring bishops unlawful. They made the signing of the National Covenant compulsory in Scotland (Montrose was present and agreed to this). Again, no bishop attended. Very quickly parliament followed, meeting in the new but not quite finished Parliament Hall on 31 August. Again, Traquair presided. Again, no bishop attended.

That meant procedural problems. In fact, procedural discussion about the selection and functioning of the Lords of the Articles prevented any real meeting of parliament for some time.[15] This kind of thing seems trivial, but it was not. No parliament works without agreed procedure and every arrangement had a meaning.

Choosing the lords without royal input, as was initially suggested, was cutting the king's influence, or rather, as Charles would have been the first to say, his rights, which were as old as time. Sure enough, not much later Argyll proposed that for the future the selection of the Lords of the Articles be taken out of the king's hands entirely; that each of the parliamentary estates (nobles, lairds, burgesses) should elect their own candidates. Argyll's measure passed by one vote. Two notable voices of opposition were the legal expert Sir Thomas Hope and the Earl of Montrose.

So it was in Scotland that the parliament first explicitly cut the king's power.[16] This was later taken up in England but it was the Scots who led. Montrose was against it. Control of the Royal Mint was transferred to parliament. So was the power to appoint officers of state.[17] The assembly resolutions were ratified including the abolition of the bishops. On 14 November the king ordered Traquair to prorogue parliament, that is to say close current proceedings for the time being.[18]

Without Charles I's agreement the session would resume in June 1640, this time with the covenanter Lord Burleigh in the chair. It passed a Triennial Act, which required a parliament to sit every three years, in other words without the king's summons. And it organized general mobilisation – raising an army to fight the troops of Charles I. All with the 'presumed allowance' of the king.[19]

Montrose liked none of what he saw. He spoke against this second session, arguing that parliament could not sit without the king's explicit consent. He was heavily outvoted. Montrose was always a Reformed Protestant aristocrat with deep aversion to bishops. But he questioned tactics. He found himself extremely reluctant to support the attack on the king's prerogative. He thought the National Covenant and the king could and should co-exist as the text said: the 'true religion' and 'the king's majesty' went together.

Did they? There was no shortage of people ready to think the worst by this time. Even before the Scottish parliament tore up the rulebook, at the court of England Henrietta Maria's Lord Chamberlain the Earl of Dorset wrote to a friend in September 1639:

All things that discontented, rebellious minds can ask is granted in Scotland, and yet they daily breath new liberties and more and more study the dethroning of their sovereign.[20]

17

On a Windowpane

To defeat the Scots, Charles I recalled his fixer Thomas, Viscount Wentworth, Lord Deputy of Ireland since 1631, a man known as Black Tom Tyrant. Having run the north of England as President of the Council of the North (appointed in 1628) through promotion of friends and family, Wentworth faced the greater challenge of Ireland in the same spirit. He increased royal Irish revenues to the highest level yet, while keeping the third Stuart realm at peace.

Wentworth's tactics of undermining, fining, imprisoning, even sentencing to death[1] those who did not fall in line were the definition of strong-arm tactics. He was exceptional, but the price of success – and his success included amassing great personal wealth – was making enemies such as the Marquess of Hamilton and the Earl of Holland. Wentworth blocked both from receiving grants of Irish land. His great ally was Archbishop Laud.

The viscount arrived back in England in late September 1639. He was appointed to the new committee formed for Scottish affairs in December. In January 1640 he was made Lord Lieutenant of Ireland, which meant Irish responsibilities (and opportunities) continued but he could govern from England through his own deputy.[2]

The same month Wentworth became Earl of Strafford. With this he chose the subsidiary title Baron Raby, the latter being a fantastically arrogant insult to Sir Harry Vane, whose main estate was Raby Castle in County Durham. Vane was about to become one of the two Secretaries of State. By agreeing these titles Charles I needlessly sowed discord among his ministers.

In a masque which played during the Whitehall winter season on 21 January 1640 the king resumed his broadcast. This was *Salmacida*

Spolia (the spoils of Salmacis), written by William Davenant and designed by Inigo Jones. The title played on the myth of the spring of Salmacis at Halicarnassus (today's Bodrun) whose waters had pacifying powers when drunk by invading barbarians. The idea that the ancient kingdom of Scotland was peopled by barbarians in need of a civilizing drink was hardly the message to send north at this juncture, but it was in a way sincere.

Charles I appeared as Philogenes ('lover of the people'). Henrietta Maria descended from heaven as an Amazonian heroine dressed for war, armed with an 'antique sword... environ'd with her martial ladies' and surrounded by rays of light. Special effects and scenery included a head of the wind god Zephyr 'whose breath converts in mid-air to buds and flowers', 'two-storied palaces with Doric colonnades', 'trees of strange forms such as only grow in remote parts of the Alps, and 'a crescent-shaped cloud on which are thirty-one figures'.[3]

The masque begins with the fury Discord summoning riotous anti-masquers. Their antics are dispelled by Philogenes whose reward will be partnership with the heavenly queen. The harmony the two of them bring is hymned in the final scene, which plays before the depiction of an idealised London, with the river running through it – both the Thames and the spring of Salmacis. England under Stuart rule is the source of peace, of civilisation, good for everyone.

There is some evidence that the reception of *Salmacida Spolia* was restless. Even by the standards of court theatre it was wishful thinking. The Scots were by no means pacified or in any way under control. Rather than peace, the king for the second time was planning war as Strafford's return so clearly showed.

Failure made Charles I's position more difficult. If he was to enforce his will by summoning another army he would have to make better plans and they must be financed. Because the previous campaign ended early he got away with it, but even the posturing army of 1639 drained the Exchequer. He would need fresh money in large amounts. His Scottish policy undermined his English policy of not calling parliament. In the first part of his reign Charles I made England his preoccupation so that the Scots were second-class citizens, with the results so far described. Having provoked a rebellion in Scotland, the king needed to give that country his full attention, so he made mistakes in England.

Pressure for a parliament in England was strong anyway. Strafford was in favour because of his own experience with Irish parliaments, which he managed rather in the same way Charles I dealt with the 1633 Scottish parliament. Encouraged by Strafford and Laud, Charles I therefore changed tack and agreed the way ahead was an English parliament. They all thought that it could be managed.

In late February 1640 the writs were sent out. On 13 April 1640 the English parliament met for the first time since 1629. At the opening session, Lord Keeper Finch, in the king's presence, made a speech which outlined the Scottish situation loosely. The covenanters were described as rebels and traitors, but the prayer-book was unmentioned. It was as if the Scots had risen without provocation. The parliament was summoned to raise money ('supply') for the king in the face of a rebellion founded on nothing. The reality was well known in London, prayer-book and all.

The king had an ace up his sleeve. When Finch concluded his speech, the king handed him a letter addressed to the King of France which he, the king, and he, Finch, regarded as conclusive on Scottish treason. The letter was signed by Scottish lords including the Earl of Montrose. They were approaching a foreign king for help against their own.

(Because of his French experience, Montrose had helped write the letter. Nonetheless, there were mistakes which included using the words *rayes de soleil* for 'rays of sun,' which should have been *rayons de soleil*. This mistake meant the Scottish nobles had invoked, presumably to describe the king's majesty, the image of 'a sort of fish'.)[4]

At the English court was a party of men who favoured an English alliance with Spain, the enemy of France. In 1640 these included Strafford who thought he could raise money for Charles I that way. The presence of Marie de Médicis in St James's Palace leavened the mix. She had arrived in October 1638. She received the honourable, generous and very expensive treatment demanded by her status. She attracted to her court at St James's French enemies of the man she hated above all, Cardinal Richelieu. She was supported by her almost as high-profile and equally strong-minded friend Marie, Duchesse de Chevreuse. She also favoured Spain.

The complications of this unique situation are mesmeric. For instance, Strafford was wooing Spain while his friend Laud hated and feared Marie de Médicis. Charles I had himself gone to considerable lengths to keep his mother-in-law away (another failure). But the long and short of it all was that the policy of the French court was anti-English for good reasons.

The upshot was that in early 1640 the Tables, alive to French antipathy to England, sent a letter to King Louis XIII. It asked for the King of France's help. The letter fell into the hands of royal agents and reached King Charles. This was the document read out by Lord Keeper Finch to the assembled parliament in order to secure his master. Charles I triumphantly took the view that the way the letter was addressed was an act of treason in itself. That is to say it was addressed 'au roi' – to the king. 'The king' rather than 'the King of France' implied the Scots thought their king was Louis XIII. This interpretation was correct in a pedantic sense, even though the Scots obviously did not think Louis was their king. Was the wording carelessness? Was it flattery? Did it just signify that in France, where the letter was sent, Louis was the king? It was certainly less than an offer. The last time a French king wanted to govern Scotland a Protestant revolution resulted.

Once again, we find Charles I pushing the logic – and extremely touchy. Louis XIII, if he ever saw the letter, played his cards close to his chest. He did not offer help to the covenanters although Richelieu was already encouraging them, in order to distract England from Spain.

The English House of Commons reacted not at all to the king's *coup*. What did it matter to Englishmen if the King of Scots had a rebellion on his hands? Anyway, the King of Scots had had his chance the year before (spending English money) and fluffed it. Parliament was not a one-way street. Members of Parliament had their own rights. These included putting their grievances to the king – that was the problem of not having parliaments, it silenced rich, influential men – and now they had their opportunity. They were meant to debate wartime supply, but they launched their own debate.

So there was a connection between England and Scotland in what became known as the Short Parliament, but not the connection wanted by Charles I. Rather than attack the Scots as rebels, a well-organized group found common ground with the Scots. They had begun to do this before the parliament even met.[5]

John Pym, member for Tavistock, and his stepbrother Francis Rous, member for Truro, made speeches in which Catholic encroachment was blamed for everything wrong in England. Everything apparently included the various financial complaints of the 1630s from Ship Money to the abuse of monopolies. These were opening shots which took the discussion away from Louis XIII to English unhappiness about religious change.

Pym and Rous were uncompromising from the start – Rous was incandescent – but a further hardening of the so-called Pym junto was evident when the Commons refused to accept a huge compromise offered by the king, proposed in parliament by Harry Vane on 4 May 1640, which was to give up Ship Money altogether in return for supply.

On 5 May Charles I dissolved parliament. It had not lasted long, but evidently the king had given his opponents the oxygen of publicity.

A council meeting immediately followed. Charles I had to decide how to handle Scotland in the absence of parliamentary support. Now English politics were visibly infected by the Scottish situation. The Earl of

Strafford spoke brave words that we know because of the notes taken by the younger Harry Vane:

> Go vigorously on... no defensive war, loss of honour and reputation... Go on with a vigorous war, as you first designed, loose and absolved from all rules of government being reduced to extreme necessity, everything is to be done that power might admit... Confident as anything under heaven that Scotland shall not hold out five months.[6]

The Archbishop of Canterbury supported his ally. The Earl of Northumberland won no friends when he questioned the financing of the enterprise. Strafford's conviction carried the day. It was to be an offensive war, an invasion of Scotland, the rebels would be crushed, the king's honour redeemed, there would be an end to the National Covenant.

Strafford also returned to the theme of Irish troops. He told the king 'You have an army in Ireland you may employ here to reduce this kingdom,' which would be fateful words.

The hope of at least two armies attacking the covenanters at the same time on different fronts never went away. Since Strafford had been sceptical of the Earl of Antrim in 1639 it is interesting that in 1640 he thought Ireland could supply a working army, indeed that it was safe to arm the Irish. But things had moved on. A greater effort was needed this time. Also, Strafford had secured funds from the Irish parliament. All the time therefore, the invasion of Scotland from the west was longed for, sneaking in behind the front line.

Not long after the dissolution there were a number of arrests including the Earl of Warwick, Lords Saye and Brooke, and the parliamentarians John Pym and John Hampden. Homes were searched for documentary evidence of correspondence with the Scots (nothing came up). Four alderman of the City of London were imprisoned after the king asked for and was refused a loan as part of his new financing.

The reaction was rapid. On 11 May 1640 a violent street protest took aim at Archbishop Laud, 'William the Fox'. It was organized, promoted by street placards. A crowd of apprentices gathered in Southwark and marched to Lambeth. One of the young men battered the gate of Lambeth Palace with an iron bar. For this he was arrested and would be executed. On 14 May the mob assembled again. Some of the boys made it to Croydon to see if Laud was in his summer palace. In fact, he was holed up in the heavily protected Whitehall. The riot was explicitly anti-Catholic as well as again trying for Laud. The plan was to attack St James's Palace, home of Marie de Médicis, the Catholic chapel of Henrietta Maria at Somerset House, and Arundel House nearby. The Earl and Countess of

Arundel were not openly Catholic, but their faith was suspect. Aletheia Arundel was a close friend of the papal emissary George Conn who said she was 'Catholic in all but outward profession'[7] (and was probably her confessor).

Even in the inner sanctum of Whitehall Palace the Scottish agenda found support. On a window pane in the king's ante-chamber someone scratched the words 'God save the King, God confound the Queen and all her offspring, God grant the Palatine to reign in this realm.'[8]

18

Ford of Lyon

Montrose was a member of the Scottish committee of estates, formed in early summer 1640, as were his brother-in-law Lord Napier, and his nephew by marriage Sir George Stirling of Keir. The committee was set up by the parliament to replace the Tables. Because it was parliamentary, it was correct constitutionally. It was the new Scottish governing body.

The Earl of Argyll was not on the committee. As a privy councillor he could not be part of a rebel committee but invisibility was a help anyway. Committee members were bound by majority rule. In a sense therefore, Argyll was not. He was in a class of his own. By now the rebels trusted him fully.

In 1640 the covenanter government was more aggressive with the north-east. Huntly was out of the picture having joined the king in England on his release from Edinburgh Castle. Colleagues did not think Montrose had done enough the previous year. They were not going for another gentleman's agreement. In the preparation for a second round with the king, Montrose had the command of two regiments, but the levelling of the north-east was entrusted to the German veteran Colonel Robert Monro. Monro was tougher. This time the citizens of Aberdeen suffered physically as well as financially. Some were pressed into the army. There was rape. The country around Strathbogie was soon left 'almost manless, moneyless, homeless and armless'. That was a pacification in a way.

Also to be secured was Angus, south-west of Aberdeen. Here the Ogilvies had a similar position to the Gordons further north. They were influential royalists. At this time the Earl of Airlie was also with the king in England. His son Lord Ogilvy was in Scotland minding their possessions, with him the pregnant Lady Ogilvy. For a second time Montrose tried his brand of noble diplomacy, leading his men into Angus, placing a garrison in Airlie Castle, and obtaining a promise of good behaviour from Ogilvy.

Argyll meanwhile obtained from the committee of estates a commission of fire and sword for the central highlands. That meant a mission to terrorise. He took it to include Angus. Montrose wrote to him explaining the Ogilvy threat was dealt with. Argyll ignored the letter. He marched into Angus, ejected Montrose's garrison from Airlie Castle and burned the house to the ground, personally supervising the work, including the destruction of the expensive roof. He marched on to Forthar where Lady Ogilvy had taken refuge in another Ogilvy house. He burned that also.

> Lady Ogilvy looks o'er her bower window,
> And O she looks warely!
> And there she spied the great Argyll
> Come to plunder the bonnie house of Airlie.[1]

Lord and Lady Ogilvy and the unborn baby escaped, but their two existing children, 'the eldest of them not being much above three or four years of age', were taken as prisoners to Dundee.[2]

Argyll was mild in meetings but in action was highly aggressive, and now it was evident that he had his own wars to fight, against other nobles. The challenge to Montrose could not be missed. Ogilvy's grandmother was another Ruthven, Montrose's great-aunt. He and Ogilvy were cousins and old friends, the same age, were at St Andrews together and travelled together in Italy. The story is they even both wanted to marry Magdalen. Argyll's destruction of Ogilvy possessions was an attack on Montrose's extended family.

Argyll wanted to secure the territory under his commission for the revolution. Nonetheless the fact this had not been done the previous year with no ill effect, suggests the central highlands did not offer risk to the committee of estates. Argyll's ambition came into it. He wanted to take possession for himself of land in Badenoch and Lochaber, to the north of his existing estates. He argued this new territory was owed him under mortgages he had provided to Huntly, which now fell due. With 4,000 men Argyll marched through the area securing his position by violence. The earl was on a roll. Looking back, we can see he uncharacteristically miscalculated in what came next.

Argyll continued his campaign into Breadalbane, the Highland area due north of Glasgow. At the Ford of Lyon (a tributary of the River Tay) he took the Earl of Atholl prisoner by offering talks then making the arrest, as happened to Huntly a year before. Breadalbane was Campbell territory but had once been part of Atholl. Perhaps atavistic thoughts filled Argyll's head crowding out good sense. Everything was going so well. His midsummer camp in beautiful Glen Lyon made him speculate. In his tent on the riverbank Argyll had a conversation with Atholl, in front of witnesses, in which he spoke of changes at the top: 'That they had consulted both lawyers and divines anent the deposing of the king and gotten resolution that it might be done in three cases (1) Desertion (2) Invasion (3) Vendition (betrayal).'[3] In this campaign his men liked to refer to Argyll as 'King Campbell'. He spoke of his lineage, as the 'eighth man from the Bruce', in other words the direct descendant of Robert the Bruce. He was a noble with that elixir, royal blood.

In a world in which an apprentice could be executed for banging on the door of a palace with a crowbar, in which Lord Balmerino could be sentenced to death for possession of a document he had not written, words like these were treason against the king. It did not matter how generic the conversation was (a defence later put forward). If Argyll was wondering about deposing kings there was only one king who came into it. These events took up July and the first days of August 1640.

On return to Edinburgh, Argyll obtained an indemnity which protected him and his heirs from any claims relating to what he had just done. The fact that he did this shows that he had inflicted considerable damage to property, and probably people had been killed: he had to protect himself. Argyll was not a man to leave things to chance, he had learned that in his early life. Everything must be anticipated. Then he called for Montrose to be impeached for his Ogilvy trade-off. In this way he started a direct attack on the Grahams.[4] From being the supportive royal privy councillor Argyll was transformed into a marauding power striking out, by this time, at no fewer than four major families: the Gordons, the Ogilvies, the Murrays (Earls of Atholl and Tullibardine), and now the Grahams. His crusade was sincerely presbyterian but as sincerely Campbell; he was always the clan leader out to increase family power. It was a case of revolution letting loose the furies.

Nothing came of the impeachment attempt. There was an enquiry which resulted in no charges being brought against Montrose.

—◦◦◦—

The covenanters raised money efficiently.[5] It was done by fear and violence as well as conviction and inspiration, but it worked. As noted already, the poverty of Scotland in a way helped. It was because Scotland was poor that so many Scots had experience of war in Germany (now returning tried and trained), and there were Scots earning their way as merchants on the continent of Europe (sending money home). Nationhood reached beyond national boundaries.

The spirit of effectiveness, getting things done, inspired a political initiative. The committee of estates was a start – but committees are slow. Could some other structure be better? Everyone knew that King Charles was not going to accept the status quo, that he would try again. Was there an argument for a leaner government to fight him? In search of inspiration some looked back to pagan Rome. Where else? One idea was a triumvirate. The country would be divided into two zones, north and south of the River Forth. The northern area would be governed by the Earl of Argyll; the southern by the Earls of Mar and Cassillis.

There was a more extreme proposal, to appoint a single and supposedly temporary 'dictator'. The most famous dictator of the classical world was Julius Caesar, whose career put an end to the republican Roman oligarchy and cleared the way for the first imperial dynasty under his great-nephew and adopted son Augustus. In ancient Rome the office of dictator was temporary, to get the state through a crisis. Caesar subverted it. He was killed but his family took up a permanent dictatorship. The candidate for dictator of Scotland was never named but Argyll was the only choice.

Solutions like this were outrageous novelties. So proud of their history, the Scots had only ever known royal government. It is not clear what support there was for either the triumvirate or the dictatorship. There was no formal discussion on the committee of estates, but it was a leaky world. Montrose heard of the plans and did not like them. He managed to water down the triumvirate idea so that he would be included as a member of a larger governing group, if it was accepted (which it wasn't). But he had to face the reality of Argyll's attacks on himself and his family, while news of the talks at the Ford of Lyon spread. Montrose tried to form his own faction to balance Campbell ambition.

In July 1640, the Cumbernauld Band was signed at the home of the Earl of Wigton, Cumbernauld Castle.[6] This was a moderate presbyterian manifesto. Signatories pledged loyalty to 'Religion, King and country' and the 'Covenant already signed'. They did so because of the 'particular and indirect practising' of a few which was causing Scotland to suffer. 'And this band they made because they perceived that religion was but a mere pretext and not the true cause of this rebellion.'[7] The nineteen signatories pledged to defend each other if necessary. The text was a statement of loyalty to the National Covenant but emphasised the King with no qualification. By accusing unnamed persons of 'indirect practising' it said there was something rotten in the state of Scotland.

In several ways the Cumbernauld Band was built on sand. First, there was no major figure in support other than Montrose himself. Second, there were few signatories. Third, it was not public. More signed but who cared, nobody else knew. Fourth, the nature of the covenant movement was changing. What began as a noble revolt had a momentum by summer 1640 which drew in others, more Kirk ministers, and the burghs (urban business communities), who needed to stand up for their own interests in a new world.

But the main problem with the Cumbernauld Band was timing. July 1640 was no time to undermine the revolution.

Early the same year an embassy was sent from Scotland to Whitehall. These men, led by Lord Loudoun, were to find an agreement with Charles I after the various autumn and winter decisions of the Scottish parliament. Triumphant in his discovery of the letter to Louis XIII, the king arrested them on 11 April 1640. Loudoun, a Campbell kinsman of Argyll, was taken to the Tower and nearly executed for treason. Which came first, the king's refusal to negotiate or the covenanters' suspicions of the king? Did it matter?

Contacts between the English and Scottish opponents of the king increased after the Short Parliament. The presence of leading Scottish nobles in London provided every opportunity to explore tactics and to bond. We know that Lord Savile, a rich Yorkshire peer, suggested to the covenanter leaders an invasion of England, promising support from the Yorkshire gentry. In a letter sent to Argyll, Rothes and Wariston, Savile went so far as to forge the signature of six other peers in support of this proposal. Probably Savile was pushed by hatred of his Yorkshire rival, the Earl of Strafford, more than anything.[8]

Invasion became the preferred option. It would take the Scots off the moral high ground and meant an extended line of communications, it was tactically harder. But with English support it would pile the pressure on King Charles. Taking the initiative would force the issue. They went for it.

In this decision the leaders of the Scottish revolution showed their mettle, taking a big risk to force events. All the time they had in mind that England, if it came together under the king, would easily field larger armies – it was a bigger, richer country. Again, the Scottish leadership showed courage, clear decision-taking, a risk appetite much greater than that of Charles I. They began the Second Bishops' War.

On 20 August 1640, the Earl of Montrose led the invading army across the River Tweed into England. Lots were drawn to decide who would have the honour. It is tempting to speculate they were rigged. If it were a test, Montrose passed with flying colours. Cheerfully he waded alone across the river at Coldstream, then waded back, showing the river could be safely forded. Unlike everyone else, he had to cross three times in total – that was a very visible show of leadership and physique. The army, 20,000 strong, followed his example, crossing with only one casualty, one man drowned. Alexander Leslie was in command overall.

This substantial force marched 'at leisure through Northumberland' in three bodies of men, divided to make provisioning easier. This was a march 'after the Swedish manner, in small bodies'. The infantry carried 'half pikes called swans feathers'.[9] They expected a hostile reception but met no opposition. Local people kept well away.

On 28 August the Scots arrived outside their destination, Newcastle. The invaders stood at Newburn on the north bank of the River Tyne, opposed on the other side by English troops under Lord Conway. Their objective was to cross so they could attack Newcastle from the south, where the defences were poor. If they could take Newcastle, they would control the coal supply to London.

Charles I had his defensive war. The King of England's first duty was to protect his people from invasion, but he was far from ready. Helped by loans from supporters, including Strafford, the king found enough money to summon an army. York again was the rallying ground. He would raise 16,000 men but could he keep them in the field? Raising more loans from city merchants had proved impossible. The City of London was against the Scottish war. In Ireland, Strafford had raised another 9,000 but transport had not been arranged, and the difficulties of an Irish army coming to England were all the time a barrier to full deployment. The men remained in Ireland.

The command of the English army was new. The Earl of Northumberland replaced the Earl of Arundel as commander-in-chief, while Strafford was his Lieutenant-General. Pleading sickness, Northumberland in fact dodged all involvement. The whole thing was shaky to say the least.

Meanwhile at Newburn Conway commanded 4,500 against four times as many Scots. The invaders were on higher ground, which was a better disposition. Again, the artillery made the difference. The Scottish bombarded the English who were forced into a disorderly retreat. Montrose was of course present and saw the artillery in action.

Arriving on the south side of Newcastle on 30 August, Leslie found the town empty of English troops because Conway had withdrawn to Durham. Newcastle fell at once to the Scots. If there was no agreement before the winter, London would be in serious difficulty. In addition, the king's share of revenue from coal sales was in Scottish hands. The covenanters struck with panache at his capital city, his finances and his credibility.

—⟨∞⟩—

Almost at once Charles I accepted the need for a second negotiated peace. In the talks at Ripon the English commissioners were sympathetic to the Scots in early October. Among other things, the covenanter representatives complained about the influence of Henrietta Maria on the king.[10] On 28 October, the humiliated king accepted terms. This was the end of the Second Bishops' War. The Battle of Newburn was the only encounter in which the king's army was involved. There was barely any more fighting in 1640 than there had been the year before.

Covenanter courage was vindicated. The English agreed to pay the costs of the Scots while they were on English territory. The peace was made conditional on the summoning of another English parliament. This new parliament met for the first time on 3 November 1640.

On the Borders the previous year, Charles I might have won his war with Scotland. There was a chance for the Earl of Holland at Kelso, another for the king at Duns Law. But the sheer lack of professionalism – and especially the untried royalist commanders – meant the king had no idea what was happening on the Scottish side, he just did not know he could win. Now everything was lost.

The meeting of the second 1640 English parliament started a new phase. Black Tom Tyrant, the man who was meant to cut through it and deliver victory, found himself outplayed. Strafford stayed with the English army in the north but returned to Whitehall to take his seat in the Lords. At once the Pym junto moved against him. Before he could take the initiative, Strafford was arrested. Impeachment charges were prepared by a committee of the Commons (11 November 1640). For the Scots, Strafford was a primary target because he believed that Scotland should, like Ireland, be governed as an English dependency. His fall was part and parcel of the peace. The arrest of Archbishop Laud followed. The troubles of Scotland led to the arrest of the king's main supporters in England.

Happy or not, the Earl of Montrose was with Leslie's army in Newcastle.

19

'His majesty is the sun'

Landing treason charges on Strafford was quite an ask. The process of impeachment consisted of prosecution by the House of Commons and judgement by the House of Lords. While the earl had enemies in both houses, they had to beware their spite. Splashback from the trial could drench them all. High treason was a crime against the king – but the whole point was Strafford's devoted loyalty to Charles I.

The understanding of sovereignty would later change. In Great Britain the sovereignty of parliament, as the originator of laws, would come to be accepted in conjunction with that of the king.[1] If parliament was sovereign, you could commit treason not just against the king but against parliament. However, in 1641 that was thinking outside the box.

Even if you allowed for parliamentary sovereignty, Strafford had not attacked the English parliament. Quite the reverse, it was Strafford who advised Charles I to summon the first 1640 parliament. In the second he took his seat in the Lords. He was parliamentary.

The first day of his trial was 22 March 1641. In the arrangements in Westminster Hall, and in Strafford's own conduct, we find ourselves back in the theatre. In order to house Lords, Commons, spectators and royal family an elaborate structure was built with seats all around – similar to the arrangement in Glasgow Cathedral for the 1638 assembly. Strafford conducted his own defence from a desk in the middle. The king, queen and some of their children sat in a box which was originally partitioned off for privacy, but the king broke the screen so that he could be seen.

Every day, Strafford '... was always in the same suit of black... At the entry he gave a low curtsey, proceeding a little he gave a second, when he came to his desk a third, then at the bar, the fore-face of his desk, he kneeled – rising quickly he saluted both sides of the house, and then sat down.'[2]

He was good on detail and principle, but then the twenty-eight charges were weak. His accusers must prove treason. It was very hard. The sheer number of charges shows a kind of desperation from the start. Many were about his rule in Ireland, arising from the hostility he created there. He had been so much the strong man as Lord Deputy, his methods were resented bitterly. But Ireland traditionally was governed differently from England as a less orderly nation, so precedent was on Strafford's side.

The one accusation closer to home came from the notes of the council meeting of 5 May 1640, just after the Short Parliament was dissolved. Even this was feeble. Where, according to the record,[3] Strafford had said he had an Irish army which could be deployed 'in this kingdom' what did he mean? The accusation now made was that he intended to attack England. It hung on the words 'this kingdom'. Did it hold water? Quite apart from the context, which was war with the Scots; quite apart from the fact that England was at peace in 1640; quite apart from the fact that the Irish army was still, in 1641, in Ireland; there was also the point that sending an army to England *in the king's name* was not the definition of treason.

Tactics therefore changed. While the trial was still in progress the House of Commons introduced a Bill of Attainder against Strafford on 10 April 1641. If parliament voted in favour, Strafford would be found guilty and given the death penalty by Act of Parliament. Attainder was a way of bypassing judgement in a court of law. On 21 April, by a large majority the Commons voted in favour of the Bill. There were two more hurdles: the Lords and the king. For the attainder to pass, the Lords must also vote in favour; but even then, it would not be law until the king signed it.

When Charles I addressed the House of Lords on 1 May, asking them not to convict Strafford of treason, although, said the king, he might be guilty of 'misdemeanours,' and although he, the king, would no longer employ Strafford, he told the peers that he would never sign the Act of Attainder. That flourish is an outstanding example of the king's inability to see things from anyone else's point of view. By declaring his royal conviction, his loyalty to a good servant, his steadfastness, Charles I removed responsibility from the peers.

Boiling point came in Westminster and London. Again, crowds filled the streets. The names of the Commons members who voted in favour of Strafford were published. The apprentices threatened them with death. Yet while Strafford was detested by many of his fellow peers, most did not favour the process of attainder. If sanctioned it could be used against any of them in future. Their noble minds balanced on the one side the threats of the mob, against, on the other, aristocratic prerogative – the whole reason of their existence.

Thanks to royalist plotting the crisis became more intense. Within the army two separate intrigues had been discovered by the Pym group. One was a plan for officers to petition the king supportively and legally, the other was to mount an illegal attack on parliament. Neither bore fruit. Several courtiers and officers, mainly friends of Henrietta Maria, were summoned for questioning on 5 May, shortly before the Lords were to vote on the Bill of Attainder. They all fled either overseas or to safe houses. Escape was wise but it did not cry innocence. At the same time the king tried and failed to spring Strafford from the Tower.[4]

The king had given the peers an exit. Since he would never sign the Bill, it did not matter whether it passed the Lords. Strafford was safe! And with him the honour of English earls. Waverers did not have to stand up and be counted. The king had made that clear. He would never sign such an Act of Parliament. The result was that many stayed away. In a very thinly attended house, the Lords duly voted on 7 May to find the Earl of Strafford guilty (by twenty-six to nineteen votes).

Everything now rebounded on Charles I. Would he do as he said, and refuse royal assent?

That same day a mob advanced on Whitehall to take the royal family prisoner. They dispersed with no harm done but the point was made. On 2 May Princess Mary, aged nine, had married Prince William of Orange, aged fourteen, in a low-key ceremony at Whitehall. When the crowds gathered both children were still in London. King Charles was responsible for the protection of William while he was in England, something he owed the boy's powerful father, the Stadholder of Holland.[5] The king's other children and his wife were also in London. Henrietta Maria's mother at St James's Palace was targeted as a Catholic. Marie de Médicis had to ask for a special guard which, for the time being, parliament provided – with the proviso that she could not remain in England much longer.

After consulting bishops and judges, on 9 May the tormented Charles I after all signed the Bill of Attainder and it was law. Thanks to the king's signature, Strafford was guilty and would die. When he signed away the life of his faithful servant, the king took on a crushing burden of guilt for the rest of his life. He signed to protect his family but also to protect his people from a collapse in civil order. He signed in the cause of peace. Nonetheless, it was a personal betrayal. Strafford died on 12 May 1641 eloquently protesting his innocence of treason on the scaffold, then stepping 'from time to eternity'.

The drama of Strafford's death should not hide what it meant. He really was Charles I's most capable minister. That was why the king's opponents insisted on his execution. The king was more and more isolated: '... the Storm was not over with this Death.'[6]

There were two other important losses at this time leaving dangerous gaps: the moderate and constructive Earl of Bedford (Pym's patron) died of smallpox just three days before. Had he survived, his influence could possibly have prevented further deterioration. On 23 August the Earl of Rothes died in his early forties 'of a burning fever'. He was at Richmond, having been at the English court since November 1640. The sincere leader of the early rebellion in Scotland, in the last year of his life Rothes showed a courtier's facility, popular with both king and queen. Rothes, too, might have sought a middle way but it was not to be.

———*◁•◦•▷*———

Scotland was still unsettled.

After Archbishop Spottiswoode's death at the age of seventy-four in November 1639, Scotland made do without a Chancellor. Instead there was a committee. Traquair was dismissed as Treasurer in the course of 1641 on the insistence of the covenanters. These were the two top posts in Scottish government. Although parliament had stated its claim to make appointments, the necessary authority still lay with the king. The Scottish army was still in England. Their costs were covered by England, but an unemployed army was high risk. Nor was there agreement with the king on religion, the original quarrel. In short, there was no fully worked out peace. The covenanters had won the strange Bishops' Wars but terms had not been agreed in detail. English and Scottish commissioners talked in London. The extreme politics of England caused delay.

While Charles I stuck to his losing battle over Strafford, Montrose therefore wrote to the king suggesting that he visit Scotland. Montrose's idea was more than a way to tackle the outstanding issues. He was agitating for what he really felt – as he now saw – he wanted to help firm up the royal position in Scotland. This eloquent letter began:

> Your ancient and native Kingdom of Scotland is in a mighty distemper. It is incumbent on your Majesty to find out the disease, remove the causes, and apply convenient remedies. The disease (in my opinion) is contagious, and may infect the rest of your Majesty's dominions. It is the falling sickness; for they are like to fall from you, and the obedience due to you.

From the tree of liturgical reform poisoned fruit had sprouted. An obedient nation now refused to obey. Disobedience tends to spread.

In other words, the king must get on top of things in Scotland to keep England under his control.

Without, perhaps, adding to the sum of Charles I's knowledge, he told his sovereign 'They (the covenanters) have no other end but to preserve their Religion in purity and their Liberties entire.' By 'liberties' Montrose meant traditional rights, and this really meant the rights of the nobility. He was trying to show that while things had gone too far, the cause was not unreasonable and not anti-royal, whatever it looked like.

> You are not like a tree lately planted, which oweth the fall to the first wind. Your ancestors have governed there [in Scotland] without interruption of race, 2,000 years or thereabout... It is easy to you in person to settle these troubles, and to disperse these mists of apprehension and mistaking, impossible for any other... Suffer them not to meddle or dispute of your power; it is an instrument never subjects yet handled well. Let not your authority receive any diminution of that which the law of God and Nature, and the fundamental Laws of the Country alloweth... On the other side aim not at absoluteness.[7]

The letter was certainly written with the assistance of Lord Napier, the old court hand. The text is interesting for its dishonesty. We know that Montrose had deep suspicions of Argyll, this was about to become unmissable. But he reassured the king that the Scots were loyal: 'That they intend the overthrow of monarchial government is a calumny.'

Was it Montrose's eternal optimism? Generosity? Or flattery? Or putting Argyll on one side as an exception? Or street smartness since, as he knew very well, letters could be intercepted and copied and reach an unintended public.

On 10 August 1641, the Treaty of London was signed, the detailed settlement of the Bishops' Wars. It was a covenanter triumph except in one thing. The hope that England would also become presbyterian in religion was dropped. It was a purely Scottish treaty. On the other hand, the king accepted the abolition of Scottish episcopacy, he issued a general indemnity to all who had subscribed to the National Covenant, he accepted that Scottish 'incendiaries' could be tried in Scotland, and agreed a payment of £300,000 to the Scots from the English exchequer, as 'brotherly assistance'.

By this date Charles I had already decided to preside over the next Scottish parliament in person. Montrose's letter encouraged him but was only one voice. The King of Scots had an obligation to return Scotland to peace and order. It would be good government and it would look good. By rising above above faction – above the issues which he had himself raised – Charles I could show himself a generous monarch. The king could disperse the mist. The vision of Charles I as Sun King well in advance of Louis XIV was not Montrose's alone. One of the royalists in the Short Parliament told the house 'His Majesty is the Sun, which though it ever shines in itself gloriously, yet by reason of Clouds it doth not so many times appear.' In 1639 an English gentleman said that the rebels when faced with the king 'like a mist with the breaking forth of the sun would dissipate and vanish.'[8]

For Scottish royalists the weight of their national myth was more weighty than the squabbles of the day:

>...this uncurable combustion; uncurable since it seems to fight directly against the only complete and heaven-imitating rule of monarchy under which this kingdom hath been this nineteen hundred years... Fergus the First... from him a glorious, royal and unconquered chain of kings are without intromission of breach of blood descended, in number a hundred and seven.[9]

20

Time to Write Poetry

By the time Charles I arrived in Edinburgh on 11 August 1641, Montrose and his associates were in prison.

After the 1640 crossing of the Tweed, Montrose's drift out of the rebel mainstream accelerated. From Newcastle he wrote to Charles I in general terms, showing that his support for the National Covenant did not preclude loyalty to the crown. As a Scottish noble he might at any time contact his lord, but as a soldier in the Scottish army Montrose was forbidden to correspond with the enemy. The correspondence was betrayed by someone close to the king (possibly the ambivalent Will Murray). A copy of Montrose's letter was sent to Argyll.

There was an outcry. An offical enquiry quickly took place. The familiar difficulty was that the king was the king and despite appearances could not be treated as the enemy. From the enquiry no action came, but the spotlight on Montrose threw up shadows.

Through the deathbed mutterings in November 1640 of the young Lord Boyd, reported to Argyll, the truth came out about the Cumbernauld Band, too. Argyll pursued that with Lord Almond. The document was discovered. The text of the Cumbernauld Band explicitly supported the National Covenant but the existence of a secret pact was the true crime. Montrose came through a second time, battered. People were reminded of his 'intolerable pride'. We know what the band said because a copy was found in the nineteenth century.[1] At the time very few people knew because it was burned on the order of the committee of estates. It was easy to think that Montrose had conspired.

His reputation emerges in a hostile account of a paper he submitted to the committee of estates 'after the burning of the band, full of vain humanities, magnifying to the skies his own courses, and debasing to hell his opposites.'[2]

In summer 1641 the storm broke. Beginning with a March 1641 meeting at Scone Palace near Perth, Montrose was part of several conversations in which he was open about his horror at the constitutional innovations (the triumvirate, the dictator), and said he would attack attempts against the royal prerogative in parliament, he would even make his own accusations. He spoke of Argyll's words at the Ford of Lyon. So sensational were his remarks, they could not be brushed under the carpet. The committee of estates launched the third enquiry into the Earl of Montrose.[3]

Sure of his ground, Montrose told the committee he knew of the Ford of Lyon exchange thanks to John Stewart of Ladywell, who had been there. When Ladywell was interrogated on 31 May he confirmed what Montrose said. Ladywell accused Argyll to his face of talk of deposing the king. After the meeting, Ladywell was arrested and imprisoned. Montrose also said Lord Lindsay had told him about the plans to make Argyll dictator before the Scottish army had crossed the Tweed into England, but this was a less important charge, and it was agreed Lindsay had not said this plainly but had somehow implied it.

While in custody and probably after torture, Ladywell changed his story. He now said he had misconstrued 'innocent speeches': Argyll had really been talking about deposition in a general sense, referred to kings, not to King Charles I. Argyll shored up his own position by producing counter-witnesses to his innocence. The problem remained of Montrose's intentions. His persistent challenge to Argyll could not be ignored.

By this time, Montrose was running a campaign. He had sent to Traquair in London a copy of Ladywell's original deposition. If Traquair had a copy, the king would see it. Argyll's confidence had led to unintended consequences. He was at risk of treason charges.

The next move was the interception of a messenger from London, Walter Stewart. This man was taken to Lord Balmerino's house and found to be carrying a letter from Charles I to Montrose. In the letter the king only said that he intended to come to Scotland to promote 'a firm and solid peace'. He said he would satisfy the Scots 'in their Religion and just Liberties', exactly as Montrose had suggested. Other than being a letter from the king, which implied privilege – but nobody could deny the privilege of an earl – there was nothing to complain of. But there was more in Walter Stewart's pockets. There were strips of paper written in code.

Obligingly, Walter provided the key. The messages were incoherent. They seemed to testify to a different exchange between Montrose and Charles I in which the king more openly gave his support to the moderates and asked for details of the Argyll allegations. In the code Hamilton appeared not very flatteringly as 'Elephant' while Montrose was glamorously cast as 'Genero.' Could it be a plot?

On 11 June, Montrose and his closest political allies were arrested and imprisoned: Napier, Keir and Keir's brother-in-law Archibald Stewart of Blackhall. No charges were made. Montrose's houses were search for documents with no success, except supposedly the discovery of old love letters which showed he was immoral. Mugdock Castle was 'demolished'.[4]

On 28 July, Ladywell was beheaded. Just before he died he said that his original deposition had been correct. He had been found guilty of 'leasing making', or seditious libel. That was a crime against the king, certainly a capital crime. But Ladywell accused not the king but Argyll, which said everything about Argyll's position in Scotland. Argyll's insistence on killing Ladywell was political. There was no moral – no Christian – argument for the death of this otherwise inconsequential man. The legal case against him was slight. The revision of his testimony did Ladywell no good whatever – there was no gratitude, he received no mercy, he must die to set an example. Argyll could not risk more dreadful chatter. Better the silence of the grave.

—◊◊◊—

On 14 August 1641 King Charles arrived in Edinburgh. He came as a Scot with 'not passing 100 persons in his train'.[5] The principal courtiers in attendance were the Duke of Lennox, the Marquess of Hamilton, and Hamilton's brother William, the Earl of Lanark, the king's secretary of state for Scotland. He also brought his nephew Charles Louis, the Elector Palatine. The elector came to England to block the marriage of Princess Mary with Prince William of Orange (he wanted to marry her himself – and was so irritated when the Orange wedding occurred that he sulkily refused to attend the feast afterwards). The elector was a Stuart prince and Reformed Protestant icon who might impress Scottish opinion.

The local interests of Lennox and Hamilton led them to sign the National Covenant not long after arrival. They can only have done so with the king's knowledge. The trip was all diplomacy. The king wanted to settle Scottish affairs; he would be a bringer of peace. Evidently the Treaty of London had been signed by this time. What was needed now was soft politics – but soft politics can be hard to keep malleable, as events showed.

On 14 September, a Day of Thanksgiving for the peace was held throughout Scotland. 'The weather being wonderful fair, the poor country people rather wishing to have been at home bringing in their corns... thus

through this covenant is both burgh and land held under daily vexation...
thereafter there was nothing but tempestuous rains.'[6]

Appointments still had to be made. This required haggling. Charles
succeeded in preventing Argyll from being named Chancellor. The king
first tried to secure the earl's father-in-law, the Earl of Morton, for the
office, but settled on Lord Loudoun. He failed in his wish to make
Lord Almond Treasurer. A committee was appointed to run the Scottish
treasury. The appointments were far from a royalist triumph, but at least
Argyll had to remain in the shadows.

Before he left Edinburgh to return to London, Charles I scattered
honours over his opponents. Argyll was made a marquess, Loudoun an
earl, Alexander Leslie became Earl of Leven, Wariston was knighted.[7]
Soft power indeed. Only kings could give honours. In an age of hierarchy,
honours were supremely valued. With his generosity Charles I shored up
monarchy, confirmed his unique rank, but did so at the cost of endorsing
his critics. Nor was this the only damage.

Untying the Montrose knot was not easy. It was in the king's interests
for Montrose to survive, first of all. He also wanted him out and about.
What good would it do if his foremost supporter were locked up for
years? Allowing for the politics, that meant holding a trial. If they were
accused of crimes the Montrose group must know the accusations and
be able to defend themselves in public. If that trial had ever happened, it
would have been the Scottish equivalent of Strafford's. The Scotch mist
would have cleared if so. Instead, the murk deepened.

From his prison in Edinburgh Castle Montrose sent letters or messages to
the king through Will Murray, who was both servant and friend of the king
and nephew of one of the ministers involved in the earlier correspondence row.
Will had the best royal connections and close relations in the Kirk; he was on
both sides, for better or worse. These letters became linked with a plot against
Argyll – a plot which may or may not actually have existed. Montrose had said
before he would challenge Argyll in parliament. Probably, the correspondence
with the king was about this plan. Charles I did not write back.

Hamilton became involved. In the English parliament the marquess sat
as Earl of Cambridge. From the House of Lords he worked hard at the
politics of reconciliation, which meant being friendly with the opposition
leaders. So English royalist hawks were suspicious of him. The same
happened in Scotland. Hamilton thought there could be no peace in
Scotland unless a deal were made with Argyll, and he made that clear.
Although he was of the king's retinue, he reached out to the covenanters
and became compromised.

On 11 October 1641 Hamilton approached Charles I in Holyrood
gardens and told him that he, Hamilton, had been traduced to the queen.[8]

For his own safety he would have to leave court. Thanks to, again, Will Murray, Hamilton had read Montrose's letters to the king. In fact, it is very hard to connect Henrietta Maria, in the south of England with letters written in Edinburgh Castle and delivered to Holyroodhouse down the hill.

The shadowy plot against Argyll developed into a plot against Argyll, Hamilton and Lanark, too. Or the accusation levelled at Hamilton somehow included his brother and Argyll. There was a story that army officers were asked to arrest the three of them at Holyroodhouse in the king's apartments. They would then be taken to a waiting ship and transported, presumably to English custody. Or killed on the spot.

In the evening of 11 October, after a conversation with Alexander Leslie, the three noblemen left Edinburgh for Kinneill, a Hamilton house ten miles west of the city. There they stayed until their return on 1 November as popular celebrities under the protection of parliament. Their flight was a huge event, which fomented every sort of rumour. Had they escaped arrest or murder? Had King Charles ordered their assassination?[9] What was the involvement of Montrose? Was he, from his cell, the puppet-master?

Listing the endless honours he had lavished on Hamilton, Charles I protested his innocence before parliament on 12 October. Yet another enquiry was held, again involving the Earl of Montrose, but the report was not published. Again, there was guilt by association. These fragmentary events and non-events became known as 'the Incident', a name which appropriately gives nothing away.

The intervention of Alexander Leslie could be a pointer to what really happened. He would be very much in the picture as to what happened in a plot which really did happen, in the German wars, this being the assassination of the imperial general Albert von Wallenstein seven years before. It was a famous story and he almost certainly knew one of the assassins.

In 1634, Wallenstein had been killed, along with several of his most important officers, on the orders of his master the Emperor Ferdinand II. Wallenstein had won a super-eminent position within the empire by military success. He was a Bohemian whose efficiency saved the imperial cause, but after receiving fantastic rewards he became a power in his own right and developed his own policy for ending the German war, against the emperor's wishes. Ferdinand ordered and rewarded his assassination, which took place on 25 February 1634.

The events began with deception, an offer of dinner – just as one of the versions of the Incident involved an invitation to the king's apartments. The assassins were Scottish and Irish officers, one of them the Scot

Walter Leslie. If only through the expatriate network in the empire, the two Leslies are likely to have known each other: they were both Scots, they were both in Stralsund in 1628, there was the name and probable kinship.

Did Alexander Leslie, a man good at tricks, good at managing men (and especially nobles), draw on German memories to furnish the details of a non-existent plot that would cast a shadow on Charles I (and Montrose)?

This sequence of events, the arrest and execution of Ladywell, the arrest of Montrose and his friends, stories of further plots – true or false – were a degradation of a principled rebellion. It was in 1641 that the covenanters truly left the moral high ground.

—◦◦◦—

Even the Incident paled by comparison with the Irish news brought to the king on 27 October 1641 as he played golf at Leith.

Starting in Ulster under the O'Neill family, a rebellion had spread across Ireland. Irish troops attacked and destroyed English forts and plantations (colonies) and killed their inhabitants. It was a reaction to English policy, which increasingly preferred new settlers to the native Catholics, the 'Old Irish', and also the result of purely English politics, because only Strafford's iron will had been enough to keep the lid on Ireland.

Strafford's deputy Wandesford had died before he did, so for nearly a year there was a vacuum at the top of Irish government. Subsequent holding appointments were inadequate. The ever-present tensions (new settlers vying for land with a long-established, and itself conflicted, local population) led to the insurrection. Strafford's Irish army complicated the situation, viewed from England as another threat.[10]

As petrifying news poured in of Protestant men, women and children being massacred by Catholic tribesmen, the king's Protestant reputation was again on the line. Her faith sucked Henrietta Maria in. In some quarters the Irish rebellion was called the 'queen's rebellion'. Sir Phelim O'Neill caused the maximum confusion by falsely announcing that he had a commission from the king to represent the Old Irish against recent settlers.

Nor did the king react dynamically. After sending a message to the House of Commons, which heard the news on 1 November, he focussed on the problems immediately before him hoping that the rebellion would win him support in England. Some people thought he was at heart in favour of murderous Irishmen, or at least did not mind.[11] Charles I left Scotland on 18 November 1641. He had just kept his head above the water but overall, his time in Edinburgh was hard work for little reward. Yet on return to London he had a hero's welcome.

To roars of acclaim the king made a triumphal entry into his English capital on 25 November as though he had won a war. He made a speech proclaiming his loyalty to the Protestant religion and to the City of London whose aldermen, on whom he bestowed knighthoods, for a short time ensured the crowds were all royalist. He was re-established as the fount of honours, of justice, of government.

It made sense. He had fought two wars with rebels in Scotland then created peace, listening to his people. The stunning irony was that the king's Scottish trip worked as well for him in London as it did for his opponents in Edinburgh.

The price was the casting aside of Montrose, who was released from captivity on 16 November but did not see the king. He and the others had to wait until the end of January 1642 before they saw the formal list of charges. One was an accusation of leasing-making, for which Stuart of Ladywell had died. Another made agreements like the Cumbernauld Band, if they were against the estates (which the Cumbernauld Band was not), leasing-making, sedition. So anyone conspiring against the estates was a traitor. That was new ground, new status for the estates (or parliament).[12] Also, it was tidying up after the execution of Ladywell.

The trial never took place. The Montrose group did not have the chance to mount their defence. The king agreed not to employ them in any office without the agreement of parliament, nor would any be given a personal audience. It was a good way of thrusting them all to the outer margins. Not long before, Montrose had been a leader of Scotland. Now he was a country gentleman with time to write poetry.

These were big events and much emotion and blood had been spent, but the king's visit to Edinburgh marked no conclusion. The mood in Edinburgh did not lighten. Presbyterian women spoke again. There was more to come.

... the Inferiors began to talk and call it our duty to press Reformation in *England*; and the Wives at Edinburgh... cried out against all, especially the Ministers, who were for peaceable Temper... and when the vulgar sort began thus to vent themselves (it being well enough known that they used not to speak by guess, but first had their Lessons given them) Men began more clearly than before to discover and foresee what might be the Design of the Great Ones.[13]

Dating the verse of Montrose is hard, but it is tempting to think that it was at this time that he wrote his poem 'In praise of Women', which reads

149

as a reflection on love but is shot through with politics – and indeed Kirk politics:

> My dear and only love I pray
> This noble world of thee,
> Be governed by no other sway
> Then purest monarchy.
> For if confusion have a part,
> Which virtuous souls abhor,
> And hold a synod in thy heart,
> I'll never love thee more.[14]

PART THREE

BATTLEGROUNDS

'Wake up wake up you hard world, open your eyes before terror comes upon you in swift sudden surprise.'

Paul Gerhardt

21

'The generosity of your character'

The king and queen left Whitehall Palace hurriedly on 10 January 1642. When they arrived at Hampton Court no beds were ready (they had not been sent ahead). With them were the three eldest children, Charles, Mary and James, eleven, nine and seven respectively. The two youngest, Elizabeth (five) and Henry (eighteen months) stayed at St James's, the nursery palace. The king did not see these younger children for another five years. Henrietta Maria did not see Henry for another eleven years. Elizabeth she never saw again.[1] They were left because any move across the park, sending for the children, transporting them, would give a warning to the enemy. Whereas a departure from Whitehall by river could not be stopped: a few steps down the pier and onto the royal barge.

Every move was watched. Six days before, in the afternoon of Tuesday 4 January, King Charles had walked into the chamber of the House of Commons so that he could himself arrest his main opponents on treason charges. These were the 'five members': John Pym, John Hampden, Arthur Hazelrigge (who introduced the Bill of Attainder against Strafford), Denzil Holles, William Strode. Forewarned, the five members left shortly before he arrived. Famously, the king looked around the chamber red-faced to see that 'the birds were all flown.'

Various whistleblowers have been named but none was needed. The king had left Whitehall Palace with a large retinue to support him. Petitioners stopped him before he reached Westminster. With regal gravity he listened to them. Anyone in the vicinity knew the king was on his way. Anyone could have cried a warning. Any number of radical sympathizers were in the streets.[2]

Face to face with his Majesty, the sitting members had a bad fifteen minutes. They were terrified that Charles I would order a bloodbath. Through the open door they could see the king's men armed with swords, muskets, pistols. However, courteously, if angrily, he accepted his own failure. His absolutist tendency did not stretch to cold-blooded murder. It was not a time of gratitude and the gentleman of the Commons would not be thankful. The opposite, there was bitter resentment at the king's intrusion. The unwritten rule was the king could not enter the House of Commons. His presence alone was an attack on the rights and privileges of parliament – the place of the subject, not the sovereign. At Charles I's side stood the Elector Palatine, that rather powerless figurehead. He should not have been there either, but nobody complained about him.

Charles I could not make his arrest. The combination of threat, insult and weakness provoked nothing so much as contempt. The five members found safe lodgings in the City of London where their presence cemented City loyalty to parliament. The fiasco tipped the scales against the king. The next day, 5 January, Charles I addressed the Mayor and Aldermen in the Guildhall to justify what he had done, and to ask for the surrender of the Five Members. The response was surly. He went home empty-handed. On 8 January there was a committee meeting of the Commons in the Merchant Taylors' Hall at which Pym and the others were welcomed. Later (17 January) the committee ruled that anyone who arrested a Member of Parliament without the authorisation of the house he belonged to, would be an enemy of the country.

The 10 January dash to Hampton Court was Charles I's best answer. He wanted to get away from a dangerous place, to regroup. But when the king ran away from London he abandoned England's largest port and richest reserve of cash, quite apart from the arsenal in the Tower. And he broke another unwritten rule, by which the presence of the king was bound up with the loyalty of the people. If he left them, why should Londoners trust his goodwill? If the king did not want to live at their side, what should the citizens expect from him? Desertion was rejection. Influential courtiers – the Earls of Holland and Essex, the Countess of Carlisle – begged king and queen to stay. Others thought he would be safer away.[3] Whoever was right, this was the time the king decided he had been pushed too far and must fight parliament.

———✥———

To the covenanters, the English news confirmed that the 1641 settlement was just a start. Nor were things easy in Scotland. People were afraid. Northern weather in January and February 1642 was tempestuous, gales and driving rain. The River Dee flooded. As the campaigning season approached, people in Bankafair heard spectral drumbeats. A scarcity of fish was reported in coastal regions thanks to a monstrous 'sea-dog' that consumed the bodies of the fish caught by lines, leaving only the heads for the poor to eat.[4]

When Charles I in April attempted to occupy Hull, the biggest arsenal of north England, and Sir John Hotham kept him out, his intentions were undeniable. By now Henrietta Maria was in the Dutch Republic, where she had delivered their daughter Mary to her new home in the Hague. The queen stayed to raise money and buy arms for her husband. By selling jewellery and with the help of the Stadholder Frederick Henry, the queen was a success as royal fund raiser and arms trader. Surrounded by Calvinist Dutch, she could hardly conceal what she was doing.

The Scots resurfaced in England. In May 1642, with Airlie and Keir, Montrose rode south to York where the king was holding court. Charles I did not see him. In July, after debate at the General Assembly, Lord Maitland came to England in order to deliver a supplication to the king for England to accept Scottish religion. The king heard Maitland but did not commit to a presbyterian England.

On Monday 22 August, 'a very stormy and tempestuous day',[5] Charles I raised his standard at Nottingham Castle. A herald read out the royal proclamation, appealing for support against the Earl of Essex, the general-in-chief of parliament's army. It was the formal start of civil war in England – five years after the Edinburgh prayer-book riots.

The first pitched battle was fought on 23 October at Edgehill in Warwickshire. Prince Rupert of the Rhine, the king's nephew, led a successful cavalry charge against the left flank of Essex's army. That could have made the battle a decisive royalist win. However, the cavaliers lacked the discipline to regroup, instead galloping on in pursuit of the fleeing troops on that wing. A parliamentary advance in the centre threatened the safety of the king's sons, Charles and James, who had to be escorted from the field. The king's failure to provide himself with a reserve, and the ill-disciplined cavalry, led to heavy royalist losses.

Families would split. It had started. At Edgehill Montrose's old friend Basil Feilding fought under the Earl of Essex, while his father, Denbigh, fought for the king. The outcome was indecisive but at least the king was undefeated. He advanced on London to reclaim his capital but was blocked at Turnham Green and retreated to Oxford, which became his wartime headquarters.

Trying to return to England, Henrietta Maria was twice nearly killed. She first attempted the crossing in January 1643. There was a ferocious storm in the North Sea. Two of her flotilla of eleven ships went down and the others were driven back to Dutch shores. She tried again in February and landed at Bridlington on the Yorkshire coast. Here the house she was staying in was bombarded at close range by a parliamentary ship (the captain knew the queen was inside). 'She got up out of her naked bed in her night gown, barefoot and bareleg, with her maids of honour (of which one, through plain fear, went straight mad)... and on the bare fields she rested, instead of stately lodgings, clad with curious tapestry.'[6] The queen made it. She travelled on to York where she granted Montrose an audience. What advice did he give?

Montrose urged military action against the covenanter government who were as dangerous as the English House of Commons. He told Henrietta Maria the Scottish royalists needed a commission from the king to make action legal, that was all. This must be done before another rebel army was raised, it must be pre-emptive: 'the only risk was in delay.'[7]. The king must act now.

At York there was a quarrel between Montrose and the Marquess of Hamilton, who came to give his own, different advice. Montrose was so irritated that later he wrote a short poem to celebrate the killing by Hamilton's 'maiden sword' of a young noble's dog there.[8] With hindsight, he appears so right and the queen so wrong to listen to Hamilton, who counselled his now highly developed brand of temporizing diplomacy with the aim of keeping the peace. On the other hand, Scotland *was* at peace and England at war. England was the natural priority. To confirm the good sense of that line of thought, during 1643 Charles I enjoyed a winning streak. It was a year of royalist victories: the Battle of Braddock Down (19 January), the Battle of Adwalton Moor (30 June), the Battle of Roundway Down (13 July), Bristol falling to Prince Rupert (26 July).

Charles I's English successes increased Scottish stress. People had visions of armies at night 'sometime appearing near hand, sometime appearing afar'. Armies of men were seen in the air, and drumbeats heard. The apparitions vanished as the sun came out, but there they were in the minds of men and women.[9]

Montrose was stressed too. His warnings about Scotland fell on deaf ears. The court did not believe he was being straight. The Earl of Antrim thought Montrose was a royalist but even he had his doubts, writing 'I am not entirely desperate of Montrose...'[10]

Henrietta Maria did not lose hope of keeping Montrose's support. On 31 May 1643 she wrote from York promising to help. She told him she had always had confidence in the 'generosity of your character'. She said that despite rumours of his intriguing with the king's opponents, she would remain his 'very good friend'.[11]

Henrietta Maria had good information. He was being wooed. More than that. He was offered a commission in the covenanter army.[12]

In June, Alexander Henderson agreed to a meeting. They met on the banks of the River Forth close to Stirling. Montrose came with his closest friends: Napier, Ogilvy, Keir. Henderson came with Sir James Rollo who had been married to Montrose's sister Dorothea, and after her death (very young, in 1638), married a sister of Argyll. Rollo had a foot in both camps.

While Montrose is known for being frank, this encounter shows him capable of deception. Clearly, he could not tell Henderson about his meeting with the queen. Instead he explained that he had been living quietly in Kincardine, hoping the charges brought against him by his enemies could be forgotten. He said he was out of touch with current affairs. Could Henderson bring him up-to-date?

Henderson could. He said the plan of the Scottish government was to raise an army to help the 'English brethren' against the king: 'The covenanters in both kingdoms had unanimously resolved either to die or to bring the king to their terms.' They wanted Montrose's help. It would bring him material and spiritual profit. If only he gave active support, others 'who yet respected the empty shadow of royalty' would follow him. Unified, they would pop the king's balloon.[13] This was the moment.

Had Henderson spoken more softly, Montrose might have hesitated. Had there been a note of regret for the attacks on his reputation, for the imprisonment, for the dodging of an open trial, perhaps Montrose would have been attracted. He had signed the National Covenant in 1638 sincerely.

Not only was there no apology by Henderson, but Montrose found himself correct in every detail. His advice to the queen was sound. The covenanter leadership was ready to tear up the Treaty of London and march against Charles I in England.

He asked whether this plan was agreed with the estates. Rollo said yes, the estates agreed it. The exact Henderson said no, there was no formal plan, yet he was certain of support. That gave Montrose an absolute confirmation and his desired escape. He could not commit to something unofficial, he said. That was the end of the riverside meeting.

Not long after, Montrose gave up on Scotland and rode south across the border with his cousin Ogilvy to join the king in Oxford. This was late July or early August 1643. He had failed to persuade other Scottish royalists to rise against the covenanters. These men 'were resolved to have no further concern in these civil commotions, but to live quietly at home, and offer up prayers to God Almighty for better times.'

Now Charles I broke the previous year's agreement with the Scottish government and at last saw Montrose. Had Henrietta Maria encouraged him? In August the king was overseeing the siege of Gloucester. Montrose found him watching the siege lines and was granted an audience. Charles I heard his report but still refused to provide the royal warrant to support Scottish royalists. Not only could the king not drop his confidence in Hamilton, he was still wrestling with the whispering campaign against Montrose, which warned of his 'youth, rashness and ambition'.[14]

—◈—

In summer 1643 the war balance was against the English parliament.[15] To win, win, win again and then, when it came to fighting, to lose... But they had militant friends. In August 1643 the General Assembly of the Kirk in Edinburgh received an appeal by the parliament of England for joint action. In hand-wringing the supplication held nothing back:

> Surely if ever a poor nation were upon the edge of a most desperate precipice, if ever a poor church were ready to be swallowed up by Satan and his instruments, we are that nation... we looked for peace but no good came, and for a time of healing, but behold trouble! ... be pleased to advise us further, what may be the happiest course for uniting the Protestant part more fairly.[16]

A committee of the General Assembly drew up the response, which came to be called, somewhat confusingly, the Solemn League and Covenant. It was quite different from the purely Scottish National Covenant of 1638. It was international, an agreement between the English parliament and the Scottish government to promote and defend the presbyterian form of Calvinism in both countries.

The Solemn League and Covenant sought 'the preservation of the reformed religion in the Church of Scotland... the reformation of religion in the kingdoms of England and Ireland'. It was of course explicitly anti-bishop, anti-Catholic. It was not anti-royal. With conditions, the text revered the king. The signatories would 'preserve and defend the King's Majesty's person and authority in the preservation and defence of the true religion and liberties of his kingdoms...'

The king is always a bastion. If only he can change his mind...

On 25 September 1643, the document was signed by both chambers of the English parliament and by Scottish commissioners in Westminster. Now there was a godly alliance, treaty-bound. Hopefully, Calvin's God would smile on the three realms of the Stuarts once they were unified by the true religion's simplicities – obviously the smile would not extend to papists such as the queen. The extreme neurosis of the time can be seen in a series of witch trials at this time. In Anstruther, Dysart, Culross and St Andrews, and in other towns, people were put on trial, found guilty and burned to death.[17]

Ironically, the ardent wish of King James VI and I, which he never achieved, the union of England and Scotland, appeared to be almost a possibility thanks to the furies attacking his son. The Solemn League and Covenant went on to urge 'firm peace and union' between the two countries.

What happened immediately was the reinvigoration of the Earl of Leven (Alexander Leslie) who had spent an unsuccessful few months fighting Irish guerillas. Leven sent to Europe for experienced officers. He duly raised an army of 20,000 – 18,000 infantry, 2,000 cavalry – which he led across the Tweed into England on 19 January 1644. The costs would be met by the English parliament; in other words, the English taxpayer would fund the Scottish invasion.

The Scottish estates threw their all behind the expansion of their religious system, for if that were adopted in England, they would be safe spiritually and militarily. The English thought otherwise: they were hiring mercenaries.

22

Advance and Retreat

Two months before Leven's army crossed into England, Charles I showed Montrose letters from Hamilton and Lanark. They confirmed the new army being formed in Scotland would help parliament in England. The king asked Montrose for advice.[1] Montrose's reply was not a model of tact. He had warned the king, he said, for the past year and had not been believed. Instead, his sovereign had trusted the Hamiltons who 'had yielded everything to the rebels'.

Nonetheless, he was upbeat. He offered a solution. Montrose told the king that 'though matters seemed to be in a very lamentable state, yet, if it pleased his Majesty, he promised to reduce the rebels to obedience, of which he did not yet altogether despair, or lose his life in the attempt.'

Two days later he was granted another audience in which he sketched a plan involving the old favourite, an invasion from Ireland; with cavalry supplied by the Marquess of Newcastle (then in the north of England); with more cavalry from Denmark (King Christian IV being the uncle of Charles I); and arms supplies from 'abroad'.

The king was sanguine. He ordered Antrim, also in Oxford, to put in motion the Irish invasion. Antrim was more sanguine still. He told Montrose that he would himself land on the Argyll coast with 10,000 men by 1 April 1644,[2] a date that would give anyone pause today. Sir John Cochrane was ordered to procure arms and cavalry from abroad. Instructions were drawn up for the Marquess of Newcastle, which Montrose would take to him.

The next excitement for the Oxford court was the unpredicted arrival of the Hamiltons in person. With his brother, Hamilton left Scotland complaining they were hounded out because of their loyalty to the king. Of course, they had not calmed the unmanageable covenanter leaders.

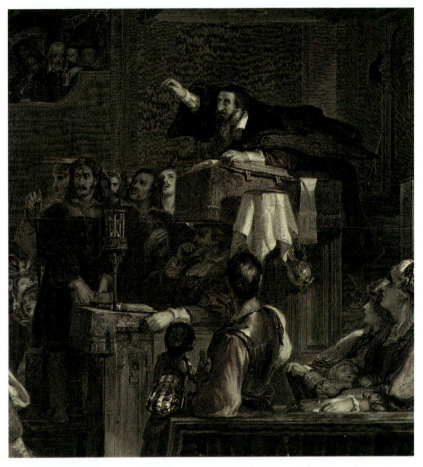

1. John Knox preaches to the Lords of the Congregation in 1559. (Rijksmuseum)

2. Dunfermline Palace, where Charles I was born on 19 November 1600. (Author's collection)

THE DEUCALIDON SEA

THE KINGDOME OF SCOTLAND

The Yles of Hebrides
Caled of Pliny
Hæbudes, of
Beda Meuanae

LEWYS

Rona Iland

James King of Great Britain,
Fraunce & Ireland.

Henry Prince of Wales
& Ireland

THE SCALE OF SCOTISH MILES

PART OF IRELAND

IRISH SEA

THE

Previous spread: Map of Scotland, 1610, by John Speed. The figures on the sides are King James VI and I, his wife Anne of Denmark, their two sons Henry and Charles. (Reproduced with the permission of the National Library of Scotland)

Above: 3. The Ruthven brothers, Montrose's uncles, meet their fates on 5 August 1600. (Rijksmuseum)

Left: 4. James VI and I is described here as King of Great Britain, France and Ireland, although he never united England and Scotland into Great Britain. The claim on France was a historic dream. (Yale Center for British Art)

5. The Winter King and Queen, living in Dutch exile, riding with members of the Orange-Nassau family. (Rijksmuseum)

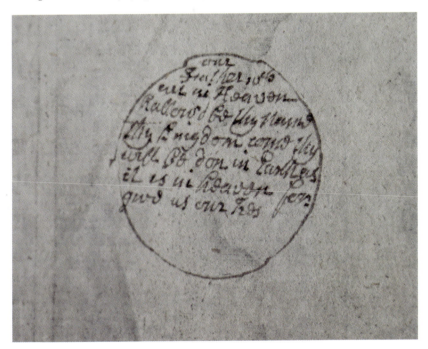

6. Within a coin's outline, on the back of an illustration in his copy of Raleigh's *History*, Montrose wrote most of the Lord's Prayer – a spiritual doodle. Probably during his student days. (Author's collection)

LA BIBLE,
QVI EST
TOVTE LA SAINCTE
ESCRITVRE DV VIEIL ET
NOVVEAV TESTAMENT.

Autrement,

L'ANCIENNE ET LA
NOVVELLE ALLIANCE.

*Le tout reueu & conferé sur les Textes
Hebrieux & Grecs.*

A SEDAN,
Par IEAN IANNON Imprimeur
de l'Academie.

.M. DC. XXXIII.

Above: 7. Holyroodhouse, showing the ruined abbey church, where Charles I was crowned King of Scots in June 1633. (Author's collection)

Below: 8. Montrose's personal Bible measuring about three by five inches. (Author's collection)

Left: 9. Title page of Montrose's Bible: a Protestant French language text, published in 1633. (Author's collection)

10. The castle at Angers. Montrose attended the military academy in the town in 1633. (Wikipedia)

Above left: 11. The statue of the philosopher-emperor Marcus Aurelius was among the classical antiquities that Montrose would see in Rome, probably in 1635. (Rijksmuseum)

Above right: 12. A decorative arch of the kind erected for court entertainments, and for triumphal entries, such as that of Charles I into Edinburgh in 1633. (Yale Center for British Art)

13. Montrose in full armour. Probably painted while he was in Oxford in 1643-1644. (Flickr)

Above: 14. The saltire, or Cross of St Andrew. Scotland's national flag, thought to be the oldest national flag in Europe. (Author's collection)

Right: 15. Mary Ruthven, Montrose's niece, wife of Sir Anthony van Dyck. The inscription says she was born in Scotland but that is unlikely. (Rijksmuseum)

MARIA RVTEN

NATA IN SCOTIA.VXOR ANTONII VAN DYCK PICTORIS.

Ant. van Dyck pinxit.   E RVTORVM FAMILIA NOBILISSIMA ORIVNDA.   *S. à Bolswert sculpsit.*

16. 'Cutty Stool' by Merilyn Smith (1992). This one is bronze. The original was wooden, thrown, according to tradition, by Jenny Geddes at the Dean of Edinburgh, when he started to read from the new prayer-book in St Giles' on 23 July 1637. It was still heavy. (Author's collection)

Above: 17. Montrose's signature on the title page of a 1637 edition of Camden's *Britain, a chorographical description...* (usually called *Britannia...*). (Author's collection).

Below: 18. A seventeenth-century musket. (Rijksmuseum)

Above: 19. Blair Castle was Montrose's base during his glorious year 1644-1645. At the time the building was much smaller, a fortress rather than stately home. (Author's collection)

Left: 20. A drummer boy, like the child killed before the Battle of Aberdeen. (Rijksmuseum)

Carolus D̃g Ang. Sco. Fra. et Hib Rex

A. van Dyke pinx; I. Beckett fe: Sold by I. Smith at the Lyon & Crown in Russell Street Covent Garden

21. King Charles I. The inscription describes him as King of England, Scotland, France and Ireland. (Yale Center for British Art)

Right: 22. Statue of Montrose in Montrose High Street. (Author's collection)

Below right: 23. Inverlochy Castle, the scene of Montrose's defeat of the Marquess of Argyll on 2 February 1645. (Yale Center for British Art)

Below: 24. Dunnottar Castle, where the Earl Marischal, surrounded by ministers of the Kirk, sheltered in March 1645 while Montrose burned his land. (Author's collection)

Above: 25. Site of the Auldearn battle-field, looking from Castle Hill onto Garlic Hill. (Authors' collection)

Left: 26. Montrose as Lieutenant Governor of Scotland. (Rijksmuseum)

Above: 27. Seals of Montrose from 1639 and 1650, the latter with cypher of the lion poised to leap across an abyss. (Author's collection)

Right: 28. The Heart of Midlothian, a pavement mosaic, marking the old Tolbooth of Edinburgh, very close to St Giles' Cathedral. (Author's collection)

Below right: 29. Today's junction of East Preston Street and Dalkeith Road, Edinburgh, where Montrose's mutilated trunk was buried in May 1650. (Author's collection)

30. On 23 May 1660 (Julian calendar) Charles II set off from Scheveningen for England to reclaim his throne. Huge crowds watched.

31. The elegant memorial to Montrose in St Giles was built in 1887-1888 after Queen Victoria indignantly asked why there was nothing in the church worthy of him. (Author's collection)

They had altogether failed. Hamilton and Lanark had to get out before Leven's army crossed the border. If the two of them were north of the border when another Scottish army invaded England, they really would be implicated in treason. Having nourished their friendship with Argyll, Loudoun and the others, they wanted to preserve their relationship with Charles I. If only! The arrival of the brothers was hard for the king. He had trusted Hamilton so much that he had made him a duke the previous April and now had to admit his mistake. Some urged treason charges.

Montrose told the king that he would ask to leave court and go into exile on the continent if the two Hamiltons resumed their places on the privy council 'for he would never stand by and see his country ruined.'[3]

On arrival in Oxford, that is on 16 December 1643, Hamilton and Lanark were arrested. The duke would be out of action for the next two years, although he was never put on trial.[4] Lanark did not help his family's reputation by escaping soon after to parliamentary London. He would return to Edinburgh and sign the Solemn League and Covenant. The arrest signalled a new royal policy for Scotland.

On 1 February 1644 the king appointed the Earl of Montrose his Lieutenant-General in Scotland, subordinate only to the Captain General, Prince Maurice of the Rhine (the king's nephew, younger brother of Rupert and the Elector Palatine, at twenty-three much younger than Montrose). With the gushing enthusiasm of the convert, Charles I offered the senior commission to Montrose who deflected the honour by suggesting Prince Maurice. It was good politics to appoint a royal prince as figurehead, which was what it amounted to since Prince Maurice had never been to Scotland (and never went).

In recognition of his strength in the north-east, the Marquess of Huntly was at the same time made Lieutenant of the North, subordinate to Montrose. Huntly's loyalty to the king was always evident, although it seemed a matter of predilection rather than commitment as he hardly ever did anything.

The combination of Prince Maurice, Huntly and Montrose appeared vastly authoritative, but the problems arising from Huntly's escapist and proud nature were not understood. Under these terms Huntly was bound to obey a younger man (by twenty years) and, although to us the difference must seem modest, by rank the junior noble.

A further difficulty was the elevation of Montrose to a marquessate. This happened on 6 May 1644. The honour was a slap in the face for existing Scottish marquesses (who were, if the ducal Hamilton is set aside, only Huntly, Douglas and Argyll) and for the many earls of Scotland, whom he now outranked. The three existing marquesses were still senior because they were older titles, but it was annoying. From this time, Montrose is the Marquess of Montrose, the title of the history books.

A final comment can be made on his Oxford months. Having arrived in August, Montrose was a 'Scot in waiting' until the king asked for his help. He was there seven months in total. He had to live in wartime Oxford, a place of political and love intrigue, where the king held court in Christ Church and the queen in Merton College and cavaliers caroused. Having been dispossessed (also excommunicated) in Scotland, Montrose lived largely on credit, although his lieutenancy may have brought an income. How did he spend his time?

We know he organized yet another band or pact, which rejected the Solemn League and Covenant, and asked other resident Scots to sign (they all seem to have done so, although both Traquair and Will Murray initially would not).[5] Probably he joined cavalier raids from Oxford which would add to his military knowhow.

Historians are drawn to Montrose's undoubtedly generous, idealising nature but a thirty-one-year-old man, far from his family, would possibly not spend free time in contemplation alone. His friend the Earl of Rothes had been both dedicated covenanter and promiscuous; just as the English Earl of Holland was a puritan patron but had many affairs. Did the handsome Montrose join the games? From his own verse we know his romantic taste. His work is filled with metaphor, often political, but his idiom is the love song:

> But if thou will prove constant then,
> And faithful of thy word,
> I'll make thee glorious by the pen,
> And famous by my sword;
> I'll serve thee in such noble ways
> Was never heard before,
> I'll crown and deck thee all with bays,
> And love thee evermore.[6]

Montrose was nevertheless displeased by the hedonism of another court where later he found himself, or it would be more accurate to say he was uncompromisingly disapproving.[7] He had high principles, even a degree of austerity. He expected chivalry, not indulgence:

> But yet fair ladies you must know
> Howbeit I do adore you so;
> Reciprocal your flames must prove
> Or my ambition scorns to love.[8]

For the period it is an unusual insistence on reciprocity.

—⟨∽⟩—

It was the end of February 1644, still winter, when Montrose started the mission of his life. His first stop was with a highly coloured bloom of cavalier society, William Cavendish, the Marquess of Newcastle, a man then fifty-one years old.

Grandson of the famous Bess of Hardwick (1527-1608) by her second husband, Newcastle was unusually rich. He had large estates in Derbyshire (Bolsover), Nottinghamshire (Welbeck) and Northumberland (Ogle). Himself author and playwright, he was a patron of the arts – in particular of Ben Jonson – but also a passionate horseman, skilled in the French school of equestrian *manège*,[9] also a dedicated practitioner of the art and sport of fencing. He was a supremely well-funded intellectual, 'amorous in poetry and music to which he indulged the greatest part of his time.'[10] He was fiercely anti-puritan for courtly as much as spiritual reasons. He had a deep belief in ceremony and tradition, although his interests were up-to-the-minute modern.

Newcastle had been the governor of the Prince of Wales (the future King Charles II) from 1638 to 1641, whom he advised 'to study things [rather than] words, for too much contemplation spoils action.' He also told the prince, 'Beware of too much devotion for a King, for one may be a good man but a bad King.' He was obliged to cede that role to the Marquess of Hertford because of puritan pressure.

As wartime royal lieutenant of much of northern England, he enjoyed several military successes around the time he met Montrose, including a defence of York (April-July 1644) against the massed forces of parliament. Newcastle was courageous, but the generalship was down to his lieutenant, the professional soldier James King (another veteran of the German wars). Lord Clarendon's later verdict was that Newcastle 'liked the pomp and absolute authority of a general well... but the substantial part and fatigue of a general he did not in any degree understand.'

According to the instructions of King Charles, this gifted but not predictable grandee was to provide Montrose with a cavalry escort. By the time they met during March 1644 (in Durham), Newcastle was facing the threat of Leven's army, now camped close to his own smaller force, while parliamentary troops under Lord Fairfax were advancing across the Pennines from Cheshire towards royalist York (shortly before the siege). So he was reluctant to part with troops. However, he provided 100 of his cavalry, 'very lean and ill-appointed'[11] and provided authority to raise more troops from the Cumberland and Westmorland militia.

When Montrose crossed into Scotland (13 April) he had an army of 1,300 behind him. He also had senior officers including the Earls of Crawford, Nithsdale, Kinnoull, Traquair, and Lords Aboyne and Ogilvy.[12] Things slid pretty quickly.

Offered the lieutenancy of Clydesdale by Montrose, the Earl of Carnwath refused even to read the letter and cast it aside because he was insulted by Charles I's favour to Montrose.[13] His pride did not prevent him from supplying support, but it may have been only the troop of Captain Francis Dalyell, apparently the earl's illegitimate son, or rather daughter. Captain Dalyell was a woman soldier dressed as a man. Her cornet (subaltern) held her banner, all black and displaying a naked man hanging from a gibbet. The motto appropriately was 'I dare.' Her married name was Mrs Peirsons. She and her soldiers were financed by Carnwath. Briefly she appears to history in 1644, allowing us a glimpse of pure gutsinesss and unexpected privilege.[14]

Two days into Scotland the Cumberland and Westmorland men deserted. The king's champion was left with a few hundred men. Montrose advanced to Dumfries, which surrendered without a fight. Here he awaited news of Antrim's army, which was meant to have landed in Scotland two weeks before. There was no news because there was no Irish army. Nor were there arms supplies from abroad.

Friends encouraged him to advance further to Sterling, saying the garrison wanted to support the king. He decided against. That was ninety miles due north, three times further than his journey from Carlisle to Dumfries. There had been no support from the border earls. The further into Scotland Montrose marched, the more cut off he would be. What if his friends were wrong?

He has been criticised for bad planning. But he could not predict the desertions, and he could not predict the behaviour of the border earls. It was their duty to follow the king's commission. Resentment, caution, self-interest came first.

Now there was a timing issue, also a communications issue and a personality issue.

On 16 March, a month before Montrose entered Scotland, the Marquess of Huntly issued a proclamation that he would not pay taxes to finance Leven's army or any backup recruitment; or raise men himself against the King of Scots. Junior Gordon leaders galloped into Aberdeen and seized four of the citizens most prominent in organizing Covenant support, including the town provost. On 24 March, Huntly occupied Aberdeen and started raising an army including bringing in supplies from the citizens and from the countryside. He did very little more. Again, younger men among his supporters led raids including to Montrose (the town) and appealed to the Ogilvies for support.

By the time Montrose (the marquess) was in Dumfries, it was clear that Huntly's attempt was half-baked. He had jumped into the water, creating a splash, and there he stood as the ripples died away. Having seized the moment, Huntly let it go. That is what the Ogilvies saw. They did not join his cause. They did not have confidence in him.

By the end of April Huntly decided to retreat. Thanks to his inaction he suffered desertions. On 30 April he left Aberdeen for Strathbogie, then disappeared to take refuge in Strathnaver, on the north coast of Scotland, under the protection of the Reay family. That was as far north as you could get and still be on the mainland.

Probably, Huntly thought Montrose was coming with an army and actually he was right, but that army deserted. He may well have concluded that Montrose had once more let him down. Nor is it impossible that his family connection with Argyll came into it: the late Lady Huntly was Argyll's sister, their children were Argyll's nephews and nieces. Was Huntly trying to square the circle by remaining distantly royalist without confronting his brother-in-law? Was he jealous of Montrose?

The brother-in-law used the weeks of nothing happening to raise an army against the Gordons. Huntly had gone by the time Argyll arrived, so he eluded capture, but the Covenant again gripped the north-east. Argyll's men wasted land around Aberdeen. Sir John Gordon of Haddo, hated by the covenanters since the outbreak of the troubles, was captured, put on trial and executed in July 1644.

⟞ᴑᴑᴑ⟝

By now Montrose was back in England, hard at work. The royalist garrison of Newcastle was under siege by the Scots (divisions of Leven's army led by the Earl of Callendar). Montrose helped supply the garrison. He took Morpeth Castle, fifteen miles to the north. He took a fort at South Shields on the coast. This was two months of manoeuvring to reduce the pressure on the besieged garrison, no major actions, everything a success.

Then a transformative battle was fought. After a skilful and rapid flanking march that avoided the parliamentary armies blocking him on Marston Moor west of York, Prince Rupert entered and relieved the city from the north on 1 July. It was a brilliant conclusion to the siege. Because the prince thought his uncle Charles I had commanded him to fight the northern armies of parliament and defeat them, he then forced a confrontation the next day on Marston Moor, to the west of the city.

The battle involved five armies, three for parliament (all the soldiers were asked to wear something white), two for the king. Approximately 46,000 troops joined battle, rather evenly matched.[15] After a day of manoeuvring, the action started very late indeed, close to half past seven in the evening. Although both sides were drawn up for battle, the attack at this time was yet another unexpected move from the Earl of Leven who had supreme command on the parliamentary side (because of the size of the Scottish army). Possibly because a dip in the ground concealed some of the parliamentary troops, Prince Rupert did not expect the parliamentarians would advance. The fighting lasted two hours and concluded by the light of the moon. In a very tough contest. The decisive element was the training of Oliver Cromwell's cavalry, soon to be called Ironsides after his own nickname, but the Scottish regiments were also critical to what ended in a victory for parliament.

An unusual feature of Marston Moor was the circulation of stories about the parliamentary generals. It was said that Leven, Lord Fairfax and the Earl of Manchester all fled the field, so uncertain was the outcome. The gossip was probably an attempt to glorify Cromwell and dish the Scots.

The battle was a disaster for Charles I, who lost control of the north of England. Cromwell's new highly disciplined and meritocratic[16] approach to soldiery, an outstanding example of new military thinking, was triumphantly vindicated. Cromwell himself thanked God: 'an absolute blessing... God made them as stubble to our swords.'[17]

Montrose nearly fought at Marston Moor. He had been summoned by Prince Rupert, who needed all available help, but arrived the day after the battle. The two conferred at an inn in Richmond. After first unrealistically offering Montrose support, the prince took from him the greater part of what was already a modest force to add to the king's Oxford army.

With a hundred or fewer followers, Montrose returned to Carlisle. He complained that he found it hard to commandeer accommodation for himself, let alone his men.[18] At this time he seems to have received further information on the scale of Huntly's lost opportunity, writing that the marquess had raised 5,000 men at the peak[19] (probably an exaggeration). He was ruminating on what might have been, never a good sign.

He must decide what next. With his officers he discussed the depressing options. After receiving more intelligence about pervasive covenanter power, Montrose had to accept that the hopes of keeping his promise to Charles I – 'to return the rebels to obedience' – were vanishingly thin. The glorious commission as the King's Lieutenant in Scotland was finished. His choice was between returning to Oxford or retreating to the Continent. The latter was tempting. If the Marquess of Newcastle could retire to Europe, as in a fit of pique he did, so could the Marquess of Montrose.

He gave his decision. He would lead his men back to Oxford. It made sense to follow Prince Rupert south.

23

A Burning Cross

Actually, Montrose had seen enough of Oxford. Two days passed on the march, then he doubled back to Carlisle, leaving personal servants, spare horses, weapons and clothes with his men.

He gave command of the troop to Ogilvy. Montrose now travelled only with Colonel Sibbald and Major William Rollo (brother of Sir James), a man lame in one leg, not apparently disablingly so. It was no entourage for the king's representative, it was so modest as to hide his identity entirely. He was incognito.

In Carlisle Montrose conferred with Viscount Aboyne. He had not given up on the Gordons. We glimpse the unquenchable hope of Montrose. Argyll had destroyed swathes of Gordon property, had killed Gordon of Haddo. Neither this nor the vanishing act of their clan leader made Montrose think the Gordons a lost cause. On 18 August 1644 he left Carlyle heading north. Montrose was returning to Scotland.

As nothing had gone well, nothing had been supplied, not one of his requests had been met except by Lord Newcastle – and that in the end amounted to almost nothing thanks to desertions – as he now had no army, not even a regiment or brigade or troop, and such men as he had were on their way to Oxford, as there was not the least sign in Scotland of the covenanter grip loosening... the decision seems unhinged.

Montrose had told Charles I he would return Scotland to obedience, or he would die. He would return Scotland to obedience, that is, if he had the support he requested. Yet now, apparently, he would return Scotland to obedience with no help at all. He was breaking his own rules.

Outside Montrose's self-belief, there was nothing. But confident he always was. That spirit gave him charisma. A contemporary bears witness to this non-condescending charm:

[Montrose had] a presence graceful, courtly, and winning upon the beholder as it seemed to claim reverence without suing for it; for he was so affable, so courteous, so benign as seemed verily to scorn ostentation and the keeping of state, and therefore he quickly made a conquest of the hearts of his followers... [He] did not seem to affect state nor to claim reverence nor to keep a distance with gentlemen.[1]

He was in disguise. His escort was just Rollo and Sibbald, travelling with roles reversed. The marquess was the servant who followed his two inferiors as Sibbald's groom: 'He rode upon a lean, jaded horse, and led another in his hand.'[2]

Not long after they crossed the border, a servant of Sir Richard Graham fell in with them. Sir Richard had started life as a servant himself. As such in 1623 he travelled on a similar adventure with the Prince of Wales on his trip to Madrid to woo the Infanta. This led to royal preferment including the baronetcy which now distinguished him, as his loyalty did not.

At Edgehill, Sir Richard fought for parliament. Now his man told the travellers that his master was in favour with the committee of estates. He 'had undertaken to be their spy' and to inform the authorities about travellers in the district. If there was one traveller they wanted to find it was the Marquess of Montrose. Since he, Rollo and Sibbald continued unrecognized and unreported, since the man thought they were from Leven's army, the meeting and apparently quite prolonged conversation was not that alarming.

Another man straightaway recognized Montrose. This soldier, a Scot who had fought under Newcastle, respectfully saluted the groom: 'Do not I know my lord Marquess of Montrose well enough? But go your way and God be with you.' Montrose gave him some money. They parted. Had the soldier reported them, there was no possibility of resistance, it would be capture or death. They rode on with more determination.

Four days later the three of them arrived at Tullybelton, five miles north-west of Perth close to the Highland line, a house belonging to Montrose's cousin Patrick Graham of Inchbrakie. They had travelled (quickly) through Montrose's own estates to get there. The decision clearly was to avoid the obvious. At remote Tullybelton, Montrose was relatively safe but could not appear openly.

Sibbald and Rollo went scouting for intelligence. Not merely, as we read, 'of the state of the kingdom' but to see whether there were pockets of royalist resistance. They probably visited the Napier and Keir families to tell them that Montrose was now in Scotland. They appear not to have visited Magdalen and the children at Kincardine Castle, unless she was at Kinnaird. This protected Montrose's immediate family (by now there were three boys).

These were days of retreat in the wooded countryside, the life of a hermit – or outlaw. In the seventeenth century a man of Montrose's status was never by himself. Servants, family, petitioners crowded in. Bedrooms, beds, were shared. A grand marquess would be at court (always crowded), in parliament, entertaining or being entertained by his peers. Being solitary was impossible. Yet now Montrose, although protected by his cousins, was utterly alone. He spent the long summer days in the hills where nobody could find him, the short nights in a cottage, surrounded by the abundant life of the natural world.

When Rollo and Sibbald returned, they only confirmed that 'the tyranny of the rebels' was complete. 'Ruinous fines, imprisonment and death, was the certain portion of every honest and active loyalist that fell into the hands of the committee of estates.'[3]

Theirs was not the only sense of foreboding:

...the sun in divers parts was seen to shine with a faint beam, yielding a dim and shadow light even in a clear heaven and sometime did show like a deep and large pond or leak of blood. The beating of drums and sounding of muskets, with salvos of canons and musket, was ordinarily heard in many places as seeming to foretell the large loss of blood that was shed soon after.[4]

In England, Montrose's cavaliers continued south to Oxford.

They included several Ogilvies and Harry Graham, Montrose's illegitimate half-brother. Lord Ogilvy carried written instructions from Montrose as to what to say to the king on arrival. At some length the instructions insisted on Ogilvy explaining to Charles I the refusal of the border earls to give support. Again, Montrose administered a frank rebuke to his sovereign. He pointed out that none of his requests had been supplied, from Antrim's Irish to the ammunition from abroad. He complained that Prince Rupert had stripped him of men. Yet with his baffling optimism he concluded that Ogilvy should show Charles I 'how feasible the business is yet...'[5] How was Ogilvy meant to do that? From this ticklish instruction Ogilvy was unhappily delivered.

The troop met a group of 400 of Prince Rupert's cavalry, who had survived Marston Moor and were riding for refuge in Lancashire (15 August 1644). Outside Preston, having dispersed a group of parliamentary troops on Ribble Bridge, the joint body was surprised by a much larger detachment of Lord Fairfax's army and taken prisoner to a man.

The royalists were held in Hull for some time, then transported to Newcastle, which fell to parliament in October. Joined by other Scots from Newcastle, including the Rev. George Wishart, who would be Montrose's first biographer, the men were sent to Edinburgh and imprisoned in the

Tolbooth.[6] Had he continued with them, Montrose would have been captured, too, and we would have a different history.

The covenanters took all his papers from Lord Ogilvy including the letter of instructions. They saw that the King's Lieutenant was somewhere else, but where? They learned that Charles I's plans for Scotland were a mess, they were not really plans, just imagination. They read that Montrose still thought success possible but Montrose, wherever he might be, was obviously deluded.

It must have filled the committee of estates with satisfaction.

———◦◦◦———

In Methven Wood, on the edge of the Tullybelton estate, according to a gentleman who later heard his account, melancholy flooded Montrose.

> He became transported with sadness, grief and pity to see his native country thus brought into miserable bondage and slavery through the turbulent and blind zeal of the preachers, and now persecuted by the unlawful and ambitious ends of some of the nobility.

A sign of a change in fortune was sprinting into view.

A vision appeared, a man running along the path holding a fiery cross. Montrose approached and asked what was happening. The man said he was a messenger on an urgent mission to Perth. The news was this: a chieftain known as Coll MacGillespick, son of the famous warrior Colkitto, was entering Atholl 'with a great army of Irishes' and was about to plunder the land. Perth officials had to be warned as soon as possible so that the town could help organize resistance before disaster struck.[7] It was as if a mythical giant had come to trample Scotland underfoot.

Coll MacGillespick went under various names, of which Alasdair MacDonald is the best approximation to his Scottish identity.[8] He was indeed a giant, at least according to rumour, standing a head taller than the average. He was ambidextrous, fighting with his sword as happily in his left hand as his right. His also ambidextrous father Colkitto (Col Ciotach), lord of the Isle of Colonsay near Kintyre, was at this time a prisoner of the Marquess of Argyll. In the words of a contemporary, Alasdair was 'of a grave and sullen carriage, a capable and pregnant judgement, and in special in the art military, and for his valour, all that knew him did relate wonders of his actions in arms.'[9]

Alasdair and his father were Hebridean Scots, MacDonald chiefs, related to the Earl of Antrim – would-be heirs of the Lords of the Isles. The imprisonment of Alasdair's father was due to Antrim's attempts to mobilise the MacDonalds against the Campbells earlier. The arrest was pre-emptive. Alasdair would also have been taken but escaped, fleeing to Ireland where he fought on both sides, returned briefly to Scotland in November 1643, was again chased away by the Campbells.

Now he was back because Antrim had delivered his invasion force at last. In May-June 1644 Antrim in Ireland gave Alasdair MacDonald the rank of Major-General and supplied him with letters from Charles I appealing to Scottish chiefs. In July 1644 Alasdair transported something like 1,600 troops from Ulster to land at Morvern and Ardnamurchan, wild country on the west coast of Scotland to the north of the Argyll estates. In this way he avoided interception.

It was a smaller army than planned – various figures were proposed at different times – but they were experienced and disciplined men, blooded in the Irish war that was now three years old and still running. Alasdair commanded both Irish and Hebridean Scots like himself.

His invasion began with modest success. Taking several local strongholds Alasdair gathered a store of booty (sheep and cattle), which he put on a small island to retrieve later: he took the precaution of ensuring his men would be paid. However, his royal letters were not enough to persuade local chieftains. Either he must return to Ireland or take the risk of plunging into Scotland, which would arm against him. But retreat was impossible. The Marquess of Argyll summoned his own highland troops and destroyed (or put to flight) the ships that had brought the invaders from Ireland. The invaders had no option but to turn inland. The Campbells followed in pursuit.

Alasdair found more hostility from the Earl of Seaforth, the magnate of the north and north-west, although Seaforth did not fight the increasingly desperate Irish. Having provided them with food, he allowed them to travel on into Lochaber and further into Badenoch, which took them away from Mackenzie (Seaforth) territory. They travelled onto land which originally belonged to the Marquess of Huntly but, according to recent claims, was now the Marquess of Argyll's. In the central highland region, the invaders added to their numbers through appeals to anti-Campbell solidarity.

The men must be fed. So must the wives and families with whom the Irish always travelled. Alasdair's options narrowed. From the west, Argyll's army approached. Escape to the north was blocked by the combined forces of the Earl of Seaforth and the Laird of Grant, both determined to keep the Irish away from their own holdings. Lord Elcho was raising an army to the south-east.

If only he could find the King's Lieutenant. Alasdair was not a pirate chief. He was tied into the command structure, was a royal officer. Once in Scotland his commander was Montrose.

Subordinate to the marquess, MacDonald would be better placed for two reasons. Other Scottish lords and lairds were more likely to listen to a high-status noble of Scotland with a commission from the king than to an island chief. Just as important, the poisonous issue of religious identity would be trimmed. Alasdair and his men were Catholic. Montrose was Protestant.

Hardly anyone knew Montrose's whereabouts. Alasdair may have thought he was on the Borders, say at Carlisle. He sent out letters, presumably to different places, and one quickly reached the Graham house of Tullybelton. Whether the man with the fiery cross came first we do not know. What we do know is that in mid-August 1644 Montrose realised his army was here, heaven-sent and not far, forty miles away.

Montrose replied to Alasdair telling him to find his way to Atholl, not quite twenty miles north of Tullybelton. Alasdair took on a guide and led the soldiers and their followers there and occupied the castle. It was the only course, although, having led his men out of the path of the northern clans, he now challenged the Atholl Murrays, Stewarts and Robertsons who banded together against the invaders. Out of the frying-pan into the fire. Each group occupied a hill. Both were ready to fight. Alasdair had more men, but the locals were in better shape.

On 29 August the arrival of Montrose put a stop to that. For the King's Lieutenant it was not a stately entrance. With his cousin and guide Patrick Graham of Inchbrakie the younger, he walked through the heather like a labourer. Montrose was wearing simple country clothes – 'highland dress'[10] – suitable for his scramble through the wild. The Irish could not believe this was the illustrious Scottish marquess trusted by King Charles.

But he had with him the king's commission, which he showed to Major General MacDonald. The two men were about the same age, which perhaps helped. The Atholl men recognized Patrick Graham, well known as 'Black Pate' thanks to an earlier accident with gunpowder, and put two and two together. First the Irish, then the Atholl men, cheered their new leader, threw their caps in the air and fired musket salvos. Both sides rallied to Montrose, who now had an army of 2,000 to 2,500. Montrose and Alasdair MacDonald spent the night in the House of Lude, the Robertson home bordering on the Blair Castle estates.

The next day Montrose raised the royal standard on a mound close to Blair Castle and read out a prepared statement:

I, in his Majesty's name and authority, solemnly declare that the ground and intention of his Majesty's service here in this kingdom (according to our own solemn and national oath and covenant) only is for the defence and maintenance of the true Protestant religion, his Majesty's just and sacred authority, the fundamental laws and privileges of Parliaments, the peace and freedom of the oppressed and thralled subject; and that in thus far and no more, doth his Majesty require the service and assistance of his faithful and loving-hearted subjects.[11]

His declaration repeated his commitment to the National Covenant. He did not mention the Solemn League and Covenant: the Reformation of England was no part of Montrose's credo. He struck an impersonal note, committing to defence of the king's 'sacred authority'. He supported parliament and the subject, but he spoke on Charles I's behalf. The King's Lieutenant in Scotland would lead in the name of the traditional values of the Protestant ruling class.

In this way Montrose returned civil war to Scotland.

There is evidence that he now sent to his family. Quite soon we read about the elder children being in his company, that is to say John and James, respectively fourteen and eleven.[12]

24

Tippermuir and Aberdeen

To the committee of estates, the arrival of Alasdair MacDonald's army on the west coast was a shock. Yet by comparison with Leven's army, with the armies which fought on Marston Moor, with those at this exact time fighting around Lostwithiel in Cornwall, he did not field many men. Although Montrose attracted more from Atholl, the royalist force was not large.

The covenanters had men on the ground to deal with the King's Lieutenant: the Marquess of Argyll raised three highland regiments, Lord Elcho was at Perth with lowland levies, there were burgh militias. The highlanders of Lord Seaforth might also come in.

But by comparison with the king's indecisive manoeuvres of 1639 and 1640 and with the Marquess of Huntly, Montrose moved fast. Having raised the standard on 30 August 1644, he fought his first battle two days later, having decided to strike at Elcho, 'who was not reputed an extraordinary soldier'.[1] From Blair Castle to Perth was a march of thirty miles. Montrose's army covered it in two days.

On the way he fired cottages and stores of corn on the land of the Menzies family and picked up recruits. At the River Almond his way was blocked by a large armed group led by Lord Kilpont, eldest son of the Earl of Airth and Menteith. However, when Kilpont and his companions, who included Montrose's brother-in-law David Drummond, Master of Maderty, discovered that it was not marauding Irish that they had been summoned to fight but the King's Lieutenant, they saw things in a new light. They deserted the Covenant and joined Montrose to fight for 'the best of kings'. In this way he augmented his troops by 500 and received good information on covenanter deployment.

When he reached the plain of Tippermuir, two miles west of Perth, at seven o'clock in the morning of Sunday 1 September, 'The day was very fair... and pretty hot for the season.'[2] Montrose had a numerical advantage over Elcho: slightly more than 3,000 men against something like 2,500.[3]

Elcho had 400 cavalry where Montrose had, according to the primary, if very friendly, source, three.[4] He also lacked artillery while Elcho had some. But Montrose had the advantage of commanding Alasdair MacDonald's disciplined and tried troops against new recruits – 'freshwater soldiers, never before used to martial discipline'.[5] Royalist sources record much higher numbers for Elcho but these are exaggerations to glorify the outcome. What the covenanters had in spades was the support of Kirk ministers, one of whom unwisely said that 'if ever God spoke truth out of his mouth, he promised them, in the name of God, a certain victory that day.'[6]

Montrose first sent David Drummond to parlay under flag of truce. He made an appeal to Elcho to join the royalist cause so that no Scottish blood would be spilled. Ignoring the conventions of war, Elcho arrested Drummond and sent him to the prison in Perth, promising a rapid beheading after the battle.[7] By sending a member of his family to talk with the opposing generals, Montrose was paying them a compliment. He must have been angry.

On the covenanter side, the infantry was drawn up in the centre, where the Earl of Tullibardine commanded, flanked by cavalry. Elcho was on the right flank. For the royalists Montrose put Alasdair MacDonald in the centre. Lord Kilpont commanded the left. His troops included a number of archers. Montrose himself was on the right wing. To protect from cavalry encirclement, the troops on the two wings were extended by being drawn up three deep.

After initial skirmishing Montrose ordered a general advance. The Irish contingent fired upon their inexperienced opponents. This was a conventional exchange of musket fire, but the discipline of the Irish probably meant they reloaded and fired more quickly and more accurately. In the essential psychological confrontation Elcho's troops panicked and broke as the Irish charged. There was a chaotic retreat of the covenanter centre.

On Montrose's side of the field, where he led the Perthshire (Atholl) levies of Patrick Graham the younger of Inchbrakie, the confrontation was similar. They were facing cavalry, on whom they fired once, with not much result. Some also threw stones. Then the Athollmen charged and used their swords once they were at close quarters. The inexperienced covenanter troops broke and fled. On the left wing there was little fighting. Possibly Elcho, having retreated in order to attack the harder, was swept away by the general retreat of the army.

That was a rapid battle. It featured the 'highland charge' – a frightening full-frontal infantry attack. Covenanter artillery played little part because of the speed of the action, their pieces quickly captured. Elcho's troops performed poorly despite being better armed than many of the royalists. Alasdair's contingent had arrived in Scotland ready for war, an infantry force equipped with small pikes and matchlock muskets. The Hebridean Scots, who formed a relatively small part of his army, carried broadswords and targes (small round shields). On the royalist side the new levies were not so well equipped. The entire royalist army was probably short of gunpowder. One of the results of their victory was that the royalists re-equipped from booty.

A final comment on the battle itself is that Montrose's army had marched a couple of hours before they fought – we read they set off for Perth that day at dawn.[8] The physical toughness of these men is impressive. Royalist casualties were very light. On the Covenant side maybe 500 had been killed. Perhaps as many as 1,000 were taken prisoner.

Covenanter propaganda spread stories of massacre after the battle, of panic so great that soldiers and citizens collapsed and died without any wounds.

Witness statements, depositions to the committee of estates, paint a calmer picture: enough surviving members of the Perth militia to mount a night-time guard as usual that evening,[9] the imprisonment (not slaughter) of 300-400 of the Fife regiment, 'three or four score slain' on the battlefield and unburied in the immediate aftermath (ie three per cent of Elcho's army). Although there was some plundering of the town, although the dead soldiers had been stripped, these statements show the King's Lieutenant insisted on good order. The sheriff-clerk of Perth was 'forced' by Montrose to write a general protection for the citizens and for the lands around.

Perth still had to pay a price. Montrose requisitioned cloth and ammunition and the town was required to find £50 for Alasdair MacDonald. Incidentally, the amount of cloth he required, four thousand marks' worth, shows how poorly dressed many of his troops had been.[10]

David Drummond, Master of Maderty, was released and rejoined the army. It was at Perth that Montrose's two elder sons joined him, also his old tutor William Forrett (to help with administration).

Montrose returned to the idea which obsessed him, the raising of the Gordons, and decided to march north to Aberdeen. Since Huntly was in Strathnaver, his eldest son Lord Gordon was a covenanter, and the next son Aboyne was in Carlisle, that was not promising; but what was the alternative? If he were to raise a sizeable force, he needed reliable troops in numbers and especially he needed cavalry.

After Tippermuir the Atholl levies went home with their plunder – normal for highlanders, they fought for gain – and to bring in the harvest. The men might return, they might not. Unless Montrose could summon a more disciplined lowland army this would always be a problem, as he fully understood. Nor did the local gentry flock to him as he had hoped, although the Earl of Kinnoul came, also some Ogilvies. But Tippermuir made an impression on the covenanters. The initial news that arrived in London was of a calamity.[11]

The shock was reflected in a very nasty incident soon after the army left Perth. On 5 September the royalist army camped at Collace, a few miles north-east of Perth. At daybreak the next day it became apparent that Lord Kilpont was dead.

The discovery of the body, stabbed several times, caused an uproar in the camp, the men 'running to their arms'. The murderer was quickly identified. In the night fog, John Stewart of Ardvorlich had left the camp, killing a sentinel to get out in the dark. Ardvorlich was close to Kilpont. They shared a bed (not unusual). Ardvorlich was the junior officer described as Kilpont's vassal. He never denied the crime, indeed he would be exonerated by parliament of murder. He found a post in the Marquess of Argyll's army, which looked like a reward since he was not a professional soldier. Royalist sources speculated about Ardvorlich's intention to kill Montrose or Alasdair MacDonald and about Ardvorlich trying to involve Kilpont (who had access to the generals); the murder resulting from Kilpont's refusal. Certainly, the covenanters welcomed the fugitive, which showed an alarming acceptance of assassination.[12]

The committee of estates went further. On 12 September 1644 it set a price of £20,000 Scots on Montrose's head, dead or alive. The proclamation said he had joined with 'a Band of Irish Rebels and Mass-priests... for establishing of Popery'. He was excommunicated at the same time.[13] Not only could he be legitimately killed but he must go to hell.

Montrose's distress at losing a friend by midnight murder was considerable. Kilpont was one of his own. He valued him 'besides his knowledge in polite literature, philosophy, divinity and law ... for his probity and fortitude'.[14] Kilpont's men took the body back to his father for burial, so Montrose lost more soldiers.

Since the victory, his army went on shrinking. In fact it was about sixty per cent of its original quite modest size: 'The Irish he only was sure of because they had no place of retreat.'[15]

At Aberdeen Lord Balfour of Burleigh wanted a battle.

He could have defended the town from within the walls, but the odds were in his favour. When on 13 September 1644 his men confronted those of Montrose, Burleigh had 2,000 infantry and a little over 300 cavalry. He chose his ground well, drawing his army up on the top of a steep ridge less than a mile outside the town centre. Among his officers was Huntly's third son, Lord Lewis Gordon, leading a small cavalry troop.

Montrose had 1,600 infantry and 80 cavalry of mixed quality, the latter led by Sir Thomas Ogilvy and Nathaniel Gordon. They were looking uphill on the other side of a stream, the How Burn.

To get an idea of the array on both sides one has to think of the space needed between the soldiers. In order to load, aim and fire with their unwieldy weapons, musketeers needed at least a metre of leeway around them. Where there were cavalry it is a mistake to think the horses jostled up against each other as one sees in epic movies. In fact there was a good space between the horses, they needed room.

With his numbers, Burleigh should have won. Yet other than the Aberdeen militia his men were inexperienced. He had some artillery, but it is possible the gunners were untrained.[16] This time Montrose's troops were better armed and refreshed, better fed, after Perth. Also, the Irish and Hebridean contingent of Alasdair MacDonald made up more of the smaller royalist force. At Tippermuir Alasdair's men had been about half of the royalists. At Aberdeen they were the great majority. Burleigh was facing a cohesive, well-drilled army.

Once again Montrose sent a messenger under flag of truce urging Burleigh to surrender in order to spare life. This was rejected. The messenger was courteously received this time. The written reply to the King's Lieutenant told him the burgh would not 'abandon nor render our town so lightly, seeing we think we deserve no censure,' claiming to be loyal subjects of the king.[17]

Yet as the man with his accompanying drummer boy returned, a shot rang out. The child fell dead. It was not ordered by the commanders but for the second time the covenanters showed an exceptionally hard face. Montrose was outraged: 'He grew mad, and became furious and impatient.'[18]

Both sides deployed their main infantry in the middle. Burleigh seems to have concentrated his cavalry on his left wing, where the slope was less steep: a charge would be easier. In the conventional way he also had some cavalry on the right. Montrose positioned his small cavalry contingents on each wing but placed with them musketeers interspersed, in the new manner of continental thinking.

At the beginning of the battle there was an artillery exchange. A grisly story arose according to which an Irishman had a leg blown off by a cannonball – or blown off ninety-five per cent. It was still attached by some flesh, which he hacked at himself to detach the useless limb while, supposedly, saying that he hoped Montrose would now provide him with a horse.[19]

On the right wing of the covenant army, the left wing of the royalists, stood some buildings, the Justice Mills (a name also used for the battle). It was around the mills that the first action was fought. The buildings provided cover. They were a good position for musketeers. At the outset the lower mills were occupied by royalist infantry, who came under attack from covenanter cavalry.

The action spread towards the centre. Provocation by Lord Lewis Gordon's cavalry drew in the royalist infantry of Colonel O'Cahan on the left of the centre. Lord Lewis's men performed the *caracole* manoeuvre. That pulled the royalist infantry out of the centre and exposed them to a cavalry charge. Parting ranks the Irish allowed the covenant cavalry through, then turned and fired on them from behind. To part ranks they had to bunch together in groups – they did not extend, they contracted, leaving lanes open between the clusters of men. Again, one sees how the first deployment of infantry was spread out. The battered covenanter cavalry were then charged by Nathaniel Gordon, who routed them and took prisoners. On the royalist right wing, the covenanter left, something similar happened. Covenant cavalry twice charged to limited effect but drew in the infantry of Colonel McDonnell, on the centre right, in defence.

That left the third Irish infantry regiment, placed exactly in the centre under Colonel Laghtnan, free. After an exchange of musket fire, Montrose ordered Laghtnan to charge uphill using only their swords and daggers (ie casting aside pike and musket). As at Tippermuir, the effect was devastating. The inexperienced regiments opposite were more numerous but broke and fled and that was the conclusion, a second Montrose victory in two weeks.

The Battle of Aberdeen was harder fought than Tippermuir, lasting about two hours. It was a greater success because Montrose won against the odds. Evidently the contribution of the Irish was enormous.

They had their reward. Montrose allowed them to plunder Aberdeen, as he had not allowed a wholescale plunder of Perth. He was influenced by the imprisonment of his brother-in-law, the murder of Kilpont, the shooting of the boy. And he had to give the Irish their due, although that came at a price. It reinforced his image as a leader of barbarous Catholics.

The looting lasted four days:

> ...nothing heard but pitiful howling, crying, weeping, mourning through all the streets... some women they proceeded to deflower, and other some to serve them in the camp... the wife dared not cry nor weep at her husband's slaughter before her eyes, nor the mother for the son, nor daughter for the father, which if they were heard, then they were presently slain also.[20]

Casualties in the battle and rout were closer to 500 than 1,000, the number found in several sources, most of them on the covenant side. Different numbers were given for those killed inside the town. It was probably something like 150.

Montrose maintained his modest style of dress. At Aberdeen he was 'clad in coat and trews, as the Irishes was clad...'[21]

25

Taking on the Campbells

Montrose's victories at Tippermuir and Aberdeen achieved nothing much strategically. Certainly they surprised, and certainly they added to a reputation. That was important if Montrose were to recruit. Reputation is a weapon. Yet the reality is that in 1644 Montrose started all but hopeless, won two battles, then went on the run. He left Perth and Aberdeen soon after occupying them. He could not put in garrisons because he did not have enough men. In fact the covenanters reinforced Aberdeen's defences, building entrenchments around the town.[1]

Much mocked by royalist sources, the slow approach of the Marquess of Argyll let the covenanter army swell. Having originally set off in pursuit of Alasdair MacDonald with his own levies, Argyll now had nearly 5,000 men beneath him. Two regiments withdrawn from the Scottish army in Ireland joined him,[2] so that he had 4,000 infantry. The regular cavalry of the Earl of Dalhousie and other cavalry, adding up to 900, also came under his command.

It can be seen that troops were withdrawn from other theatres to give Argyll the numbers. Something was working for Charles I's cause: Montrose was an effective diversion. But the diversion had to keep one step ahead. He could not win against so large a force. At the end of October 1644, Argyll came close to snapping up the King's Lieutenant.

As autumn advanced, weeks went by in marches and manoeuvres. The days shortened. First, Montrose led his men away from Aberdeen due west, towards Rothiemurchus in the heart of the Grampians. They were carrying booty, which slowed them, but once they had hidden (buried) their captured cannon, the smaller army was still quicker. By going into the highlands they disempowered the enemy cavalry.

The plan was to move north. If Montrose reached the coast of the Moray Firth he would be able to hide in the northern highlands assuming the natives accepted him, or even if necessary escape by sea. However, at the fast-flowing River Spey he was blocked by, among others, Lord Gordon at the head of a cavalry regiment, with levies from the Grants and other northern families.

Montrose had to keep moving. He therefore turned south. About this time the strain told. He fell ill. News of his death spread. Quickly he was back in the saddle leading the men to Atholl once more. Atholl remained securely in the hands of royalists who disliked Campbell imperialism and who had listened to Montrose's August declaration. You would expect his base to be Kincardine Castle, or Old Montrose, but it was Blair Castle in Atholl. Even in his own territory he was not confident.

At the same time Montrose ordered raids on land belonging to covenant families. In Gordon territory, Argyll had run a brutal scorched earth policy. By marching south, Montrose led him away from that. He could not himself resist the logic of violence. If he rose above Argyll's example he only made it easier for his enemies.

There is nothing heard now up and down the kingdom but alarms and rumours, rendezvous of clans, every chieftain mustering his men, called weaponshows... The spring well above the town of Beauly had the stream of it running blood three days.[3]

From Atholl, Alasdair MacDonald took 500 men on an expedition to protect the garrisons he had left in the west to protect his line of retreat. Argyll similarly split his army. To keep a grip on Moray he installed two regiments in Inverness as a garrison. With the rest of his men still outnumbering the royalists, he followed south. Montrose marched south-east to Perth, then north-east again to Aberdeen, where Sir James Ramsay occupied the Brig o' Dee against him. Montrose moved upriver, crossed and continued north-west to Strathbogie.

Although the Gordon chiefs kept their heads low, probably because Lord Gordon openly sided with his uncle Argyll, Montrose managed to recruit a regiment at Strathbogie. Through this and other levies he compensated for the 500 gone with Alasdair, but recruiting was severely limited by the chase. Geographically, Montrose had gone round in a circle. Many miles were covered. Nothing much was done.

On 24 October Argyll entered Aberdeen. On the 26th Montrose reached Fyvie Castle, a large fortified house belonging to the Earl of Dunfermline, standing above marshy land enclosed by a bend in the River Ythan. Fyvie is several miles due east of Strathbogie, twenty miles north of Aberdeen.

We do not know Montrose's intentions at Fyvie. He may have meant to make it his winter quarters. In November the weather would start to close in and campaigning would come to an end. Armies must be fed. The bigger army of Argyll had many mouths and stomachs including those of hundreds of horses. Fodder on this scale was hard to find in late autumn. Perhaps these reflections account for Montrose's carelessness. He had only to dig in at Fyvie: Argyll must retreat to his own winter quarters.

But Argyll moved quickly on from Aberdeen. On 28 October his cavalry arrived outside Fyvie Castle, taking the royalists by surprise. It was a shock to see armed troopers trotting up and forming a line under the covenant banner, with the certain knowledge that thousands of infantry were following. The horsemen were quick, but it seems that Montrose failed to have the approach roads properly watched. Now he was caught.

Originally a fortress, Fythie had lost defensive strength with the addition of a new tower and ornamental entrance at the beginning of the century. Abandoning the house, Montrose took his position on the high ground overlooking the house, where the terrain was uneven, wooded, and divided by turf walls – good for defence. That was a quick, improvised manoeuvre, drawing up hundreds of men fired by adrenaline. The covenanters outnumbered the royalists as much as five to one.

Argyll swiftly sent a foot regiment in. At this point Montrose's Strathbogie regiment defected. Still the covenanters were beaten back. Argyll then sent cavalry, which did better but had to retreat when they faced a barrage of musket fire. Another regiment of foot attacked but also failed to get through. Skirmishing continued the next two days. The royalists held their position. The action petered out. Needing fodder, Argyll retreated a few miles. That allowed Montrose to take his men safely in the other direction, back to the better fortified Strathbogie.

At Fyvie, Montrose failed on the intelligence, he was in the wrong place, and failed on the supplies. The royalists were so short of shot that they had to melt pewter from the house to make their own musket balls.[4] Presumably they had very little to eat those three hard days. They escaped the trap thanks to Montrose, but equally they were in it thanks to him.

Nor did the situation improve. While the royalists occupied Strathbogie, the opposing generals agreed a truce. Under cover of talks Argyll offered pardons and safe conducts. In this way he enticed almost all the gentry and nobility who had gone over to Montrose in the past two months. Defections included Lord Kinnoull, William Rollo, Colonel Sibbald. With the defecting officers went their men. On 6 November Montrose retreated further to Balvenie Castle, twenty miles due west, closer to the uplands.

Montrose's strength was now a few hundred. The Ogilvy family and Patrick Graham were loyal. The Athollmen remained, also the Irish and Hebridean Scots who had not left with Alasdair.[5]

Our primary source concludes his account of the autumn campaign with Montrose trying to attack the Marquess of Argyll at Dunkeld, a few miles north of Perth, after he had sent his cavalry to winter quarters. Montrose 'in one night travelled with his army no less than twenty-four miles, through a wild uninhabited country, by unbeaten tracts, and almost impassable for rocks and depth of snow; intending to fall upon Argyll while he had no horse with him.'[6] However, Argyll left Dunkeld, retreating to the walled city of Perth. The attack did not take place.

Alasdair MacDonald had deserted other leaders. This one he trusted. The young Montrose had grown into a thoughtful adult, now thirty-two years old. His good manners and goodwill (to everyone) signified respect. He was calm in a crisis. He fought with his men. He had won two battles. This was persuasive to the independent-minded Irish and highlanders. At the end of November Alasdair rejoined Montrose in Atholl. He brought back the 500 men he had taken, and another 1,000 recruits from the western clans. John Moydartarch Macdonald, Captain of Clanranald, the largest MacDonald sept (clan subdivison) came with his son. As quickly as it had withered, Montrose's army was back to fighting strength, something like 2,500, maybe as many as 3,000.

Now what should have happened was winter quartering, seeing out the bad weather in a safe place. But the enlarged army was quickly on the move again. The winter campaign, something very rare, can be attributed to Alasdair. He wanted to waste Campbell heartlands. He wanted Campbell plunder. He was a MacDonald. That was his natural war. His new recruits were similarly Argyll haters. He also wanted to strike a blow for Catholics everywhere by attacking the clan that had a history of killing Catholics in Ireland and Scotland.[7] By contrast Montrose wanted to lead the army into the lowlands and winter where there were easy supplies (maybe at Strathbogie) – ready to move in the spring. A council of war discussed the options.[8]

In one version of the debate, Montrose asks if there were in the western highlands 'cities... wherein we may enrich ourselves.' The answer from Angus MacAilen Duibh of Glencoe is no, not even half a city, but 'if tight houses, fat cattle and clear water will suffice you will never want.'[9] Montrose warned his officers against the difficult terrain of the west highlands, the mountains that must be crossed, the peninsulas jutting into the sea, each of which could be a trap. He did not know this part of Scotland, but he knew descriptions such as this:

> Argyll is the wildest country of all... And even before it is reached, a short distance takes many days to traverse, with no regular road, with continually alternating ascents and descents, and numberless streams to be crossed... There are few trees to conceal or adorn the landscape. There is no track which the traveller can follow, except along the shore, and this is frowned upon by rocks, and interrupted by pools of water, alternatively spreading and subsiding.[10]

Alasdair said he and his men knew the land well and argued that the Marquess of Argyll was the leader of the rebellion against Charles I and was therefore the perfect target.[11] The upshot was a midwinter march into the Campbell kingdom.

The commander is limited by his troops and the moment must be seized. Where would the highlanders in fact go? Montrose knew these men would follow him up to a point only. Military discipline was new throughout Europe, and highlanders had less of it than lowlanders. If they lost heart, they would melt away.

Montrose could command in battle, but he could not dictate. A soldier's life was not comfortable. For instance, a few years before, a soldier not far away had written: 'I had nothing to keep me from the cold, wet ground but a little bundle of wet, dried flax... And so with my boots full of water, and wrapped up in my wet cloak, I lay as round as a hedgehog, and at peep of day looked like a drowned rat.'[12] Montrose had to accommodate his troops' need for action and plunder, which made such misery worth it.

What about his friends? What would their position be if his winning streak evaporated? If, for example, he lost his new army through desertion? Lord Ogilvy and the others were in prison in Edinburgh at risk of their lives. Whether or not Montrose knew, the Napier family had also been put under house arrest (8 October 1644) at Holyroodhouse where Lord Napier still had rooms.[13] Another hostage would soon be William Forrett whom Montrose sent home for safety. He, too, was arrested.[14] We know Montrose had all these people very much in his thoughts in the winter of 1644-1645. He would not help them by sitting on his hands.

For these reasons, he overcame initial reluctance and agreed the plan.

———

On 11 December 1644 the royalist army marched out of Atholl. It was very cold but fine. There was action on the way. The royalists burned the lands of the Menzies family. By Loch Tay they burned Campbell dwellings on the southern side of the loch and captured the island castle of Eilean nam Bannaomh on the northern side, where Sir Robert Campbell of Glenorchy had taken refuge, then savaged the surrounding land. At this season there were no crops in the fields but there were cattle and stores. It was destruction and loss at the worst time of year for the people who lived there.

When Blair Castle was sixty miles behind them, and Argyll's headquarters at Inverary Castle was twenty-five miles ahead, the army found the way blocked by a Campbell island fortress, close to the shore of Loch Dochart. It dominated the only possible track. On one side was the water, on the other the steep side of Ben More. Here was exactly the kind of bottleneck feared by Montrose. The castle was fortified with cannon trained on the track. The advance stopped well short. A group of men came forward offering to join the royalists. These were MacNab clansmen ready to fight against their Campbell lord. Because they were known to the soldiers in the castle they gained access on a pretext, killed the guards, and handed the castle over to Montrose.

The march covered icy, rocky wastes, natural barriers that turned out not to be impenetrable – it could be done, just as Alasdair said. Not that it was easy. Nearly a hundred miles must be crossed. Although cold the weather held, no storms, no snow showers. Montrose arrived at Inverary not long before Christmas 1644, according to tradition arriving on such a cold day that the sea water froze.[15]

The plan was to cover as much of the inhabited part of Argyll as possible, fire as much as possible, including the town of Inverary, take as much as possible. Three war parties did exactly this. 'They went through the whole shire of Argyll, the Baronies of Lorne and Glencoe, and a part of Lochaber, driving all the cattle before them... They likewise fired the Villages and Hamlets where they passed.'[16]

The violence was not unmitigated, there were acts of mercy,[17] but it was an attack on the civilian population executed to perfection, a shock assault on unprepared and vulnerable communities in the middle of winter. Perhaps we cannot imagine the fear the warriors inspired, the pain inflicted. We do not know how many died (including deaths from want later). There was no intention to fight battles or conduct sieges or win territory. Montrose did not try to take Inverary Castle.

What about the Marquess of Argyll? We read of his escape from Inverary in a fishing-boat to Rosneath Castle.[18] The appealing story is found in several sources but may be royalist propaganda. From Inverary to Rosneath by sea is quite a trip; Argyll might more naturally have stopped at Rosneath on his way from the lowlands, three-quarters of the way from Edinburgh to Inverary. Perhaps Argyll never made it back home before the royalists came but stopped helpless at Rosneath.

Either way he was humiliated. Under pressure he quarrelled with William Baillie of Letham, the man just chosen by the committee of estates to head the next army against Montrose. This quarrel took place at Dumbarton. Argyll imposed his authority on Baillie, an experienced professional soldier, and took from him 1,100 lowland troops to start the counter-attack. With these men he would return home and raise more.

In January 1645 the marauding royalists regrouped in Inverary. Montrose led them out of the ravaged Campbell capital probably on 15 January (three days later a letter was read out in parliament which said they had left Argyll for Lochaber).[19] Captured cattle and food stores encumbered their retreat. They had also taken arms and armour.

They did not retrace their footsteps but marched due north. At the northern end of Loch Awe the Irish released Alasdair's father and two brothers from the castle where they had been held captive since 1639. The expedition was a MacDonald high. Once they were safely away from Inverary, many highlanders left the army to take their booty home.

26

Inverlochy Castle

In late 1644 the Scottish commissioners in the Westminster Assembly (whose meetings started in July 1643) gave their backing to a negotiation with Charles I. On 29 January 1645, talks between parliament and Charles I started at Uxbridge.

The aim of the Scots had always been a presbyterian Church of England. England and Scotland would join in the Reformed Protestant island of Great Britain. That was the unity they longed for, spelled out, they thought, in the Solemn League and Covenant. But the second English Reformation was not what all the English wanted. Some did but there were many sectaries or independents: 'multitudes of Anabaptists, Antinomians, Familists, Separatists...' They did not want uniformity, they wanted a meadow of a thousand flowers (not too brightly coloured), multi-faceted Protestantism. Their champion was Oliver Cromwell, who was increasingly anti-Scot. Nor was parliament as a whole content to allow an *independent* Church of England on the model of the Kirk. Parliament was mainly Erastian (believed the national church should be governed by the state).

The Earl of Leven's army had not brought the war to an end. Marston Moor was not a knock-out blow. In Cornwall, the Battle of Lostwithiel (21 August to 2 September 1644) was as great a royalist victory and a humiliation for the Earl of Essex, who after days of fighting abandoned his men and his artillery by escaping in a fishing-boat. The Battle of Montgomery (17 September) was a parliamentary victory. But the sieges of Basing House (June to October) and Donnington Castle (July to October) failed. The Second Battle of Newbury (27 October) was inconclusive.

Charles I had learned enough to know he must engage in the talks at Uxbridge. He was never hopeful about their success. He was not asked to meet in the middle. He was asked to cede too much. By January 1644 he knew of Montrose's victories at Tippermuir and Aberdeen, and he knew that Montrose still had an army and was in the field, which made it even less likely that he would accept the peace. He did not yet know of the wasting of Argyll. It would have encouraged him further.

—◦⁄◦⁄◦—

To stay alive Montrose must move or fight – move *and* fight and move again. He could not rest. He had the legality of the king's commission on his side but was outlawed in Scotland. There was no retreat. Of his army only Alasdair's men were reliable because they could not get away easily.

In late January 1645, as he moved out of the heartland of Argyll, two armies were raised in Scotland against him. Ahead was the 5,000-strong force of the Earl of Seaforth who took a pro-covenant (or pro-Seaforth) position: 'consisting of the garrison of Inverness... and the strength of the shires of Murray, Ross, Sutherland and Caithess, and the clan of the Frasers'.

At first Montrose targeted this northern army, thinking new recruits would crumble when attacked by his battle-tempered men. His plan was to attack 5,000 with 1,500, the number left to him after desertions:[1] '...he made no difficulty to encounter Seaforth's disorderly army; for, though he knew that the Inverness garrison were veteran soldiers, yet the rest of the army were but levied men... altogether raw and unfit for service.'[2]

The other army was the Marquess of Argyll's. The great covenanter was wounded, materially poorer (after the devastation rents could not be paid), but not disabled. Argyll added his own highland levies to the 1,100 taken from Baillie. He was reported to have 3,000 infantry, so he also outnumbered Montrose. Again, he moved quickly. Before the end of January he was installed in Inverlochy Castle, near the present-day Fort William, thirty miles behind the royalists. They came to rest at Kilcumin, today's Fort Augustus, at the southern end of Loch Ness.

When he learned of the approach of Argyll's army, Montrose changed his mind. He decided to confront his primary enemy. He later told Charles I: 'I was willing to let the world see Argyll was not the man his highlandmen believed him to be, and that it was possible to beat him in his own highlands.'[3] If he could win that battle he would have trounced Argyll twice over.

Rather than march to Inverlochy by the obvious route, Montrose decided on a feint. If he backtracked along the Great Glen, the easy route, Montrose would be visible from miles away. Inverlochy Castle was a medieval building, partly ruined at this time, built on the south bank of the River Lochy to control the entrance to the Great Glen. It commanded a view. Instead, Montrose disappeared on 31 January 1645 by marching eastwards out of the Great Glen 'over the mountains'. It was high risk: 'If I had been attacked but with one hundred men in some of these passes, I must certainly have turned back, for it would have been impossible to force my way, most of the passes being so strait that three men could not march abreast.'[4]

His exact route is disputed. Probably it concluded with a march down Glen Roy, parallel to and east of the Great Glen, bringing the army down just north of Ben Nevis. It seems to have involved his men walking along flowing riverbeds and over snowbound highland plateaux. He needed the help of local countrymen as wilderness guides.[5] It continued to be very cold. It had become gusty. The two-day march required extreme endurance. Again, the men had little to eat.

In the early evening of 1 February his vanguard had Inverlochy Castle in sight. They were looking down from the east from the flanks of Ben Nevis, the summit to their south. To the men on watch they were unexpected and unknown. They seemed to be MacDonald scouts as at first they were few in number. The trek was hard. The army was strung out. It took time to mass. The worn-out royalists passed the night on the icy mountainside.

By the time the winter sun rose on 2 February – appearing about eight o'clock in the morning – the covenanters saw clearly. A considerable force was camped above them flying many banners; not scouts but the Marquess of Montrose. Because the castle was no longer a stronghold, the covenanters had to fight. They could not pack the fortress and hold him off. ,

In his personal galley Argyll removed himself from the battleground. With him came the committee that represented the government. When the Battle of Inverlochy was fought Argyll was safe on the waters of Loch Linhe – a spectator. He looked like a coward. The story was put out that he had dislocated his shoulder in a fall.

Montrose commanded 1,500 men, against perhaps 2,500 covenanting troops. For the first time he had the advantage in cavalry, having a small (50-strong) troop led by Sir Thomas Ogilvy, whereas the covenanters had none. The full strength of the covenanting army was reduced thanks to the way the troops had camped overnight: one contingent was still on the other side of the River Lochy when fighting started. It is agreed the covenanters had the numerical advantage even so. They also had urgent motivation: revenge for the dreadful damage just done by their traditional enemies.

Their commander was Sir Donald Campbell of Auchinbrech, called back from Ireland to support Argyll. He drew up his troops with about

1,500 in the centre in two bodies, all highlanders. Stationed ahead of the main force was a well-armed group of 500, thought to be Argyll's personal regiment. Behind these were 1,000 highlanders, Campbell levies, less well armed. On the wings were the lowlanders taken from Baillie, some 500 on each side.[6]

Montrose's deployment was similar. He split his army in four. The centre was all highlanders, with a reserve positioned behind, possibly to the right. On the left was a block of Irish troops. Thomas Ogilvy's cavalry troop seems to have been on the right wing.[7]

The Campbell front troops fired at long range upon the advancing royalists, wasting their shot. Then the royalists (under Montrose in the centre) fired at close quarter and smashed into them. The royalist infantry charge was very rapid, helped by running downhill. The covenanter army was positioned on a ridge, but the momentum was still with the royalists. The ferocity of the attack panicked the supporting troops on the Covenant side, the men behind the front regiment. They broke and ran. That meant their higher numbers were never used – which was perhaps the essence of the battle. A fast and violent charge broke the line and broke the spirit. It also seems the covenanters were quite tightly packed in a defensive formation, which limited their ability to move and fight.[8]

By this time the same thing had already happened on the royalist (Irish) left, which started the action: delaying musket fire until reaching close quarters then crashing through. Here, too, the speed of the attack was critical, allowing the enemy musketeers time only for one round of fire before fighting hand-to-hand. Thomas Ogilvy's horse, charging to the covenanting left, cut off a group trying to take refuge in Inverlochy Castle and forced them onto the open shore. In this action Ogilvy himself was severely wounded. The royalists had won in every part of the field.

——✿✿✿——

The Battle of Inverlochy was a third outright victory for Montrose. It made him the most successful general in all the British theatres of war. Nobody else had decisively won three battles in a row; nobody else had turned the tables in the way the Argyll campaign did. Although there was a difference of scale, in the size of the armies,[9] Montrose now compared with the great names of the German and Dutch wars – with Princes Maurice and Frederick Henry of Orange, with Count Tilly, even with Gustavus Adolphus and the extraordinary Wallenstein.

The next day Montrose wrote an account of the Battle of Inverlochy for Charles I.[10] He said that 'the rebels fought for some time with great bravery... as men that deserved to fight in a better cause.' He said the rout after the battle had gone on for nine miles with great slaughter, 1,500 dying on the covenant side. He explained he would have prevented that if he could, another indication of the general's partial control – he also understood that killing fellow Scots was a bad tactic. Montrose had taken prisoners where he could and, in his high-minded way, took their parole 'never to bear arms against your Majesty'. Though he kept a number to bargain with.

He told the king 200 royalists were wounded and only four dead! Perhaps it was true. There would be at least one more. Thomas Ogilvy would not survive his wounds. The letter ends:

Only give me leave, after I have reduced this country to your Majesty's obedience, and conquered from Dan to Beersheba, to say to your Majesty then, as David's general did to his master 'Come thou thyself, lest this country be called by my name.' For in all my actions I aim only at your Majesty's honour and interest, as becomes one that is to his last breath, may it please your Sacred Majesty, your Majesty's most humble, most faithful, and most obedient subject and servant, Montrose.

He also counselled his king against settling the English conflict by negotiation. His words must have been music to the royal ears:

The more your Majesty grants the more will be asked; and I have too much reason to know that they will not be satisfied with less than making your Majesty a King of straw... I must declare the horror I am in when I think of a treaty, while your Majesty and they are in the field with two armies, unless they disband and submit themselves entirely to your Majesty's goodness and pardon.

The king's goodness and pardon... In a way this exuberant letter goes to the heart of the matter. The eloquent prose should not be read as emotion run wild. Montrose expressed very clearly what he believed, that there was no compromise. Again and again he had seen the obstinacy of the presbyterian élite in action and could not trust them. He was generous to his sovereign. Was he right? Would Charles I in fact extend forgiveness to rebels?

Montrose was decisive, energetic, but war also confirmed in him the power of mercy. Had the king learned the same lesson? How merciful was the bruised heart of King Charles? History never allowed Montrose's judgement of his sovereign to be tested.

27

Night Marches

The letter reached Charles I on 19 February 1645. On 22 February the Uxbridge talks ended with no deal.

It was not Montrose's words that swung the balance. Charles I had been asked to give up all control of the army and the church, which he would not contemplate. Much earlier and more than once he said he could not accept the status of a Doge of Venice. But his Scottish champion's warning about a king of straw struck a chord.

Continued war in England meant continued war in Scotland.[1] With the wasting of Argyll and the defeat at Inverlochy the committee of estates stepped up. Regiments were recalled from England to defeat Montrose. The new commander William Baillie was a professional soldier who fought for years in Germany, then under Leven in England. In the New Year Baillie was joined by another professional Scottish officer, Sir John Hurry, as his cavalry commander. Hurry was also a German veteran. He had fought on both sides in England.

The General Assembly voted for reprisals, sending a group of ministers to ask the parliament for the execution of royalist prisoners in Edinburgh. These included Lord Ogilvy, the older Graham of Inchbrakie, the Earl of Crawford and the Reverend George Wishart. They all survived because more thoughtful men in government thought of the prisoners held by Montrose. It was not accepted practice to kill prisoners when a battle was won.

The Scottish parliament quickly endorsed the partial account of Inverlochy presented by their tarnished angel Argyll on 12 February 1645. He spoke with his arm tied in a sling to show his disability. He was commended by the parliament. The narrative changed again when Lord Balmerino next day said that Argyll had lost no more than thirty men in the battle, which hardly explained the outcome.

Sentences of forfeiture were voted against Montrose and others. Not only was he dispossessed of his material possessions but also of his titles and, if he were caught, of his life, without trial.

When he heard of the Battle of Inverlochy, the Earl of Seaforth made his peace with Montrose and retreated. His 5,000-strong army disbanded. Montrose's assessment of Seaforth was right. Turning back and fighting at Inverlochy was the correct decision, it was a greater victory against Argyll than it would have been against Seaforth (and it would have been a victory against him). Even better, Lord Gordon abandoned his uncle and declared for the king. Gordon, Seaforth and others subscribed to yet another bond drafted and signed by royalists earlier, when Montrose was at Kilcumin.

Gordon did not bring huge numbers with him – about 200 cavalry, together with his kinsman Nathaniel Gordon who returned to the royalists, also his younger brother Lord Lewis Gordon. Lewis was a fighting Gordon but was ungovernable. In 1640-1641 he left home (at about fifteen) having stolen his father's jewels to pay his way and gone to the United Provinces to start his own career.[2] Having created a horrific family rift, of which he appeared forever unheeding, he was back in Scotland before Montrose's campaigns.

Lord Gordon himself was much more than a trophy. First, he had fighting experience, second, as future Marquess of Huntly he could rally the Gordons if anyone could. It meant a lot that all the adult sons of Huntly were now declared royalists.[3] The third reason for the importance of Lord Gordon was that he commanded cavalry. If there were to be lowland victories, cavalry must be part of the army. Infantry could carry the day in country unsuited for massed troopers, whose mounts must get across the terrain and must feed, but in the lowlands Montrose needed real cavalry support – and to reduce Scotland for the king Montrose must take the fight to the southern lowlands. He would ideally descend on Edinburgh. Another 300 men came to Montrose with the Laird of Grant.

These meetings took place at Elgin, in Moray. Montrose arrived there on 19 February 1645. He allowed Grant to loot the town but not to burn it. The land of covenanting lairds in the area was wasted, more stores taken or destroyed, more hungry mouths the result. He tried to recruit but had little further success. He therefore moved south to the Gordon stronghold Bog O'Gight, arriving on 4 March.

Here his eldest son John fell ill and died, possibly from typhus. He was fourteen years old. It has been assumed the boy was exhausted from the Argyll campaign and assumed that Montrose took him along, that his collapse was the result.[4] If so, Montrose emerges as worse than blinkered. The challenges of Argyll were always exceptional, as he had himself argued. Yet John may not have been on that campaign. We know that in spring 1645 Montrose's second son, James, was at Old Montrose. Perhaps both children were safe in the lowlands throughout the winter.

The shock cannot have helped his relations with Magdalen. She is one of the mysteries of his life, an absence. After the earliest days of the marriage, she is forever unmentioned. There is no record of his trying to see or contact Magdalen at this time when their first child died young.[5]

———※———

Arriving empty-handed in Scotland the previous summer, Montrose's confidence was built on air. In early 1645 he was victorious, battle-hardened, determined. Before, he was confident he could win and he surprised the world. Now he knew it and everyone knew it. His opponents also changed. Under new command the covenanter troops in Scotland were quicker, more daring, selectiveThe new campaigning season would be a different kind of conflict.

Aberdeen returned to the fore. Montrose was sympathetic when at Turriff, he met emissaries from the city pleading the constant, always conflicting demands from both sides. Of all the Scottish towns Aberdeen had the worst of the Scottish civil war.

On 9 March Nathaniel Gordon rode in on a blustery day to receive the keys of the town. While he accepted the keys, the King's Lieutenant kept the feared Irish troops out of Aberdeen entirely. It was another gentleman's agreement. But boys will be boys. On 15 March Nathaniel and others returned to Aberdeen to have some fun, to drink, to indulge… It does not seem to have occurred to the young men that there were bound to be enemy sympathizers within the walls. They posted no guards.

> Hurry, whose horse were encamped at no great distance, learning that some of the principal cavaliers from the camp of Montrose were amusing themselves carelessly in Aberdeen, came down upon them in person with eight score of dragoons at his back and took them completely by surprise.[6]

By staying inside whichever tavern, Nathaniel survived, but Donald Farquharson, one of the better royalist captains, was cut down and killed in the street. Hurry took prisoners and precious horses. He then rode on to Old Montrose where he knew that James, the second son and now the heir of Montrose, was staying with his tutor. He took them both as prisoners to Edinburgh.

Through carelessness Montrose lost a good officer, hostages, some horses. One son died, the next was betrayed. Then his cousin Lord Airlie fell seriously ill and had to be sent to Strathbogie with a large armed escort who would stay with him as protection, which took men from the main army. All this within a month.

His campaign of destruction continued. He fired the Dunnottar estate around Stonehaven, a few miles south of Aberdeen, the property of the Earl Marischal (who was barricaded in the castle). 'The people of Stonehaven and Cowie came out, man and woman, children at their foot and children in their arms, crying, howling and weeping, praying the Earl (Marischal) for God's cause to save them from this fire... but the poor people got no answer'[7]

Montrose then marched south in the hope ultimately of meeting Charles I on the Borders. Although the meeting never happened, it was something the king himself wanted.[8] Baillie and Hurry could not ignore that risk. They wanted to pen the Scottish royalists in the north, to defeat them in detail. Baillie and Hurry flanked Montrose, moving with him within reach, always a threat, but never drawing up the lines. They were playing for time, to wear him down.

Montrose started with about the same infantry (3,000) as his opponents. He had 300 cavalry while Baillie/Hurry commanded 700. However, the Gordon element in his army was a two-edged sword. Not only were the haughty young men – most of all Lord Lewis – easy to offend and liable to disobey. The Huntly estates were always vulnerable to attack from ancient enemies (Frasers, Forbeses, Mackenzies), which could draw the Gordons off.

On 29-30 March the two armies camped on opposite banks of the River Isla, which flows into the Tay ten miles north of Perth. Neither could cross in the face of the other. Montrose offered Baillie safe passage provided he agreed to battle afterwards. Baillie declined. It was a game of raising and dashing expectations. Evidently there was nervousness on both sides. In fact, Montrose was the more vulnerable. A coalition of Gordon enemies was indeed assembling, so the Gordons wanted to leave and defend their own and Montrose allowed it. He was bound to – they would have gone anyway.

After the stand-off by the Isla, the armies lost sight of each other, but there was intelligence from scouts and other sources. Montrose marched to Dunkeld (west) while Baillie, the scouts said, turned and crossed the Tay to take up a position thirty miles south along the River Forth to block the fords. Baillie's move put pressure on Montrose, who had lost both momentum and part of his army. By the beginning of April, the royalists were roughly 2,000 strong. They were now outnumbered.

Montrose's overriding problem was that he had limited cash to pay the soldiers, except for the occasional 'donations' from towns. They had to live off the land and could only be rewarded with plunder.[9] To prevent desertions he had to do something.

The distance from Dunkeld to Dundee, going directly east (not via Perth) is about thirty miles. This was the route Montrose took overnight, arriving at Dundee in the morning of 4 April 1645. He had with him 600 infantry and 150 cavalry. It would have taken something like eight hours, the speed limited by being for half the time a night march. It could have taken longer. After that demanding exercise the royalists invested and entered 'the disloyal town of Dundee'. The attack started not long after ten o'clock in the morning. The royalists rested some hours before the action. They broke through both the West Port and North Port. Street fighting followed. 'The Irish burnt the west part of the town, but the inhabitants from within killed divers of their men.'[10]

It was not until the afternoon that the royalists had real control of Dundee. Some buildings were fired and '… had not the common men, by an unseasonable greed of plunder and desire of strong liquors, immediately fallen to pillage and drink, this opulent town had undoubtedly been soon burnt to the ground.'[11] Given the hard fighting which took up the morning, 'soon' was not really the word, nonetheless Montrose's men did eventually get their hands on what they were after. There was time for many to get drunk.

But time was quickly up when the lookouts saw men approaching from the west, following Montrose's tracks. These were cavalry coming as vanguard. A large army was a few miles away and closing fast. Baillie had not gone south after all. Possibly he had detached some troops who crossed the Tay as reported, or it was false intelligence. As he approached Dundee, Baillie had effectively his entire force with him, five times the men under Montrose's command.

The only option was escape but how? So bad was the situation that some in the rapid council of war advised the King's Lieutenant to save himself and forget the men (others advised suicidal resistance). Montrose asserted himself in quite a different way. Against impossible odds he decided to get his people out.

Hundreds of men milled around Dundee, worn out, many drunk, most disorderly, some panicked. Montrose and his officers collected them and marched them out of the East Port at the same time as Baillie entered the West Port. The royalists left Dundee marching to the east. They found themselves on the road running parallel with the coast, which lay on their right-hand side. If safety could be found it would be in the high ground twenty to thirty miles north and west, that is to say behind them and to their left.

The very difficult exit from Dundee was the easy part. Montrose must now keep ahead and put enough distance between his men and the enemy to exit the coastal lowlands. Everything was against him except the exceptional physical condition of the soldiers and the time of day. And the methodical conservatism of Baillie helped. He waited at Dundee for his infantry to catch up with the cavalry. Pursuit was delayed. Baillie's men were also tired. He had just put them through a forced twenty-mile march to save Dundee. By the time Baillie sent Hurry after Montrose it was evening.

The covenanting cavalry caught up with the royalists but were repeatedly beaten off. In a reversal of normal deployment, the men in worse (drunken) condition were marching at the front of the column, while the men at the back were alert. The cavalry, too, were at the rear, led by Montrose himself, who took on the personal risk. He deployed his men in ranks spaced very wide, so that musketeers could take up positions among them (remembering the lessons of Angers).

> ... the foremost of the [covenanting] horse were up with his rear; but these excellent musketeers, who were mixed with his horse, brought down three of the most forward, one after another; and the rest becoming more cautious by their fate, they slackened.[12]

As darkness fell, Hurry withdrew his men some distance.

The first pursuit was only that. While Hurry chased the royalists with his cavalry, in his methodical way Baillie marched due north out of Dundee to cover the ground that Montrose needed to cross if he were to reach the hills. If he could not make his own successful attack, Hurry would drive the royalists into the jaws of Baillie's infantry.

But Montrose turned north off the main road in the middle of the night. He wanted to rejoin the other part of his army, which he had sent to Brechin (twenty-five miles north) two days before. In fact, it seems he sent cavalry messengers ahead because these men left Brechin and made for the hills before he reached them.

In the dark the royalists passed Baillie's large force at Forfar. To reach high ground Montrose had to continue marching north. He did it undetected. He escaped the notice of Baillie's scouts and reached Careston Castle, a couple of miles west of Brechin and eight miles north-east of Forfar. He was now within a few miles of security – but the men were shattered and he had to rest them.

As amazing, the royalists had escaped the still pursuing Hurry. He, too, was leading tired men and horses and evidently fell some way back. It was still a feat of command that Montrose gave the slip to the covenanting cavalry, who continued on the coastal road up to Arbroath before realising their mistake. He eluded them again after they raced ahead to block the way at Friockheim, just to the east of Forfar. The much larger forces of Baillie and Hurry, only a few miles apart at this stage, should have created an unbreachable barrier. Admittedly Montrose had fewer men, but his group, allowing for losses in Dundee, was still 700, hardly a band to creep in total silence. All these were night manoeuvres, which makes the adventure the more remarkable. His men kept going through two night marches running.

Was local knowledge Montrose's secret? Some commentators have failed to observe that the countryside here would be familiar. Kinnaird Castle, the home of his early married life, is just outside Brechin. He had three years to learn the lie of the land. He would know the geography inside out.

There was a final rush when Hurry's cavalry approached Careston in daylight. One last heroic effort roused the exhausted royalists. Again, Montrose made an orderly retreat, the last few miles to the hills. Hurry snapped at his heels, there was a skirmish at Edzell, but he could not break through. He made no attempt to follow the royalists onto the high ground.

28

Auldearn

While the retreat from Dundee was very greatly admired by other generals – those who knew what military command was really like, who understood night-time operations, and the morale of men on the run – it was indeed a retreat, not a 'strategic withdrawal', the label attached to the retreat from Mons in 1914. The covenanters exaggerated Montrose's losses. Although they quarrelled about the escape of the royalists – Hurry was blamed – Baillie and Hurry enjoyed the faint scent of success.

Reconstituted in the highlands, the royalist army amounted to some 2,000, not enough to take on Baillie. At the end of the first week of April 1645 Montrose split his forces in order to recruit. Patrick Graham was sent to Atholl, Alasdair MacDonald to the Cairngorms, Lord Gordon to his Aberdeenshire base. In command of 500 infantry and 50 horse, Montrose went in search of Viscount Aboyne who had broken out of Carlisle and was back in Scotland.

Montrose thought that Charles I would send reinforcements from England. He needed to be closer to south Scotland to rendezvous with the expected 500 royal cavalry. With his mobile band of men, Montrose disappeared into the hills in the second week of April. He emerged a few days later in the woods near Crieff, fifteen miles west of Perth. That was another of his rapid marches, covering sixty-five miles undetected.

However, Baillie was very nearby, in Perth itself, and learned of Montrose's arrival. He marched overnight on Crieff. This time, Montrose's scouts were well posted. Warned of the enemy approach Montrose safely conducted another retreat, until he reached and occupied a pass into the hills. The covenanting cavalry could not force so strong a position. They turned back.

On 19 April, Aboyne and other Carlisle fugitives joined Montrose at Balquhidder[1] twenty miles west of Crieff. Aboyne was injured, having dislocated his shoulder in a fall, but functioning. Probably the same day, Montrose was also joined by his nephew Archibald, Master of Napier, who had escaped from house arrest (which would cost his father, Lord Napier, a large fine). It was heartening but it was not 500 royal cavalry. Increasingly top-heavy with officers, the royalists travelled south-west to Loch Katrine looking for those precious reinforcements in vain.

In a letter to Charles I Montrose expressed his disappointment: 'I have continued things this half year bygone without the assistance of either men, arms, ammunition, or that which is the nerves of war... though you have not assisted me, I will yet still do my best to bar all assistance coming against you.'[2] This letter was intercepted and the messenger hanged.

It was cheering for the committee of estates. They saw that Montrose should be kept as far north as possible to stop the king from joining forces with him. They could hope his morale and supplies were low. Sir John Hurry had already arrived in Aberdeen (on 11 April, before Montrose arrived at Crieff). He came with only 160 cavalry.[3] There he was delayed because one regiment mutinied in protest at the preferential treatment given another. Having settled this, Hurry marched north on 19 April to meet the covenanting lords. Hurry was sent to face down the Gordons, always at the centre of the struggle. But this was the same as threatening Montrose himself who, again moving fast, returned to the north to protect his allies.

The depression expressed in his letter to Charles I notwithstanding, the King's Lieutenant was upbeat when he met his own lieutenants, all of whom had raised men. The royalist strength was recovered and the fact that Baillie and the main covenanter army remained at Perth provided him with a plan: he only had Hurry to confront. Thanks to Aboyne, who conducted a raid on Aberdeen, he had new supplies of gunpowder.

By the end of April both sides were growing in confidence. On the covenant side, Baillie had driven Montrose back north, and Hurry's diplomacy was a success. He raised troops from the northern covenanters who would combine with the Inverness garrison, all trained men. Hurry built an army very quickly. If he had not been delayed in Aberdeen, he would have been in the field well before Montrose's return.

Royalist recruitment worked, too. Alasdair Macdonald, Patrick Graham and Lord Gordon all came back with fresh troops. When at Skene in late April 1645 Montrose met with all three, he was leading an army of more than 2,000. It was not enough to beat Baillie and Hurry combined, but it was enough for the north. And after Montrose had gathered in Viscount Aboyne, the three adult sons of Huntly were with him.

There was guerrilla activity against the Gordons by the covenanters, which included an atrocity, the murder of the wounded James Gordon of Rhynie (aged eighteen), as he recuperated in bed. This happened in early May and was a rallying cry to the Gordons.

Both sides wanted to fight it out. Both needed to.

The prelude to the Battle of Auldearn[4] was another chase with roles reversed. This time it was the covenanter Hurry who retreated parallel to the Moray Firth coast, from Elgin through Forres and Cawdor, in the direction of Inverness, where reinforcements waited. In pursuit Montrose found himself on the receiving end of a skilful rearguard. At this point he commanded more men than Hurry, but could not break the discipline of Hurry's army.

South of Nairn, he broke off. The closer to Inverness, the better his opponents' chances. If Hurry could collect the Inverness garrison the numbers would change, Hurry would then have the larger army. Because the garrison consisted of seasoned professionals, Hurry's army would also be of higher quality.

On the night of 8 May 1645, the royalist army camped near the village of Auldearn, south of Nairn. We do not know quite how Montrose saw things when he ordered this break. He must have assumed Hurry was still on his well-ordered march to Inverness, with another twenty miles to go. If he was right, then Hurry would have to march over forty miles before catching up with the royalists, much more than a night's work. He would have to reach Inverness, rendezvous with the garrison, march back. Pace could be forced but a hard march would need the men to rest afterwards for perhaps a couple of hours or more. That was a false assumption. Hurry did not go anything like the whole distance: he summoned the garrison to meet him near Cawdor, which gave him plenty of extra time.[5] He was a good eight or ten hours ahead.

The same night Hurry met his reinforcements, the Inverness garrison and northern levies, which gave him the advantage, he quickly reversed course and marched back to surprise the royalists, who thought the enemy too distant to worry about. In this manoeuvre, a night march in driving rain, Hurry showed gritty professionalism. He was a more experienced officer than Montrose.

Before dawn in the morning of 9 May the covenanting army came close to the royalists. They were four or five miles away before anyone noticed. Because it was wet, Hurry ordered his men to clear their muskets of damp charges. Not all his firepower was musketry. A significant body of covenanter highlanders was armed with bows and arrows. But the musketeers must be ready when battle was joined. Wet weather was potentially disastrous for muskets.

Hurry's army left the main road, marching towards the sea for cover. In order to keep momentum he ordered the men simply to fire and reload. The crash of the discharge was heard by scouts sent out first thing by Alasdair Macdonald. If Alasdair had not tried to remedy the situation the moment he was up, the royalists would have faced a surprise attack unprepared.

As it was, they had something like forty-five minutes' notice. The other difficulty was that Montrose's army had camped 'commodiously,' some of the men in Auldearn village, many on the ground to the east. The village was small, the weather bad, they found what shelter they could in barns and cottages. They spread out. When the Battle of Auldearn began, the royalists were scrambling to deploy (and never did really deploy in the normal sense).

Action started about eight o'clock in the morning. Hurry had 3,000 men under his command of whom a maximum of 300 were cavalry. Montrose had 2,000 of whom 600 were cavalry commanded by the two Gordon brothers, Lords Gordon and Aboyne. The numbers overall gave a huge advantage to Hurry, but only half his men were really experienced soldiers. The balance of battle-hardened troops was probably equal between the sides, while Alasdair's Irish and Hebridean Scots were unusually tough. It seems that some of Montrose's recent recruits either did not take part or had not actually joined the army. Hurry may have been distracted, rather than supported, by the presence of the Earls of Sutherland and Seaforth (who provided his northern levies).

Hurry rushed across country to surprise the royalists and could not properly reconnoitre.[6] He took up a position on the low rise of Garlic Hill to the west of Auldearn, which seemed as commanding a position as was available. Yet the ground at the bottom of the hill was marshy, which would be a problem for troops coming down to fight. Because he insisted on using Garlic Hill, his numbers did not count as much as they ought to have. In the battle neither side formed a battle line, so superior numbers were not brought to bear in the way a classic deployment would have permitted. The covenanting army, arriving from the west, came onto the hill regiment by regiment, it never spread out. Neither side had artillery. Hurry may have left his behind so as to move more quickly. So the battle took place eccentrically, as it were. No artillery barrage, no lines drawn up, just a series of extremely hard-fought encounters.

Alasdair MacDonald advanced to meet the covenanters while they were still to the west of Garlic Hill, which blocked their view of the village. With as many men as he could summon, mainly his own Hebridean highlanders who had been quartered in the village itself, he moved to the top of the hill to be met by the discouraging sight of the larger army on the other side.

Hurry sent both cavalry and infantry against the challenge. The infantry were probably Sir Mungo Campbell of Lawer's veterans from Ireland, who had a particular hatred of Catholic opponents. There was a long fight on Garlic Hill in which several successive standard bearers on the royalist side were killed. Force of numbers pushed Alasdair back down towards Auldearn.

Because Hurry held his main army back, Alasdair was able to break contact and take up a new position in the backyards of the village. What Hurry did made perfect sense, but a fully manned pursuit might have been better. The marshy ground and the lie of the land made this part of the battleground hard to cross. It was not obvious from Garlic Hill, but the houses and enclosures of Auldearn village were sited higher than the marshy ground up a steep slope.

When the covenanter infantry reached the marshy ground, their advance was therefore checked. They could not scale the slope against the vigorous defence. Part of this was raking musket fire that hit them from the left. On nearby Castle Hill – higher than Garlic Hill – Nathaniel Gordon was directing Monymore's regiment in a superb contribution to what was now a holding action. Castle Hill was easy to defend itself and perfectly positioned on the flank of the attacking covenanters.

Despite having fewer troops than his opponents, Alasdair's position was very strong. With relatively few men Alasdair stood his ground so well that he decided to counter-attack. This was about eleven o'clock in the morning. At once he ran into difficulty crossing the marshy ground, 'all quagmire and bushes'. Nonetheless some of his men advanced up the hill. There was then a second assault by the covenanters, this time with two infantry regiments, the first Sir Mungo Lawers' and behind them the highlander bowmen who shot volleys into the air over the heads of their advancing colleagues. This time it was a successful advance.

The covenanters drove the royalists back into the village and succeeded in scaling the slope and advancing into the backyards. They were pikemen supported by musketeers. The fighting was intense, both on the hill and in the village. Alasdair broke one or maybe two swords hacking at pikes stuck in his shield, was rescued by his brother-in-law who gave him his, and was then promptly cut down.

Although the exceptional quality of the royalist troops, supported by the musketeers on Castle Hill, held the ground to begin with, they were facing determined opponents backed by more regiments. To Alasdair the 'symptoms of a disastrous and dreadful overthrow' were evident. He urged the men fighting round him to die bravely. It was now about one o'clock in the afternoon. So far, there had been no support from the rest of the royalist army, which Montrose was desperately trying to organize.

The fact that it took Montrose so long to do this suggests something more than their dispersal overnight. He also had to work out how best to intervene, not easy because sightlines were obscured by the fight itself, including musket smoke, on a dull day. But he did rally other royalists. What he could see was that that Hurry's army was literally stacked up on Garlic Hill, prevented by the terrain from doing anything except advance slowly behind the two hard-working infantry regiments who had been fighting for hours and were apparently about to win the battle alone. It was clearly a unitary advance by the covenanters with no attempt at attacking from the flanks. Montrose saw the opportunity, divided his men into two units, sending one around the village to the north, the other around the village to the south.

His counter-attack came just in time and was devastating. First, from the south Aboyne led a cavalry charge into the right flank of the covenanting infantry. They were covered by a cavalry troop which wheeled away in terror, trampling their own side. The Gordon cavalry slammed into the men and took several colours. On the point of taking Auldearn, Sir Mungo Campbell now ordered a retreat up Garlic Hill, which must have been a slow process because of the marsh.

The second cavalry attack then hit him from the north, led by Lord Gordon 'with swords only', not bothering with pistol fire. He similarly put the covering cavalry on that side to flight, then attacked the infantry. In this way the greater number of royalist cavalry combined with Gordon spirit turned the battle around.

Montrose was still on the southern side of the village. He was at the head of a completely fresh infantry body consisting of the professional Strathbogie regiment and the Irish troops of Alasdair under Colonel McDonnell, about 600 men ready to fight. All were highly experienced. He ordered an advance up Garlic Hill where in the crisis of the battle the covenanters were suddenly desperate. There was prolonged fighting with musket, pike and sword, which ended with the retreat of Hurry to the west. With that Montrose won his fourth victory. Leading some truly formidable troops, Hurry should have won, but he failed to use his numbers.

Casualties of the Battle of Auldearn are variously recorded. Each side may have lost 600-700 in the battle, killed and badly wounded, although mythologizing royalist sources indicate Montrose's losses in the improbable tens. Although much was exaggerated after the battle, the covenanters must have lost more because many would have died in the rout. Perhaps in total they lost as many as 1,000 as was reported (higher figures were also given). Among their officers Sir Mungo Campbell of Lawers died. The fighting came to end as dusk fell. It was a very long, exhausting struggle, which left the committee of estates without a northern army and reinforced the legend of the Marquess of Montrose.

Sixteen colours were taken and 'much money and riches'. What was not paid out to the men was stored in Blair Castle.[7]

That was four battles fought and four battles won by the King's Lieutenant in Scotland, but there was no political conclusion. Baillie's army was intact. Leven's army was intact, still in the north of England, but a Scottish army that could come back. Charles I was still in the field in England but had not been able to supply Montrose, nor join him.

In England, Oliver Cromwell's New Model military drill, his meritocratic attitude to army appointments, his willpower, his faith in God and himself and his success at Marston Moor made him the coming man on the parliamentary side. He wanted to defeat the king first, and second he wanted a tolerant Protestant settlement. If Charles I had more insight, if he had been a flexible politician, he might have seen that Cromwell and the Independents were opening a rift with the presbyterian Scots, but he did not.

Montrose probably understood little of England. When his thoughts strayed from the endless demands of the campaign, he must have worried about the members of his family in danger from the vindictive committee of estates and from plague. There was a bad outbreak in Edinburgh and Leith (probably typhus, spread by fleas, lice and mites). Anyone in close confinement was especially at risk.

Lord Napier was put under full arrest along with Sir George Stirling of Keir on 21 April 1645. His daughter-in-law and his daughter were taken in for questioning. All were held in Edinburgh Castle. Another member of the Napier family, John Napier of Easter Torres, had also been arrested as a royalist courier, a charge for which others had been executed.

Harry Graham, Montrose's half-brother, was in Edinburgh Castle. Montrose's eldest surviving son James was there. His youngest, Robert (about seven years old), was treated more leniently. With Montrose's father-in-law, Southesk, the child was put in front of the committee of estates (19 April) but was permitted after that to live with his mother Magdalen.[8]

Robert's delivery to his mother 'exonerated' his grandfather. Was she living independently of Southesk? Magdalen was not herself in trouble with the government, but her husband was dispossessed of land and titles as an enemy of the state, her eldest son had just died and her second son was in prison. 'When sorrows come...'

29

Victory in the North

The committee of estates wrote to Baillie, criticising him for not pursuing Montrose hard enough. He had in fact moved quickly north after the news of Auldearn (and was rejoined by Hurry).

There was more actionless confrontation between the two sides at Strathbogie, which led to another pursuit of the royalists by the covenanters. Montrose led his men away by night to Balveny, then to Badenoch holding a pass in the hills. Baillie followed energetically enough, but it was too strong a position to attack. Eventually, Baillie had to retreat to provision his men. They had eaten nothing for two days.

Montrose did not want to fight Baillie then and there, but he wanted more success. The covenanter Earl of Crawford-Lindsay[1] was in command of three newly raised regiments, currently at Newtyle of Angus, eleven miles north of Dundee. New recruits were a soft target.

The royalists marched south through the highland country to pounce, but Alasdair MacDonald at this point left to recruit in the west, taking with him a number of his men (incidentally showing the damage of Auldearn). At the same time, or shortly before, the Gordons left the army, again to protect their homes in Aberdeenshire from Baillie. That put paid to plans of attack.

The next two or three weeks were spent trying to bring the Gordons back, with some disagreement between the brothers Lords Gordon and Aboyne but ultimately with reasonable success. Montrose was now camped at Corgarff Castle, safely in the hills twenty miles due west of Aberdeen. It was a lot of manoeuvring since Auldearn and nothing achieved.

Meanwhile, the committee of estates ordered Baillie to hand over 1,200 veteran troops to Crawford-Lindsay who in return gave him 400 new recruits. With his improved army Crawford-Lindsay set off for Atholl, which he wasted, but he did not take Blair Castle.

With his reduced army Baillie threatened Bog O' Gight; a good move, as it brought Montrose out of the hills. At Keith the two armies confronted each other but there was no battle. Montrose marched away, trying to draw Baillie into a more vulnerable position.

Baillie now knew that Montrose's Irish component was much reduced, that Alasdair was away in the west. Because the Irish were especially feared, Alasdair's absence was an opportunity. Baillie therefore followed with alacrity. There was another confrontation at the foot of the Coreen Hills but again no action. The royalists moved away and contact was lost.

On 1 July 1645 Montrose ordered a halt outside Alford, a small village just south of the River Don, ten miles west of Aberdeen. He stayed overnight at Asloon Castle. On 2 July he awoke to fight his fifth battle.

Montrose took up a position early in the morning on Gallows Hill outside Alford, his rear protected by a marsh. Accounts vary but it is likely (from ballad 'evidence')[2] that Baillie approached from the east, having marched south not down the main road, the Suie Road, which Montrose had used, but on a parallel track to the east. That would be a more thoughtful approach, crossing the Don downriver of the obvious ford.

After the battle Baillie said he had been outnumbered, but probably he had the advantage with about 2,800 troops, of whom 380 were cavalry. Montrose had something like 2,300 men of whom 500 were cavalry. Both sides were drawn up this time in a regular battle line, infantry in the middle, cavalry on the flanks. Baillie deployed his men three deep because he was worried about being outflanked. He had no reserve, while Montrose had a reserve behind his main force commanded by Archibald Napier.

At first it looked as though there would be a third stand-off. Neither general was at his most confident, but the covenanter Lord Balcarres evidently was. His cavalry were veterans of Marston Moor. Lord Gordon on the royalist right wing, and Balcarres on the covenanting left, engaged first with an exchange of fire and then, probably moving at a trot to start with, clashing and locking together.[3] The two sides pushed against each other in a contest of will and strength. There was no room to draw swords and swing them. The men urged their mounts on, some clubbing the enemy with their pistols. If the line broke, then the riders could be shot at, slashed and, should infantry arrive, speared. The moment the tight-packed body broke, the killing would begin. Until then it was hard shoving.

When Balcarres's second squadron under William Forbes of Craigievar joined on the covenant side by adding its weight at the back of the first squadron, it looked as though the royalists would collapse, but Colonel Laghtnan ordered his infantry, the remaining Irish, to attack the covenant horse (which were virtually stationary) with sword and dirk. Thanks to Nathaniel Gordon, that turned into an attack on the horses themselves, hacking at their legs to hamstring them. On the other wing, Aboyne's for the royalists, Sir James Halkett's for the covenant, the two forces kept apart, although they exchanged fire.

In the Gordon/Balcarres struggle the Irish infantry attack on the animals succeeded in panicking the covenanting cavalry. After ten or twelve horses had been lamed, their riders presumably then being savagely dispatched, the cavalry withdrew. With no enemy reserve to stop him, Gordon then led his men around the back of the covenanter infantry. That was an unusual manoeuvre that doubled the odds against the other covenanter flank and meant their infantry in the centre were surrounded.

Gordon first attacked the covenanter cavalry on that wing, which broke; then he turned to savage their infantry, who had also been engaging with the royalist infantry directly opposite. For this bravado Lord Gordon paid with his life, shot, it was said, in the back.

The double attack snapped the resolve of Baillie's infantry. They broke and ran. The Gordon cavalry had decided the Battle of Auldearn, but Alford was even more of a cavalry battle, the first such in the Scottish civil wars. Nonetheless, there was also a meaningful infantry struggle. We do not have an accurate idea of the time scale. The cavalry push on the royalist right was not a rapid action and the infantry struggle in the centre was similarly hard fought. Perhaps it was two or three hours of fighting. In the end, the royalists held the field. Baillie had lost.

This was Montrose's fifth victory running, achieved without the galvanising presence of Alasdair MacDonald, although partly due to the remaining Irish troops and their leadership by Laghtnan. Casualties are not clear. Conservative estimates are 300 dead on the covenant side, and perhaps 100 among the royalists. There were two heavy qualifiers to this success.

The loss of Lord Gordon had a deep effect on Montrose: 'He could not command his grief, but mourned bitterly over the fate of his only and dearest friend.'[4] The bond between the two men, who had known each other less than six months, was intense. A man who knew them both wrote 'So real was his (Gordon's) affection and so great the estimation he had for the other (Montrose) that, when they fell in to any familiar discourse, it was often remarked that the ordinary air of his countenance was changed from a serious listening to a certain ravishment or admiration of the other's witty expressions.'[5] (This mutual affection must have made the position of the younger brother, Aboyne, difficult. He had known Montrose earlier and had always been loyal to the king but was less loved.)

The second overshadowing event was the defeat two weeks before Alford of King Charles in England at the Battle of Naseby (14 June 1645). Like Marston Moor, like Lostwithiel, the scale of this battle was much greater than anything in Scotland. Although exact numbers are not known, it was something between 20,000 and 25,000 men who fought at Naseby in Northamptonshire. The action did not at a stroke end the first English Civil War, but it destroyed Charles I's Oxford army, so it was the beginning of the end. His stores and artillery were captured, with his private papers, which gave parliament exceptional propaganda material. Military action did not stop in England in June 1645, but the question increasingly was, where was the political solution?

Immediately after Naseby came an attack on women. Charles I left the battlefield at about midday, with the cavalry troops left to him. Royalist camp followers, mainly women, tried to get away, walking north to the next village, East Farndon, hoping to reach the royalist garrison at Leicester. Pursuing parliamentary cavalry overtook them in Farndon Field near the village and attacked them with their swords. At least 100 women were killed. Many of the survivors were disfigured by cuts to the face.[6] An unprovoked attack on non-combatants was no part of any code of war. It has to be explained.

On the parliamentary side there was a widespread belief, fuelled by pamphlets, that the cavalier army was debauched: the camp followers were therefore whores. In fact, many would have been wives of officers and soldiers, there would be cooks, laundresses and so forth. There would also be prostitutes but there is no reason to think they predominated. Nonetheless it seems the women slashed in the face were considered whores who must be marked.[7] Then there those who died.

They were mainly Welsh. There were Welsh soldiers in the king's army accompanied by their Welsh wives. English parliamentary soldiers did not distinguish Welsh language from Irish (and probably did not distinguish the two nations). There may also have been some Irish women on Farndon Field but the point is the confusion of the two. Parliamentarians were not going to smile upon Welsh camp followers, but the Irish were she-demons. It was an old fear, or contempt, recently revived. The Irish rebellion of 1641 had terrified the English. Stories of atrocities against English settlers included atrocities committed by women. Apparently, armed with long knives called skeins, Irish women habitually cut the throats of wounded English soldiers. Being with the royalist army in England, they threatened law-abiding English in Kingston-upon-Thames with death.

Pamphlet writers worked up their material to make the women of Ireland murderous furies who must be struck down before they attacked.

Other factors were perhaps a belief that the royalist army was supported by witches. Another element was revenge. After the Battle of Lostwithiel the previous year, parliamentary women had been attacked.[8]

—⌁⌁⌁—

After Alford, Alasdair MacDonald came back from the west with substantial reinforcements. Aboyne had also been sent to recruit in Aberdeenshire but was slow to return. Without more cavalry Montrose could not risk a move away from the hills. But he must keep moving, he must show fighting spirit. Highlanders needed the inspiration of action.

He had 100 cavalry until Aboyne rejoined him. That compared with Hurry's 400, who now protected Perth, where a parliament was to meet on 24 July (away from the plague). Montrose could not challenge Hurry. He could not fight. But he could tease.

He mounted musketeers on baggage ponies to fill out the numbers, set them to ride with his real cavalry, and put on a show at a distance, just as Alexander Leslie had created his 1639 illusion at Kelso. For a time, this kept the covenanting cavalry within the walls until the scouts worked it out, and Baillie marched out of Perth to attack the royalist camp at Methven Wood.

Montrose beat a retreat to Dunkeld, leaving the camp to the covenanters. Here '...having gained no credit by this expedition... and because they could not cope with men, therefore exercising their impotent rage on women, and shamefully butchering such of the wives of the Highlanders and Irish who followed the army as fell into their hands,'[9] the godly soldiers repeated the experiment of Farndon Field.

Two comments can be made. First, the men who had just fought at Naseby had their blood up and were desensitized by battle. That excuses nothing but nonetheless mentally they were in fight mode. The slaughter in Methven Wood was cold-blooded. Second, there was no confusion about nationality in Scotland. The women were most certainly either Irish or highland and Hebridean Scots. By killing them the covenanters showed a pitiless contempt for papist foreigners based on fear.

This was the weakness of Montrose's position. Although he held the king's commission, Montrose could not campaign without the Irish and Hebridean Scots. He led an invading army. We know that Baillie had problems with his men after Auldearn, because a number wanted to support the king.[10] But the majority support for the covenant in almost all lowland Scotland shows people might fear, and could not trust, the man who led Catholic barbarians.

30

His Biggest Army

Montrose told Charles I he would reduce Scotland to obedience. That was a sound bite, not a war aim. We may think reducing Scotland to obedience meant changing the government (which needed support from parliament), pacifying the nobility, satisfying (disciplining?) the Kirk, disabling Argyll. It meant at least one other battle that he must win (in south Scotland), then a constitutional settlement against the new vested interests. And more. Thanks to Naseby, by late summer 1645 Montrose's challenge had just expanded to an English campaign. Only a Scottish army could win the king's cause now.

There is not the smallest indication that he was taken aback by these realities.

Before the episode at Perth, Alasdair MacDonald returned with recruits from the western highlands. He brought welcome reinforcements, but they were infantry. Aboyne did not return until a week after the massacre of Methven Wood. He had with him something like 350 men, of whom 120 were dragoons, which is to say mounted infantry – not experienced cavalry. Gordon infantry followed later.[1] The Earl of Airlie, aged nearly sixty, also returned to the royalist army. With him were other Ogilvies and 80 cavaliers.

These were reasons for cheer. Montrose's new force was 4,400 infantry and 500 cavalry, his biggest army yet. It created its own momentum, a lot of mouths to feed, a lot of men to satisfy. Having brought the men together he had started the ball rolling. He could only provide for them through war: he could not fight without an army, and once he had an army its existence obliged him to fight, or the ground would disappear from beneath his feet.

Baillie was waiting in Bridge of Earn, due south of Perth, for three new regiments from Fifeshire and highlanders from Argyllshire. The Scottish government was efficient at raising money. His difficulty was not how to pay the men, or at least it was not a particular difficulty. Baillie's particular difficulty was political interference. Nominally, he was commander, but the committee of estates took decisions, for instance about exchange of prisoners, without asking for his opinion. He was not autonomous and was sometimes ignored.

After Alford, Baillie tried to resign his commission. He was persuaded to stay by a vote of confidence from the Perth parliament. Nonetheless, he could not campaign as he wished. A new committee was appointed to supervise him, including the Marquess of Argyll, Lord Balfour of Burleigh, Lord Elcho, all of whom Montrose had beaten in battle, also the Earl of Crawford-Lindsay.

Montrose offered battle at Bridge of Earn. Baillie refused. Montrose marched on to Kinross, then west to Stirling, a place to avoid because it was 'consumed by pestilence'.[2] The army crossed the Forth north-west of Stirling at the Fords of Frew. That was the main geographical barrier to the southern lowlands. This was the furthest south Montrose had yet led an army.

On 14 August 1645 the royalists camped on high meadows a mile outside the village of Kilsyth in north Lanarkshire. Kilsyth lies fifteen miles north-east of Glasgow and is forty miles due west of Edinburgh. Montrose was now within easy reach of the major cities.

Less happily, he was positioned between two covenanting forces. Having received his reinforcements, Baillie was in pursuit. In Clydesdale, to Montrose's west, the Earl of Lanark was raising troops. As usual the trick was to stop the two enemy armies combining. The Lennox was wild country close at hand, but it provided less cover than the highlands proper. If things went wrong, Montrose would be caught in a trap of his own making.

During this journey south the paradoxes of war continued. Before reaching Stirling, the royalists marched through Campbell possessions centred on the fortress called Castle Campbell but known as Castle Gloom. This building with its land was wasted by the Macleans, Campbell enemies. In the neighbouring estate of the Earl of Mar, the Macdonalds similarly laid waste while the earl and his family entertained Montrose, Airlie and others to a feast in their castle.[3]

When he arrived in the area with Baillie's army, the Marquess of Argyll took his revenge by destroying the Earl of Stirling's house and a Graham property there. He sent a letter to Mar telling him to expect retribution.

General Baillie lacked Leven's ability to manage noblemen. It is not clear whether he knew that Lanark was relatively nearby with his levies, according to one account only twelve miles away by the morning of 15

August (the Catholic feast of the Assumption). Whatever Baillie knew, he did not wait for Lanark, who had raised 1,500 men. The sources tell us the reason was the supervising committee. They insisted on Baillie engaging with Montrose then and there.[4] We read they even dictated the initiating tactics.

In the coming battle the covenanters had a slight advantage, just short of 4,000 men of whom nearly 400 were cavalry. Their Fife levies were 1,200 of the infantry and untried, but the others were battle-hardened. Montrose had the cavalry advantage with 460 regular cavalry troopers under Aboyne, Airlie and Nathaniel Gordon, and in addition 220 dragoons. There were a little over 3,000 royalist infantry (of which 1,400 came from the highland levies and 620 were Irish). So Montrose had an army of nearly 3,700.

The 15th of August 1645 was a very hot day. Montrose '...ordered all his men, both horse and foot, to throw off their upper clothes and fight stripped to their shirts; which they cheerfully and readily obeyed.'[5] He drew them up in line facing the road.

But Baillie marched to Kilsyth across country. So Montrose's deployment on the meadow was wrong. Baillie came from the east and occupied a ridge that looked down on the meadow. He was placed to turn Montrose's left flank. Rather than Montrose rushing down onto the road to attack the advancing Baillie, he found a large army on his left-hand side. The difficulty for Baillie was that the ground was uneven and, in August, overgrown.

The big decision now taken by Baillie, probably forced on him by the committee, was to continue the flanking movement by occupying the hill which lay to his right, to the north, where there was a farm, or farm buildings, barns and enclosures, called Auchinviroch. If he could do that the royalists would be very poorly placed because Auchinviroch was behind them. They would face two bodies of enemy on higher ground and could be attacked from two directions.

It was not in Montrose's power to redeploy his whole army now that he could see, or partially see, where the enemy were. Because a substantial part of Baillie's army was behind the ridge he could not see everything, but he saw enough. Montrose could not redeploy because reorganizing with the enemy in battle order nearby was an invitation for him to strike during your inevitable confusion. On the other hand, redeployment was exactly what Baillie was obliged to do. He ordered an advance up the hill to Auchinviroch starting from behind the ridge – so that the royalists would not at once see what he was doing. The manoeuvre depended on discipline. To take this second area of high ground the men must move as quickly as possible without being disturbed.

Discipline broke. The man at fault was Major John Haldane, who was in charge of a covering musketeer battalion. He was ordered to move with the army on their left flank, between the men heading for Auchinviroch and the royalists, to protect them should the latter attack.

Because Haldane and his men broke cover – as they must at some time – the royalists saw what was happening and evidently moved forward. The accounts of the battle do not make this clear. But it is the best explanation of what Haldane did, which was to move downhill, rather than continue northwards in defensive formation. Haldane tried to occupy another farm called Auchinvalley between the two armies, on lower-lying ground (possibly it was manned by a few royalist troops). He thought that was the best way of preventing the royalists from attacking what was now the flank of Baillie's army.

The royalist officer Euan Maclean of Treshnish advanced to block Haldane and so battle began. Baillie's outflanking manoeuvre was spoiled as the action intensified around Auchinvalley. Other highland troops rapidly supported Treshnish. Alasdair MacDonald with his main body was quickly in command of the infantry assault, the royalist line having turned without damage, covered by Treshnish's valour.

At this point Baillie was quite soon applying much greater force of numbers and might have broken through. Alasdair had 1,600 very tough men under his command, but Baillie lined up more than 2,000 infantry against him. The farm enclosures were protection for both sides, making a breakthrough difficult for either. The odds favoured the covenanters. In very concentrated action there were simply more covenant infantry who could press forward. Their Fife regiments, now on the left of what had become the line of battle, were not engaged.

The engagement, with two bodies of men pushing hard against each other head on and visibility much reduced by the smoke from musket fire, was vulnerable to an attack from either side. This is exactly what happened. At first it looked as though the covenanters would make that move. Lord Balcarres, with his cavalry, had been part of the vanguard heading for Auchinviroch, so he was now on the right flank of Baillie's army, facing the royalist left flank. He saw the opportunity to slice into that side of the enemy, which would help Baillie in the centre.

Balcarres was blocked by a small troop of Gordon cavalry, who charged and held him back. His counter-attack nearly succeeded but drew in Viscount Aboyne, who had been placed in reserve, probably to avoid the catastrophe of another senior Gordon death. Aboyne was watching and saw the danger. He galloped in support with his own troop of cavalry and came close to his elder brother's fate as, charging with his followers, he met the fire of covenanter muskets, then slammed into Balcarres's men in support of his own.

Balcarres still had the initiative and drove the massed Gordons behind the royalist battle line. But Nathaniel Gordon and the Earl of Airlie counter-attacked with the full body of royalist cavalry. The balance changed, the royalists were more numerous and were fresh. In the end, Balcarres failed. He was pushed back downhill and out of the fight.

These actions imply that attention had been quite rapidly focussed on the original northern movement of the covenanter army, which by this stage was their right flank. Very little so far had happened on their left flank (originally rearguard or reserve) where the Fife levies waited. The royalist cavalry now swung into the covenant infantry from the north – into their right flank. That shock gave Alasdair MacDonald the opportunity he needed. His infantry pushed over the enclosures and drove the enemy infantry back.

It seems the Fife regiments at last came under attack from the Gordon infantry and the Irish under Colonels Laghtnan and O'Cahan. They were quickly routed and most of them killed in the pursuit, which covered fourteen miles. They did not have the cohesion of experienced troops and could not retreat in good order. Montrose had his sixth victory.

It could be said there was not much generalship in the Battle of Kilsyth. Fighting began almost accidentally, and troops were drawn in. On the other hand, there is evidence that Montrose did what he could to be sure that Alasdair was supported in the action in the centre. And it was Montrose who ordered Airlie to charge in support of the Gordons, which was certainly a critical moment.[6]

On Baillie's side his own account suggests that the fight quite soon slipped out of his control, developing its own momentum.[7] For such an important battle, the lack of detail in the sources supports the idea that people lost grip of what exactly was happening. Yet the fighting was brutal. Casualties are hard to assess, but local tradition is eloquent. There is a patch of land at Auchinviroch still called Slaughter Howe. If the Fife levies were butchered then there would have been at least 1,000 deaths on the covenanting side. Royalist sources claim much higher figures. The royalists suffered less of course. What happened next makes the point. Montrose kept his men at Kilsyth for two days before moving on.

Soon after the battle, the King's Lieutenant spelled out his position in a formal document.[8] The 'Remonstrance of Montrose' tackles at once the issue of his excommunication, beginning 'Whereas it hath pleased the Commissioners of the pretended General Assembly summarily to excommunicate us, against our Saviour's own rule...' yet, Montrose continues, his opinions in religion were the same as those of orthodox presbyterians.

He has no difficulty stating his dislike of episcopacy. The bishops are described as 'sometime pretended prelates'. In the crisis of 1637, they '... did so abandon themselves, to the prejudice of the Gospel, that the very quintessence of popery was publicly preached by Arminians and the life of the Gospel stolen away by enforcing on the Kirk a dead service-book, the brood of the bowels of the Whore of Babel.'

He writes of his dedication to the National Covenant of 1638: 'We were constrained to renew our Covenant as the only safest and fairest way for the preservation of Religion and Liberty.' Charles I's attempts to enforce the prayer-book in the two Bishops's Wars are blamed on the advice of the bishops and even more on Hamilton who is marked out as 'the prime fomenter of these misunderstandings between the King and his subjects'. The problem was not the king, it was the advisers.

In Scotland everything changed, writes Montrose, in 1639, when parliament confirmed the Acts of the General Assembly, which had ratified those of the 1638 Glasgow assembly. Some members of that parliament liked the 'sweetness of government' and had 'far designs'.

Nonetheless, Montrose had been loyal. He was prepared 'for the sake of the country' to let things be until the Solemn League and Covenant of 1643. This he attacked as an alliance with 'Brownists and Independents' in England'. It was an attack on 'authority and liberty of the subject'. He had taken up arms in defence of the National Covenant; also in defence of the king's 'honour and greatness' and to relieve 'the base servitude of subjects, who, like Israelites, have their burdens doubled.' The last was a dig at the taxes exacted by the committee of estates.

Finally, he defends himself from the charge of employing the Catholic Alasdair MacDonald on his campaigns. Montrose here claims that the presbyterian Colonel Robert Monro had employed Alasdair in Ireland – it was true that Alasdair had fought on both sides in the Irish war – so it was pure hypocrisy to attack him, Montrose, as an employer of Catholics. It was not the strongest defence against a very damaging charge.

The Remonstrance of Montrose is a reasoned account spiced up a little, not a piece of outstanding rhetoric. Written soon after the stress of battle, that can be understood. It is, by the standards of the time, moderate. It is consistent with his proclamation at Atholl in August 1644.

If he tried to cast Argyll and others as religious independents, which was not how they saw it – they were disciplinarians – one has to accept that scrupulous fairness was not the point. Montrose had to address the difficulty that he was an unpopular winner, the man who brought war back to Scotland. In fact, thanks to the pressure of events, the Remonstrance was not published.

PART FOUR

A MAN OF CONTRARIETIES

'Come here and read varieties
A Man of Contrarieties
Most loyal to his King, although
A Traitor to the Kingdom, so
His Country-men he still oppress'd
Yet still his Prince's wrongs address'd'

Harleian Miscellany

31

Seeming Friends

After Kilsyth, the covenanter generals ran away. Argyll ran the furthest by galloping to Queensferry, on the Firth of Forth, there commandeering a boat that took him to parliamentary Newcastle. The others, including Baillie, took refuge in Stirling Castle. There was plague in the town but presumably not in the citadel. Anyway, they thought it worth the risk. Lanark disbanded his regiments and followed Argyll to England. Success led to success, failure to panic.

The political situation in Scotland was now exceptional: the lowlands were dominated by a highland army, which included Irish.[1] Montrose led the army into Glasgow to accept the city's surrender. He forbade looting. The army and he left fairly quickly and set up camp at Bothwell to the south-east. Glasgow offered to pay a tribute to keep safe, as did Edinburgh soon after. For the time being, Edinburgh was 'protected' by the plague.

On 20 August Montrose sent Archibald Napier with Nathaniel Gordon to Linlithgow to free Lord Napier, Sir George Stirling of Keir, and the ladies of their families who were imprisoned there. They went on to Edinburgh to receive the city's submission to the king.

The royalist prisoners held in the Tolbooth were released. They included Lord Ogilvy and George Wishart, who would become Montrose's chaplain. All these men were in poor shape, but they were alive. The castle was not immediately surrendered to the king. The prisoners there had included James, Montrose's eldest son. He may have been released in early August for the sake of his health. At about this time James was placed in the care of the covenanter Earl of Dalhousie, he did not rejoin his father.

Sir Robert Spottiswoode (the Archbishop's son) arrived at Bothwell at the end of August 1645 carrying a new commission from Charles I. Montrose was made Captain General, the office formerly given to Prince

Maurice, and Deputy or Lieutenant Governor of Scotland subordinate only to the king. His elevation was decided months before. Spottiswoode, the king's secretary of state for Scotland, had travelled via Wales and the Isle of Man to reach Scotland without being intercepted. It was a fine reward coming after Kilsyth.

With his new authority Montrose called a parliament to meet in Glasgow on 20 October. In a ceremony in front of the army, he knighted Alasdair MacDonald in gratitude.

There was an antechamber full of of admirers, those who had been silent when he needed them. A train of nobleman came to Bothwell to pledge loyalty. They included the Marquess of Douglas, the Earls of Hartfell, Annandale, Queensberry, Airth (Menteith) and a number of eldest sons: Lords Seton, Drummond, Fleming, Erskine, Linton, representing their fathers, the Earls, respectively, of Winton, Perth, Wigtoun, Mar, Traquair. Also Montrose's brother-in-law Lord Carnegie came for his father Southesk. The Earls of Home and Roxburgh wrote letters of submission or loyalty but stayed at home. Many burghs sent their representatives on this crucial mission. In return, Montrose wrote a number of 'protections', documents extending his (the king's) political friendship to the place in question.

The Renaissance man in Montrose reached out to the poet William Drummond of Hawthornden. He sent a protection for his property and followed up with a request for earlier compositions by Drummond that proclaimed monarchy, and a piece called *Eirene* (in Greek, 'peace'). Montrose wanted to republish these. In fact, there was a literary outpouring:

> The whole country now resounded Montrose's praise... his unshaken resolution and intrepidity, even in the greatest dangers... his faithfulness and strict observance of his promises... his clemency towards his prisoners... several poems and panegyrics were wrote upon this occasion to his honour. Most of these encomiums were sincere... but some of them, it must be confessed, proceeded merely from craft and dissimulation.[2]

The calls on his attention had consequences. Montrose had wooed the Gordons, had loved Lord Gordon, repeatedly went to support Huntly's family in the face of covenanter attack, but that family was not so important in the south of Scotland. Would they be with him if he crossed the border into England? The same, more intensely so, was true of Sir Alasdair MacDonald and his followers. Alasdair had always been loyal, repeatedly delivering recruits, an unstoppable fighter. He and Montrose must have known each other intimately. But highlanders never stayed the course. It was always war for a season with them, and for plunder.

Yet Montrose did not permit the highlanders to take Glasgow to bits. Nor did they receive any of the ransom paid by Glasgow to Montrose because he returned it to the city, trying to unify the nation.[3] There was some compensation in the booty from a 'pacifying' expedition to the south-west led by Alasdair immediately after Kilsyth,[4] but Montrose himself let the highlanders down. Obviously, the Captain General, now that he had what he wanted, preferred lowlanders. He was one himself. In his hour of glory Montrose lost most of his army.

First to go were the highlanders of Atholl who had been led by Patrick Graham the Younger of Inchbrakie. They asked permission to return to rebuild their homes, destroyed most recently by Crawford-Lindsay. Montrose agreed. Next was Alasdair MacDonald. On 3 September he led away another highland group and a number of Irish. Although he showered compliments on Montrose, he would never return. In the end, Alasdair's priority was the MacDonald cause, which he wanted to pursue unencumbered.

Despite all this, on 4 September Montrose broke camp at Bothwell and started to march south. Spottiswoode's letters from the king included instructions to join the Earls of Roxburgh and Home and head for the River Tweed in the Borders. The king would send reinforcements

The third wave then broke. Citing instructions from his father, Viscount Aboyne left the army with his cavalry. These were the troops which turned the tide in the last three battles. Although he had always been royalist, Aboyne never had the relationship that his elder brother enjoyed with Montrose. Now he saw, perfectly accurately, that the Gordon priority was gone, that lowland nobles mattered more in the south. His departure was disloyal but clearsighted.

On 10 September Spottiswoode wrote to Lord Digby in England:

> You little imagine the difficulties my Lord Marquess [Montrose] hath here to wrestle with. The overcoming of the enemy is the least of them; he hath more to do with his own seeming friends... The Earls of Roxburgh and Home... when he was within a dozen miles of them, have rendered their houses and themselves to [covenanter] David Leslie... All these were great disheartenings to any other but to him, whom nothing of this kind can amaze.[5]

Spottiswoode also told Digby about the departure of the highlanders and Aboyne who, he said, 'took a caprice'. Roxburgh and Home had indeed left the scene, now being imprisoned in Berwick. All the sources state this was by friendly agreement with David Leslie, the covenanter general who marched smartly up from England against Montrose. Leslie was another professional soldier from the German wars, where he had learned under the command of Alexander Leslie. He came back and fought in the Scottish army in England, with distinction, at Marston Moor. The Marquess of Douglas was loyal to Montrose, but he, too, suffered desertions.

Although probably written earlier, perhaps in late 1641, Montrose's own verse on false friends seemed to apply:

> Some friends as shadows are, and fortune as the Sun,
> They never proffer any help till fortune hath begun;
> But if in any case, fortune shall first decay,
> Then they, as shadows of the Sun, with fortune pass away.[6]

It is tempting to think Montrose reflected on the difference between theory and reality. If war is the continuation of politics by other means, politics always takes over in the end.

—◦◦◦—

On 12 September 1645, the master of Scotland arrived at Selkirk, twelve miles from the English border. He commanded about 1,600, less than half the army that won Kilsyth, but by the standards of the campaign a good-sized force. 1,000 of these were the moss-troopers of Douglas, mounted troops recently levied, something like the Borders equivalent of highlanders. They were cavalry but they were not professional soldiers.

To the west of Selkirk, Ettrick Water flows north into the Tweed. South-west of the town, on the other side of the river is Philiphaugh plain, where the army camped. Montrose and other officers found quarters in the town.

Montrose knew that David Leslie was nearby with an army. We can be sure of that because the covenanter force was mentioned in Robert Spottiswoode's letter quoted above. In fact, Spottiswoode told Digby that Montrose was 'resolved to pursue' Leslie (who had marched further north, reaching Prestonpans, near Edinburgh, but turned back to find the royalists). Elsewhere we read that Montrose was especially worried by Leslie's 'strength in horse'.[7]

He clearly was thinking of the threat and yet... We may speculate that Montrose was, as we might put it today, psychologically confused – distracted, worn down.

Within twelve months, against huge odds, he had achieved what he promised to the king. The risks he took, his unfailing energy and optimism, had no like. He lost his eldest son and he lost Lord Gordon, who was like a son. He fought six battles and saw at close quarters what happened to the men who died in the fighting and the men who were wounded – the gaping injuries, the final agonies, the moment of death. Charles I at least three times said he would send reinforcements and did not. The king promised the support of Roxburgh and Home, which was never there. While Montrose won, the king lost. For a few days he had accepted tribute as viceroy, yet victory weakened his army.

George Wishart, who was there, wrote that Montrose on the night of 12 September 1645 did not supervise the setting out of look-outs and spies. 'It was his custom to see all these things done himself, but that night he could not, being obliged to write letters to the king by a faithful messenger he had fallen upon, whom he was to dispatch before day.'[8] If so, the letters have not survived.

There was a stunning failure of vigilance. David Leslie was very near. The story is that he was told of Montrose's whereabouts by Montrose's brother-in-law the Earl of Traquair, whose son Lord Linton was with Montrose's army that night.

By night Leslie came closer. Advance troops of his ran into a royalist outpost commanded by an officer called Charteris of Amisfield and provoked a fight. Amisfield and two others managed to get away. Back at the royalist camp, whatever these three said, no senior officer believed they had been surprised by the enemy; obviously there had been a drunken brawl.[9] Even that was not investigated.

During the night Linton and his men left the royalist army. In the night, fog came up. At daybreak on 13 September 1645 visibility was very bad. Even so the failure of the lookouts was so total as to suggest some were paid to be blind. The royalists had no idea that a large enemy army was about to attack. Soldiers and officers prepared and ate their breakfast as they would on any peaceful day.

Leslie's official report says that he attacked at 10.00 am,[10] more incriminating evidence against the sluggish royalists. Montrose's total army of 1,600 consisted of about 500 Irish infantry, 1,000 of Douglas's cavalry, and a few more than 100 experienced cavalry under Airlie and Nathaniel Gordon. David Leslie was leading what was basically a cavalry army, something which Montrose had not yet faced. Leslie had a reasonable body of foot, something in the region of 700, and 400 dragoons (mounted infantry), but more than 3,000 cavalry proper.

Leslie split his army in two. His operations started at the Linglie Burn, half a mile north of Selkirk. Even allowing for poor visibility, his ability to be so close to the town where the royalist officers were mostly quartered before the alarm was raised is astonishing. Perhaps local sympathies explain this. Leslie sent one part of the army into Selkirk to clear the town of royalists, who were killed, captured, or fled.

Montrose himself jumped onto a horse and galloped to the plain where the men were spread out with hardly an officer to guide them. The other part of the covenanting army trotted round the base of Linglie Hill and charged the royalists on Philiphaugh plain.

The Irish infantry had the leadership of Colonels Laghtnan and O' Cahan, who formed 200 of them (less than half) into a unit positioned in relative security facing north, the direction of the attack. They were covered on one side by the Philhope Burn, on the other partly by the River Ettrick. In front were agricultural enclosures. The royalist professional cavalry under Nathaniel Gordon covered the part of the right flank which was open to attack.

The initial action centred on this formation. Nathaniel Gordon led his troopers forward to engage the enemy with pistol and carbine fire but was quickly driven back. A body of Irish musketeers advanced to cover their retreat but they, too, were quickly repulsed.

Because the Irish had found a good position, Leslie's options were limited. He attacked again and was driven back. However, on the royalist counter-attack his numbers told. A number of Irish were cut off from the main body and ran off north to escape. Leslie ordered a final charge on the infantry, which he led himself. This smashed into the Irish and broke them.

Meanwhile Montrose, supported by his cavalry commander Crawford, put together another line from the remainder of the royalist troops. Leslie paid no attention while he drove home his attack on the Irish. The other wing of his army, having cleared Selkirk, then crossed the Ettrick under Lieutenant Colonel Agnew. This had a large infantry component who attacked the royalists from the rear and quickly destroyed their cohesion. It was the end of the battle proper.

Although it sounds like a sudden catastrophe, there was a lot of manoeuvre and delay. Agnew's men had gone into Selkirk and cleared it of the royalists they could find, which was time-consuming, then they had to cross the river before attacking. The defensive position of the Irish at the outset made Leslie's job a lot harder than the numbers would suggest. It was two to three hours of fighting.

Leslie's men fell on the royalist baggage train. The sources agree that another massacre of camp followers now followed, one of great violence:

> ... there remained now but boys, cooks, and a rabble of rascals, and women with their children in their arms, all those without commiseration were cut in pieces... There were many big with child, yet none of them were spared, but all were cut in pieces with such savage and inhuman cruelty.[11]

A large number of Irish women had already left Philiphaugh, presumably having set off the moment they saw the covenanter army approach. It must have been obvious how the battle would end. There were apparently eighty of them. They had children with them. All were rounded up by local people and taken some distance, to Linlithgow. Here they were thrown off a high bridge into the River Avon. The survivors from this fifty-foot drop were speared by pikemen standing on the banks or pushed back until they drowned.[12]

A number of Irish soldiers escaped from the battlefield. One group, commanded by the army adjutant Stewart, surrendered and was taken prisoner. Orderly surrender implied safe conduct but again, the rules were broken. Somebody ruled that only the officer was included in the formal agreement of surrender. The men were lined up and shot. About fifty died, the numbers are not clear.

For the first time, Montrose saw defeat with his own eyes but was characteristically decisive. He fought in the midst of his men until he saw that it was escape or die, whereupon 'he determined to live for the service of the king.'[13] His immediate companions told him to get off the battlefield because he was the life and breath of Scottish royalism.

The fighting around Montrose was intense. Yet oddly there was no concerted attempt to capture him, a failure on the part of Leslie. With twenty or so companions Montrose fought his way off the Philiphaugh plain. He was recognised and followed by a detachment of covenanter cavalry, but some miles away, the royalists turned and confronted them. Some of the covenanter troop were killed, others captured with two standards.

Both the royal standards (cavalry and infantry) of Montrose were saved, one thanks to the courage of an Irish solder who returned it to Montrose himself afterwards. The other was saved by the Earl of Kinnoul's brother, William Hay, who took it to England when he went into hiding. He came back to Scotland later and gave it to Montrose.

The Earl of Airlie and Marquess of Douglas also escaped. They joined Montrose soon after. In total, he had a group quite quickly of 500 fugitives whom he led back through Scotland. Within a week they were back in Atholl.

Royalist losses at Philiphaugh were surprisingly light, probably a few hundred soldiers. The men who had mounts were able to gallop away and were not seriously pursued. The hardest hit were the Irish infantry and of course the defenceless camp followers. It was a mysterious action, since David Leslie could surely have done better. That is testimony to the fighting power of the core of Montrose's followers. What Leslie did achieve was to push Montrose back north, so Edinburgh and Glasgow were safe, and Charles I was isolated.

A tradition grew that David Leslie's tactics were advised by an old man whom he met early in the morning of the battle. It is an example of the tendency always to mythologise, although who knows, perhaps Leslie really was helped by someone with good knowledge of the lie of the land.

When they came to the Lingly burn
As daylight did appear
They spy'd an aged father
And he did draw them near...

'But halve your men in equal parts
Your purpose to fulfil
Let ane half keep the water side
The rest goe round the hill...'

Now, let us a' for Lesly pray
And his brave company!
For they hae vanquish'd great Montrose
Our cruel enemy.[14]

32

The Minister's Servant

Two days before Philiphaugh, Prince Rupert surrendered the port of Bristol to parliament. This caused a rift with his uncle, who could not admit that Rupert had no other option if he were to save lives. Bristol was bound to fall, but the king thought it was betrayal.

On 24 September 1645, Charles I lost the Battle of Rowton Heath near Chester, which was under siege by parliament. Here he watched his twenty-two-year-old cousin Bernard Stuart being cut down. That defeat led to the fall of Chester, the last of the royalist ports, in early 1646.

The time was past for intervention from royalist Scots. However, thanks to the intervention of the French royal government a Scottish deal of a different sort was brokered by the French ambassador Jean de Mareuil. Charles I, defeated, could take refuge with the presbyterian Scots. This would keep him out of the hands of the English parliament (of whom King Louis XIII was nervous).

In spring 1646 Charles therefore had three options: escape abroad, surrender his person to parliament, or to the Scots camped at Newark. After dithering he chose the last. On 18 April he wrote a letter to Montrose[1] expressing the hope that the Scottish presbyterian army 'have really declared for me' thanks to the French; and asking Montrose to march south, if he was satisfied with the good faith of the covenanters!

It was a poor understanding. As soon as the king was in Scottish hands (from 5 May 1646) he found himself a prisoner. Soon Oxford surrendered to the parliamentary army on 24 June 1646)

Charles I was taken to Newcastle. There the covenanters tried to bring him on board (Alexander Henderson spent hours arguing with him). They wanted Charles I to take the National Covenant and to accept the terms of the Solemn League and Covenant.[2]

The king coolly observed and assessed the different strands of Scottish politics, writing to his wife on 17 June 1646 about

> ... the several humours of the Scots. I divide them into four factions: Montroses, the neutrals, the Hamiltons, and the Campbells... The three first seem to correspond, the two last are avowed enemies, the second keeps fair quarter with all, and none of them trusts one another.

The letter tells us about the different power bases of these factions. 'At the committees in Scotland the Hamiltons are the strongest, but here the Campbells. Most of the nobility are for the Hamiltons... but most of the ministry, gentry and towns are for the Campbells.'[3]

At no time did Charles I abandon his belief in an episcopal Church of England. The king never altered his conviction expressed in a letter of 26 August 1646 to the Prince of Wales:

> As the Church can never flourish without the protection of the Crown, so the dependency of the Church upon the Crown is the chiefest support of regal authority... My first direction to you is, to be constant in the maintenance of the Episcopacy not only for the reasons above said but to hinder the growth of Presbyterian doctrine, which cannot but bring anarchy into any country.[4]

Charles I's words show how hollow the concessions were that he made in Scotland in 1640 and 1641. He had always been tactical and always intended to return to his vision of a royal church with bishops in Scotland as well as England (just as his father had).

Faced by royal stubbornness on a heroic scale, the covenanters at last washed their hands, receiving £ 100,000 from the English parliament as an up-front payment (another £ 100,000 to be paid shortly, and a further £ 200,000 later); and handing over the King of Scots to the English at the end of January 1647. The covenant army marched out of Newcastle as the women of the town shouted 'Judas' after them.

In early February Charles I was escorted to Holdenby House in Northamptonshire, where he resumed his courtly routine. There was another step change at the beginning of June 1647 when a junior officer of the New Model Army, Cornet Joyce, with armed escort, essentially kidnapped the king and took him south from Holdenby to Hampton Court.

First, the king was in the hands of the presbyterian Scots; then, at Holdenby, of the English parliament (presbyterian in sympathy); then, because of Cornet Joyce, of the English army (the Independents). These were the different power groups, of which the last was the strongest, and becoming stronger. By now, each had serious disagreements with the others.

While he had no real freedom, Charles I surprisingly started to gain ground at this time. The further he moved away from the covenanters, the better he was treated. At Holdenby he attracted crowds. He was allowed to hunt and play bowls. He touched the sick for the King's Evil.[5] But with his surrender to the Scots, Charles I had to accept that the war was over. Long before he went to Holdenby the king was obliged to call a halt to all military actions in his name.

On 19 May 1646 the king wrote to Montrose from Newcastle commanding him to disband his forces and go into France. He repeated the instructions on 15 June. He wrote again on 21 August promising to reward Montrose when it was possible, adding the characteristically baffling and very unhelpful postscript: 'Defer your going beyond seas as long as you may, without breaking your word.'[6]

—◦◦◦—

Since Philiphaugh, Montrose had been through a depressing cycle of disappointment, clashes where clashes were least needed, and one near miss.

In October 1645 he briefly led an army of nearly 3,000 thanks to Gordon recruits, but the project failed because Montrose wanted to wage war in the south, while Huntly and his sons were preoccupied with defending their land against the new covenanter commander Middleton. And they wanted to attack a number of their traditional local enemies.

In a very cold winter Montrose led his faithful Atholl men into Aberdeenshire and met Huntly in person to force a deal. For a time, there seemed to be an accord between the two men. A plan was formed to take Inverness. But Huntly was reluctant, when it came down to it, to support a winter campaign. There was also the old difficulty of seniority. Since Montrose had lost all his papers at Philiphaugh, he no longer had the recent commission from Charles I appointing him Captain General. Although in time he was sent a copy, it was an excuse for Huntly to refuse Montrose's authority.

Not everyone holed up in the bad weather. The actions of the winter included an unexpected invasion of Menteith by 1,200 Campbells, supported by other highlanders (apparently displaced by the actions of Alasdair MacDonald in the west). Patrick Graham the Younger of Inchbrakie led the Athollmen against them, driving them away. One of the results of this incursion was, somehow, the occupation of Kincardine

Castle in early March 1646 by Archibald Napier the younger and others, which attracted the attention of General Middleton, who took Kincardine in a fortnight and tore it down. Napier and his friends escaped and rejoined Montrose, but the garrison was captured. Twelve of them were executed on the spot.

By spring relations with the Gordons were in shreds. Montrose had offered the joint command to Huntly despite his own senior commission, but it was refused. On 29 April Montrose besieged Inverness without their support, investing the town from the west, which left him with an escape route into the highlands. The Gordons wasted their traditional enemies' land to the east without supporting the siege. They dug up the cannon buried by Montrose in October 1644, after the Battle of Aberdeen, and used it themselves.

Lord Lewis Gordon especially let rip. He 'ravaged up and down the country on all suspect persons, burning cornyards and pillaging all towns and villages... Lord Lewis was a merciless cruel man, and had his master burner with him, who upon the sign given him would instantly set fire to the cornstacks.'[7]

Middleton relieved Inverness in early May 1646, Montrose withdrawing into the highlands. Either the Gordons took no pains to warn him of the approaching covenanters or, as some thought, Lord Lewis deliberately misled the squadrons Montrose had sent to keep watch. Huntly seems to have thought the weakness of Montrose gave him an opportunity to extend his own influence. In May he led an attack on Aberdeen, whose citizens had suffered again and again, and occupied the town. This violent and pointless episode did no good to anyone and that in the end included Huntly himself.[8]

The near miss happened earlier. It involved Lord Digby, one of the trusted English courtiers. In a last throw of the dice, Charles I did succeed in sending reinforcements to Montrose. With 1,500 cavalry Digby made it through north England and across the border in October 1645. With him were the Earls of Carnwath and Nithsdale. They got as far as Dumfries (22 October) but could not make contact with Montrose and had to retreat. That was a lost opportunity indeed. Their joint numbers could have been enough for Montrose to intervene in the lowlands and prevent the royalist executions in Glasgow.

Almost all the Philiphaugh captives were executed. In Edinburgh, shortly after the battle, Colonels Laghtnan and O'Cahan were hanged without a trial – they were mere Irish. On 28 October 1645 Sir William Rollo and Sir Philip Nisbit were hanged in Glasgow, having been tried and condemned by a committee of parliament. The eighteen-year-old Alexander Ogilvy of Innerquhartie was hanged the next day. On 26 January 1646

Nathaniel Gordon, Andrew Guthry and Sir Robert Spottiswoode were beheaded, also after a form of trial. On 29 January the nineteen-year-old brother of the Earl of Tullibardine, William Murray, was executed.

At this time Montrose came under pressure from his own men to exact revenge by killing his own prisoners. He would not do it.

> He desired them seriously to consider, how great would be the injustice to make those prisoners, who were guiltless of the murders committed by their party, suffer the punishment of others' crimes; especially when assurances of safety had been given.[9]

The most celebrated escape was Lord Ogilvy's. He was imprisoned and tried in St Andrews on 16 January 1646. The date set for his execution was the 20th. The day before, his mother and sisters visited him. He exchanged clothes with one of the girls. 'She, at the same time, put on his night-cap and lay down in bed in place of her brother.'[10] *En travesti*, Ogilvy walked free.

The Fraser chief Lord Lovat at this time lamented the state of both Scotland and England: 'England is an Aceldama or field of blood, and Scotland is following fast upon the tract; blood is terrible, and who can think on it and not quake, that our land is defiled with blood, and not shed by an alien's hand.'[11]

Montrose suffered two family losses at this time. His wife Magdalen died in November 1645. He went home to bury her.[12] We do not know where she was living at this time, but the likelihood is that she was at Kincardine in its final days. As previously mentioned, from start to finish Magdalen is an enigma. Her death is unremarked by the main sources including George Wishart, to whom her husband was a hero and who was with Montrose at the time. Perhaps the death of their eldest son earlier in the year was a terminal shock.

Wishart did write about the death of Lord Napier the elder, Montrose's brother-in-law. He says the marquess lamented Napier's death 'as if he had been his own father.'[13] Napier also died in November, at Fincastle at the age of seventy. He was one of the greatest friends of Montrose and was surely an immense influence, very much the moderate presbyterian, a patriot.

—◈◈◈—

Montrose thrashed out the terms for peace in a long conversation with Middleton on the banks of the River Isla on 22 July 1646. They knew each other since Middleton fought for Montrose as a captain on the side of the then recent National Covenant, at the Brig O' Dee in 1639. Middleton's father had been killed in March 1645 by a band of Montrose's Irish, who broke into his house near Fettercairn and found the old laird sitting by the fire with his family.[14] There was no obvious reason for this random murder. Nonetheless, the terms which Middleton the son agreed were generous.

Other than Montrose himself, the Earl of Crawford and Sir John Hurry (with bad timing he had joined Montrose after Philiphaugh), the royalists, including Lord Ogilvy, would be pardoned. Most of those declared forfeit would suffer no loss and could return to their normal lives. Montrose himself must leave Scotland before the end of August. It was specified that he must depart from the port of Montrose – so that he could be tracked.

As the deadline neared, he tried to obtain an extension of his permitted presence in Scotland but had 'nothing but doubtful and evasive answers'. It was not until 31 August that the boat appointed to take him overseas came into port under a captain who was 'a violent and rigid covenanter', who eventually admitted that he had instructions to sail to certain ports agreed with the government and nowhere else, and that English ships were waiting in the open sea. His boat was in bad repair and needed, said the captain, several days for cleaning and repair.[15] It was a good trap.

Some of the group with Montrose said he should at once return to the highlands. He took the view that breaking the terms of the peace would put his friends in danger. Their security was covered by the same terms. He decided to make his own arrangements.

Twenty miles to the north, in Stonehaven, a Norwegian pinnace, a small boat, was found, whose master was ready to ferry the royalists to Bergen. Montrose sent his remaining followers to travel on that. They included his brother Harry, Sir John Hurry, John Spottiswoode (nephew of Robert), and George Wishart, whose account we have.[16] They sailed on 3 September 1646.

He did not go with his friends. It was time for another disguise. The Marquess of Montrose put on 'a coarse suit' and pretended to be the servant of the minister James Wood. The two of them boarded a ship moored outside the port of Montrose, which followed the route of the pinnace. In due course they, too, landed at Bergen. In all this he evaded covenanter spies partly because he still had a good many friends and admirers 'even among the covenanters themselves'.

33

The Fears of King Charles

Montrose's departure to Norway was as perilous as the queen's flight to France two years before. At Oxford, she became pregnant and decided to protect herself and the king by going away. She left the city on 17 April 1644, saying farewell to her husband at Abingdon; she travelled west out of the frying pan and into the fire.

The Earl of Essex led an army to relieve the siege of Lyme and if possible to intercept her. On 16 June 1644, Henrietta Maria gave birth to her last child, a girl, in Exeter. She immediately left the baby to the care of nurses to escape England. Her pregnancy had been difficult, so was the labour. The queen collapsed physically and mentally but made it out of Falmouth in a royal vessel fortunately docked there. As they left the port, Henrietta Maria and her party were at once attacked by parliamentary ships, one of them armed with fifty-eight pieces of canon, but her vessel sailed out of the harbour at full tilt and outran the pursuit.[1] The queen landed safely but not easily in France. Having reached the shore in a longboat provided by the Cornish captain of the main vessel, Henrietta Maria with her small entourage had to scramble across rocks to reach the nearest village.

When Exeter later surrendered, the abandoned baby, Princess Henrietta, was taken into parliamentary custody under the supervision of Lady Dalkeith. This state of affairs lasted as long as Lady Dalkeith put up with it, for she decided in summer 1646 to leave England with the princess and (in disguise) deceived the authorities and did so. This remarkable woman returned the toddler to her mother in France about the same time that Montrose arrived at Bergen.

Henrietta Maria was established in Paris thanks to the generosity of her sister-in-law Anne of Austria, the Regent of France (for her seven-year-old son King Louis XIV). Now she was paid a French income. She lived in the Louvre. Anne of Austria lived in the Palais Royal nearby.

Henrietta Maria's court was led by her Lord Chamberlain and Treasurer Henry Jermyn, a hate figure accused of greed and corruption by those whose influence he blocked. Men such as Edward Hyde and Edward Nicholas, who had been at the king's side in England, disagreed with the policies pushed by Jermyn, which truly were the policies of Henrietta Maria. They included variations on the theme of Catholic powers assisting Charles I.

In Paris, the Prince of Wales had recently joined his mother, which distanced him from his father's advisers. They stayed away. She was keen that Prince Charles, aged sixteen, should marry his first cousin, the extremely rich Bourbon princess Mademoiselle de Montpensier. His clumsiness and La Grande Mademoiselle's dreamy arrogance – was she not destined to be either Queen of France or Holy Roman Empress? (no) – and his either real or pretended inability to speak French put paid to that. In short, the Stuart cause was weighed by new court politics, those of the English Louvre.

At first, Montrose kept his distance from the queen. At Bergen the governor of the castle was a friendly Scot, Thomas Grey, which helped with the next steps. The royalists decided to find Charles I's uncle, King Christian IV of Denmark, who also governed Norway.

Having travelled to Christiania (Oslo), 'over the tops of high and rugged mountains, frightful to look at, and constantly deep with snow',[2] Montrose and his band boarded a boat across the Skagerrak to Denmark where they still failed to find the king. He was in Germany where they followed and again failed to make contact. They went to Hamburg where they stayed for several months.

Probably this was a time of financial reorganization, including conversations with bankers. We know how important finances were to exiled royalists from correspondence between the younger Archibald Napier, now Lord Napier, who joined Montrose, and his wife,[3] who was still in Scotland. We do not know Montrose's financial situation, but it must have been difficult. His costs included those of the group with him. However, famous generals made fortunes. Montrose was in his prime, only thirty-four. He could find a new life and continental riches – excellent security.

From Hamburg he travelled south to the Dutch Republic. He had received letters from both king and queen. The first told him to find Henrietta Maria in Paris. She wrote and reassured Montrose of her confidence in him. Nonetheless, there was an attempt to divert him back to Scotland from one of the Paris courtiers, probably at Jermyn's initiative. Montrose ignored this and came on to Paris arriving in late March or early April 1647.

——⟨*୬/୬/୬*⟩——

The English court of Henrietta Maria was jealous and stand-offish, while France embraced Montrose's celebrity.

He was given precedence at the French court over regular ambassadors. He had access to the most powerful man in France, Cardinal Mazarin. He made new friends such as the Jean François Paul de Gondi the co-adjutor[4] of Paris. This highly political man judged Montrose to be 'the only man in the world who ever made me think of certain heroes that you only see in the Lives of Plutarch, having worked for the King of England's cause with a greatness of spirit which has no equal in this century.'[5]

In the course of the next year a job was negotiated. On 14 June 1648 his nephew Archibald Napier told his wife that Montrose 'was in treaty with the Frenches'.[6] Mazarin offered him the post of Lieutenant General in the French army with command of the Scottish bodyguard of the king. For this he would be paid and on top of the pay he would have a pension of 12,000 crowns a year. Within a year, Mazarin told him informally, he would be promoted to the top rank in the French army as Marshal of France.

By now Montrose's fame was magnified by the work of George Wishart who had composed an account of his deeds in Latin, which was quickly a European best-seller. The first edition, dedicated to the Prince of Wales, was published in the Netherlands in October 1647, the second in Paris in January 1648, with an English edition later that year. As events transpired, Wishart went on writing and brought out updates.

Montrose now stood on a pedestal: a unique hero, a brilliant general always fighting against the odds, a romantic royalist. Wishart's *tour de force* infuriated other top people. Since he presented Montrose as being right about everything, that meant that others must have been wrong, including King Charles every so often. The Hamiltons did not welcome the publicity, nor did Argyll, obviously. They were shown to be variously warmongers, traitors, cowards, incompetents. The book is a good read but partial to say the least. So partial that the Prince of Wales wrote to Montrose on 5 March 1648 complimenting him on his achievements but asking him to suppress publication, which Montrose did not.

As for his wider relationship with the Stuart family, in the fourteen or fifteen months when he lived in or near Paris, Montrose found the court of Henrietta Maria far from welcoming and not to his taste. As early as July 1647 he wrote to his nephew by marriage, Sir George Stirling of

Keir, saying the queen's court was a 'lewd and worthless place'.[7] He was utterly opposed to the plan to find a place in the queen's household for his unmarried niece, Lilias Napier. We do not know how he got on with the Prince of Wales personally in this period. The king's eldest son was only sixteen. Later he would be famous for his many girlfriends.

While Henrietta Maria had confidence in Montrose, she turned to her old friends. 'The Hamiltons' soon emerged as the strongest royalist grouping in Scotland, because the two Hamilton brothers were both there on the ground and could hopefully raise troops. Montrose's glitter put others in the shade, but he commanded no army. The Duke of Hamilton was back in play having been released from Pendennis Castle in April 1646.

As already noted, the position of Charles I improved after he moved from Scottish to English custody. From the end of June 1647, he was permitted his own chaplains, which at first had been forbidden. More amazing still, commissioners came from Scotland, reflecting the changes in sentiment noted by the king himself. After his horrendous experiences in Newcastle, Charles I negotiated an agreement with them called the Engagement.[8]

This was concluded in Carisbrooke Castle in the Isle of Wight in December 1647. From Hampton Court he had escaped to the Isle of Wight, but the governor of Carisbrooke had parliamentary sympathies, so Charles found himself a prisoner once more. He was still king nevertheless, both in England and Scotland. The paradox was that he still had power.

The Hamiltons were behind the Engagement, which Henrietta Maria supported in March 1648. Help from Scotland was now seen as the best hope for Charles I. Scottish opinion had been outraged by the actions of Cornet Joyce, because that was taking the king into the hands of the detested Independents. While religion catalysed the politics, finance was never far behind. The balance of the large sum owed to the Scots, another £200,000, was never paid: they found they had sold the king at half-price.

To be fair to the queen, it is not obvious that Montrose was a better option at this juncture. If the Stuarts wanted a second round of war there must be an army that would travel into England and fight there, something Montrose had not accomplished. The mutual dislike of Hamilton and Montrose made it hard for the two to work together, and yet it was now Hamilton doing the legwork in Scotland. The second round of war therefore came without Montrose.

In May 1648, Hamilton persuaded the Scottish parliament to raise troops to fight for the King of Scots. Argyll and the General Assembly of the Kirk did not support the levy. The politics were so heated that Argyll and the Earl of Crawford-Lindsay very nearly fought a duel. Crying off (by mutual agreement) Argyll was both accused of cowardice and criticised by the Kirk for being involved in an ungodly row.[9]

The Scottish army marched into England. In very wet weather the extended Battle of Preston was fought from 17 to 19 August 1648 and won by the English led by Cromwell. In the latter part of the encounter, the Battle of Winwick Pass, Cromwell defeated an army more than twice the size of his own. Cromwell then marched into Scotland to make sure an anti-engager régime was installed under Argyll.

For a second time, King Charles had unleashed war on his people. That convinced the senior army command in England that he was a man of blood. Was he? The truth was more complex. Distrust of the king took root among the senior army command when he escaped from Hampton Court and fled to the Isle of Wight the previous November. He appeared to be relentless against them.

In fact, his escape was triggered by the Putney Debates (28 October to 11 November 1647) within the New Model Army, chaired by Cromwell. In the debates army radicals (not the grandees) put forward proposals for a constitutional settlement which included an extended suffrage and – in the most extreme case – the trial of the king. Cromwell was so far from wishing the king's death that he sent a letter to the governor of Hampton Court warning of the risk of an assassination attempt (11 November 1647).[10] It was this letter more than anything else that persuaded the king to look for safety elsewhere. The final agreement with the Engagers followed.

The Engagement confirmed the fears of the senior officers, who were certainly not radicals. Yet it came about because of the fears of Charles I.

Privately, Montrose poured scorn on Mazarin's offer. He told Napier the only rank in the French army that he would accept was Marshal of France and this was not formally offered. Nor was he convinced that the French royal government would help Charles I.[11] He was surely right about that. Probably Mazarin wanted Montrose in French service to keep him away from the Habsburgs.

How much Montrose was influenced by personal dislike of the Louvre court we do not know, but we do know that he left Paris secretly and travelled to Geneva, then into the Austrian archduchies to Vienna and from Vienna to Prague, where he found the Emperor Ferdinand III, who gave him a splendid welcome. Here Montrose received the most senior appointment. He was made Marshal of the Holy Roman Empire with a commission to raise his own regiments. Ferdinand agreed to send him to

Flanders, where his brother the Archduke Leopold was governor. This required the agreement of the Spanish ambassador, which was obtained. All this Montrose accepted. The emperor wanted the most famous general in the world on the Habsburg side to keep him away from Bourbon service.

After a circuitous trip through east Europe to avoid the confusion of Germany, where armies milled (although peace was being negotiated) – and of course to avoid France – Montrose reached Flanders from Denmark, where at last he was received by Christian IV. Arriving in Flanders shortly after the Battle of Lens (20 August 1648) he found the Archduke licking his wounds. In a summer of decisive battles, Lens was a considerable French victory, which added the final touch of momentum to the imperial peace negotiations. Three separate peaces were in fact agreed in 1648: between Spain and the Dutch; between Sweden and the emperor; and between France and the emperor. These treaties jointly made up the Peace of Westphalia.

Montrose spent autumn and most of winter in Flanders. Leopold was in no condition to give him much assistance, being preoccupied with the defence of Flanders (part of Spain which continued to be at war with France). He was friendly but delegated the requests of the Scottish Imperial Marshal to the attention of his senate, which did nothing much.

Not long after his arrival in Flanders Montrose received letters from the Prince of Wales in the Hague asking for his help. The Battle of Preston had closed off the chosen royalist strategy. By leaving his mother's court, the young Charles found some independence but now there were two centres of Stuart intrigue on the continent. Henrietta Maria was still the senior representative of her husband the king. Rejoined by Hyde and Nicholas, the prince was in competition with his mother. Montrose at last decided to go to the Hague. We read that Montrose was about to set off to join the prince when he heard of Charles I's execution.[12] The king died on 30 January 1649, so Montrose must still have been in Flanders at the beginning of February.

The impact of this news across Europe can hardly be understood today. The death of a king in battle was serious, the murder of a king very shocking, but the trial of an anointed king on treason charges, his being found guilty, his being beheaded on a scaffold outside his own palace...

When he heard the news Montrose 'fainted and fell down in the midst of his attendants, all the members of his body becoming stiff, as if he had been quite dead',[13] wrote George Wishart, continuing his chronicle as eyewitness. When Montrose came to, he said he wanted to die, but Wishart, himself very shocked, said his master must live to avenge the king. 'He heard me patiently in his usual complacent manner; but at the mention of avenging the king's murder, the very thoughts of which gave him new life, he revived from his former disorder.'

Montrose went to his private rooms and stayed there three days without seeing anyone. When Wishart was at last allowed in, he found a poem just written. At his worst moment Montrose turned to his muse.

> Great, good, and just! Could I but rate
> My griefs to thy too rigid fate,
> I'd weep the world to such a strain,
> As it should deluge once again;
> But since they loud-tongu'd blood demands supplies,
> More from Briareus' hands than Argus' eyes,
> I'll sing thy obsequies with trumpet sounds,
> And write thy epitaph with blood and wounds.[14]

In Greek myth Briareus was a monstrous giant, with fifty heads and a hundred arms, who assailed Mount Olympus. Argus was also a giant, with a hundred eyes, a good watchman but not a fighter. Montrose is saying he would again fight for his king.

34

Montrose's Last Declaration

On 5 February 1649 a proclamation was read out at the Mercat Cross, Edinburgh:

> Forsomuch as the King's Majesty who lately reigned is, contrary to the dissent and protestation of this kingdom, now removed by a violent death... we, the estates of the parliament of the kingdom of Scotland, do therefore most unanimously and cheerfully, in recognisance and acknowledgement of his just right, title, and succession to the crown of these kingdoms, hereby proclaim and declare to all the world that the said lord and prince Charles is by the providence of God and by the lawful right of undoubted succession and descent King of Great Britain, France and Ireland.[1]

The Scots were the first of all nations publicly to accept Charles II as king, admittedly with a certain amount of qualification and some colouring of the past.

The latter came in the claim that the Scottish parliament had tried to preserve the king's life. Although Scottish commissioners in London claimed to have formally protested when Charles I was sentenced,[2] nobody much noticed at the time; and it was the Scots who handed Charles I over to his English enemies two years before. 'Violent death' was an exceptionally concise phrase for what had happened. Another choice of words, 'unanimously and cheerfully', grabs the attention, the Scottish parliament on the whole lacking both qualities and especially the second.

Parliament urged obedience to the new and young king (eighteen) 'according to the National Covenant and the Solemn League and Covenant'. As before, King Charles II must be Reformed Protestant and must subscribe to presbyterianism everywhere. The king would only be king if he were the covenanters' own.

The title 'King of Great Britain' is striking. It sent a defiant message to the English leaders, that the Scots accepted Charles II as King of England. It strangely harked back, because both his father and grandfather liked to use the title – although nobody had yet been crowned King of Great Britain. It tried to forge the future with words alone. A presbyterian Great Britain was the aim of the Solemn League and Covenant. (As for 'King of France', the title was claimed by all English monarchs since Edward III (1312-1377). The French government under Cardinal Mazarin accepted the old claim for what it was, nothing at all.)

The régime in England trod a different path. On 17 March 1649 the Rump Parliament passed an act abolishing the monarchy and two days later abolished the House of Lords. On 19 May parliament passed an act declaring England to be a Commonwealth. The English did not accept Charles II or anyone else as king.

All common ground was gone. England and Scotland were squaring off.

———◈◈◈———

When he learned of his father's death Charles II was in the Hague. Thanks to her not especially happy marriage, his sister Mary had been based there nearly ten years, living in the Binnenhof, a large complex in the centre of the city. Their aunt, Elizabeth, Queen of Bohemia, also lived there, in the House of Wassenaar-Duivenvoorde. There was a lively Stuart interest in the Hague, a faction. Yet the hopes of raising a Dutch army were zero. The Dutch had just concluded peace terms with Spain. Their eighty-year struggle for independence was at last finished. There was no appetite for another war.

Nor was there a French option despite the hopes of Henrietta Maria. Although freed of war in the empire, the royal French government was facing its own civil war, the Fronde, which began in 1648, while continuing to fight the war with Spain. (And French coffers were empty.)

If he was to reclaim at least one of his kingdoms, Charles II must look to his own. Admittedly the manner of his father's death caused a huge royalist upswell in England and Scotland, but in 1649 England was in the iron grip of the army. For instance, on 9 March 1649 Hamilton was executed as a traitor. He was a Scot, and therefore could not betray the English parliament legally speaking – he was executed under his subsidiary title Earl of Cambridge. The duke's epitaph was written by a politician of the day: 'His natural darkness and reservation in discourse made him be thought a wise man, and his having been in command under the King of

Sweden, and his continual discourse of battles and fortifications made him be thought a soldier; and both these mistakes were the cause that made him be looked upon as a worse and more dangerous man than, in truth, he deserved to be.'[3]

Ireland and Scotland provided possible platforms for Charles II, but Ireland would be ruled out by English parliamentary militancy. Cromwell's military successes there – disasters to the locals, bitterly remembered today – such as the siege of Drogheda (September 1649), the sack of Wexford (October 1649), finally put an end to the plan for Charles II to go to Ireland.

While 'the Montroses' continued to urge military action in Scotland, a royalist military invasion, others favoured the so far rejected presbyterian deal: combining forces with the existing government. Perhaps it was more realistic.

Since the Battle of Preston, the Kirk party was in the ascendant. Their reaction to the execution of Charles I showed they were angry at the presumption of the English parliament.[4] It is important to understand the two plans were opposites: an invasion was an attack on the *de facto* Scottish government, accepting their terms was supporting them.

Not surprisingly, the Kirk party behaved with the same harshness as the English army, for instance executing the Marquess of Huntly on 22 March 1649, 'because they had not in their power another king to murder.'[5] Having shown their hand in this way, commissioners of the Kirk wrote to the Hague in spring 1649 to ask Charles II whether he would agree their program.

Montrose was asked to advise. On 21 May 1649 his memorandum was read to the king's council.[6] First, it says there was no need for the king to reply to Kirk commissioners at all since their authority came from 'pretended judicatories'. Charles II might choose to reply out of a healing spirit. That would be his free choice.

Then there was the National Covenant of 1638. His Majesty was asked to subscribe. The Kirk commissioners argued that it was based on the Negative Confession of 1581, which his grandfather had agreed; surprisingly, they said that his father had assented to it.[7] Montrose does not contest this but points out the Negative Confession included 'no bond or league of mutual defence'. It was not militant. For that reason, he had no objection if Charles II 'should be pleased to seem to dispense with it', meaning the king might smile on the National Covenant with no harm done.

Montrose's loathing for the 1643 Solemn League and Covenant is trenchantly expressed in his memorandum: '...it is so full of injustice, violence, and rebellion, that, in my humble opinion, it were your Majesty's shame and ruin ever to give ear to it.'

Comments are made on the hypocrisy of the Kirk commissioners who seek to impose their form of private worship on the king, exactly as they had complained his father sought to do to them. Montrose does not deny the late king's responsibility, but only says the commissioners are hypocrites.

A similar twist is identified in their promise of faithfulness to Charles II, to be modelled on the faithfulness they showed his father! Montrose pointed out that their 'faithfulness' included an insistence that kings could be tried by process of law. And the commissioners have asked Charles II to agree that all civil matters should be decided by parliament, and all ecclesiastical matters by the General Assembly – leaving the king with no powers at all.

The gist is clear. Montrose advises adherence to the traditional position of the king. He denounces the commissioners as 'the fountain and origin of all rebellion'. He insists on the horror of the betrayal of Charles I when he was handed over to the English parliament at Newcastle in January 1647. And he urges Charles II 'to trust the justice of your cause to God and better fortunes; and use all vigorous and active ways, as the only probable human means that is left to redeem you.'

Montrose speaks for royal power against theocracy, against the combination of England and Scotland, and very much for Charles I whatever his shortcomings, and for vigour. That meant attack.

At the Hague Montrose found a new friend. Elizabeth of Bohemia was totally committed to the Stuart cause, and a hundred per cent for Montrose himself. She is a cheering voice. We know what she was like because of the letters that have survived, as well as many contemporary tributes. In her portraits – Gerard van Honthorst was her in-house painter (she and her daughter Louise took painting lessons from him) – she appears tall, dark blonde, pale-skinned, eyes widely spaced. At the beginning of 1649 she was fifty-two.

Elizabeth was Reformed Protestant, but religious belief did not for her preclude court entertainments, hunting expeditions and so forth, all such things broadcasting royal sophistication and incurring occasional Dutch displeasure. After the events of 1646 to 1649 she showed nothing but disdain for the Scottish presbyterians.

Glamour, upbeat charm and fizzing energy combined in her and did not fade, despite her being at the centre of what was by now a poverty-stricken court in the house Wassenaar-Duivenvoorde.[8] Elizabeth's finances were never strong, and were further dashed by the 1648 peace, when the

Dutch stopped paying her an income. Evidently, royal poverty was not like real poverty. She also had a country palace at Rhenen in the central Netherlands, where the Utrecht Hill Ridge meets the River Rhine.

In 1649 Elizabeth was a widow. She dedicated her time to promoting the careers of her children, including that of the eldest surviving son Charles Louis, Elector Palatine by inheritance but not possession, until the Peace of Westphalia. Unlike his brothers Rupert and Maurice, Charles Louis had hedged his bets in England and became friendly with parliament (and was even in England when – to his horror – his uncle Charles I was executed). Elizabeth had her difficulties with Charles Louis but could not fault him in that. She herself had written in 1645 to the speaker of the Commons, William Lenthall, to ask, as an English princess, for financial help.[9]

Among the Winter Queen's trials, after the loss of Bohemia and the Palatinate in 1620, were the death of her greatly loved husband in 1632, the death of four children including her eldest son Frederick Henry in a boating accident in 1629, and of course her brother's death in 1649. There would be more blows but never enough to dull the lustre.

Also chiselled by misfortune, also constantly optimistic, Montrose was a natural visitor to the house Wassenaar-Duivenvoorde where a rapport grew, even to the extent of marriage being somehow contemplated between him and Elizabeth's daughter Louise.[10] If so, that would be an extraordinary compliment to Montrose, but the match did not happen.

In June 1649 Montrose sent the Queen of Bohemia his portrait for which she thanked him: 'I give you many thanks for your picture. I have hung it in my cabinet to fright away the Brethren.'

In their correspondence, and presumably when they met, Elizabeth was informal. From a queen (a Stuart princess) to a noble, the correct form of address was 'Cousin'. Elizabeth called Montrose 'My Lord,' also 'Jamie Graeme' and 'my Highlander'. This was the address of an equal.

They wrote to each other after Charles II left the Hague, taking Montrose with him. The young king appeared to have accepted the advice of Montrose on Scotland but was not focussing. In spring and early summer 1649, he was thinking more of Ireland.

With Charles II Montrose went as far as Brussels (where Elizabeth wrote). It is possible he continued in the king's suite to Paris but not likely. There he would have to face Henrietta Maria and Jermyn. If he did go to Paris, he did not stay long. While he made his plans for a descent on Scotland, travelling to Hamburg, Copenhagen, then Gothenburg in Sweden, his correspondence continued with the Winter Queen. She told him what she knew, for instance in a letter of 12 September: 'The king is still at St Germains... I would he were well gone from there.' Elizabeth never saw eye to eye with her sister-in-law Henrietta Maria.

On 2 October Elizabeth wrote 'My Lord Jermyn is coming hither, it is said, to take order about the Jewels. Others think it is to meet with Duke Hamilton (previously Lanark, who had inherited after his brother's death), Latherdale (Lauderdale), and your other friends, to have new commissioners sent to the king from the godly brethren, to cross wicked Jamie Graeme's proceedings.'

On 9 December she wrote 'I doubt not but you have seen... the proclamation against Morton and Kinnoull and all the adherents of that detestable bloody murderer and excommunicated traitor, James Graeme. The Turks never called the Christians so.'

———

By this time the Scottish plans were well advanced. Montrose and the Earl of Kinnoull first formed them at a meeting in Rhenen in September. At that time they were not royal policy, however as information and misinformation dribbled through from Ireland, the Scottish plan was all that was left.

Kinnoull's father-in-law was the Earl of Morton,[11] a power in the Orkneys, islands so far north that they were ungarrisoned by the Scottish government. What emerged was a plan to land in the Orkneys with an army mainly supplied by European princes, to recruit further on landing – Kinnoull would go in advance to do this – then cross to the mainland and march south.

By late autumn Montrose was truly on his way, but three things now militated against him.

First was Scottish and English diplomacy. Ambassadors travelled from both countries to European powers; and for both, the objective was to make their case as legitimate states best not interfered with. Montrose had already met Scottish commissioners in the Hague, or rather not met them, since they walked out of the room whenever he walked in. The fact that he had been excommunicated made him the arch-enemy. The activities of these emissaries reduced the propensity of the Protestant princes, including the Prince of Orange, to support Scottish (and English) royalism.

Second was the deaths of Kinnoull and his father-in-law. Kinnoull arrived in the Orkneys in September 1649. On 12 November Morton died. Then Kinnoull himself fell ill with a respiratory complaint and died soon after, still in his twenties. For once, nobody alleged poison. It was just bad luck. Montrose did not give up, but the death of Kinnoull was a problem: it was the loss of a friend and meant there was no local leader for the men he had raised.

Problem number three – by far the most difficult – was Charles II. Because of his age and because of his character and, in fairness, because of the difficulties of his situation, the king was keeping his options open.

He did not discourage Montrose. On 19 September he wrote to him from St Germain-en-Laye: 'I entreat you to go on vigorously, and with your wonted courage and care in the prosecution of those trusts I have committed to you, and not to be startled with any reports you may hear, as I were otherwise inclined to the presbyterians than when I left you.'[12]

Why would there be reports that Charles II was warming to the presbyterians? For good reason. The king was indeed in touch with the Scottish government, dangling before them the possibility of his agreeing their terms.

Having reached Gothenburg on 15 November, for several reasons, one being that in mid-December the entrance to the harbour was blocked by pack ice, Montrose found himself stuck. He was gathering arms and supplies, but it did not always go to plan. He waited for supplies that never arrived. One of his emissaries absconded with the money. Others raised men but could not transport them to Gothenburg. But he had some success.

That gave the provincial governor, Per Lindorson Ribbing, a headache. Having a foreign aristocrat on his doorstep building a secret if small army – not that secret, given the size of Gothenburg – Ribbing had no idea what to do. The royal government of Queen Cristina gave him no guidance because they were turning a blind eye. His superiors finally responded to his entreaties and sent formal instructions to leave Montrose alone.[13] The foreign aristocrat did everything possible to minimise embarrassment by sending his mercenaries out of Gothenburg to the island of Marstrand, fifteen miles north (still in Sweden);[14] but Ribbing's worry shows that Montrose's plans were pretty obvious to any observer. Scottish spies reported back to Edinburgh.

Not that Montrose was a sphinx. He had very openly published his own Declaration in late November 1649. Copies were sent to Scotland and distributed in Edinburgh in December 1649. He did not want secrets. This document[15] is the authentic voice of Montrose, now visionary, angry. It accuses 'an horrid and infamous faction of rebels within the kingdom of Scotland' of stirring up their neighbouring kingdom of England. He says in this they 'did still thrust in, as oil to the fire, and ganger to the wound'.

He charges them with a senseless aggression, '...neither were they contented in the fox-skin alone to act this their so brutish tragedy,' but they went on to invade England even though everything requested had been granted – prayer-book and canons withdrawn, episcopacy abolished.

In England the Scottish rebels 'persecute their prince, in a foreign nation (and) assist a company of stranger rebels against their native king.'

He finds the words for the betrayal at Newcastle: 'They, contrary to all faith and paction, trust of friends, duty of subjects, laws of hopitality, nature, nations, divine and human... to the blush of Christians and abomination of mankind sold their sovereign over to their merciless fellow-traitors to be destroyed.'

The declaration blasts the Scottish government for their provisional proclamation of Charles II 'robbing him of all right'. Most interesting of all, it explains the new king is ready to pardon everyone except those guilty of regicide. Did Charles II actually see the exuberant text? That seems impossible. More likely he agreed (sincerely) that Montrose could announce a general pardon in this way. The document ends with an appeal to

> ... all who have any duty left them to God, their king, country, friends, homes, wives, children, or would change now at last the tyranny, violence and repression of these rebels... let them as Christians, subjects, patriots, friends, husbands and fathers join themselves forthwith with us in this present service, that is so full of conscience, duty, honour, and all just interests.

This eruption of certainty is magnificent but a bit mad. There is not the slightest shift away from furious hostility to the incumbent government of Scotland. Montrose's beating heart was firmly and visibly on his sleeve.

He had not raised the people of Scotland before, had not come close. But his outrage at the death of Charles I seemed to make all things possible: it transformed him and the world. After such a crime people would flock to the royal standard and justice would be done, apparently with no reprisals. From the soil of Scotland a royalist army would rise. He was giving himself to the dream.

35

Nil medium

Sailing from Bergen, Montrose landed on the Orkneys at the beginning of March 1650.[1] He had with him 500 men, Danish and German mercenaries. On arrival he picked up another 1,000 locals, strong and hardy no doubt but recent levies with no experience of fighting. As in earlier times he had few cavalry, just forty horsemen, all of them officers and gentry who had been with him in Gothenburg.[2] Since he stayed on the islands for a month, it is likely that he started to drill the recruits.

He would need to recruit again on the mainland. His glorious campaign five years before had failed because of desertions – owing to the reluctance of Scots from the north to fight in the south. This time he had at last the support of the Earl of Seaforth, whose Mackenzies might come when called, but they, too, were northerners with a limited reach.[3] And they had not come in yet.

Another flaw was the cause itself. While Charles II was rightful king, he was unknown because of his age, because he had never been to Scotland, because he was an exile. He was half-French – and was he half-Catholic? Nor was he crowned. Although there was a surge in royalism after his father's death, although the Kirk party's zeal – and its accommodation of Cromwell – lost it support, Charles II was an unformed king. He might be malleable but that is not leadership. Yet for Montrose, fired by a sense of dreadful injustice, by love for the dead king, right was might.

On his cloak he wore the star of the Order of the Garter that Charles II had recently awarded him – the greatest possible royal honour (and one especially favoured by Charles I). Montrose's personal standard was white damask 'with a lion rampant on the top of a rock, with another steep rock on the other side of a river'. The flag did not display the Graham family motto. It displayed words that said it all: *nil medium*. Literally 'nothing in the middle' – the lion must leap from rock to rock and not fall between

– it can be paraphrased as 'all or nothing.' The same device was shown in the seal on letters he sent at this time. It had become his personal motto.[4]

There were two standards for the king: one for the minuscule cavalry, the other for the infantry, both of black taffeta. The infantry standard featured 'a man's head in the middle, bleeding as if cut off from a body'. This flag had the motto *Deo et victribus armis*: 'for God and victorious arms'.

There was no doubt in Montrose's mind that the cause of Charles II was the cause of Charles I, and it was holy.

———

As his future hung in the balance, the young king looked in two directions. He wished to negotiate properly with the committee of estates, and he wished to come out of that negotiation fully accepted as King of Scots, with their support for an attempt on England. He agreed to talks. But he did not want Montrose to hold back. In fact, he thought that Montrose would help his talks by applying pressure.

The fame of Montrose dazzled Charles II, he thought his general capable of anything. Before the marquess set off for Orkney, when he was still at Gothenburg, the king (now in Jersey) therefore wrote him two letters (dated 22 January 1650, European style – the equivalent British date being 12 January).[5] One was private. Charles II reassured his most loyal servant that there was no slackening in his support: 'I will never fail in the effects of that friendship I have promised, and which your zeal to my service hath so eminently deserved.' He said Montrose must not be discouraged by hearing anything which suggested otherwise but should 'proceed in your business with your usual courage and alacrity'.

The other was public. The whole point of this letter was that other people should see it. A whole lot of other people would undoubtedly quite soon see it, because it would be circulated in Scotland. In the second letter the king said that he had agreed to receive the representatives of the committee of estates and was hoping for a treaty with them 'to produce an agreement and present union of that whole nation in our service'.

In other words, he would shortly talk to the Scottish government so as to forge a pact with them to secure his Scottish throne. These talks would be held at Breda, on the Dutch side of the border with Flanders. This second letter optimistically said the king did not expect the talks to impede Montrose's campaign.[6]

Charles II could not walk away from a double strategy, nor did he see that a double strategy worked only if it was kept private. If he talked with the covenanters in order to come to an agreement, the king could not *in fact* support Montrose's campaign, since Montrose's campaign was directed against the covenanters in the most honest, open and aggressive way. Conversely, if the king supported Montrose's army, then he could not negotiate in good faith with the committee of estates – and they would know it. Perhaps doing both at the same time might have worked better if he had not insisted on telling everyone. The publicising of the second letter meant that Charles II found that instead of cunningly applying carrot and stick, he had tied his own hands. Thanks to battlefield events, he soon lost the initiative in any case. But his public message influenced those events.

Is it right to think that Montrose, having risked everything for Charles I, having been promised help by that king which was never delivered, having lost his possessions in royal service, and lost even the hope of a continued campaign when Charles I ordered him to disband his army in 1646, was now, four years later, the helpless pawn of Charles II? Yes of course. All royal servants were pawns in the end.

Nonetheless, it would be wrong to think the young king was duplicitous. He was merely deceived about his own cleverness. Later history would show Charles II to be more than capable of duplicity, but at this time he was alarmingly open. That was the problem. What he could not see was that Montrose could not apply much pressure if he could not raise support in Scotland, and he could not do that without unconditional backing from Charles II. Always it was all about the king.

One can point the finger at Montrose. Surely he should have been certain that his sovereign was properly briefed? But he had so much on his hands, trying to raise an army, appealing to the King of Denmark, the Queen of Sweden, the German dukes for help, maintaining the men that he had. He was improvising all the time; and anyway, it is hard to tell one's lord that he must back you in the way you choose, on your terms not his. After all, the whole struggle was about the king's autonomy.

There was an English spy, Henry Manning, in Charles II's exiled court. The new English Commonwealth was probably better informed than the Scots about royalist plans, but the latter were in the picture, too. Ships were sent to intercept Kinnoul when he arrived in the Orkneys in September 1649. They failed to engage. Since the 'fleet vessel' the Kinnoul party sailed in had no cannon (although that had been promised) the royalists would have come off badly in a fight, but a gale drove the enemy away. One of Kinnoul's officers, John Gwynne, was inspired to versify:

> The waves so stirr'd about, still mounting high,
> To guard the fearful road, as we passed by;

And Boreas even burst with freenes to blow,
We were toss'd (Lord knows how), to quit the foe.[7]

Once on shore the landing party had further weather protection. David Leslie was sent to Caithness by the committee of estates, to occupy the Orkneys. However, 'When he had boarded several boats-full of horse and foot, to come and fall upon us, there arose so great and sudden a storm, that they could not stir.'[8] Then Leslie was called away, having left garrisons in the distant north. By sailing in March 1650, maybe setting off in the dangerous month of February, Montrose himself crossed the North Sea unharassed. He may have benefitted by his distance from the king's horribly indiscreet court.

In April the royalists crossed the Pentland Firth to Caithness on the mainland. Sir John Hurry led a vanguard of 500 men. Their job was to secure the route south, which they proceeded to do by taking the Pass of Ord on the east coast. They were unopposed. On 11 and 12 April Montrose followed with the main army, maybe 800 (he left garrisons in the Orkneys). He set up his headquarters in Thurso and found there was no mass reaction to his second attempt to bring civil war to Scotland, neither resistance nor support. Some members of the Sinclair and Mackay clan joined him with their followers, but it amounted to little. He set off south.

On the 16th or 17th of April he arrived outside Dunbeath Castle on the east coast of Caithness. Leaving a garrisoned fortress behind him would be a mistake. He laid siege. After a few days the castle surrendered. The defence had been led by Lady Sinclair. She was now permitted to leave with her possessions. Her husband Sir John had set off earlier in order to warn the government.

The immediate reaction of the committee of estates was to rely on the Earl of Sutherland to defend his own. His main residence Dunrobin Castle lay twenty miles further south. By 25 April David Leslie was back, having raised a large force in Brechin. Forced marches would bring him into Sutherland in three or four days but no quicker. Leslie sent instructions to local covenant commanders, Colonels Strachan and Hackett, to do what they could to block the royalists.

Montrose by this time had reached Carbisdale, now the site of a much later castle,[9] on the borders of what are now Sutherland and Ross and Cromarty. He was roughly thirty miles north of Inverness. He camped in a very secure place. The waters of the Kyle of Sutherland (an estuary fed by several rivers) protected his left flank. Behind and to his right was a range of hills, his favoured high country. He would be able to retreat into a narrow pass if necessary. He ordered the men to throw up a defensive breastwork in front. We know at this point Montrose was preoccupied by the risk of Charles II cutting a deal with the covenanters, so much so that his unhappiness was evident to others[10] – this in the man known for unperturbed confidence.

He had left his half-brother Harry in Caithness with some of the soldiers, trying to drum up recruits. He had garrisoned Dunbeath. Some men were lost, taken prisoner by the Dunrobin garrison when they incautiously wandered away from the main force. That castle was too secure for him to attempt, so he risked leaving a hostile presence behind him. The army with him at Carbisdale was about 1,100.

In the immediate vicinity, the leadership of the covenant side had been taken by Colonel Strachan, a fervent presbyterian. He led a group much smaller than Montrose's army, slightly more than 250 men, all mounted, some experienced cavalry, some dragoons. The Earl of Sutherland was tasked with taking on Harry Graham who was reported to be moving south, so he was marching north towards Dunrobin and would not be involved in the coming action.

In the afternoon of Saturday 27 April 1650, Strachan arrived at Wester Fearn, four miles away from Montrose's camp. Partly because delay would take them into Sunday, the Lord's Day, partly because he wanted to show Leslie that he, Strachan, could handle the situation, the decision was taken to provoke a battle. Since he must have had reasonable intelligence from Sir John Sinclair about the size of Montrose's army, this was a courageous choice by Strachan. Though he knew that there were few royalist horse.

The Battle of Carbisdale was quickly fought.[11] Strachan sent a troop of horse into the open while the rest of his men were concealed in thickets of broom, covered at this time of year with bright yellow blossom. On seeing the few visible troopers Montrose conferred briefly with Major Lisle, who commanded his cavalry (who outnumbered the enemy that he could see); then committed his entire force to advance out of the camp. It seems he decided these covenanting horse were a troop previously reported to him as travelling alone through the countryside. If they were, he would easily win the skirmish.

Once the royalists were on the plain, Strachan ordered his hidden men to charge. They at once smashed Lisle's few troopers and panicked the Orcadians, who were the majority of Montrose's infantry. These ran away. A number crossed the estuary in a single boat. The mercenaries made a stand but were also put to flight very quickly.

Strachan had been joined before the battle by 400 infantry from the Ross and Monro clans, who were almost certainly intending originally to fight with Montrose but who discreetly went with Strachan so as to avoid immediate trouble. They did not take part in the initial fighting at Carbisdale, but the collapse of the royalists drew them in for the plunder. Suddenly the fugitives were pursued by a force of nearly 700.

Like a number of his officers Montrose was seriously wounded in the initial charge. His horse was killed under him. Viscount Frendraught,

Sutherland's nephew, gave him his own horse, trusting to the family relationship for his own safety. Montrose at once saw that it was flight or death. Perhaps as a reflex he chose flight. On Frendraught's horse he swam across the Kyle of Sutherland together with several others. The next day they decided to separate (one of them apparently succumbing to his wounds).

By now the great marquess was on foot. Was his horse exhausted? Did he think his chances better as a walker? He had changed clothes with a countryman. Just like the time when he strode through heather on 29 August 1644, to take up his first royal command at Atholl, he dressed in 'Highland habit'.[12] He had thrown away his cloak with the Garter star on it as he fled the battlefield. He could not easily be identified.

On 29 April he found a shepherd's enclosure. For the first time in two days he was given food. The story is that Montrose had to hide while the shepherd spoke with a party of covenanter soldiers searching for royalists. The shepherd did not betray him but did speak about him to one other person at least.

Having left his benefactor Montrose was overtaken by a servant of the Laird of Assynt and led to Ardvreck Castle on Loch Assynt. Montrose had covered twenty-five miles in three or four days. Loch Assynt is no more than ten miles from the west coast of Scotland. Whether he knew exactly where he was is not clear. Ardvreck was not Montrose's destination – he had hoped to get through into the territory of the royalist Lord Reay – but it was shelter.

Here he was joined by one of his officers, Major Edward Sinclair, also found lost in the mountains. The two of them did not know whether they were in friendly hands, but there was nothing obviously hostile so far. It seems very likely that Sinclair would have spoken to Montrose with a natural respect and this was noticed.

The royalist failure at Carbisdale was much worse than at Philiphaugh. Montrose's men were trounced by a far smaller army, if Strachan's group even merits the word. It was the ultimate lesson in the superiority of cavalry, but that was something Montrose knew perfectly well. In his 1644-1645 campaign he always was careful to think of the cavalry equation. There was certainly bad luck involved in various ways, but that is no excuse – warfare always involves luck.

Casualties were almost all on the royalist side. Tradition is that only one of Strachan's men died, by drowning when he pursued the Orkadians across the Kyle of Sutherland. Strachan himself was harmlessly struck by a bullet which hit the buckle of his belt. Wishart writes that 1,200 were taken prisoner, among them Sir John Hurry, and 200 killed. Others have higher numbers. More royalists were rounded up after the battle. Harry

Graham escaped back to the Orkneys and then to the continent before the islands were at last garrisoned with covenant forces.

Montrose's decision to leave his excellent defensive position at Carbisdale tells us all we need to know about his state of mind. He was so keen on success that he could not contemplate anything else. Evidently he had no idea that there was a substantial body of horse hiding in the broom thickets, so historians have pointed to yet another intelligence disaster. But cavalry could travel quickly giving little advance warning. It was much easier to be surprised by horsemen.

In addition, this part of Scotland was supportive of the covenanters, thanks to the influence of the Earl of Sutherland. In some campaigns commanders could be helped by local people freely offering information. There is no record of Montrose ever benefitting in this way, and certainly not in his short 1650 campaign. His passionate commitment to the Stuarts was quite simply not shared. Local people kept their heads down and hoped for the best.

Finally, the whole situation was down to the great game tactics of King Charles II. His cunning plan to use Montrose as a negotiating ploy only meant that hardly anyone dared openly support Montrose. People knew that if the king came to an agreement with the committee of estates – and he did, in the Treaty of Breda of 1 May 1650 – he might have to offer sacrifices. Why volunteer in advance for that?

36

21 May 1650

The Laird of Assynt, Neil MacLeod, was not a power player. His home Ardvreck Castle, the melancholy ruins of which can be seen today, was a fortress out of necessity, but it was small. Like other lesser chiefs in north Scotland, MacLeod was a kind of modest robber baron always in practical awe of the material power of men such as the Earl of Seaforth (Mackenzies), the Earl of Sutherland (Gordons, but traced back through the female line to Sutherlands), and Lord Reay (Mackays).

It is not clear whether MacLeod was at Ardvreck when Montrose arrived there.[1] The tradition is that the half-starved marquess was met by MacLeod's wife. Nonetheless what happened must have happened at MacLeod's direction – indeed, while his position varied over the years, he proudly took credit for it at the time.

A messenger was sent from Ardvreck to David Leslie, now at Tain, fifteen miles from Carbisdale. This was how Leslie learned of the capture of the great enemy. By playing it safe MacLeod received a reward, variously described. Leslie sent his subordinate Major General Holbourn to secure the prisoner. Montrose was arrested on 4 May 1650. He travelled south as a captive on display.

While he was at the mercy of his enemies, many of whom detested him, the marquess was a popular giant – an immense person, that is, in the eyes of the people. Whether he was feared or admired, and whether admired reluctantly or sincerely, he was the only man who had chalked up six battle victories in a row in the recent wars, the only man to cow the Marquess of Argyll. Even if propaganda branded him an excommunicate murderer, Montrose stood for the king and nobody could deny it. Unlike Argyll, he made no personal gains out of the wars, in fact the opposite. As the smoke slowly cleared, and thanks to his own constantly courteous behaviour under abject humiliation, he appeared as a man of principle.

Although forfeited, always referred to only as James Graham when named by the government, he was also a marquess by the gift of Charles I, let alone the head of one of the old Scottish houses. At Skibo Castle, north of Tain, Lady Gray physically attacked Holbourn, hitting him with the nearest thing that came to hand – their supper in fact, a roasted leg of mutton – because Holbourn had seated Montrose between himself and another officer rather than next to her.[2]

At Inverness he was gazed at by the crowd as an object of wonder. A woman not unreasonably scolded him, presumably with real anger and a kind of triumph, for the destruction of her property during his abortive siege in 1646. 'Yet he never altered his countenance; but with a majesty and state beseeming him, kept a countenance high.' Friends greeted him on the way such as Thomas Mackenzie of Pluscarden, and at Elgin the parson of Duffus, Alexander Symons, with whom he had been at St Andrews University.

On 12 May another parson took a different line. At Keith, William Kinanmond used his sermon to lay into Satan's brood. 'This unnatural merciless man so rated, reviled, and reflected upon the Marquess in such invective, virulent, and malicious manner, that some of the hearers, who were even of the swaying side, condemned him.'[3]

On the way to Edinburgh Montrose was allowed to see two of his children at Kinnaird. That cannot have been easy but '...neither at meeting nor parting could any change of his former countenance be discerned, or the least expression heard which was not suitable to the greatness of his spirit.'[4]

There were attempts to help him escape. At the House of Grange near Dundee, Lady Grange plied officers and soldiers with a dangerous combination of 'ale and aquavite'. The men were mainly highlanders. By midnight they were 'stark drunk'. She arranged for Montrose to dress in a woman's clothes (he was not very tall) and in this he made it past the first and second rows of sentinels but was stopped by a trooper who was not part of the guard, and therefore was sober, and unfortunately knew Montrose having been to Ardvreck with Holbourn. That was that.

'With much rudeness' Montrose was returned to captivity. Because of the sheer embarrassment to the authorities, after a tricky night Lady Grange was let off scot-free.[5] Here is another historical what-if. Who knows what his chances were, even if he had got away?

The party came through Dundee, one of the few towns Montrose had allowed his men to plunder five years before. The citizens 'were so far from insulting over him, that the whole town testified very great sorrow for his woeful condition'. Here for the first time he was allowed to change his clothes into something 'suitable for his birth'.[6]

On 18 May 1650 Montrose arrived at Edinburgh, coming from Leith through the Water Gate. A committee of parliament had met the day before to decide how to deal with him. They wanted their prisoner to look ridiculous, powerless before his death. The committee made recommendations about his treatment on arrival, and proposed that he be hanged, the punishment of a common criminal, not a noble (who would normally be beheaded).

They also decided that at his execution a copy of the famous book about his triumphs, that is to say Wishart's history, and also his own declaration of late 1649, should be hung around his neck. After death he would be buried in hallowed ground if he had repented his sins, otherwise in the common grave. When dead he would be butchered. His head would be placed on a spike on the Edinburgh Tolbooth, and his limbs would be sent to different cities, to show people what awaited enemies of the state.

He was now put on a cart, raised above the crowds on a chair, and driven through the streets to the Tolbooth by the hangman, who rode the horse. Montrose was bareheaded while the hangman, wearing official livery, wore a hat, an inversion of the rules of respect. He was tied to the cart with a rope and could not protect himself.[7]

He displayed a transforming acceptance. There were in the crowds

> ...great numbers of women, and others of the lower sort, who were hounded out to abuse him with their scurrilities, and even to throw dirt and stones at him as he passed by; but there appeared such majesty in his countenance, and his carriage and behaviour were so magnanimous and undaunted, as confounded even his enemies, and amazed all the spectators; so that their intended insults and reproaches were converted into tears and prayers for his safety.[8]

As Montrose rumbled past, the Countess of Haddington overplayed her hand by jeering from her vantage point. Nobody joined in. A man in the crowd shouted back that she should be in the cart as an adulteress (a dangerous charge with the Kirk party in control).

The cart stopped by the Earl of Moray's house where three enormously powerful men were watching from a balcony. It was important for them to be seen. They were the Chancellor of Scotland (the Earl of Loudoun), his kinsman the Marquess of Argyll, the great power behind the scenes, and Archibald Johnston of Wariston. More than anyone, they had made the revolution in the first place.[9]

The capture of Montrose should have been their great moment. Montrose looked up at them. They said nothing and 'presently crept in at the windows'.[10] 'His Resolution confounded them.'[11]

On arrival at the Tolbooth Montrose paid the hangman for his trouble. A group came to interrogate him, both members of the parliament and ministers. He refused to answer their questions, asking them how they stood in relation to Charles II. Montrose was told that the Scottish government and Charles II were in agreement (untrue, as there were two weeks of haggling to go before the Treaty of Breda was signed).

The next day was Sunday. The ministers returned. They wanted him to recant so that they could lift his excommunication (this had been discussed at the committee meeting two days before). The point was not the saving of his soul, it was to show that they were right. Perhaps they only wanted to reassure themselves. Montrose did not co-operate.

Parliament could not meet on Sunday. So it was on Monday 20 May 1650 that proceedings resumed. At eight o' clock in the morning the delegation of ministers was back, trying again. This time there was more of a conversation.

Montrose's sins were put to him, a mixture of the political and personal. These were the things that would 'mar his light'. They accused him of being 'aspiring and lofty', of being 'given to women'. They said he had brought 'Irish and Popish rebels' into Scotland and 'taken them by the hand against his own countrymen'. They said his followers had killed many people and destroyed property.[12]

Montrose did not reply to the charge of womanising – nobody else made this accusation, and it was a conventional slur – but was prepared to admit that 'he was one of those that love to have praise for virtuous actions,' quite an endearing confession. He said that God had made men 'of several tempers' and he hoped that God would not withhold light from him on account of his. This remark perhaps shows a much broader and more generous understanding of human nature than was ever displayed by those on the other side of the argument.

He responded also to the political charges, defending Alasdair Macdonald and his followers as loyal to the king at a time when others were not; and saying that he, Montrose, had done what he could to protect innocent lives and private property, but unpaid soldiers must have compensation somehow.

Oddly, perhaps necessarily, the ministers accused him of breaching the National Covenant. Montrose made a robust reply. He reminded them of his enthusiastic support and assured them 'Bishops I care not for them. I never intended to advance their interest.' As for the Solemn League and Covenant, for they also charged him with denying that, he repeated his scorn for the deal with 'a party in England... against the King'.

None of this was the repentance the ministers wanted. James Guthrie told him they could not lift his excommunication and must leave the fate of his soul to the mercy of God, the risk being that things bound on earth would also be bound in heaven (that his destiny as an excommunicate was eternal damnation). That was interesting given the Reformed doctrine of predestination – which taught the fate of the soul after death was decided before life began, not dictated by the Kirk in a political struggle.

Again, it is telling that Montrose responded. He told the ministers he was very sorry to quarrel with the Kirk and longed to be reconciled. But he could not call what he saw as his duty a sin.

In these exchanges Montrose outclassed his visitors. He spoke from the depths while they were caught in the moment.

At ten o'clock parliament met, chaired by the Lord Chancellor, the Earl of Loudoun. Montrose was brought before the assembly, wearing a black suit and over it a scarlet cloak trimmed with silver and lined with crimson. He wore a hat trimmed with silver, which he took off to show respect. He wore scarlet silk stockings and shoes with ribbons on them.[13] He was 'somewhat pale, lank-faced and hairy',[14] having not been permitted to shave. Nor should one forget that he had been wounded at Carbisdale three weeks before.

Loudoun repeated the charges of Montrose breaking the National Covenant and the Solemn League and Covenant, of rebelling against his native country, of bringing in the Irish, and committing 'many horrible murders, treasons and impieties'.

Montrose asked to speak, was permitted to do so and gave his defence at some length. He said that his first campaign, that of 1644-1645, had been under a commission from King Charles I, which he was bound to obey, and that he had disbanded his army and left the country when commanded to do so by the king. He emphasised that his recent campaign was on the command of King Charles II. He spoke calmly and clearly.

Loudoun responded, saying that he was 'the most cruel and inhuman butcher and murderer of his nation'. He was told to kneel, which he did. His punishment was then read out by Wariston, the Clerk Register, death by hanging as already decided, and the details: book, declaration, head, limbs and all. He was sentenced by committee. Legally, the view was that Montrose had been found guilty when forfeited. There was no trial.

He behaved himself all this time in the house with a great deal of courage and modesty, unmoved and undaunted, as appeared, only he sighed... several times, and rolled his eyes along all the corners of the house, and at the reading of the sentence he lifted up his face, without any word speaking.[15]

After hearing the sentence he was taken back to the Tolbooth, where the relentless ministers came, again pressing for penitence. Montrose only said that he considered parliament had done him a great honour and he wished he had more flesh so that more body parts would be available for distribution 'to every city in Christendom' as witness to his loyalty to the king.[16]

During his time in the Tolbooth, the prisoner was permitted no visits from friends and family. He was isolated but not alone because a 'rude guard' was left with him in the cell, to make sure he did not kill himself and cheat the scaffold.[17] On the Monday night Montrose resorted to verse, just as he had when absorbing the news of Charles I's death. On the window of his cell he scratched the following lines:

Let them bestow on every airth[18] a limb
Then open all my veins, that I may swim
To thee, my Maker, in that crimson lake,
Then place my par-boil'd head upon a stake;
Scatter my ashes, strow them in the air.
Lord, since thou knowest where all these atoms are,
I'm hopeful thoul't recover once my dust
And confident thou'lt raise me with the just.[19]

Juggling his thoughts about bodily resurrection on his last night on earth, the always optimistic Montrose showed confidence that he had the love of God. The poem reads like a challenge to his tormentors. Not only does he play with their grotesque decision[20] to dismember him after death, he also announces that he is saved. It was light touch defiance left behind, most provokingly, for them to read.

———

The next morning Montrose was taken to the scaffold which had been erected by the Cross of Edinburgh near the recently completed Tron Kirk (a place of presbyterian worship built on the Dutch model). It was not far from the Tolbooth. The scaffold was a very sturdy construction, four-square in the base. The gibbet was thirty foot high. It would be used repeatedly in the coming weeks to dispatch many royalist prisoners. The prisoner was dressed as he had been the day before 'more beseeming a bridegroom than a criminal going to the gallows'.[21]

Montrose's radiance bathed observers: '... there appeared in his countenance so much beauty, majesty and gravity, as amazed the beholders; and many of his enemies did acknowledge him to be the bravest subject in the world.'[22]

It is absolutely believed that he hath overcome more men, by his death in Scotland, than he had done if he had lived. For I never saw a sweeter carriage in a man in all my life.[23]

At the scaffold he was allowed a speech, or it may have been closer to a dialogue with near spectators.[24] He said that many greater than he had died unjustly. He forgave his enemies but in his characteristic plain-speaking mode said they 'oppressed the poor and violently perverted judgement and justice'. He surrendered himself to God. For the last time he said that what he had done, he had done to 'honour the King, according to the commandments of God, and the just law of Nature and Nations'. He repeated that he was sorry to have quarrelled with the Kirk, and he regretted his excommunication. He desired that to be withdrawn but 'if they (Kirk ministers) will not do it, I appeal to God, who is the righteous judge of the world, and who must and will, I hope, be my judge and saviour.' He described his powerful moral sense, which was unarguably evident in his career, as steeped in spiritual conviction, something transcending the world: 'I do but follow the light of my conscience, my rule, which is seconded by the working of the Spirit of God that is within me.' He concluded with 'my love and charity to you all.'[25]

In the terrible way that had become customary[26] Kirk ministers now railed against Montrose in his last moments. They could not pray for an excommunicate and had to rub it in publicly. Nonetheless with baffling sincerity they wanted him to pray now himself, but he must do so alone. At first he said he had 'already poured out (his) soul before the Lord' but then stood a few moments in silent meditation. After that he was ready.

He gave the hangman four pieces of gold, which was usual. His executioner hung Wishart's book and a copy of the declaration around his neck. Montrose said this was his greatest honour, even greater than the Garter star. His arms were tied behind him. He mounted the scaffold. He forgave the executioner and told him to open the trapdoor when he lifted his bound hands: these seem to have been his last words. He lifted his hands and in that way he died.

Throughout, according to a witness, the hangman was weeping.[27]

37

Funeral Rites

The body was left hanging for three hours. Then it was taken down and the head and limbs lopped off. The trunk was transported to Burghmuir, or the Burrow Mure, to the south of the city, 'a place where malefactors are interred,' and buried with no ceremony. The head was set on a spike on the Tolbooth to rot as carrion in public view. The limbs were distributed to the main Scottish cities for display: the arms went to Perth and Aberdeen, the legs to Glasgow and Sterling.

Very soon after, the mangled stump was illicitly dug up again on the orders of Elizabeth Napier, wife of Archibald, Montrose's nephew. She had stayed in Scotland to mind the family interests while her husband joined Montrose in Paris. Being closely associated with the cause, having herself been imprisoned, and being devoted to her husband, who adored his uncle, Elizabeth had no intention of letting matters rest. She wanted a legacy – or rather she wanted to add to the already rather blood-soaked legacy that had so far been retrieved, which is to say Montrose's hat, and the handkerchief and stockings that he wore when he died (and when he was cut into pieces).[1]

As she instructed, Montrose's heart was cut out of his chest and sent to the 'skilful chirurgeon and apothecary Mr James Callendar' who embalmed it and set in a 'rich box of gold'. Elizabeth had the preserved heart in its beautiful cradle sent to Flanders, to the dead man's son James, now second Marquess of Montrose.[2] Or possibly she took it with her when she joined her husband there and handed it over personally. The now even more damaged trunk of Montrose's body was returned to its burial place.

These risky moves were made easier by location. Merchiston Castle, the Napier residence, now surviving as Merchiston Tower, is less than a mile to the west of the place where Montrose's mauled remains were buried. There was not much ground to cover. In the circumstances no other act of defiance was possible, but perhaps this can also be thought of as nurture for a young man of seventeen as much as loyalty to Montrose himself.

In this way, the Napier and Montrose families at a raw time turned to the ancient Catholic custom of revering relics of the saints. Neither Elizabeth nor her cousin James would have put it that way. They were Scottish presbyterians and did not think that Montrose's heart had miraculous properties. They did not pray to it and regard it as holy, but it was a precious relic in that traditional sense.

Politics spun on. In the Treaty of Breda (1 May 1650) Charles II agreed to accept the authority of the Scottish parliament[3] and the Kirk; and reluctantly said he would take the National Covenant. He did not agree to impose presbyterianism in England. In return he would have Scottish support for his attempt to win back England and Ireland, although the latter was grit in the oyster because of the Catholic element. After the fury of rebellion, the Catholic Irish Confederacy currently was, in the face of Cromwell, rather desperately aligned with the king's Lord Lieutenant the Marquess of Ormond.

By now, to establish goodwill, Charles II had also agreed to call off Montrose's campaign. He did this before discovering that it had imploded. We do not know exactly when the king learned of Montrose's death but it was probably before signing the Treaty of Breda. While his balancing act failed, Charles II sincerely meant to save Montrose. The speed with which the Scottish parliament rushed Montrose to the gallows was to pre-empt the king. There was an attempt by the French royal government to intercede for the great hero, a letter signed by Louis XIV, dated 10 June 1650 (European date – 31 May Scottish date),[4] in other words after he died. The speed of the execution surprised everyone.

On 8 June Charles II wrote to the dead man's heir as follows: 'Though your father is unfortunately lost, contrary to my expectation, yet I assure you I shall have the same care for you as if he were still living, and as able to serve me as ever; and shall provide for your subsistence.'[5]

It is curious, as one reads these words, to think the two men, king and second marquess, were barely adults. The first was twenty, the second seventeen.

On 23 June Charles II arrived in Scotland to continue his talks. His difficulty was that Argyll and his supporters held most of the cards. Theirs was that the Kirk was dominated by zealots who had a nasty streak.

It would be a very difficult time for Charles II. He had a crowd of courtiers and advisers, cavaliers who appalled the Kirk party, but the pressure was very much on him personally. After resisting fiercely, he at last signed a humiliating public declaration in August. He had to say that he was committed to the cause of the National Covenant, that he disavowed the agreement Ormond had made with the Catholic Irish, and he had to express his shame at his father's faults and his mother's idolatry.

The hard-core Kirk more and more alienated the growing royalist party. Argyll was political leader of the Kirk party but found himself impatient with unreasonable and impolitic theocratic tactics – in the end he was hoist with his own petard. One of the problems was that Kirk discipline was extended by emboldened ministers to the upper classes, which was at least consistent, but it was not acceptable.

Royalism was a unifying force among the Scots after Cromwell invaded Scotland and won the Battle of Dunbar on 3 September 1650. As he advanced into Scotland Cromwell wrote to the General Assembly suggesting that the Kirk party suffered from 'spiritual drunkenness' and telling them to consider whether their treasured agreement with God might be 'a Covenant with death and hell'.[6] At Dunbar he fought against the two Leslies, David and Alexander, Earl of Leven.[7] Unexpectedly, the battle ended in English victory: Cromwell's army was weakened by sickness and lack of food but prevailed. After the battle Cromwell was consumed by uncontrollable fits of laughter.

Invasion and defeat triggered a Scottish reaction centred on the king, although it took time to gel. Charles II tried a coup against the Kirk party on 3 October, which was a flop, but it made the point that he could not be taken for granted. After this his position improved. On 1 January 1651 he was crowned King of Scots at Scone by Argyll himself. Neither that, nor the offer of Argyll's daughter in marriage, created a bond. Argyll did not accompany the Scottish army which tried to outflank Cromwell by invading England in August 1651, the fourth Scottish invasion of England since the prayer-book rebellion.

This army was commanded by David Leslie and inspired by the king, who came with them as a fighting officer. At the Battle of Worcester (fought on the anniversay of Dunbar, 3 September 1651) the invaders were defeated by Cromwell. The invasion was what he wanted. He knew it would be easier to confront the Scots in England.

These two victories led to the Stuart dream without the Stuarts, the formal political union of England and Scotland for a short time under the Commonwealth[8] – the first ever state of Great Britain. Scotland was occupied by an English army commanded by General Monck from 1654 to 1660: *Britannia Triumphans* after all.

Charles II fought very bravely at Worcester and after the battle only just avoided capture by hiding, at one point, in an oak tree at Boscobel House in Shropshire. With a new resilience and with remarkable good humour, helped by royalist supporters but very much relying on his own instinct and courage, the conspicuous king, a very tall young man, evaded detection despite near misses and reached the coast. He returned to France in October 1651. By all this he was remade.

The second Marquess of Montrose, his cousin Lord Napier, and Harry Graham did not take part in the Worcester campaign. They did not attempt to come to Scotland at all in 1650 or 1651 because they were too controversial. Even the king was unlikely to welcome them.

———*◊◊◊*———

The death of Oliver Cromwell on 3 September 1658 and the inability of his son Richard to maintain the Protectorate, led to another short period of military rule by three generals, which people found intolerable. The army in England was unpaid, the system was not working. At last, the misery of extreme Reformed Protestantism was rejected.

In the very cold winter of 1659-1660, the English army of occupation in Scotland commanded by George Monck crossed the border and marched south. Monck had been loyal to both Cromwells but saw that the English parliament[9] was the solution and not without difficulty engineered a fully reconstituted House of Commons. There were new elections, the 'Convention Parliament'[10] met on 25 April 1660 and recognized a House of Lords. On 1 May parliament voted for the unconditional return of the Stuart monarchy.

Charles II came back from the Dutch United Provinces where he had issued his unifying Declaration of Breda on 4 April 1660. In this he gave a 'free and general pardon' from which he excepted only those identified by parliament as not worthy of pardon, by whom he mainly meant the regicides. So, as a condition of his restoration, he gave parliament that essential role, an astute political move. He landed at Dover on 25 May and entered London on his thirtieth birthday, the 29th. The return of the king was the first step. The settlement of both England and Scotland required accurate navigation and was not quickly done. For instance, like his father and grandfather, Charles II wanted an episcopalian church in Scotland.

One thing that was rapidly accomplished was the rehabilitation of the king's incomparable Scottish champion. On 4 January 1661 Charles II ordered the reburial of Montrose's remains. On 5 January what had been buried at Burghmuir was for the second time dug up, then taken to Holyrood Chapel:

The town of Edinburgh early, about nine in the clock, set out four of their captains with their companies, all of them in their arms and displayed colours... after a long span marching up and down the streets, went out thereafter to the Burrow mure... his body and bones taken out and wrapped up in curious clothes, and put in a coffin, which, under a canopy of rich velvet, were carried from the Burrow mure to the town of Edinburgh and many thousands beside conveyed this corpse all along, the colours flying, the drums touking [banging], trumpets sounding, muskets cracking and cannons from the Castle roaring.[11]

The skull, still stuck on its spike on the Tolbooth, was taken down and joined the body. At the beginning of February Lord Maderty (husband of Montrose's sister Beatrix) fetched back the other remains, which were also placed with the body and enclosed in a coffin. There was a report that the embalmed heart was brought in at this time but that was probably not what happened: Montrose's heart would have its own travels and troubles.[12] In the chapel the remains were displayed with honour. On 8 February the Scottish parliament rescinded Montrose's forfeiture. This cleared the way for his son to take on the estates and to start to tackle his father's huge debts.

On 11 May 1661 the 'true funeralls' took place 'with a greater solemnity than any of our kings had at their burial at Scotland.'[13] The new burial site would be St Giles' Church. Montrose would be placed to rest with his grandfather, the third earl, Chancellor of Scotland.

There was a procession from Holyroodhouse to St Giles'. It was stormy and wet but when the coffin emerged into the light of day the rain stopped. When it reached St Giles' and disappeared into the church, the rain started again. As the cortège trudged up the hill into the centre of the city, the trained bands on either side of the street fired their muskets in the air, and the cannon of Edinburgh Castle boomed.[14]

At the head of the procession were two 'conductors in mourning' holding black staves. Twenty-four poor followed, dressed in gowns and hoods and carrying a funeral banner, or gumpheon, displaying the Montrose arms. Then came a group which stood for the broader clan Graham led by Harry Graham in full armour on a horse, featuring a number of flags such as a streamer with the Montrose arms, a full standard with his arms, four smaller banners with the same arms, another gumpheon 'of black taffety' and a 'pincel (streamer) of mourning'. These were carried by different Graham relations. The smaller banners were carried by trumpeters.

In the same group were Montrose's domestic servants and his friends, who all walked two by two. There was a horse decorated with his badges of parliament. George Graham of Drums carried a gauntlet on the point of a lance. Mungo Graham of Gorthy carried a helmet, also on the point of a lance. George Graham of Monzy carried a casket. At the end wads another banner of mourning carried by John Graham of Balgown.

In the next group was the Scottish civic establishment: the Lord Provost, the Bailiffs and Burgesses of Edinburgh, the members of parliament and Scottish nobles. All these walked two abreast, the nobles at the end as the highest caste.

Then was a heraldic display of Montrose noble connections. For Montrose's mother's side the arms were shown of Lord Dirleton, the Earl of Angus, Lord Methuen and the presumably still slightly controversial Ruthven of Gowrie (the titles had not been returned to the family). For his father's side the same was done for the Earl Marischal, the Earl of Wigton, the Earl of Perth, and finally – the last place was the most honourable – the Marquess of Montrose. All these were carried by members of the family concerned.

The heraldry continued with the next group led by James Graham of Bucklevy carrying a banner showing the arms of Montrose in mourning. A horse in full mourning followed led by 'two lackeys'. Then came trumpeters, pursuivants, heralds. Other Montrose household officials followed including two secretaries, William Ord and Thomas Saintserf (or Sydserf) and a chaplain (possibly Wishart). Further emblems followed: Montrose's parliamentary robes, a baton to show his military command, the star of the Order of the Garter, his marquess's crown, and a purse, each carried by Grahams.

The coffin approached. In front walked Sir Alexander Durham, the Lion King of Arms, carrying Montrose's Coat of Honour. The coffin was carried by fourteen earls: Mar, Morton, Eglinton, Caithness, Winton, Linlithgow, Hume, Tullibardine, Roxburgh, Seaforth, Callendar, Allendale, Dundee, Aboyne.[15] The canopy above the coffin was carried by eleven lesser nobles: Viscounts Stormont, Arbuthnott, Kingston; and Lords Strathnaver, Kilmaurs, Montgomery, Coldinghame, Fleming, Gask, Dumlanrig, MacDonald. Twenty-one gentleman followed in order to relieve the coffin carriers if necessary.

By the side of the coffin walked Montrose's two sons James, second Marquess of Montrose, and Lord Robert Graham. After came the nine men nearest in blood: the Marquess of Douglas, the Earls Marischal, Wigton, Southesk; the Lords Drummond, Maderty, Napier and Rollo; and the Laird of Luss. We do not know the order they walked in but probably the nearest places to the coffin went to the most senior nobles.

Behind it all was the king's commissioner, driven in a coach. He came at the end as the highest ranking person present, standing for the king. It is not clear who this was, possibly the Earl of Lauderdale.

Rather oddly the remains of the great marquess were re-buried at the same time as those of Sir William Hay of Dalgety, also a royalist casualty of the wars, but not a man of Montrose's unique stature. However, the double funeral emphasised the royalist point and did honour to the Hay family. Nobody seemed to mind the glory being shared: 'The friends of both the deceased had wedding countenances, and their enemies were howling in dark corners like owls.'[16]

After the funeral the young second marquess gave a feast in his house at which a sermon might have been expected, for this was a religious occasion, but it was not permitted. The presbyterian age was far from over – but even so it was a sign of the times.

38

Magnificat

In the course of Montrose's career, names recur. What became of them?
The longest lived was his father-in-law Southesk. He died at eighty-three in 1658. He was a moderate royalist whose relations with his son-in-law were uncomfortable. Other family members fade into the penumbra but we know that James, second Marquess of Montrose died in his mid thirties in 1669. The line continued and is represented today by James, Duke of Montrose.

The year 1669 also saw the death of Henrietta Maria at not quite sixty in France. She was given what turned out to be an overdose of opium – to help her sleep – by the doctor of her nephew Louis XIV. It was a calm end to a far from calm life. Elizabeth of Bohemia, the Winter Queen, had died in 1662 of sickness aged sixty-five, having at last returned to England with her nephew Charles II in 1660. She had been away fifty years.

Of the Palatine children who are on the edges of Montrose's life – though he and Prince Rupert had quite a correspondence after he left Scotland in 1646 – the three eldest boys met different fates. Charles Louis, the Elector Palatine, died peacefully in 1680 having lived a complicated married life and, like his parents, having had many children. At almost sixty-three Rupert died of sickness in 1682 after a life of adventure both physical and intellectual. In a way he was the child most true to his mother's spirit. Maurice was lost at sea in 1652 aged thirty-one.

As for the children of Charles I and Henrietta Maria, two would be kings – Charles II and James II – but two died of sickness in 1660, the year of Stuart triumph: Henry, Duke of Gloucester, and the beautiful Mary, Princess of Orange. They were twenty and twenty-nine respectively.

The baby girl who came dramatically into the world in Exeter in 1644 died aged twenty-six in France in 1670. On her deathbed she thought she was poisoned but the cause of death was probably a perforated ulcer. Henrietta, also called Henriette-Anne, was raised at the French court by her mother – the 'Anne' was a tribute to Anne of Austria. She married, for better for worse, her first cousin Philippe d'Orléans, brother of Louis XIV.

The second Lord Balmerino died in 1649 of 'apoplexy', which means a stroke or heart attack – a sudden collapse. The Earl of Loudoun died in 1662 of sickness, so he lived to see the reinstatement of Montrose, which must have given pause for thought. Alexander Henderson had died in 1646 after trying to woo Charles I in the presbyterian cause. He was sixty-three. There is reason to think he found the king's stubbornness exceptionally distressing.

Covenant generals survived to die in relative peace. The great survivor the Earl of Leven died at home in Balgonie Castle in 1661, about eighty years old. Leven was a supporter of the Kirk party and took no part in the Engagement nor in the Worcester campaign, but even in his seventies continued some involvement in Scottish military affairs.

David Leslie died at home in 1681. He joined the engagement and was captured and imprisoned after the Battle of Worcester and was only released in 1660. Charles II made him Lord Newark in 1661. William Baillie died peacefully in 1653, also having taken part in the Engagement, also fighting at Worcester. Very much against his will, he surrendered to Cromwell, so he escaped without imprisonment. Sir John Hurry had changed sides at the wrong moment. He was beheaded in Edinburgh not long after Montrose was hanged.

Argyll survived until the Restoration. He was beheaded in 1661 on the charge of collaboration with the Cromwellian régime in Scotland, a fate he met calmly enough. Although he has his admirers, and was not the cardboard cutout villain, it is not easy to make him a sympathetic character. At the last minute Argyll stood back from direct involvement in the committee which decided Montrose's fate, although there is no doubt he agreed with them. The reason may have been that his wife was due to give birth at any moment and he wanted to be with her. She did so on the day Montrose died (producing a daughter).

From his youth Argyll was wrapped in politics, was obliged to be if he were to preserve his inheritance (which was his duty). His verdict on Montrose was characteristically severe and surely utterly mistaken: 'He (Montrose) got some resolution after he came here how to go out of this world, but nothing at all how to enter another, not so much as once humbling himself to pray at all on the scaffold.'[1]

Wariston was hanged in 1663. Lanark, who became second Duke of Hamilton, died after the Battle of Worcester during which his leg was smashed. It was probably gangrene that led to his death. His elder brother, as noted already, had been executed in England soon after Charles I.

Of the Gordons, Viscount Aboyne died in Paris in February 1649 'of an ague'. Like his elder brother George he predeceased their father Huntly (executed in March 1649). So it was the violent Lewis who succeeded as third Marquess of Huntly. He also died young, in 1653 in his thirties, as the result of sickness. At the time he was under pressure from his uncle Argyll who, through financial engineering, was trying to take possession of the Huntly estates – which would have made him even more a Scottish superpower. In time, the land was returned to the Huntly family. Archibald Napier the younger died in the Netherland in September 1658, of sickness. He was thirty-four.

Not least was Alasdair MacDonald who died in 1647 in Ireland, after being taken prisoner in battle. He was shot dead, perhaps in the course of a quarrel between his captors, an obscure death for an exceptional warrior. He, too, was in his thirties.

———

If we are to believe the story, and successive Napiers did, Montrose's embalmed heart moved on. The package was like a Russian matryoshka doll. The heart itself was wrapped and enclosed in a steel case, which was inside the gold box, which was inside a silver urn. Precious as it was, the heart was lost – perhaps the urn was stolen – and turned up in a Dutch collection, from which it was returned to the Napier family in the eighteenth century. By this time the urn had gone but the golden box and steel case remained.[2]

Then the gold box was destroyed in a situation worthy of Montrose himself. By the early nineteenth century the relic was in the possession of Hester Napier, who married Samuel Johnston, an officer in the East India Company. On their way to India the ship they travelled in was attacked by a French squadron. Hester and Samuel stood on the deck facing the danger.

She had packed her most valuable items, including the heart of Montrose, in a velvet reticule to which she clung. French cannon shot struck one of the English quarterdeck guns. Splinters flew. Two sailors were killed. The Johnstons were hit, both were wounded, but happily the velvet reticule took most of the blast. The golden filigree box was shattered, although the steel case and its contents were undamaged.

When they reached their journey's end in Madura, south India, Hester commissioned another gold box from a local craftsman, and another silver urn (the original was recorded in family papers).

On the new urn a short account of Montrose's life and death was engraved, in Tamil and Telugu. The multicultural whole was displayed in the Johnstons' drawing-room. It was quite small: 'The steel case was the size and shape of an egg. It was opened by pressing down a little knob... inside was a little parcel, supposed to contain all that remained of Montrose's heart, wrapped in a piece of coarse cloth, and done over with a substance like glue.'[3]

It, too, was stolen – probably for its talismanic power. The urn and contents were taken or sold to a tributary chief of the Nabob of Arcot – a person with influence similar to a seventeenth-century highland chief.

Yet the Johnstons' son Alexander recovered it. He went on a hunting expedition with this chief and saved his life when the party was attacked by a wild boar. The noble later asked him how he could repay the debt. Alexander told him about his ancestor's heart and explained what it meant to his mother. His host replied that he did not know the urn had been stolen and said he would of course return the heart of Montrose to the family: 'The next day he stood by his promise and sent the young man home with six of his finest hunting dogs, two matchlocks, a gold dress and some shawls for Lady Johnston and the silver urn accompanied by a letter apologizing for having innocently been thus the cause of her distress.'[4]

Having beaten vigorously through the Scottish Revolution the relic was later caught up in the French Revolution. The Johnstons were returning home in 1792. They were in France when the new French government ordered that all gold and silver was to be surrendered so that it could be melted down to help finance the war. In order to save Montrose's heart, Hester gave the silver urn to a Mrs Knowles, who promised to keep it safe.

Mrs Knowles died unexpectedly soon. The urn and its contents were never again found.

—◦◦◦—

From Montrose's life a legend grew of honourable royalism. This was in tune with the romantic movement of the late eighteenth and first part of the nineteenth centuries and the remoulding of Scotland in English eyes, and especially of the highlands, during the reign of Queen Victoria.

The monument to Montrose in St Giles' is owed to Victoria who on an 1886 visit expressed her astonishment that he had no real memorial there. By 1888 it was built and on view. By this time the remains of his body had disappeared, probably thrown away when a coal cellar was added to the church in 1829.

The prolific novelist (and poet and critic and lawyer) Walter Scott (1771-1832) was the most important figure in the cultural redefinition of Scotland during that period. His fascination with Scottish legend and history made him a trailblazer. Scott wrote about England and Scotland at different periods. He was a huge popular success through to the early twentieth century. He was involved in Scottish cultural affairs including the rediscovery of the Honours of Scotland, the Scottish crown jewels, in 1818. They had not been seen since 1707 but were safe in a box hidden in Edinburgh Castle which, on a warrant from the Prince Regent, Scott with others found and opened.

One of Scott's novels, *A Legend of Montrose* (published 1819) is set during Montrose's campaign. In the next century John Buchan wrote a novel with the Montrose campaigns as background and Montrose himself appears as a cameo: *Witch Wood* (published 1927). Other novelists who found inspiration in the story of Montrose are Margaret Irwin, Nigel Tranter, James Dow, Robin Jenkins. Biographers of the nineteenth and twentieth century have followed the narrative of the noble marquess.

Does that get him right?

If one plays devil's advocate it is tempting to redraw, to see in Montrose a man of ambition looking for success, who went full speed ahead in whichever direction seemed gainful. More than one contemporary thought he suffered from 'intolerable pride'. In 1637 and 1638 it was the National Covenant or nothing, until the personal successes of others, mainly Argyll, made him jealous. Then royalism gave him a way ahead against his natural opponents.

Personally, he was considered 'pleasant and witty in conversation' and 'frequent in his devotions'[5] which suggest something a bit different from this. Looking at the Bible he bought in France, with the notes he made, we have confirmation of the religious interest.

Montrose was thought to be learned but also ambitious, even dreamily so. 'He had taken upon him the part of a hero too much...'[6]

Earlier work on Montrose has bypassed his split heritage. He was half Ruthven, half Graham. His position came from the latter but the politics of his mother's family were respectably Scottish, even if they went against the Stuart program. Dispossessed and proscribed, the Ruthvens were still there, as Mary Ruthven's court position shows. Is it fanciful to think he was torn by his own family history?

Even if reconstruction as a narrow careerist were a satisfactory narrative, one would still have to grant Montrose's success in the field.

Commanding disparate regiments that were not filled with natural friends was not straightforward. The Irish who came with Alasdair MacDonald were potentially as much trouble within the army as to the enemy. But there was no such difficulty. And evidently Montrose won six battles in a row and avoided defeat until Philiphaugh, even when caught in tight corners like Fyvie, Dundee and Crieff.

His appetite for risk was colossal, as evidenced by the winter campaign of 1644-1645, the march before Inverlochy, the determination to continue south in late summer 1645 after his best troops had deserted. Another talent was Montrose's sheer speed of manoeuvre, his ability to melt into the highlands and resurface miles away before anyone thought it possible, his night marches, his feints. All this in charge of large bodies of men crossing huge expanses.

Montrose's leadership skills were outstanding. He had an ability to command and inspire lacking in others of similar background (for instance the covenanter leaders at Tippermuir and Aberdeen, or Argyll himself). A big part of that was his own courage, his driving energy, his being an involved general – but it was more than example. Leading soldiers requires thought, discipline, understanding. It is also a matter of personal style. His was low-key, unassuming. And he took big decisions quickly.

One of the critiques is that Alasdair MacDonald was responsible for much of Montrose's achievement and has been airbrushed out. Montrose won Alford without his presence. Otherwise, it is true that Alasdair was an extraordinary soldier – and saved the army at Auldearn when he sent out lookouts first thing. Montrose owed him a lot.

Yet the proud Gordon lords also played a big part in the 1645 battles. They would not have agreed to fight side by side with Alasdair unless Montrose was in command. Nor would the Athollmen.[7] Nor were the essential marches and manoeuvres the work of Alasdair. Montrose's officers were part of the command structure, notably Alasdair himself with his outstanding Irish colonels, but there is a skill to working with subordinates, winning respect. Undoubtedly Montrose had huge charisma – and he delivered.

There is nothing in the sources which make us think that Montrose had a cynical drop of blood in his veins. He could stop and think, he could deceive – as when he met Alexander Henderson on the riverbank in spring 1643 – he could be a courtier, as he was with Henrietta Maria and Charles II in exile. But we see from his exchanges with Charles I that he was happy to speak plainly to a king, and, judging by the letters of Elizabeth of Bohemia, with a queen too.[8] That was his natural mode.

By preventing the sack of Aberdeen at the end of the first Bishops' War and of Glasgow after Kilsyth, Montrose showed he was a principled general. He was not squeaky clean. His year of success included a later sack of Aberdeen, the devastation of Argyll and destruction of a lot of property elsewhere. Yet he held his men back when other generals would have let rip, and when his own ability to pay them was very limited.

By preserving the lives of prisoners when he was urged to take revenge, he remained morally steadfast under pressure. He was generous to his opponents, for instance when he wrote to Charles I after Inverlochy that the Campbell army 'fought some time with great bravery... as men that deserved to fight in a better cause.'

By contrast, the moral standards of his opponents fell away. At Tippermuir, Montrose's herald (his brother-in-law) was imprisoned before the battle and promised a beheading; after that first battle Lord Kilpont was murdered and his killer exonerated by parliament; at Aberdeen the drummer boy was shot dead, again before the battle; after Inverlochy the Kirk bayed for innocent blood (the execution of prisoners); there were the massacres of defenceless camp followers in Methven Wood and after Philiphaugh.

Wariston's nephew, a bishop of the Church of England, found words to describe what the covenanters had tragically become:

> They affected great sublimities of devotion... they had but an ordinary proportion of learning among them; something of Hebrew and very little Greek; books of controversy with papists, but above all with the Arminians, was the height of their study [ie they were mainly concerned with the internecine Protestant war]. True morality was little studied or esteemed by them.[9]

Montrose is criticized for lazy intelligence work. It was poor at Fyvie Castle, at Dundee, very poor before Auldearn. Before Philiphaugh it was negligent. Also at Carbisdale, although Strachan's cavalry would be fast moving. Yet historians who criticize him do not scrutinize his opponents' record as closely.

The winter raid on Argyll was entirely unexpected and undetected by the Campbells. At Inverlochy, the Marquess of Argyll – now on the warpath, when he should have been alert – was taken by surprise. The night march from Dundee to safety, when Montrose should have been captured and killed, was accomplished undetected by Baillie's scouts. After Auldearn, Montrose escaped from Strathbogie, again at night, when he should have been trapped. Not long after that, Baillie's faulty intelligence meant that Montrose deceived him (initially) about the true size of the royalist cavalry outside Perth.

Montrose made mistakes but the truth it that one might expect many more. All the time, from beginning to end, his chances were so low against a well-organized and vindictive enemy that could pay soldiers, that his phenomenal success makes us expect perfection.

Montrose's character weakness was naivety – yet without that apparent flaw nothing would have happened. He entered Scotland in 1644 without a hope, trusting in the shining light of the king's commission, and in himself. Rescued by the arrival of Alasdair MacDonald, he did not question the risks of Catholic soldiers at war in the presbyterian lowlands. But if he had, so what? Where would that have left the king's cause? Wrongly, he hoped for lowland support aftert Kilsyth, but what was the alternative? The confidence we see after Inverlochy and his final admission that he liked to be praised are very human qualities which frankly bring the man to life.

His devotion to the king – which increased with time – was a kind of blindness. Very few students of the period believe Charles I was sincere in the concessions he made to the covenanters after his unwarlike Bishops' Wars and in 1641. Yet Montrose always took the view that the king had granted what was asked, with the result that the covenanters only pushed further. They ripped up the Treaty of London and in the end sold their king to the English. For him, both were treasonable acts. Yet the covenanters had good reason to fear royal duplicity. If Charles I had been able to, he would have ridden roughshod over any deals.

The execution of Charles I would be a wound to Montrose so deep that it killed him. In 1649 he could have continued his career in French or Habsburg service and made his fortune, but he chose to return to Scotland for the Stuarts. He was troubled by Charles II's determination to negotiate with Argyll and the Kirk extremists and was badly compromised by the young king's attempt to do two things at the same time; but he continued regardless. This was selfless, almost thoughtless loyalty.

The mystery of Magdalen, the death of their son John and the imprisonment of their second son James remind us that behind Montrose stood almost invisible people. The abduction of his sister Katherine by Sir John Colquhoun in 1631 led to him missing the coronation. In 1638 another sister, Dorothea, died. We do not hear of his reaction. As far as we can tell, he did not give his close family much priority by comparison with his campaigns, his projects of glory. Not that this was unusual in an élite man of the time. Their privileged world was hard.

Montrose was a man who led, who acted, who directed, who proposed, who fought. As a condemned prisoner he had to be passive, the opposite of his nature. Taken captive, condemned, harangued, led to the scaffold, he could have been, should have been, humiliated. That was not what happened. He faced death with an acceptance so complete it could be felt through the crowds, it made the hangman cry. It was his grandest, most tranquil, most generous triumph. As a last impression, it overwhelms the rest.

Montrose Timeline

1612	Birth of James Graham, Lord Graham (probably in October).
1624	James is sent to study in Glasgow (Michaelmas term).
1625	Death of James VI and I (27 March), accession of Charles I. Charles issues his Revocation (October).
1626	Death of fourth Earl of Montrose (14 November), James succeeds as fifth Earl of Montrose.
1627	Montrose starts at St Andrews University.
1629	Montrose marries Magdalen Carnegie (10 November).
1631	Montrose's sister Katherine elopes with – or is abducted by – her brother-in-law Sir John Colquhoun (September).
1632	Sir Thomas Hope starts prosecution of the absent Sir John (October). Montrose sets off for France.
1633	Coronation of Charles I as King of Scots in Edinburgh (18 June). Montrose is at the Angers military academy.
1634-1635	Trial of Lord Balmerino (starts 3 December 1634).
1634-1636	Montrose travels in France and Italy.
1636	New Book of Canons introduced in Scotland (January). Montrose returns home, meeting Charles I for a formal audience in England on the way.
1637	Prayer-book rebellion (starts 23 July).
1638	Launch of National Covenant (28 February). General Assembly at Glasgow (November-December).
1639	First Bishops' War. Covenanter Montrose defeats royalist Viscount Aboyne at the Brig O' Dee; Pacification of Berwick. Both on 19 June.
1640	Second Bishops' War. Scottish army invades England and occupies Newcastle. Treaty of Ripon (28 October) – the agreement insists on an English parliament being summoned.

1641   Execution of Strafford (12 May). Montrose and associates arrested (11 June) and held in prison on suspicion of plotting against the Scottish committee of estates. Treaty of London provides Scottish settlement after Bishops' Wars (10 August). Charles I visits Edinburgh to appoint ministers (14 August-18 November). The 'Incident'.

1642   Montrose retires to private life. Charles I raises his standard at Nottingham Castle, beginning the first English Civil War (22 August).

1643   In York Montrose warns Henrietta Maria about covenanter aggression (March). His fears are confirmed in a personal meeting with Alexander Henderson (June). He joins Charles I in Oxford (July-August). Solemn League and Covenant signed (25 September).

1644   Leven leads Scottish army into England (19 January). Charles I makes Montrose Lieutenant-General in Scotland (1 February), and elevates Montrose to marquessate (6 May). In England, Battle of Marston Moor (2 July). Montrose meets the army of Alasdair MacDonald in Atholl and raises the royal standard (29 and 30 August). Battles of Tippermuir (1 September) and Aberdeen (13 September). Winter campaign in Argyll begins.

1645   Battles of Inverlochy (2 February), Auldearn (9 May), Alford (2 July), Kilsyth (15 August) and Philiphaugh (13 September). In England Battle of Naseby (14 June).

1646   Charles I, held in captivity by the Scots at Newcastle, orders Montrose to disband the royalist army (19 May and 15 June). End of first Civil War. Montrose retreats to Norway (September).

1647   Montrose arrives in Paris (spring). George Wishart publishes the first edition of his account of Montrose's campaigns (October). Montrose travels to Prague where he is made Marshall of the Holy Roman Empire. The Engagement, agreed in Carisbrooke Castle (December), marks the beginning of the second Civil War.

1648   Battle of Preston (17-19 August) ends the second Civil War. Montrose travels through east Europe and reaches Flanders (August).

1649   Execution of Charles I (30 January). Montrose plans an invasion of Scotland through the Orkneys in support of Charles II.

1650   Montrose lands in the Orkneys (early March) and crosses to the mainland (early April). The Battle of Carbisdale (27 April). Montrose is captured and hanged (21 May).

1660   Restoration of Charles II.

1661   State funeral and reburial of Montrose in St Giles' (11th May).

Reformed Protestant Beliefs

I have made a selection of points from the teachings of Calvin (1509-1564) and others who developed Protestantism after Luther (1483-1546). My summary aims to give a sense of the psychology, not to analyse every point of theology, something I am not qualified to do.

1 Simplicity
The aim of Protestant reform was simplicity, to detach Christian teaching from the powers of the world, the rich, controlling hierarchies, in order to focus on the original Gospel message. Simplicity was also desired as a reaction to the intellectual tradition of scholasticism which emphasised meticulous rationality and, it seemed to the reformers, led to fruitless complexity.

2 Humility
To grasp, today, what the theologians of the time were driving at, one might consider a twenty-first century doctor, writing about a patient after several rounds of complicated surgery, 'At the depths of the most unimaginable vulnerability he has discovered that we live not by choice but by grace.'[1]

This idea that we live and thrive spiritually thanks to a greater reality which we can explore through instinct and faith but never fully know, something we glimpse – as we go through the life we directly see and feel – caused the Protestants to preach a profound humility. Catholic theology also insisted on humility, but it seemed to Protestants that Catholic leaders conspicuously lacked it.

3 Predestination
Salvation, a mystical acceptance of and by God, was – is – the purpose of Christianity. Theology develops from this conviction. In the realm of

eternity, a soul after bodily death either is joined with God in heaven or suffers damnation, the unending separation from God. The doctrine of predestination was a refinement of the belief, shared by Catholic and Protestant, that salvation lies in the hands of God alone.

Predestination taught that the fate of your soul after death was predestined by God before you were born: your salvation is entirely in the hands of God. Catholic teaching of this period included the belief that your actions during life mattered, that God observed and judged, that when it came to judgement He reviewed, or considered, or was influenced by your choices, your actions freely willed, during your lifetime. Protestant thinkers rejected this idea of winning favour with God.

The famous scriptural passage is 'For by grace you have been saved, by faith, and this is not from yourselves, but is the gift of God, not by works.' (St Paul, Letter to the Ephesians 2.8-10). In St John's Gospel Jesus says 'This is why I told you that no-one could come to me except by gift of the Father.' (John 6. 65-66).

A rich Catholic might endow a Chantry chapel where, after he/she died, prayers would be said for her/his soul.[2] One might buy an 'indulgence' which would also help after death. Reformed Protestants (and Lutherans) said 'works' like this achieved nothing, citing St Paul and St Augustine of Hippo.

Luther proposed that salvation came *sola fide* (by faith alone). He said faith was the gift of God and in no way a decision of the human will. One way of thinking about this is to reflect that faith is a surrender to God. This Lutheran idea was developed by the Reformed thinkers.

Predestination, cut and dried, seemed to destroy the incentive to do good. Taking it very simply, if you are predestined for heaven, you can do what you like on earth. The second difficulty lies in the many references in the Bible to God's forgiveness of sin, to divine mercy – a response to human behaviour.

Predestination could be elaborated strictly or permissively. According to a modulated interpretation, God's knowledge of the destiny of every human soul – God is omniscient, He has always known where everyone will end up – is a form of predestination. In that sense we are predestined by definition. It does not mean that free will has no meaning. Protestant Arminianism[3] embraced this softer approach.

4 Sola scriptura

The Protestant principle, starting with Luther, was that only Holy Scripture provided authority. Belief in God was not all instinct, there were revealed truths recorded in the Bible. Being clear about authority, meaning who should be listened to, was obviously essential.

In the Reformed tradition there was some sliding down the scale. Calvin's opinion was that scripture was divinely inspired, and therefore had a unique authority. It was others who hardened that belief into the view that authority came from scripture alone.[4]

Sola scriptura means by scripture alone. So the interpretations of theologians, of Popes, of anyone, as the centuries rolled by, had no authority. The Word of God commanded obedience. In spiritual matters the word of man did not.

Not only was the Bible enough. Anything else was too much. Evidently, the new teachings set up their own tradition and interpretation, which seemed to undermine *sola scriptura*, but the new thinkers always elevated the words of the Bible. By contrast, Catholicism allowed the development of authority mediated through the Catholic Church over time.

Sola scriptura could also lead to a certain narrowing because it set limits. These tended to tighten. Scripture itself made the point. St Paul warned against an over-defined spirituality when he wrote 'the letter kills but the Spirit gives life.'[5]

5 The vernacular

Early modern Catholic liturgy was Latin, celebrated in church at a distance from the lay congregation (separated by an elaborate carved screen). The Catholic priest as he celebrated Mass was invisible to the congregation. The language the people heard was foreign.

The Protestant preacher addressed his audience face to face, in their own language and not always in church. Preaching became a distinctly Protestant practice because it connected intensely and immediately with the people.

The drive for Bibles in the vernacular was profoundly Protestant. Different parts of the Bible were written originally in Aramaic, Hebrew and Koine Greek, translated later into Latin. Before translation into the vernacular, unless you read one of these languages you could not read the Bible. You needed a priest to tell you what it said. Protestantism wanted everyone to read the Bible for themselves (*sola scriptura*). It must be translated.

6 The Eucharist

The climax of the Catholic Mass is the celebration of the Eucharist, or Holy Communion, the primary Christian ceremony. The Last Supper of Christ, before His arrest and crucifixion, is re-enacted with the priest blessing bread and wine just as Christ does in the Gospels. History is repeated, Christ is among the faithful, incarnate again. There is no more ambitious statement of Christian mystery.

The Catholic take was that the Eucharist was a sacrament which transformed the bread and wine into something else, a different and now holy substance – in fact the body and blood of Christ. This was 'transubstantiation', the 'real presence' of Christ.

Luther believed that the Eucharist was a sacrament, that it made a real change, and agreed about the real presence. However, Lutheran teaching was that bread and wine were also present after the blessing. This is sometimes referred to as the doctrine of 'consubstantiation' although that was not the term used by Luther nor adopted by most Lutheran churches subsequently.

Reformed Protestants discarded sacrament as much as they could. They celebrated the Eucharist as the Lord's Supper but for them it was a reminder, a spiritual experience, but the bread was always bread and the wine always wine. Neither was to be worshipped.

7 Images

If a Catholic could not read, or could not read Latin, she/he could look at pictures and sculptures to understand and enjoy stories and characters from the Bible and other places. Churches were filled with frescoes and carvings, the latter inside and out. Events in the life of Christ were depicted. Every Catholic church had at least one sculpture of the crucified Christ.

Catholicism was a multimedia, multilayered religion which called upon image, ceremony (including the intoxication of incense), music, folk memory (lives of the saints), as well as the Bible text. The reformers wanted to cut things down.

Images in particular went against the Ten Commandments, especially statues. There are two versions of the Ten Commandments in the Old Testament. In both cases the second commandment forbids images – whether of 'anything in heaven above or on earth below or in the waters under the earth'.[6] Having statues (and pictures) was worshipping idols. Hence iconoclasm came, the destruction of religious art and a veto on its production.

8 Saints

To reformers, the worship of false gods was lamentably evident in the ancient Catholic tradition of saints, holy people now in heaven, to whom the believer could pray for help. Catholic prayers to saints strictly are prayers of intercession (not worship), asking that the saint will make his/her own appeal to God. Addressing a saint is not the same as worshipping a dead woman or man. It could seem a fine distinction.

The cult of saints, highly visible through the long Catholic years, was forbidden by Reformed Protestantism. Within Reformed Protestantism people still alive came to be called saints, meaning that they were predestined for heaven.

9 Structure

Not the least issue was how the Church should operate as an organisation. Calvin was very interested in this. In the Catholic world a hierarchy spiralled down from God. The Pope was God's vicar on earth. He had authority over the Church everywhere. In each country was an episcopate, archbishops and bishops, who controlled the area given to them (their 'see'), mainly through local parishes, each run by a priest, who had a pastoral duty to the laypeople. It was like a military command driven from above. It was orderly.

This linked to the parallel secular chain of command under the king who appointed bishops for instance (with occasional disagreements with Rome). The sovereign himself/herself was a kind of unique priest: coronation was like ordination.

Church hierarchy was rejected by Reformed Protestants, as being non-biblical, and with it, to varying degrees, the connection of church discipline with the king. Rejection of episcopacy (having bishops) was an important part of the politics.

Instead the emphasis was put on the local congregation (parish). Under presbyterianism the parish was the building block, superintended by ministers and lay elders. Regional synods consisted of parish representatives. In Scotland the General Assembly, a national body, was also a meeting of parish representatives, supposedly chosen by local vote. Even the presiding officials were elected by those attending, not imposed by a higher authority or tradition.

In the lay elders, presbyterian Protestantism institutionalised lay participation. This was itself different from the clerical Catholic system. It mirrored the outreach of the vernacular Bible and services.

Not all separatist Protestants – those who wanted to separate church from state – thought like the presbyterians about structure and discipline. Independents proliferated, sects with a number of approaches. None of them liked bishops.

On the other side were the Erastians, who thought church and state went together, and wanted the national church to be under the control of royal or at least secular authority. So they liked bishops. James VI and I and his son Charles I (and later Stuarts) were Erastian.

Stuart Marriages

King James VI and I arranged marriages for his children that created lasting complications. These were an important legacy.

Elizabeth Stuart, Electress Palatine and Queen of Bohemia
In February 1613 the king's daughter Elizabeth married the Elector Palatine Frederick V. The Elector Palatine governed two blocks within the Holy Roman Empire, the Rhineland Palatinate around Heidelberg, and the Upper Palatinate to the north of Bavaria, centred on Amberg. He was the most senior secular prince in the empire, and head of the German Protestant Union, a group that opposed Catholic expansion.

It is not true to say that James's son-in-law started the Thirty Years War, but he helped it along. Because of the confessional pressures in the empire there was going to be a breakdown at some time, but the problem that arose could have dissipated without the Elector Palatine.

In 1618 there was a Protestant rebellion in Bohemia. In August 1619, against the advice of most of his friends and family the Elector Palatine accepted the Bohemian crown, which the rebels had offered him. The coronation took place in November. It was a challenge to the rather militantly Catholic Holy Roman Emperor Ferdinand II who had himself been elected King of Bohemia before the rebellion (it was an elective crown). The Battle of the White Mountain outside Prague on 8 November 1620 ended in a decisive defeat of Frederick's army by imperial and Catholic League troops. From these actions, more and different instability spread within the empire.

Frederick, his heavily pregnant wife and their family fled from Prague into exile. In February 1621, he came under the imperial ban as a rebel. By imperial law he lost not only Bohemia but also the two Palatinates and his electoral title.

The Palatine family would never return to Bohemia. Because Frederick's reign had lasted a single winter, the royal couple invited the derisory nickname, the Winter King and Queen. For the rest of their lives they always called themselves King and Queen of Bohemia. A senior title was never abandoned.

Throughout, James VI and I remained peace-loving. He did not send English troops to help the Palatine family. His involvement in the early stages of the Thirty Years War was political, and only in the sense that his daughter was an exile. However, he did at last authorise a mercenary expedition against Spain – which he thought deniable – under Count Mansfeld. It took place during the last months of his life.[1] It was meant to be an attack on Spanish possessions in the Low Countries, or even on Spanish troops in the Palatinate. This costly and embarrassing fiasco achieved nothing. Many men died through disease and malnutrition. There was no fighting.

Elizabeth of Bohemia was an important figure in British politics. In 1620 she was second in line to the Stuart thrones of England, Scotland and Ireland. She was the heir, and her many children the heirs in the next generation, until 1630 when her brother had his first surviving child.

Even after that, some people preferred Elizabeth and her line as British monarchs, compared with the half-French children of Charles I. Elizabeth was impressive personally and she became a Reformed Protestant figurehead. She was always totally loyal to her brother, but the reputation of Charles I also suffered because he did nothing substantial to help her and her family to regain the Palatinate.

Charles, Prince of Wales

In 1620 it became obvious to King James that the Palatine quarrel could be resolved if the Prince of Wales married the sister of the King of Spain, the Infanta Maria Ana. The emperor was the girl's cousin. Both were Habsburgs. James VI and I thought that a Stuart-Habsburg match would create harmony in the empire as a result. This was the 'Spanish Match'.

His thinking was wrong. Spain's war with the Dutch required untroubled passage over the 'Spanish Road', which led from north Italy (Milan was a Spanish possession), flanking in its last reaches the Rhineland Palatinate, to the low countries. This was how Spanish armies reached the theatre of war; and the Dutch War was the absolute Spanish priority. So Philip IV of Spain did not want the Palatinate to return to the Protestant Elector Frederick. Nonetheless, he maintained the marriage negotiation with the Stuarts.

At the age of twenty-two the Prince of Wales decided that he could make his marriage happen by going to Madrid himself. In February 1623 he set off incognito. It was another bad idea. Far from impressing the infanta with his utterly unexpected arrival, he found himself all but a hostage, although he was treated with the greatest respect (and learned new ideas about royal etiquette while in Madrid, and also about art).

By October Charles was back in England without the bride but apparently irretrievably committed to the marriage, because a marriage treaty had quite surprisingly been signed (with his father's agreement). It did not mention the Palatinate, which was the key political point for the Stuarts.

The prince was now fiercely anti-Spanish. His always touchy sense of royal honour had been deeply offended by the situation he had himself created. The Spanish Match fell through and another bride was sought. (From the start James VI and I wanted a Catholic bride for Charles, to balance the Protestant husband of Elizabeth; and a princess of exceptional pedigree to raise Stuart international status.)

Even before Charles arrived at Plymouth (5 October) a message had been sent to France. That was revenge since Spain and France were inveterate enemies. It was also a question of availability. The youngest sister of King Louis XIII, Henriette Marie, was fourteen years old. She was more or less pledged to her cousin the Comte de Soissons, but that was soon dropped.

After hard negotiation Charles won his Catholic bride. Henriette Marie became Henrietta Maria or, officially, once married, Queen Mary. In December 1624 the marriage articles were at last agreed. The necessary dispensation from Pope Urban VIII was sent in February 1625. The wedding took place in the summer after the death of James VI and I. The Pope agreed to the ground-breaking (Protestant-Catholic) match reluctantly. He thought Henrietta Maria would be unhappy in England.

Fortunately, the terms of the marriage treaty were not widely known. James VI and I had to make enormous concessions to France, which included a promise to relax anti-Catholic laws (something he had promised parliament he would not do). Henrietta Maria was allowed a large Catholic religious household, chapels in all her personal residences and control of the education of any children up to the age of thirteen.

At first, she did not impose her Catholicism on her children or anyone else. However, in the course of the 1630s the queen became confident, even asking Pope Urban VIII to appoint an English cardinal (which did not happen). By the end of the decade she had engineered a culture of court Catholicism which included a number of converts, mainly noblewomen.

Henrietta Maria was a devoted wife. Her energy and strength of mind and her faith alarmed the English and Scottish Reformed Protestants. She was not the only cause of Charles I's complex political difficulties, but she made a contribution.

Alasdair MacDonald

Alasdair MacDonald was enormously important to Montrose in 1644-1645. In *Highland Warrior – Alasdair MacColla and the Civil Wars* (1980), David Stevenson examined what is known of his life, proposing there could have been no year of glorious success for Montrose without him. Stevenson also wrote his entry in the Oxford Dictionary of National Biography. In this appendix I draw on both these sources.

I have used the name Alasdair MacDonald. He came from one of the many branches of the MacDonalds, the family which dominated the western isles in the medieval period. The name helps place him, especially because of the enmity between Campbells and MacDonalds which developed in the early modern period. He is also called Alasdair or Alexander MacColla, because his father was known as Coll Ciotach or Colkitto.

Colkitto was one of the claimants to the chieftaincy of the clan Ian Mor, the southern branch of the MacDonalds. Because of feuds within the MacDonald family, they were incapable of defending their historic claims against encroaching neighbours, mainly the Campbells. Hence the situation described earlier whereby Kintyre and neighbouring territory became a *casus belli*. In 1636, Colkitto was obliged to submit to Lord Lorne and pay him for the lease of Colonsay (the one possession which he had kept).

Alasdair's birth date is not known. He was roughly the same age as Montrose and may also have been born in 1612. His mother was probably also a MacDonald (from Benbecula). He was distantly related to the Irish Earl of Antrim, who would play a key part in his career.

Thanks to his later fighting prowess, he had the distinction of childhood legends a bit like the infant Hercules. He was said, as a boy, to have caught a cow in one hand and killed it with an axe, for instance, and to have eaten toads (this was also said of Montrose).

He was Catholic. As an adult he had the reputation of being pious, bringing priests with him into Scotland in 1644, for example. He is described as 'most respectful and reverential to priests' and 'remarkable for zeal in the faith'. This made the Antrim plan of an invasion of Scotland from Ireland especially detestable to the presbyterian Lorne/Argyll, and Charles I's intention to reward Antrim with Kintyre and other land, by now held by the Campbells, uniquely painful.

In the late 1630s and early 1640s Alasdair was in exile in Ireland, driven away by Lorne/Argyll's campaign of defence in Kintyre (which included the imprisonment of Colkitto and two of Alasdair's brothers in 1638 or 1639). From late 1641, the rebellion in Ireland provided him with fighting work. At first, he fought on the royalist side against the rebels but the religious tensions in a mixed Catholic-Protestant force were too much for him, so he changed sides. In January 1642 he led an attack on his Protestant colleagues. However, he deserted again after a secret deal with the Earl of Leven, to release his father and brothers. When that fell through – Argyll would not co-operate – Alasdair returned to the Catholic, rebel side.

As well as their courage and strength, the men that Alasdair brought with him used the tactic for which he became famous, the Highland Charge. This took the form of one volley of musket fire followed by a rapid charge, a shock attack, before the enemy could reload, leading to hand-to-hand fighting. It appears to have been characteristic of highland warfare, although it has been argued that other armies used something similar, for instance in the early part of the Battle of Naseby.

When Alasdair left Montrose after the Battle of Kilsyth, he may have sincerely intended to return (he had on every previous occasion). He left a large body of his Irish troops with Montrose but they were mostly killed after Philiphaugh, with their camp followers. Their loss may have convinced Alasdair that the divergent aims of the two men could no longer be reconciled. Montrose wanted to win Scotland for Charles I and fight for him in England if necessary. Alasdair prioritised the MacDonald claims in west Scotland.

When in 1646 Charles I ordered royalist forces in Scotland to disband, Alasdair did not obey. He had by this time conquered much of the territory that he ardently wished to possess. But the covenanter government was now free to pursue him and did so with great savagery and success in 1647. He escaped to Ireland but most of his men were massacred.

Alasdair MacDonald died on 13 November 1647 having been captured after a battle at Knocknanuss, County Cork. He had led a successful cavalry charge and was plundering the Protestant baggage train when he was captured. Why he was shot is not known, it may have been the result of an argument between his captors.

Notes

1 Introduction

1. Dominic Pearce, *Henrietta Maria* (Amberley 2015)

1 A Pot of Gold

1. Narrative mainly from the account of W. F. Arbuckle, *The 'Gowrie Conspiracy'* Part I (Scottish Historical Review Vol 36. No 121, Part I (April 1957) pp 1-24); and *The 'Gowrie Conspiracy'* Part 2 (Scottish Historical Review Vol 36. No 122, Part 2 (October 1957) pp 89-110)
2. Probably not very effectively. That was reversed in 1641
3. *The English Thanksgiving Service for King James's Delivery from the Gowrie Conspiracy*, F. C. Eeles, in The Scottish Historical Review Vol. 8 No 32 (July 1911) pp 366-376
4. Amy L. Juhala, *Ruthven, John, third Earl of Gowrie* (ODNB) quoting J. Spottiswoode, *History of the Church of Scotland*
5. Esmé was a Scottish duke but to all intents and purposes he was French. His mother was French, He was brought up in France. His father had been adopted by a French nobleman as his heir. Esmé was Catholic, arriving in Scotland in the wake of the Scottish Reformation. And there was a body of opinion that he was the lover of the young king (probably a lie). He may have become Protestant while in Scotland.
6. For the sum owed see Amy L. Juhala, (ODNB) *Ruthven, John, third Earl of Gowrie*
7. In fact the queen was in her sixth month of pregnancy, not a good time to receive a nasty shock. And her great affection for Beatrix Ruthven, one of her household ladies, sister to the two dead men, is enough to explain why she should have been disturbed by what happened. Beatrix was dismissed. Queen Anne may have enlisted the Ruthvens as political allies against the Earl of Mar, with whom she had repeated quarrels about the guardianship of her eldest son, Henry.
8. In Scotland, James VI's bisexuality was barely an issue, unless this really is the explanation of the struggle at Gowrie House. In England it would have been more important.

2 *The Royal Family*

1. Hugh Trevor-Roper, *The Invention of Scotland* pp 11-15 and following pages on John of Fordun in particular.
2. Jacob de Wet was commissioned in 1684 to paint 111 portraits of the Kings of Scotland, of which 97 are now on display.
3. Also the Canmores.
4. Formally the child was never queen, because she was not enthroned. She was called the Lady of Scotland.
5. Both descended from Earl David of Huntingdon, who was grandson of King David I of Scotland. Balliol was the senior because he was grandson of Earl David's eldest daughter. De Brus was the more proximate (first rather than second generation) as son of Earl David's second daughter.
6. It was only formally returned to Scotland in 1996.
7. National Records of Scotland: www.nrscotland.gov.uk
8. They were originally a Norman family called Fitzalan but changed the name. 'Stuart' replaced 'Stewart' in the sixteenth century because of the Lennox Stuarts who used French spelling, the French language having no native use for the letter W. The family name of Lord Darnley, a Lennox Stuart, father of King James VI and I, is spelled Stuart. Mary, Queen of Scots, raised as a Frenchwoman, also used French spelling.
9. Robert (Stewart) II was grandson of one king and nephew of another, his mother's half-brother, David (Bruce) II.

3 *The Scottish Reformation*

1. Monteth of Salmonet, *History* p 3
2. Some were well trained theologically such as James VI and I, also the Emperor Ferdinand II. The Pope himself was of course a sovereign power.
3. Several Acts of Parliament denied papal authority, denied the legitimacy of Mary, daughter of Catherine of Aragon, and gave Henry VIII and his successors supreme authority in the Church of England.
4. In England, Mary's position was less secure because the will of Henry VIII prohibited foreigners from succeeding to the throne, which, if it held, obviously disbarred a Scot.
5. John Knox *Works*, Vol 4 p 232
6. Knox Vol 4 p 373
7. Row, *History* p 12
8. Balfour, *Annales* Vol 1 p 314. Arran was the scion of the Hamiltons who, after the Stuarts, were heirs to Scotland. Of all the husbands proposed for the future Virgin Queen, Arran was the most suitable except for his mental health. In 1562, still unmarried, he had a mental collapse and was confined as insane for the rest of his life.
9. *Scots Confession*, from chapters 11, 12, 15, 22, 24 – www.fpchurch.org.uk

4 *Lord Graham*

1. Louisa G. Graeme, *Or and Sable* pp xvii-xviii
2. Now called Old Kincardine Castle.
3 His father, son of the second earl, died at the Battle of Pinkie in 1547.

4. Their daughter Margaret married in 1619, perhaps at the age of seventeen or eighteen. Hers was the first wedding of that generation.
5. Williams, *Montrose – Cavalier in Mourning*, p 5
6. Napier, *Montrose and the Covenanters* Vol 1 p 117 quoting Sir John Scot of Scotstarvet.
7. The Witchcraft Act of 1563 made consulting witches a capital offence.
8. Napier, *Memoirs* Vol 1 p 10
9. Lee, *Road to Revolution* p 68

5 Exit King James

1. Donald, *An Uncounselled King* p 9
2. Made at the Hampton Court Conference of 1604, when the king debated religion with bishops and Puritans. The discussion led to the commissioning by the king of a new translation of the Bible, the King James Version (published in 1611).
3. Wormald, *James VI and I* (ODNB)
4. Gordon of Ruthven p 9
5. The English liturgy was introduced in the reign of Edward VI, with a break for the reintroduction of the Catholic Mass by Mary I. It was revised from time to time, notably by Elizabeth I. James VI and I also introduced some changes.
6. Row, *History* p 307
7. D. Laing (ed) *Original Letters relating to the Ecclesiastical Affairs of Scotland* (Bannatyne Club, Edinburgh 1851, vol 2 p 580)
8. Stewart, Laura A. M., *The Political Repercussions of the Five Articles of Perth: A Reassessment of James VI and I's Religious Policies in Scotland* (the Sixteenth Century Journal Vol 38, no 4, winter 2007 pp 1013-1036)
9. Mitchison, *A History of Scotland*, p 189
10. Anthony Weldon, *Perfect Description of the People and Country of Scotland*. The quotations are to be found in pp 2-6.
11. Gordon of Ruthven, *A Short Abridgement...* p 76
12. Lee pp 188-189
13. Jenny Wormald, *Court, Kirk and Community in Scotland 1470-1625*, p 161
14. See Appendix 3

6 Kinnaird Castle

1. She had married Charles I in a proxy wedding outside Notre Dame before setting off. There was no English wedding although there was a ceremony at Whitehall at which she was declared queen.
2. Napier, *Memorials* Vol I p 140-142. These are 1627 inventories, the year James went to St Andrews university. However, one describes items in the Glasgow house and the second lists possessions held by William Forret (who did not go with his master to St Andrews). The books were also Glasgow possessions moved to St Andrews.
3. The Emperor Nero thought Seneca, who had been his tutor, was involved in a plot against him and ordered him to commit suicide.
4. Napier, *Memorials* Vol 1 p 142
5. On its first publication in 1614 the *History* was briefly suppressed because of the king's irritation with his prisoner's self-publicity and the political comments, but it

became one of the great publishing successes of the seventeenth century, issued and re-issued. It was recommended by the later Lord Protector Oliver Cromwell to his son.

6. Raleigh, Walter, *History*, vol 2 pp viii-xxx, pp xvi-xvii, vol 6 pp 50-75, pp 130-136, vol 2 pp 339-352
7. The 'Emathian plains' refers to Thessaly, in the north-west of the Greek mainland, where the Battle of Pharsalus was fought in 48 BC. The English version is my translation of the Latin: Bella per Emathios plus quam civilia campos/iusque datum sceleri canimus, populumque potentem/in sua uictrici conuersum uiscera dextra/cognatasque acies, et rupto foedere regni...
8. Napier, *Memorials* vol 1 p 151-153
9. Wishart, *Memoirs of Montrose* p 220
10. Cowan p 10
11. Napier, *Memorials*, Vol 1 p 109
12. Napier, *Memorials* Vol 1 variously in pp 153-201
13. Napier, *Memorials* Vol 1 p 118.
14. Napier, *Memorials* Vol 1 pp 156-201 itemise Montrose's university spending
15. For John's age see Louisa Graeme p 141
16. Kinnairdcastle.co.uk
17. Williams p 12 quoting Sir John Ochterlony

7 Charles I, King of Scots

1. These were 'kindly' tenants who paid a low rent for historic reasons.
2. Sanderson, Margaret H.B., *The Feuars of Kirklands* (The Scottish Historical Review, vol 52, no 154, Part 2, October 1973, pp 117-136)
3. Hannay, R.K., *On the Church Lands at the Reformation* (Scottish Historical Review, vol 16, no. 61, October 1918. pp 69-70)
4. In 1624 Nithsdale was King James's emissary to the Pope to obtain the dispensation for the marriage of Charles and Henrietta Maria, which explains why both kings favoured him and the Scots did not.
5. Donald, *An Uncounselled King* pp 18-19
6. From 27th March 1625 when James VI and I died to Charles I's birthday.
7. Donald, *An Uncounselled King* p 20
8. Gregg, *Charles I* p 287
9. Cust, *Charles I, a political life* p 215
10. Lee, *Road to Revolution* p 69
11. montrose-society.ndo.co.uk/poems
12. R. Ian McCallum, *Patrick Ruthven, Alchemist and Physician* (Proceedings of the Society of Antiquaries for Scotland 2004) p 474
13. Archibald's father John invented logarithms.
14. Napier, *Memorials*, p 8

8 Hopeful Youth

1. *Charles I's Edinburgh Pageant 1633*, David M Bergeron, Renaissance Studies vol 6 no 2 (June 1992) pp 175-182

Notes

2. Alan R. MacDonald, *Deliberative Processes in Parliament c 1567-1639: Multicameralism and the Lords of the Articles*, The Scottish Historical Review Vol 81, no 211 Part 1 April 2002 p 26
3. J. Row, *History of the Kirk of Scotland* (Woodrow Society 1842) p 364
4. Spalding, *History of the Troubles...* Vol I p 21
5. Row, *History* p 368
6. Spalding Vol I pp 17-20
7. Row *History* p 363
8. Spalding Vol 1 p 18
9. Mitchison quoting Sir James Balfour p 190
10. Row p 367
11. Bergeron p 17
12. Napier, *Montrose and the Covenanters* Vol 1 p 121
13. David Stevenson, *Graham, James, First Marquess of Montrose* (ODNB)
14. Martin Garrett, *Lithgow, William* (ODNB)
15. Lithgow quoted in Williams p 14
16. See narrative in Napier, *Memorials* Vol 1 pp 96-100
17. Pearce, Henrietta Maria p 124

9 Opening the Mind

1. De Lisle, *White King* p xxv See Appendix 3 for the Prince of Wales in Madrid
2. Gordon's mother was Henrietta Stuart, daughter of the Franco-Scot Esmé Stuart, first Duke of Lennox. Because of a long family history of service to the Kings of France (under whom the Lennox Stuarts held land), the second duke, Gordon's uncle, was involved in the revival but died in 1624. It fell to Gordon to receive a second commission from Louis XIII in which he, Gordon, was named captain. He took it up in 1632, not long before Montrose arrived.
3. The marriage was declared invalid by the Parlement de Paris and would not be accepted until Louis XIII, on his deathbed, was reconciled with Gaston (May 1643).
4. Puységur, *Mémoires* vol 1 p 135
5. Marie de Médicis as regent dealt with several noble revolts in this way, although eventually she imprisoned (i.e. did not execute) Condé for his part.
6. The execution was performed by something very like a guillotine see Puységur p 137.
7. In 1638 his wife at last produced a healthy son, who would grow up to be Louis XIV. In 1640 she produced a second healthy son, Philippe.
8. Marie de Médicis' father was Grand Duke Francesco I (de' Medici) of Tuscany, her mother the Archduchess Joanna of Austria (daughter of Emperor Ferdinand I).
9. The first military academy was founded in 1616 by Count Johann VII of Nassau-Dillenburg at Siegen, east of Cologne.
10. Hastings p 44. On dancing *Harleian Miscellany* Vol 7 p 287
11. Ed. Geoffrey Parker, *Cambridge History of Illustrated Warfare* p 154
12. Ed. Geoffrey Parker, *Cambridge History of Illustrated Warfare* pp 156-7
13. John A. Lynn, *Giant of the Grand Siècle* p 517
14. Geoffrey Parker ed. Cambridge Illustrated History of Warfare p 146
15. He was Duke of Holstein, which was an imperial principality.

16. Scots travelled and settled widely; it was not just military service. When the Swedish army accepted the surrender of Würzburg in Franconia (now northern Bavaria), the local abbot delivered the capitulation, the Scot Fr William Ogilvy. See James Miller, *Swords for Hire – the Scottish Mercenary* (Birlinn 2007) pp 152-162, on Nithsdale pp 123-4.
17. Gordon of Ruthven p 76
18. Mantua and Modena were nominally independent, while Ferrara was now part of the Papal States ruled by a cardinal legate, but still displaying the treasures of the Este family. The Este retained Modena after their expulsion from Ferrara. They were a branch of the Guelf dynasty and therefore very distantly related to the north German family which became Electors of Hanover and Kings of Great Britain.
19. Ed. George Holmes, *The Oxford Illustrated History of Italy* p 119. In 1647 there was a full-scale tax revolt in Naples.
20. Burnet, *History* p 53. On Feilding see Ann Hughes, *Feilding, Basil, Second Earl of Denbigh* (ODNB)
21. Although Portland and his daughter both died in 1635.
22. See Leopold von Ranke, *Ecclesiastical and Political History of the Popes of Rome During the Sixteenth and Seventeenth Centuries* (trans. Sarah Austin, John Murray 1841), second edition Vol 2 pp 555 to 587
23. *Dialogo sopra I due system massimi del mondo* (Dialogue about the two greatest world systems)

10 Noble Lords

1. Stevenson, *Scottish Revolution* p 52
2. Lee, *Road to Revolution* p 43
3. The crown had claimed it as a male fee, a title that could only men could inherit.
4. By decision of the Court of Session. Menteith was created Earl of Airth in compensation. So he was a double earl still. Today, Prince William, Duke of Cambridge, is Earl of Strathean.
5. Literally if obscurely 'with a threefold knot, a threefold wedge'.
6. Spalding Vol I p 32
7. Charles Rogers, *A true Rehearsall...* (Transaction of the Royal Historical Society Vol 5 (1877)) p 359
8. Millstone, Noah, *Evil Counsell, the Propositions to Bridle the Impertinency of Parliament and the Critique of Caroline Government in the late 1620s,* Journal of British Studies Vol 50 no 4 October 2011 p 823
9. John A. Inglis *Sir John Hay, the 'Incendiary',* the Scottish Historical Review Vol 15 no 58 (January 1918) p 134
10. Row p 386
11. Row p 384
12. Mitchison p 182
13. Monteth of Salmonet p 9

11 Meeting the King

1. Pearce, *Henrietta Maria* pp 81 and 127
2. See Appendix 2 on Reformed Protestant belief.

Notes

3. Spicer, Andrew *'Laudianism' in Scotland? St Giles' Cathedral 1633-1639: A Reappraisal* (Architectural History Vol 46 2003) p 99
4. Clarendon *History* Vol 1 p 140
5. Cust, *Charles I* p 223 This did not survive into the final draft where 'presbyter' was used.
6. Baillie *Letters* Vol 1 p 2. The Reformed Church detested the Catholic doctrine of transubstantiation, the miraculous conversion of bread and wine into the body and blood of Christ.
7. Heylyn, *Cyprianus Anglicus* p 373
8. Napier, *Memorials* p 70
9. Pearce, *Henrietta Maria* p 129 The queen asked for an English cardinal to be appointed, but Urban VIII wanted to investigate the delicate situation more thoroughly. Although she promoted Catholicism at court the queen never tried to use her marriage treaty to raise her children as Catholics while she was in England. Later she would behave differently, but by then everything had changed.
10. A doctor also known as an alchemist. See R Ian McCallum, *Patrick Ruthven, Alchemist and Physician* (Proceedings of the Society of the Antiquaries of Scotland (2004)) pp 471-490
11. They married in 1639 or 1640 see *Ruthven Family Papers* p 57

12 *'An holy nation'*
1. Guthry, *Memoirs* p 20
2. Pearce pp 154-155
3. Baillie Vol 1 p 10
4. See Charles Rogers, *True Rehearsall...* p 359 recording secret meetings of Scottish Puritans in 1636 and 1637.
5. In March 1603 Sir Robert Carey took two and half days going at top speed, in order to be the first to tell James VI that Elizabeth I was dead. See de Lisle, *After Elizabeth* pp 126 and 136.
6. Spalding Vol I p 49
7. Guthry p 21
8. Lee p 188
9. Guthry p 24
10. Guthry p 27
11. Spalding Vol 1 pp 45-46
12. He was married to another Carnegie sister, so he was Montrose's brother-in-law.
13. Cust, *Charles I* p 229
14. Book of Exodus 19, 5-6
15. Book of Jeremiah 31, 31-34
16. Rothes, *Relation* 79
17. At this time there was a much longer gap, twenty years, between General Assemblies than there was between English parliaments.

13 *Thrusting Through*
1. Wariston, *Diary* pp 393, 395
2. Wariston p 385
3. Gordon of Rothiemay Vol 1 p 132

4. David Stevenson, *Michelson Margaret* (ODNB)
5. Burnet, *History* p 49
6. John Coffey, *Johnston, Sir Archibald, Lord Warison* (ODNB) quoting Wariston's *Diary*
7. Gordon of Rothiemay *History* Vol 1 p 45
8. Guthry p 30
9. Being Catholic was illegal in Scotland. Yet unlike in England there was no system of fines for people who refused to conform to Protestantism.
10. Charles Rogers, *True Rehearsall* p 361
11. The 1609 Statutes of Iona of James VI and I tried to tackle highland Catholicism, with other separatist problems of the area.
12. Rothes, *Relation* 81-84
13. Firth, C. H. *Ballads on the Bishops Wars 1638-40* (Scottish Historical Review Vol 3 no 11 (April 1906) pp 260)
14. Baillie p 94
15. Baillie p 96
16. Baillie p 97
17. He had already tried to trump the National Covenant with the 'King's Covenant' which was the 1580 document with which the National Covenant started. That of course did not reject later innovations such as the prayer-book. Privy councillors signed this in September but few others. The privy council did not have the same distribution as the covenanters. The greatest success of the King's Covenant was in Lord Huntly's country, the north-east.
18. Cust, *Charles I* pp 233-4
19. Claimed to be copies of the registers of early General Assemblies.
20. Baillie p 116
21. Gordon of Rothiemay Vol 1 p 152
22. *Hardwicke Papers* quoted by Williams, *Montrose* p 59
23. Guthry, pp 34-35 Hamilton had been accused of intriguing for the throne of Scotland in 1631 by Lord Ochiltree. Charles I gave that no credence to that at the time. Nor did Hamilton ever put himself forward. In the late 1640s he fought for Charles I and in 1649 died for him.
24. Nor did the legal nitpicker Sir Thomas Hope.
25. I am grateful to John Adamson for this insight. It was not the Scottish tapestries alone that the king loved, it was tapestries in general.

14 Salve regina
1. For the date see John Callow, *Campbell, Archibald, Seventh Earl of Argyll* (ODNB). The original settlement in favour of the Campbells was in 1609.
2. They descended from the first MacDonald Lord of the Isles.
3. Clarendon, *History of the Rebellion* 3.509
4. Probably devised by the Earl of Nithsdale. Fissell *The Bishops' Wars* p 3
5. Hamilton was also involved. In spring 1638 he suggested to the king using Antrim and the MacDonnells against Argyll/Campbell power. The thinking and the discussion predated the 1638 General Assembly.
6. Gordon of Ruthven p 56
7. Clarendon quoted in Willcock, *The Great Marquess* p 63
8. University of Oxford text archive tei.it.ox.ac.uk/tcp/Texts-HTML/free/A04/A04599.html

Notes

9. Nor about Ireland. Great Britain was the main island, England (with Wales) and Scotland.
10. *Book of Genesis* I, 3
11. Court Catholicism was increasing through conversion in mid- to late 1630s. It was no coincidence. Henrietta Maria's patient, low-key activism was paying dividends.

15 Silver Bullet

1. The narrative is in Fissell pp 6-7
2. Fissell pp 7-8 note 16
3. The king won his case against John Hampden but only just, by seven judges to five. The question was whether it was legal to withhold payments.
4. Spalding p 107
5. Gordon of Rothiemay Vol 1 p 222
6. Napier, *Montrose and the Covenanters* Vol 1 pp 229-230
7. There had been another confrontation between Southesk and Montrose in Forfar.
8. She was Catholic, although the covenanters may not have known, Gordon of Sallagh p 542
9. Spalding p 109
10. Gordon of Ruthven p 229
11. Spalding p 92
12. David Stevenson, *Gordon, George, Second Marquess of Huntly* (ODNB)
13. Williams p 78
14. John J Scally, *Hamilton, James, first Duke of Hamilton* (ODNB)
15. Williams p 79
16. Terms were agreed the day before.
17. On 19 May 1639 there had been a skirmish on the Borders triggered by the adventures of a young English colonel. This was the first time shots were fired between English and Scottish troops in the Civil Wars. Both the Earl of Holland on the English side and the Earl of Home for the Scots downplayed the incident. Both clearly wanted to avoid fighting. Fissell pp 24-25.

16 Theatre of War

1. Aston, *Iter Boreale* p 5
2. Fissell p 22
3. Aston p 11. It was the first time an English army was arranged by regiment, according to the new flexible philosophy of war that changed the logistics and communications.
4. Clarendon *History* vol I p 150 (ed. Macray, Oxford 1888)
5. Gregg *King Charles I* p 291
6. Fissell p 27 quoting Rawlinson MS b 210
7. Clarendon, History p 157 (Oxford 1888)
8. It is still surprising he retreated. All he needed to do was rejoin his infantry.
9. Fissell p 35 quoting the *Hardwicke Papers*
10. Firth, C. H. Scottish Historical Review, Vol 3, No 11 (April 1906) p 263
11. The king's clemency should not be overstated. There were acts of brutal suppression committed in his name, the most famous being the mutilation and imprisonment of the puritans Burton, Bastwick and Prynne in 1637; also the imprisonment of Sir Dudley

Digges and Sir John Eliot in 1629 (at the king's instigation). Nonetheless Charles I tended to be legalistic, as the disastrous attempt to arrest the Five Members of the House of Commons in January 1642 shows.

12. There was a mechanism to allow for this, the Act of Oblivion, which protected people under a general settlement.
13. Buchan, *Montrose* p 26
14. Burnet, *History* p 53
15. The Lords of the Articles (who set parliament's agenda) before included bishops who were integral to the management and indeed election of the rest of the committee. If there were no bishops, the Lords of the Articles must be selected in a new way. For this parliament it was agreed Traquair as Royal Commissioner could stand in for the bishops in the selection process – he would put forward the names of nobles to sit on the committee. That seemed to allow the king a role, as was traditional.
16. Since no Act of Parliament had validity without the king's signature nothing was absolute, but every decision was pressure against him – and clearly a public declaration.
17. As would be clear in 1641, the king nonetheless retained a considerable authority in appointments.
18. Charles I considered that the absence of the bishops from parliament gave him a get-out clause. Parliament was not duly constituted without them, so these Acts counted for nothing.
19. Williams, pp 85-89
20. Smith, David L. *The Fourth Earl of Dorset and the Personal Rule of Charles* I (Journal of British Studies vol 30 no 3 July 1991 p 277)

17 On a Windowpane

1. Lord Mountnorris in 1635. The sentence was not carried out.
2. The office of deputy had to be held by a man resident in Ireland.
3. Percy Simpson and CF Bell, *Designs by Inigo Jones for Masques and Plays at Court* (The Volume of the Walpole Society Vol 12, 1923-24 pp 16, 124, 130, 131)
4. Burnet, *History* p 54
5. Gregg p 316
6. Gregg p 310
7. DiMeo Michelle, *Howard, Aletheia, Countess of Arundel* (ODNB)
8. CSPV 25 May 1640

18 Ford of Lyon

1. From *The bonnie House of Airlie* quoted in Hastings, *the King's Champion* p 105
2. Henry Paton, *Ogilvy, James, second Earl of Airlie* (ODNB)
3. Guthry p 79. Part of the conversation treated the immediate issue, whether a parliament could sit without royal authority. Perhaps the more alarming question about the king followed naturally.
4. Williams p 91
5. Including melting privately owned silver, Guthry p 62
6. Wishart note to p 27
7. Gordon of Ruthven p 36

8. Wentworths and Saviles were Yorkshire families.
9. Gordon of Sallagh, *Continuation...* p 501
10. Pearce p 171

19 'His Majesty is the sun'
1. 1688 Coronation Oath
2. Baillie Vol 1 p 259
3. In fact, copies of the notes taken by Vane (produced by his son).
4. Not widely known but known to Pym and his group.
5. A Stadholder ('Governor') was the elected head of individual Dutch provinces – Holland was the richest and most powerful of them, so the Stadholder of Holland was in effect head of the United Provinces. Different provinces could and sometimes did have different Stadholders who had to work with the provincial estates, who elected them. The Orange-Nassau family had a kind of monopoly of the Stadholderates but they were not autocrats, there was power-sharing.
6. Monteth of Salmonet p 74
7. Napier *Memorials* Vol 1 pp 268-271. Another letter published by Napier's descendant Mark Napier in the nineteenth century was once thought to be evidence of sophisticated political analysis by Montrose about this time. This is the 'Letter on Sovereign Power' found in Napier, *Memorials* Vol 2 pp 43-53. In *The Scottish Historical Review,* Vol 61 no 171 Part 1 (April 1982) pp 25-43, David Stevenson persuasively argues for Napier as the author, and for the sentiments being based on the work of Jean Bodin, the sixteenth century French political theorist.
8. Fissell p 38 quoting Sir Francis Seymour and John Aston.
9. Gordon of Ruthven p 40

20 Time to Write Poetry
1. Williams p 95
2. Baillie Vol 1 p 313
3. Williams pp 102ff
4. Spalding Vol 2 p 51
5. Spalding Vol 2 pp 61-62
6. Spalding Vol 2 pp 68-19
7. Lord Almond was made Earl of Callendar, so it is not true that moderates were left out of the honours entirely.
8. Napier, *Montrose and the Covenanters* Vol 2 pp 125-126
9. When the king moved against his opponents in England, attempting to arrest the 'Five Members', he did so openly. He did not organize a dawn raid or try to have them assassinated.
10. No replacement Lord Deputy was appointed while Strafford was in prison. The two Lord Justices who shared responsibility for the administration came from one of the different factions and only controlled the situation briefly. Strafford's soldiers in the end largely joined the rebels.
11. Cust, *Charles I* pp 306 ff
12. Cowan p 119
13. Guthry p 94
14. Wishart p 497

21 'The generosity of your character'

1. Elizabeth died on the Isle of Wight, as a prisoner of parliament, on 8 September 1650. She was fourteen. The royal children were well treated in their captivity but Elizabeth, a superb scholar, had poor health, undermined further by the death of her father in 1649. Henry and she met and talked with him the day before his execution.
2. Names given were the Countess of Carlisle (after a conversation with Henrietta Maria), Will Murray, and a French officer, Captain Hercule Langres (on instructions from the French ambassador).
3. Pearce, *Henrietta Maria* pp 209-210; Clarendon *History*, Volume I p 508. Charles I did not return to Whitehall until 1648 as a prisoner of parliament. Henrietta Maria did not return until 1660.
4. Spalding Vol 2 pp 100, 101, 154
5. Clarendon, *History*, Volume II p 290
6. Spalding Vol 2 p 233
7. Wishart p 34.
8. Cowan p 139
9. Spalding Vol 2 pp 230, 232.
10. Spalding Vol 2 p 246
11. Napier, *Memoirs of Montrose,* Vol 2 p 380
12. Reid, *Campaigns* p 33
13. Wishart pp 39-40
14. Wishart pp 43, 44
15. Although Gloucester remained in parliamentary hands. The Earl of Essex would relieve the siege in September.
16. Spalding vol 2 p 261
17. Spalding Vol 2 p 271

22 Advance and Retreat

1. Wishart pp 45-48
2. Wishart p 49 – or else, as Stuart Reid writes, he was asked to supply 10,000 for England, and 2,000 for Scotland. Reid, *Campaigns* p 39
3. Wishart p 50
4. Hamilton was imprisoned in Pendennis, Cornwall. He was released in 1646.
5. Williams pp 123-124
6. Montrose *poems* in Appendix to Wishart p 498
7. Napier *Memorials* Vol 2 p 304
8. Montrose *poems* in Appendix to Wishart p 497
9. It means horsemanship, including what is today called dressage. Newcastle's riding schools at Welbeck and Bolsover survive.
10. Lynn Hulse, *Cavendish, William, First Duke of Newcastle* (ODNB). Hulse quotes Clarendon, and Newcastle letters.
11. Wishart pp 53-54
12. Spalding Vol 2 p 350
13. Napier, *Memoirs* Vol 2 p 394. Carnwath was a royalist but bitter, on more than one occasion, about royal favours to other people.
14. Napier, Memoirs Vol 2 p 393. On female cross-dressing see Mark Stoyle '*Give me a Souldier's Coat:' Female Cross-Dressing during the English Civil War* (History

– the journal of the Historical Association – 23 January 2018). Charles I wanted to forbid cross-dressing among the followers of his armies (a number of women probably used masculine clothes for comfort) but never went public. Possibly this was because Henrietta Maria's court theatricals had featured her ladies in masculine garb and she had herself appeared in 'Amazonian dress', so a ruling would have invited ridicule.

15. For parliament the armies of the Earl of Leven, the Earl of Manchester, Lord Fairfax; for the king the armies of Prince Rupert and the Marquess of Newcastle. On numbers see Rushworth, *Historical Collections* Vol 5, Chapter XVI
16. Cromwell was not politically egalitarian, but in the field he wanted soldiers and officers of merit.
17. John Morrill, *Cromwell, Oliver* (ODNB) quoting Cromwell's letter of 5 July 1544 to Valentine Walton.
18. Napier, *Memoirs* Vol 2 p 409
19. Williams p 126

23 A Burning Cross

1. Gordon of Ruthven pp 76-77
2. Wishart p 63
3. Wishart pp 63-65, Napier, *Memoirs* Vol 2 p 414
4. Gordon of Ruthven p 62
5. Napier, *Memoirs* Vol 2 pp 406-410
6. Williams pp 130-131, Napier, *Memoirs* Vol 2 p 410
7. Gordon of Ruthven p 72
8. See Appendix 3 on Alasdair MacDonald
9. Gordon of Ruthven p 64
10. Wishart p 68
11. Napier, *Memoirs* Vol 2 pp 146-147
12. Napier, *Memoirs* Vol 2 p 438 – in Perth shortly after the Battle of Tippermuir.

24 Tippermuir and Aberdeen

1. Wishart p 76
2. Monteth of Salmonet p 172
3. For the numbers see Stuart Reid, *Auldearn 1645* p 21 (a revision of his estimates in his earlier *Campaigns of Montrose).*
4. Wishart p 77. But Kilpont and his gentry friends were probably mounted – not much more admittedly.
5. Gordon of Ruthven p 74
6. Wishart p 77
7. Napier, Memorials Vol II p 430
8. Napier, Memoirs Vol 2 p 428
9. They tried to do so but were replaced by royalist soldiers.
10. Napier, Memoirs Vol 2 pp 434ff
11. Baillie, Letters Vol 2 pp 56-57
12. Guthry p 129, Wishart pp 83-84
13. Napier, *Memorials* pp 163-164
14. Wishart p 84

15. Gordon of Ruthven p 78
16. Stuart Reid, *Campaigns* p 67
17. Williams p 169
18. Spalding Vol 2 p 406
19. Williams p 172. The original story is in many sources, saying the man survived and Montrose made him a cavalry trooper.
20. Spalding Vol 2 p 407
21. Spalding Vol 2 p 409

25 *Taking on the Campbells*
1. James Fraser, *Chronicles of the Frasers* p 287
2. Those of the Earl of Lothian, and of Sir Mungo Campbell of Lawers.
3. James Fraser p 289-291
4. Wishart p 100
5. Numbers calculated backwards from the soldiers fielded at Inverlochy.
6. Wishart p 105
7. Cowan p 174
8. The lowlands option was not as attractive as it may appear. Lowland nobles had not supported Montrose as King's Lieutenant earlier, nor did they later, it was always the north Scots who came to him. Also, the north of England was in parliamentary hands, so a strategy of joining with Charles I in the Midlands would be tricky, even assuming what was unlikely, that the highlanders would fight in England.
9. Napier, *Memoirs* Vol 2 p 471
10. Cowan pp 175-176 quoting Fr MacBreck in Forbes-Leith *Scottish Catholics*
11. Williams pp 196-198 drawing mainly on Patrick Gordon of Ruthven.
12. Geoffrey Parker ed *Cambridge Illustrated History of War* p 149
13. David Stevenson, *Napier, Archibald, first Lord Napier of Merchistoun* (ODNB)
14. Napier, *Memoirs* Vol 2 p 471
15. Williams p 201
16. Monteth of Salmonet p 129
17. Williams p 202
18. Napier, Memoirs Vol 2 p 473. Wishart p 107
19. Napier, Memoirs Vol 2 p 476

26 *Inverlochy Castle*
1. Net of recruitment – his success in Argyllshire brought some new adherents.
2. Wishart pp 109-110
3. Napier, Memorials Vol 2 p 176
4. Napier, Memorials Vol 2 pp175-176
5. The story is they were led by a poet, Ian Lom MacDonald, the Bard of Keppoch. Montrose himself refers to 'cow-herds' (Napier, *Memorials* Vol 2 p 175)
6. Stuart Reid, *Auldearn* p 35, has lower numbers but the sources say Argyll took 1,100 men from Baillie.
7. Williams p 213 places Ogilvy in the centre around the royal standard, but there is no account of a cavalry charge from the centre, and Williams himself has them charging towards Inverlochy Castle late in the action, that is to say from the royalist right.

8. Williams p 213
9. In the empire, armies were much bigger: Wallenstein twice recruited an army of 25,000, Bernard of Saxe-Weimar had a personal army of 18,000.
10. Napier, Memorials pp 175-179

27 Night Marches
1. Ireland had a different dynamic, being a Catholic rebellion.
2. Spalding Vol 2 p 6
3. The middle brother Viscount Aboyne, still stuck in Carlyle, was always royalist.
4. Napier *Memoirs* Vol 2 p 493
5. Magdalen was alive; see Napier, *Memorials* Vol 2 p 194 (and for her death p 222)
6. Napier, Memoirs p 493
7. Spalding quoted in Napier, *Memoirs* Vol 2 p 494
8. Williams p 226
9. He raised some cash from booty and from payments by cities and towns, but it was relatively little.
10. Gordon of Sallagh p 524
11. Wishart p 122
12. Wishart p 125

28 Auldearn
1. Different locations are given for this meeting, I side with Wishart.
2. Quoted by Williams pp 233-234
3. Reid, *Auldearn* p 38
4. There are different accounts of the battle. I have followed the meticulous work of Stuart Reid.
5. Reid, *Auldearn 1645* p 42
6. Reid, *Auldearn 1645* pp 47-48
7. Spalding Vol 2 pp 318-320
8. Napier *Memorials* Vol 2 p 194

29 Victory in the North
1. The unusual title was because his relative the royalist Earl of Crawford was still alive. John Lindsay (Lord Lindsay of the Byres) was first promised his earldom (of Lindsay) in 1633 among the coronation honours. Since he was a presbyterian activist it was not conferred until 1641, as one of the honours with which Charles I wooed his enemies when in Edinburgh. In 1644, Lindsay was also given the Crawford earldom by the committee of estates, when his cousin the rightful earl was forfeited.
2. Reid, *Auldearn* p 71
3. Gerry Embleton in Reid, *Auldearn* p 76
4. Wishart p 151
5. Williams p 260 quoting Gordon of Ruthven
6. Mark Stoyle, *The Road to Farndon Field: explaining the massacre of the royalist women at Naseby* (English Historical Review, August 2006) pp 895-896
7. Stoyle *Farndon Field* pp 920-921

8. Although these attacks were made by local people and directed at soldiers as well as camp followers.
9. Wishart p 159
10. Cowan p 208

30 His Biggest Army

1. Patrick Gordon of Ruthven, who was with the army, gives higher numbers but probably he exaggerated the Gordon contribution.
2. Guthry p 152
3. Mar had been the enemy of Archibald Napier the elder, the first Lord Napier, in the early years of Charles I. But Archibald Napier the younger, who would be second Lord Napier, had married Mar's daughter. That was an instructive microcosm of Scottish noble politics.
4. Napier *Memorials* Vol 2 p 540. Probably they did not want Lanark to be part of the victory, it must be all theirs.
5. Wishart p 168
6. Wishart p 169
7. Reid, *Auldearn 1645* pp 81-82
8. Napier *Memorials* Vol I pp 215-229. The text is in Lord Napier's handwriting. It could be a copy or the original draft. The text makes it clear it is a statement by Montrose himself. And it concludes with a list of prisoners taken at Kilsyth which is conclusive on timing.
9. Robert Browne (1550-1633) was one of the first congregationalists i.e. he believed the Church (of England) should be based on individual congregations/parishes. It should not be run by bishops. By Montrose's time there was a plethora of religious Independents in England.

31 Seeming Friends

1. See Buchan p 274
2. Wishart p 174
3. Williams p 279
4. Against the Earls of Cassillis and Eglinton who were reported to be forming an army, which never saw battle and must have dispersed.
5. Napier, *Memorials* Vol 2 pp 233-234
6. Napier, *Montrose and the Covenanters* Vol 2 p 175
7. Wishart p 197
8. Wishart p 196
9. Cowan p 235, Williams p 289 – from Gordon of Ruthven, who was with the army.
10. Reid, *Auldearn 1645* p 86
11. Williams pp 291-292 quoting Gordon of Ruthven
12. Williams pp 291-292 quoting Gordon of Ruthven and Sir George Mackenzie, *Vindication of the Government of Scotland*
13. Wishart p 204
14. William Fitzwilliam Elliot, *the Trustworthiness of Border Ballads* pp 104-105

32 The Minister's Servant

1. Napier, *Memorials* Vol 2 pp 274-275
2. This was also at the heart of the Nineteen Propositions put to the king at the same time by the English parliament.
3. *The Letters, Speeches and Proclamations of King Charles I* p 182
4. *The Letters...of King Charles I* pp 205-206
5. Monteth of Salmonet p 256. The King's Evil was scrofula (tuberculosis outside the lungs, usually on the neck) which by tradition a touch from the king cured.
6. Napier, *Memorials* Vol 2 pp 277, 279-280, 284
7. James Fraser p 313
8. Huntly was captured by the covenanters at the end of 1647 and executed in March 1649, two months after Charles I died outside Whitehall Palace.
9. Wishart p 248
10. Wishart p 238
11. James Fraser p 306
12. Napier Memorials Vol 2 p 222 n. For her whereabouts, we know that her son Robert was entrusted to her by the authorities, and her father Southesk exonerated of responsbility for him (Napier, Memorials Vol 2 p 194), which suggests she was living separately from her father. If she were at Kincardine, it would be unoccupied after her death, which could explain why the younger Lord Napier went there the following March. There is a later mention of a Magdalen Carnegie in the context of Montrose's property, but this was probably her cousin, one of the daughters of Lord Northesk.
13. Wishart p 220
14. Williams p 225. The older Middleton was collateral damage as the royalists plundered the countryside north of Montrose. The town was spared on the orders of their namesake marquess.
15. Monteth of Salmonet p 243
16. Wishart pp 266-270

33 The Fears of King Charles

1. Pearce p 231
2. Wishart pp 273-274
3. Napier *Memorials* Vol 2 pp 310
4. Supporting bishop to his uncle the Archbishop of Paris and marked as the next archbishop.
5. Quoted in Williams p 320. The 'Lives' of Plutarch was a classical text of the second century AD, consisting of biographies of great men, both Roman and Greek.
6. Napier *Memorials* Vol 2 p 306
7. Napier *Memorials* Vol 2 p 304
8. Charles I agreed a three-year period in which presbyterianism would be applied in England, without bishops, to be followed by a final settlement of religion. He agreed to ratify all Acts of the Scottish Parliament since 1644.
9. David Stevenson, *Campbell, Archibald, Marquess of Argyll* (ODNB)
10. De Lisle, *White King* p 231
11. Napier *Memorials* Vol 2 p 307
12. Wishart p 335
13. Wishart pp 336 ff

14. Wishart p 495

34 Montrose's Last Declaration

1. rps.ac.uk
2. Gordon of Sallagh p 547
3. Clarendon quoted in Napier, *Montrose and the Covenanters* pp 123-124
4. Although it was really anger with the English army. The House of Commons was purged by the army of moderates on 6 December 1648. It was only this reduced chamber which tried Charles I because the House of Lords refused to take part. There was no precedent for trial by the Commons alone. Nor was the Commons now representative.
5. Wishart p 350
6. Napier, *Memorials* Vol 2 pp 376-382
7. The parliament of 1639-1640 had agreed the National Covenant with Traquair presiding as king's commissioner.
8. It belonged to the son-in-law of Johan van Oldenbarnevelt, the man executed in 1619 for supporting Arminianism.
9. The Letters of Elizabeth, Queen of Bohemia, p 165
10. Williams p 330 quoting the autobiography of the Winter Queen's youngest daughter Sophia, Electress of Hanover. Louise later became Catholic and Abbess of Maubuisson in France.
11. Until 1648 Lord Dalkeith, the husband therefore of the resourceful Lady Dalkeith.
12. Wishart pp 447-448
13. Williams pp 339-340
14. Cowan p 279
15. Wishart pp 454-458

35 Nil medium

1. Gordon of Sallagh p 551
2. There were reports that he had lost transports at sea, but they come from covenant sources with no corroboration and probably were propaganda.
3. Seaforth's brother, Thomas Mackenzie of Pluscarden, briefly occupied Inverness for the royalist cause after Charles I's death. Seaforth in early 1650 was on the continent.
4. For the standards Napier *Memoirs* Vol 2 pp 741-742; for the seals p 746
5. Napier *Memorials* Vol 2 pp 410-412
6. Oddly it also says that by talking with the committee of estates, Charles II does not intend to give them legitimacy (which obviously he did).
7. John Gwynne, *Memoirs* p 85
8. Gwynne p 87
9. Built at the beginning of the twentieth century for the scandalous Mary Caroline, Duchess of Sutherland.
10. Cowan p 283
11. I have followed the account in Williams pp 352-355
12. Wishart pp 376-377

36 21 May 1650

1. Williams p 356
2. Williams p 360 quoting Dunrobin MS
3. Wiliams p 362 quoting Wardlaw MS
4. Wishart p 380
5. Wishart pp 380-381
6. Wishart p 382
7. Balfour Vol 4 p 13
8. Wishart p 385.
9. Alexander Henderson had died four years before.
10. Williams p 363 quoting the Wigton Papers
11. Monteth of Salmonet p 513
12. For the interview see Patrick Simson's Testimony, Napier *Memoirs* Vol 2 pp 785-788
13. Wishart p 388, Napier *Memorials* Vol 2 p 447
14. Balfour Vol 4 p 16
15. Balfour, *Annales* Vol 4 p 16
16. Napier, *Memorials* Vol 2 p 442
17. *Fraser Manuscript*, in *Napier Memorials* Vol 2 p 442
18. Point of the compass
19. Wishart p 504
20. Fairly normal at the time when prominent people were executed on a treason charge, as in the Gowrie Conspiracy. Nonetheless it was Montrose's body, so he was going to think about it; and the belief in bodily resurrection was important.
21. Napier *Memorials* Vol 2 p 455 quoting the eyewitness Notary Public John Nicholl.
22. *Fraser Manuscript* in Napier, *Memorials* Vol 2 p 442
23. Eyewitness letter in Napier *Memorials* Vol 2 p 448
24. Monteth of Salmonet p 515 says he was not permitted a speech but had written his last thoughts on a piece of paper which he gave someone.
25. *Fraser Manuscript* in Napier, *Memorials* Vol 2 pp 443-444
26. Archbishop Laud was similarly assailed when he was executed.
27. *Fraser Manuscript* in Napier, *Memorials* Vol 2 p 445

37 Funeral Rites

1. Napier, *Montrose and the Covenanters* pp 550-551
2. Napier, *Memorials* Vol 2 pp 454 ff
3. Montrose during his appearance before parliament on 29 May made the point that he accepted its authority only because the king was in talks with it.
4. Napier *Memorials* Vol 2 pp 451-452
5. Napier *Memorials* Vol 2 p 450
6. www.olivercromwell.org/Letters_and_speeches/Letter_129.pdf
7. Leven was in his early seventies. He was involved in the general scheme of defence against Cromwell and present at the battle, but only nominally in command.
8. The constitutional complexity was considerable. The necessary legislation did not come into force until 1657, so the union was very short-lived.
9. Under the Commonwealth there was no parliament of Great Britain. Scotland was ruled from England.

10. So-called because it was not summoned by the king whose powers were of course abolished, or suspended, when the Commonwealth was announced.
11. Robbie, *The Embalming of Montrose* (Book of the Old Edinburgh Club, First volume) pp 36-37
12. Williams pp 388-389 There were also legends about other parts of the body including an arm, said to be Montrose's, kept in a country house in Yorkshire (my thanks to Adam White for this story).
13. David Stevenson, *Graham, James, first Marquess of Montrose* (ODNB) quoting Robert Baillie.
14. The details of the day come from *A relation of the true Funeralls of the great Lord Marquess of Montrose...* in the Harleian Miscellany Vol 7 (1746) pp 283-286
15. The earldom of Aboyne was a Restoration honour created for Charles Gordon, fourth son of the second Marquess of Huntly, i.e. he was the younger brother of the Viscount Aboyne of Montrose's campaign.
16. *True Funeralls* p 286

38 Magnificat
1. David Stevenson, *Campbell, Archibald, Marquess of Argyll* (ODNB) quoting D. Laing *Correspondence of Sir Robert Kerr, First Earl of Ancram, and his son William, Third Earl of Ancram*
2. I follow the narrative in Williams pp 388-393 which draw on a letter of 1836 from Alexander Johnston.
3. Napier, *Montrose and the Covenanters* Vol 2 p 565 quoting Alexander Johnston
4. Williams p 391
5. Harleian Miscellany p 288
6. Burnet, *History* p 53
7. Wishart p 69
8. Montrose's letters to Elizabeth do not survive.
9. Burnet *History* pp 61-62

Appendix 2: Reformed Protestant Beliefs
1. Rachel Naomi Remen, Richard Rohr, Daily Meditations, *Dying as Disorder* 20 August 2020
2. The doctrine of Purgatory taught that after death many people went to an intermediate state, neither heaven nor hell, in which the soul was further purged of sin before admission to heaven. Time in purgatory apparently could be shortened by intercession for the deceased from friends back on earth.
3. Named from the teaching of the Dutch theologian Jacobus Arminius (1560-1609). His Dutch name was Jakob Hermanszoon.
4. Mitchison p 192
5. 2 Corinthians 3: 7
6. Exodus 20: 4 and Deuteronomy 5:8-9. Quotation from the latter.

Appendix 3: Stuart Marriages
1. The king was under pressure from his son and Buckingham, both of whose Madrid experiences (see below) made them want a war with Spain.

Select Bibliography

Primary Sources

Aston, John *Iter Boreale, Anno Salutis 1639* (Six North Country Diaries, Surtees Society 1919)

Baillie, Robert *The letters and Journals of Robert Baillie*, ed. D. Laing, 3 vols. Bannatyne Club, 73 (1841–2)

Balfour, James *Annales of Scotland, Vol 1* (1824)

Bannatyne Club, Edinburgh *Original Letters relating to the ecclesiastical affairs of Scotland chiefly written by or addressed to... King James the sixth after his accession to the English throne 1603-1625* (ed. D Laing 1851)

Burnet, Gilbert *History of his own times* (1833)

The memoirs of the lives and actions of James and William: Dukes of Hamilton and Castle-Herald (1852)

Calderwood David *History of the Kirk of Scotland (1842-1849)*

Charles I (ed. Charles Petrie) *Letters, Proclamations and Speeches* (Cassell 1935)

Clarendon, Earl of *History of the Rebellion and Civil Wars in England Begun in the Year 1641* (1888 Oxford)

Cromwell, Oliver www.olivercromwell.org/Letters_and_speeches

Elizabeth, Queen of Bohemia Letters, Baker, L. M. ed (1953 Bodley Head)

Fraser, James *Chronicles of the Frasers* (1905 Edinburgh)

Gordon of Ruthven, Patrick *A Short Abridgement of Britane's Distemper from the Year of God 1639 to 1649* (1844 Spalding Club, Aberdeen)

Gordon of Rothiemay, James *History of Scots Affairs* (1841)

Gordon of Sallagh, Gilbert *Continuation of Genealogical History of the Earldom of Sutherland by Sir Robert Gordon* (1813 Edinburgh)

Guthry, Henry *The memoirs of Henry Guthry, late bishop*, ed. G. Crawford, 2nd edn (1748)

Gwynne, John *Memoirs* (1822)

Henrietta Maria *Letters of Queen Henrietta Maria, including her private correspondence with Charles I*, ed. Mary Ann E. Green (1856)

Heylyn, Peter *Cyprianus Anglicus* (1668)

Knox, John *Works* ed. David Laing (1855)

Monteth of Salmonet, Rober *The History of the Troubles of Great Britain* (1735 London)
Puységur, Marquis de *Mémoires* (1747)
Raleigh, Walter *Works of Walter Ralegh, Kt* (1829)
Rogers, Charles *Rehearsal of Events Which Occurred in the North of Scotland from 1635 to 1645, in Relation to the National Covenant.* Edited from a Contemporary MS.: *"A Litle Yet True Rehearsall of Severall Passages of Affairs, Collected by a Friend of Doctor Alexander's, at Aberdeen"* (Transaction of the Royal Historical Society Vol 5 (1877))
Rothes, Earl of *A relation of the proceedings concerning the affairs of the Kirk of Scotland from August, 1637 to July, 1638* (1830)
Row, John *The History of the Kirk of Scotland from the year 1558 to August 1637* (1842)
Rushworth, John *Historical Collections* (1721)
Rutherford, Samuel *Letters* (1891)
Spalding, John *History of the Troubles and Memorable Transactions in Scotland and England 1624 to 1645* (two volumes, Bannatyne Club, Edinburgh 1828, 1829, volume 2 1851)
Spottiswoode, John *History of the Church of Scotland – beginning the year 203 and continued until the end of the reign of King James VI* (1847 Edinburgh)
Turner, James *Memoirs of his own Life and Times* (1829)
Wariston, Archibald Johnston of *Diaries* Scottish History Society edition, eds George Morison Paul (1896), David Hay Fleming (1919), James D Ogilvie (1940)
Weldon, Anthony *Perfecte Description of the People and Country of Scotland* (London 1647)
Wishart, George *The Memoirs of James, Marquis of Montrose 1639-1650* trans Rev Alexander Murdoch and H. F. Morland Simpson (1892 Longmans Green)
The Scots Confession *www.fpchurch.org.uk*
National Records of Scotland
State Papers Domestic
State Papers Venice
Ruthven Family Papers
Harleian Miscellany Vol VII (1746)

Secondary Sources
Bell, Robin *Civil Warrior* (2002, Luath Press)
Buchan, John *Montrose* (1928, Thomas Nelson)
Carlton, Charles *Charles I – the Personal Monarch* (1995, Routledge)
Chambers, Robert *History of the Rebellions in Scotland under the Marquis of Montrose* (1828, Constable)
Cowan, Edward J *Montrose: for Covenant and King* (1977, Weidenfeld and Nicholson
Cust, Lionel *Van Dyck* (1903)
Cust, Richard *Charles I: A Political Life* (2005, Pearson)
Donald, Peter *An Uncounselled King* (1990 CUP)
Elliot, William Fitzwilliam *The Trustworthiness of Border ballads* (1906)
Fissell, Mark *The Bishops' Wars – Charles I's Campaigns against Scotland 1638-1640* (1994 CUP)
Forbes-Leith, William (ed.) *Narratives of Scottish Catholics under Mary Stuart and James VI* (1885 Edinburgh)

Fraser, Murdo *The Rivals, Montrose and Argyll and the Struggle for Scotland* (2015, Birlinn)

Fraser, William *History of the Carnegies, Earls of Southesk and of their kindred* (1867)

Graeme, Louisa *Or and Sable: a Book of the Graemes and Grahams* (William Brown, 1903)

Grant, James *Memoirs of Montrose* (1858, Routledge)

Grant, I. F. *In the tracks of Montrose* (1931, Alexander Macclehose)

Gregg, Pauline *King Charles I* (Phoenix Press, 1981)

Hastings, Max   *Montrose: The King's Champion* (1977, Victor Gollancz)

Holmes, George (ed.) *Oxford Illustrated History of Italy* (1997, OUP)

Lee, Maurice *The Road to Revolution: Scotland under Charles I* (1985, University of Illinois Press)

Lisle, Leanda de *White King* (2018 Chatto and Windus)

Lisle, Leanda de *After Elizabeth* (2006 Harper Collins)

Lynch, Michael (ed.) *Oxford Companion to Scottish History* (2011, OUP)

Lynn, John A. *Giant of the Grand Siècle – The French Army 1610-1715* (1997 CUP)

Macinnes, Allan I. *The British Confederate – Archibald Campbell, Marquess of Argyll 1607-1661* (2020 John Donald)

Macinnes, Allan I. *Charles I and the making of the Covenanting movement 1625-1641* (1991 Donald)

Miller, James *Swords for Hire – the Scottish Mercenary* (2007 Birlinn)

Mitchison, Rosalind *A History of Scotland* (third edition, 2002, Routledge)

Mullan, D. G. *Episcopacy in Scotland: The History of an Idea 1560-1638* (Edinburgh 1986)

Napier, Mark *Montrose and the Covenanters* – two volumes (1838, Duncan)

_____ *The life and times of Montrose* (1840, Oliver and Boyd)

_____ *Memorials of Montrose and his times* – two volumes (1848, the Maitland Club)

_____ *Memoirs of Montrose* – two volumes (1856, Stevenson)

Parker, Geoffrey (ed.) *Cambridge Illustrated History of Warfare* (2008)

Pearce, Dominic *Henrietta Maria* (Amberley 2015)

Ranke, Leopold von *Ecclesiastical and Political History of the Popes of Rome During the Sixteenth and Seventeenth Centuries* Volume 2, second edition; translated by Sarah Austin (John Murray 1841)

Reid, Stuart *Auldearn 1645: The Marquis of Montrose's Scottish Campaign* (2003 Osprey)

Reid, Stuart *The Campaigns of Montrose* (1990 Mercat Press)

Robbie, J. C. *The Embalming of Montrose* (1908, Book of the Old Edinburgh Club)

Stevenson, David *The Scottish Revolution 1637-1644: the Triumph of the Covenanters* (1973 David and Charles)

Stevenson, David *Highland Warrior: Alasdair MacColla and the Civil Wars* (1980, Edinburgh)

Trevor-Roper, Hugh *The Invention of Scotland – Myth and History* (2008, YUP)

Whyte, Ian D. *Agriculture and Society in Seventeenth Century Scotland* (1979 Edinburgh)

Willcock, John *The Great Marquess – Life and times of Archibald, 8th Earl and 1st (and only) Marquess of Argyll* (1903)

Williams, Ronald *Montrose, Cavalier in Mourning* (1975, Barrie and Jenkins)

The King's Only Champion

Wilson, Peter H. *The Thirty Years War – Europe's Tragedy* (209, Allen Lane)
Wormald, Jenny *Court, Kirk and Community in Scotland 1470-1625* (Edinburgh University Press 1991)
Oxford Dictionary of National Biography entries by John Callow, John Coffey, Michelle DiMeo, Martin Garrett, Ann Hughes, Lynn Hulse, Amy L. Juhala, John Morrill, Henry Paton, John Scally, David Stevenson

Articles

Arbuckle, W. F. *'The Gowrie Conspiracy'* Part I and Part 2 (Scottish Historical Review Vol 36 no 121 Part 1 (April 1957) and no 122 Part 2 (October 1957))
Bergeron, David M. *Charles I's Edinburgh Pageant 1633* (Renaissance Studies vol 6 no 2 (June 1992))
Brown, K. M. *Aristocratic Finances and the Origins of the Scottish Revolution* (English Historical Review civ 1989 pp 55-57)
Eeles, F. C. *The English Thanksgiving Service for King James's Delivery from the Gowrie Conspiracy* (The Scottish Historical Review Vol 8 No 32 (July 1911))
Firth, C. H. *Ballads on the Bishops' Wars 1638-40* (Scottish Historical Review Vol 3 no 11 (April 1906) pp 260)
Goodare, Julian *The Nobility and the Absolutist State in Scotland 1584-1638* (History vol 78, no 253 June 1993 pp 161-182)
Hannay, R. K. *On the Church Lands at the Reformation* (Scottish Historical Review, vol 16, no. 61, October 1918)
Houston, Rab *Custom in Context: Medieval and Early Modern Scotland and England* (Past and Present no 211, May 2011, pp 35-76)
Inglis, John A. *Sir John Hay, the 'Incendiary'* (Scottish Historical Review Vol 15 no 58, January 1918)
McCallum, R. Ian *Patrick Ruthven, Alchemist and Physician* (Proceedings of the Society of Antiquaries for Scotland 2004)
MacDonald, Alan R. *Deliberative Processes in Parliament c 1567-1639: Multicameralism and the Lords of the Articles* (Scottish Historical Review Vol 81, no 211 Part 1 April 2002)
Millstone, Noah *Evil Counsell, the Propositions to Bridle the Impertinency of Parliament and the Critique of Caroline Government in the late 1620s* (Journal of British Studies Vol 50 no 4 October 2011)
Russell, Conrad *The First Army Plot of 1641*, Transactions of the Royal Historical Society Vol 38 (1988)
Sanderson, Margaret H. B. *Feuars of Kirklands* (Scottish Historical Review Vol 52 no 154 part 2 October 1973)
Simpson, Percy and Bell, C. F. *Designs by Inigo Jones for Masques and Plays at Court* (The Volume of the Walpole Society Vol 12, 1923-24 pp 16, 124, 130, 131)
Smith, David L. *The Fourth Earl of Dorset and the Personal Rule of Charles I* (Journal of British Studies, July 1991)
Spicer, Andrew *'Laudianism' in Scotland? St Giles' Cathedral 1633-1639: A Reappraisal* (Architectural History Vol 46 2003)
Stevenson, D *The 'Letter on sovereign power' and the influence of Jean Bodin on political thought in Scotland* (Vol 61 No 171, Scottish Historical Review Part 1 (April 1982))

312

Stevenson, David *The King's Scottish Revenues and the Covenanters 1625-1651* (The Historical Journal Vol 17 No 1 (March 1974))

Stewart, Laura A. M. *The Political Repercussions of the Five Articles of Perth: a Reassessment of James VI and I's Religious Policies in Scotland* (the Sixteenth Century Journal Vol 38, no 4, winter 2007 pp 1013-1036)

Stilman, Alison *Angels, Demons and Political Action in Two Early Jacobean History Plays* (Critical Survey, vol 23, No 2, Angels and Demons (2011))

Stoyle, Mark '*Give me a Souldier's Coat:*' *Female Cross-Dressing during the English Civil War* (History – the journal of the Historical Association – 23 January 2018).

Stoyle, Mark *The Road to Farndon Field: explaining the massacre of the royalist women at Naseby* (English Historical Review, August 2006)

Acknowledgements

This book was partly written in coronavirus lockdown. Even when restrictions lifted it was not an easy matter to penetrate libraries for a long time. Yet the libraries did everything possible the moment they could. I am particularly grateful to the staff of the London Library and British Library who did their best for their readers with very good humour.

Amberley Publishing has backed me in a second book. I am grateful especially to Shaun Barrington for his support.

I would like to thank Lara Haggerty and Jean Ann Scott Miller of Innerpeffray Library, Perth and Kinross, and to thank the Governors. It is a historic institution richly deserving a visit if you are in the vicinity. My time there gave me unique insight into the personality of Montrose and his culture. Details can be found online at inerpeffraylibrary.co.uk.

The Duke of Montrose, who descends from my subject, was a courteous correspondent in the early phases of this book. Of the First Marquess of Montrose Society – they have an excellent website – I would especially like to thank Shelagh Noble, James Hair and Phinella Henderson for their support and help with some of the vocabulary.

Robert Bogdan, Chair of the Scottish Castles Association (and son of my father's schoolfriend Andrew), kindly helped with information about the castles of Scotland. Archie Fraser was unwittingly in on the beginning of the project, which I discussed with him over lunch: his enthusiasm was an encouragement.

In 1977 Max Hastings published *Montrose: the King's Champion*. I suggested my similar title in the early stages, before finding his excellent account. Amberley liked the title and stuck with it. I am pleased to find common ground with a distinguished predecessor.

I am grateful to Daniel Moylan for help with theology, also for comments made on my previous book which helped me structure this one. Adam White kindly sent me intriguing information on a Montrose relic. Saul David was enormously helpful with corrections to what I first wrote about the military technology. It was the comment of a moment, but I am also very grateful to John Adamson for telling me that Charles I was especially fond of tapestries (as I am myself). My brother Anthony Pearce kindly gave advice on cameras and photography, which was essential for some of the illustrations and helped me make a contribution to the visual side of this book. My thanks to him.

Evidently, mistakes, of fact or interpretation, are all my own.

Index